ARMAGNAC

The Definitive Guide To France's Premier Brandy

Flame Grape Press

FLAME GRAPE PRESS

LIBRARY OF CONGRESS CATALOG CARD NUMBER:
98-073203
ISBN: 978-1-935879-91-6
PRINTED IN THE UNITED STATES OF AMERICA

Table of Contents

Introduction 9

The *Armagnacais*: Their Customs and their Character 11

Cuisine, wine, bullfighting, course Landaise, rugby, pigeon hunting, famous Gascons, the personality of the people

The Origin of the *Armagnacais* 23

ARMAGNAC: THE SPIRIT ITSELF

The Soil 25

The relationship between soil and the vine, soils found within the Armagnac region, the subsoil

The Climate 31

The Grapes 33

Distillation 41

The history of distillation, the differences between single and double distillation

The Barrel 51

The role of the barrel, types of oak and their resultant differences, constructing the barrel, the importance of new oak

The Evolution of Armagnac in Oak 59

Alcohol evaporation, changes through the decades, aging in vat

The Role of the Enologist 65

Tools of an enologist, permitted additives, the age game of non-vintage blends, 9 steps to fool the undiscriminating consumer

Armagnac and Cognac Over The Centuries 73

A parallel look at the rise of the world's two finest brandies, major technical and taste differences between the two spirits

Armagac Today 81

Reasons for financial difficulties within the region

Vintage Armagnac 87

The importance of vintage years

Tasting Armagnac 91

An armagnac's glass, color, aromas, texture, balance, flavors, alcohol, tannin, length, overall assessment and fond de verre

Tasting Chart 97

The Bottle 98

The Label 99

VSOP, Reserve, Hors d'age...what does it mean?

Sales Statistics 101

Differences between cognac and armagnac, in France and abroad

Products Based on Armagnac 104

Armagnac blanc, floc de Gascogne, various cocktails

Armagnac and Cigars 108

Tips for creating the perfect match

21 Tips 110
Things to know before making a purchase

ARMAGNAC PRODUCERS
Listings by region and village and with tasting notes
The Bas Armagnac 115
The Ténereze 211
The Haut Armagnac 246

NEGOCIANTS 251
An alphabetical listing with tasting notes
COOPERATIVES 290
Their role within the region
Rating The Producers 293
The author's subjective categorization
Glossary 297
Index 300

For My Parents-In-Law,
André and Simone Daubin

Introduction

What Is Armagnac?

For those who do not know, armagnac was France's first brandy. Because of its concentrated, complex aromas and tremendous length, it also remains first in the hearts of true connoisseurs. Armagnac's closest relative is cognac which, although often compared, is distinctly different, not only with regard to its soil type, climate, and grapes, but also its distillation procedures, aging methods and, of course, resultant taste. As you will discover over the ensuing pages, armagnac and cognac, while both brandies, have about as much in common as Bordeaux has with Burgundy or Barolo has with Brunello.

Armagnac is also the name of the region from which the spirit comes, located about seventy miles southeast of Bordeaux, one hundred miles due east of the Atlantic Ocean, and about 150 miles south of Cognac. Its 15,000 hectares form the center of an area known as Gascony, which itself lies in the heart of Southwestern France.

The Great Brandies Of France

Traces of humanity have been evident for three million years in what is now known as Gascony. In 56 BC, the Roman troops arrived in the region and found many independent tribes speaking various dialects. The Romans soon conquered these tribes: One of the particularly brave Roman soldiers was named Hermann who, for his courageous fighting, was given a massive piece of land with Eauze as its center. The territory's name, Hermanius, was later shortened to Arminius, while over the ensuing centuries it took on a Gascon spelling and became Arminiac. Finally, around the second or third century, the name was modified and became Armagnac.

Today, on a typical summer afternoon, fluffy white clouds sprawl across Armagnac's deep blue skies. Fields are scattered along its gently rolling countryside like colored squares on a velvet-covered checkerboard. Sunflowers turn toward the hot sun in one field. Several hundred yards away, corn stalks hang limply. Golden wheat fills another square and reflects the sun's golden brilliance. Further on, long rows of green vines stretch across its crumbly soil toward the jagged horizon. Armagnac is an agricultural region, isolated from busy highways and main railway lines. Its inhabitants are closely rooted to the earth and center their lives around the products that have sprung from its soil for centuries.

All the *producers* listed in this book sell at least 250 bottles per year. However, many of their releases are available only at their domaines and will, most likely, never be exported. While frustrating for many stateside enthusiasts who will only be able to read about certain producers, it is these small, independent producers that form the backbone of the Armagnac region and give it its true soul. Because of this, I felt it necessary to document these producers if only to give them a fair voice in a domestic marketplace that is otherwise overrun with mediocre, commercialized *product* that does nothing to advance the image of Armagnac.

That being said, *Armagnac* is a guide that will make things easier for the fine spirit connoisseur to understand the most beautiful *eau de vie* in the world.

A votre santé!

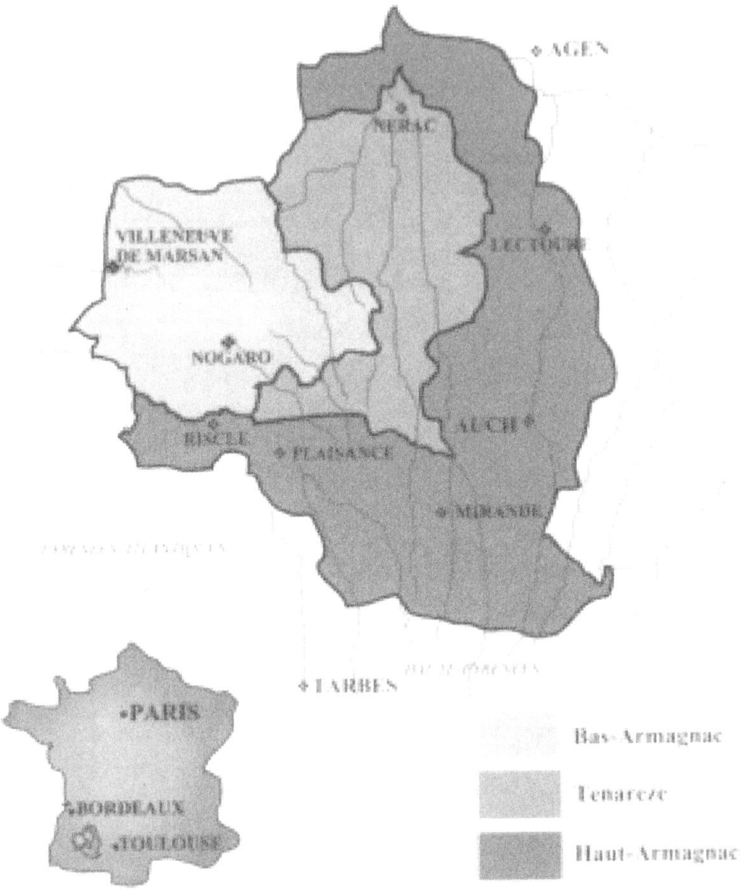

Additional Notes From The Author

In France, there are three great brandies: armagnac, cognac and calvados. With no disrespect to the latter (which can be sensational), this book concentrates on brandy made from distilled wine rather than apple cider. The exclusion of calvados is more to simplify things for the reader than demean its importance in the world of fine spirits.

Armagnac is always referred to in France in either degrees or percent alcohol, rather than proof—as in the United States. Because those numbers are what you will see on most traditional armagnac labels, I have not converted any of the degree levels to proof. You may do so, however, simply by doubling the degree to arrive with the proof level. In other words, an armagnac leaves the still at 52° or 104 proof. And an armagnac at 46° is actually 92 proof.

Alambic is the French word for still. Its correct English spelling is Alembic. But since that word is rarely used in English, I have taken the liberty of leaving the spelling in its French form.

Charles Neal

The *Armagnacais*: Their Customs And Their Character

France is often called the garden of Europe because every square mile is cultivated for a particular purpose. The reasons for these divisions stem back centuries when surveys proved that some areas were more suited to particular products than others. Henceforth, regions around France tend to have specific flavors due to the individual products grown within each one. This is of particular interest to the traveler who can, over the course of a week, enter numerous distinct areas and be spoiled by their highly original foods, wines and spirits.

Naturally, the armagnac region has its personality. And because Armagnac is considered the heart of Gascony, it is difficult to speak about Armagnac without speaking about Gascony in general. So, what exactly sets the people of Gascony apart from those in the rest of the France?

The Cuisine

Ducks and Geese provide the backbones for Gascon cuisine, and nothing is wasted: from these plump birds comes the foie gras (fattened liver), magret de canard (duck breast), confit (quarters preserved in their own fat), grease (often used in place of oil), kidneys to be flambéed with armagnac, liver to be spread on toast, and the carcass which is often grilled over hot coals.

Many people consider Gascony to be *the most important* gastronomic region of France. Certainly two of France's most important chefs—André Daguin, former owner of the restaurant at the *Hotel de France* in Auch and the first to serve *magret de canard* (duck breast) like a steak, and Landes native Alain Dutournier, chef and owner of *Carré des Feuillants* in Paris, have their roots in the Armagnac region. Michel Guérard, although not a native, owns the culinary mecca *Les Prés d'Eugénie* in Les Landes and has made Gascony his adopted home.

In the United States, Ariane Daguin, André's daughter, is the co-founder of *D'Artagnan*, which produces domestic *foie gras*, game meats, and numerous types of inventive *charcuterie*. One of America's more important chefs, Jean-Louis Palladin, grew up in the Gers and was the chef at *La Table des Cordeliers* in Condom. Later, he crossed the Atlantic and achieved tremendous acclaim at the *Restaurant Jean-Louis* at the Watergate Hotel in Washington DC. In addition, Laurent Manrique, executive chef at the acclaimed *Gertrude's* in New York, is also a native of the Gers.

It is the indigenous products that give Gascony its culinary depth. The region is easily the largest producer of ducks and geese in France. From these birds come a number of succulent delights, most importantly foie gras—fattened duck or goose liver, magret—duck breast, and *confit*—meats (normally duck and goose) preserved in their fat. Cassoulet, the luscious dish made from preserved goose, sausage, and beans, has its origins not far from Toulouse.

Of course, Gascony is known also for its fruit that grows in large orchards around the rivers Lot and Garonne, as well as vegetables like asparagus and garlic which thrive in the sandy regions toward the Atlantic. Wild pigeons are also common in Gascon kitchens, as well as game like wild boar and deer.

Another delightful delicacy coming from the earth are *cèpes*, large wild mushrooms that grow on the damp ground next to oak trees. These beefy mushrooms, somewhat similar in size to portobellos, have a sweet, nutty flavor that is delicately balanced with the wild scents of the woods. They are incorporated into numerous Gascon recipes.

Truffes noirs or Black truffles, one of the world's most expensive cooking commodities, are perhaps most known in the Perigord section of Gascony, especially the Dordogne. Many Gascon chefs include truffles in their regional plates.

When these luxury ingredients are put alongside *Jambon de Bayonne* (cured ham from the nearby Basque country) and cheese from the neighboring Pyrénées, one arrives with a tremendous arsenal of gastronomic delights.

Sauces are normally thickened with vegetables like potatoes or turnips, tomato concentrate, flour or blood. Neither butter nor cream is frequently employed in recipes: As Paula Wolfert writes in *The Cooking of Southwest France*, "until World War II, butter was rarely used in most parts of the Southwest. When rationing took place, butter was allotted in huge amounts compared to what the Southwesterners were used to; as a result, some of the cooks started using butter in their cooking."

Breakfast is rarely eaten in Gascony—perhaps just a coffee and slice of day old bread. Lunch and dinner, however, are major events; they start with a soup and are followed by a sauce or *hors d'oeuvre* (consisting of ham, dry sausage, paté and/or the vegetables of the season like tomatoes, radishes, or beans). Then comes a roasted meat served with vegetables of the season (peas, beans, new potatoes, carrots, cabbage, etc.), and desserts like *croustade* (the famous apple tart sprayed with armagnac), ice cream with prunes macerated in armagnac, fruit, or flan.

The meal is finished with a coffee; when the cup is empty, a splash of armagnac is added and its aromas are accentuated by the warm cup.

Armagnac can be incorporated into many recipes. Its flavor is subtle, and helps bring out the natural flavors of a dish. It's fun to incorporate armagnac's inherent nuances (preserved fruits, orange, apricot) into recipes that use those actual fruits in their stuffing or glaze. This is fairly easy with chicken, pork, and duck.

Armagnac is often used to flambé a dish, which not only gently sears the surface of the food but also adds complexity through the subtle flavors of the spirit. In addition, any excess fat in the pan is consumed in the flames, which ultimately leaves the dish more delicately composed.

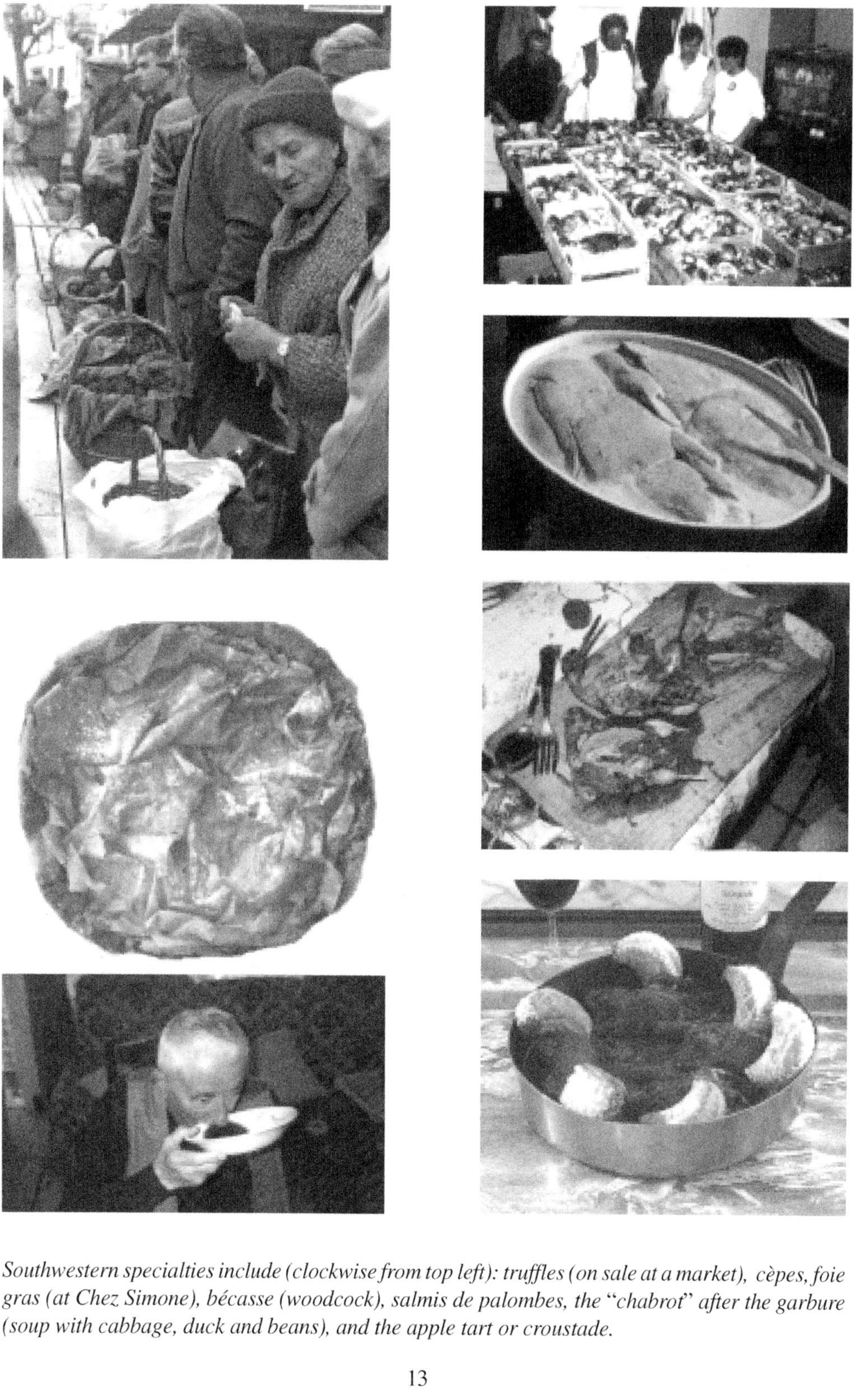

Southwestern specialties include (clockwise from top left): truffles (on sale at a market), cèpes, foie gras (at Chez Simone), bécasse (woodcock), salmis de palombes, the "chabrot" after the garbure (soup with cabbage, duck and beans), and the apple tart or croustade.

The Wine

A tremendous variety of wines are produced in Gascony, unique because most of the grape varietals employed—among them Tannat, Malbec, Gros Manseng, Courbu, Fer Servadou and Négrette—are still fairly unknown outside the region. The picturesque vineyards of Jurançon that sprawl across the foothills of the Pyrénées grow grapes for regional wines that run from crisp, light whites to highly prized thick and viscous late-harvest, botrytis-effected sweet wines. The simple yet highly aromatic whites from the Côtes de Gascogne are undoubtedly some of France's best dry white wine values. Wonderfully refreshing rosés are produced in abundance in Béarn and Fronton. A host of sensational reds also find their home in Gascony, including the robust Malbec-based wines of Cahors and the elegant Cabernet and Merlot-based wines of Buzet. In addition, the rustic yet refined reds of Madiran are some of the most exciting wines in France. In fact, Alain Brumont, owner of Château Montus and Domaine Bouscassé in Madiran, was chosen *Winemaker of the Decade* by *Gault-Millau* magazine at the end of the 1980's.

This wide range of Gascon wines serve as a wonderful accompaniment to the rich local cuisine, and have already gathered tremendous respect within France. Their international acclaim is on the horizon.

Bullfighting and Course Landaise

During the long, hot summers in Southwestern France, every town in Armagnac, no matter how big or small, sets aside a few days for the local *fête* or *party*. Normally there will be a disc-jockey who provides music, amusements for the children, and most importantly, plenty of food and drink. A different menu is featured each night, often served in the town square to scores of people; one evening people will eat *escargots* and *confit de canard*. Another night, melons filled with the local aperitif *floc* will be followed by a giant paella. A third night might have Toulouse sausages barbecued over grape vines. Local wine always is consumed in large quantities. People see other townsfolk...stay up late...get drunk...dance...and most of all have fun! Posters circulate to nearby towns announcing the activities, which often include local contests, carnival rides, dancing, and either a *course Landaise* (*Corrida from Les Landes*) or bullfight.

Spectacles that feature competition between men and animals have always had tremendous significance in the Armagnac region. For centuries bullfighting has been practiced as far west as Arles in the lower Rhone and Bayonne in the Basque country. This century, several bullfighters from the Southwest have gained recognition in Spain. The *corridas* in Mont-de-Marsan, Dax, Bayonne, Aire, Eauze and Vic-Fezansac attract the top names in bullfighting every year. Equal importance is placed on the matador and the bulls which, even though sacrificed, are tremendously admired for their beauty and bravery.

Although Spanish in origin, bullfighting is common in Southwestern France. Here Pepin Liria performs a derechazo for an appreciative audience in Mont-de-Marsan.

In a traditional bullfight, the bullfighter attempts to *perform* with an otherwise savage bull, dominate it, and ultimately kill it with grace. The *course Landaise*, on the other hand, is a spectacle where specially trained men confront the females from the same families of savage bulls used in bullfights. Like with bulls, these cows are very fast and aggressive, and the spectacle consists of gracefully avoiding the cow as she approaches at full speed. Unlike a normal corrida, however, these animals are not killed.

The *course Landaise* takes its name from where it began, the *Les Landes* region of Gascony. Cows are part of a ranch or *ganadero*; the team of men who oppose the cows are called the *troupeaux* and consist of two trainers, one jumper, seven or eight *écarteurs* (who perform the passes), and the *teneur de corde*—who holds the cow with a rope attached to the horns. All members of the *troupeaux* wear special outfits that consist of white trousers and a traditional sequined vest—somewhat similar to that of a bullfighter. The spectacle takes place in an sand-covered arena the size of a hockey rink. It is organized by the village association called *le comité des fêtes* who charge a fee to pay the contract with the *ganadero*.

When the *course Landaise* begins, one *écarteur* goes to the middle of the ring, raises his arms and calls the cow who is held against a wall by the *teneur de corde*. Because of this confinement, the cow struggles to get free. After a few seconds, the *teneur* lets the cow go and she runs straight for the movement at the middle of the ring. When she reaches the *écarteur*, she focuses on him and attempts to make contact with her horns (which have been taped to avoid fatal injury). The *écarteur* keeps his feet planted, raises his arms, and just before contact, twists his body away from the animal while keeping one foot in place. Ideally, he grazes the back of the forceful cow while avoiding direct contact. At times, however, he is drilled in the back or the thigh by the horn and suffers injury or, at very least, acute pain.

The goal is to swerve as close as possible to the cow, with as much grace and class as possible. Sometimes the *écarteur* plays to the crowd and spins a couple of times before the cow arrives. Sometimes they go toward the rope or away from the rope. In any event, it is of utmost importance when the *écarteur* makes a move that he finishes with both feet firmly planted, and without slipping or bending over to gain his balance. Depending upon his level of skill, risk and grace, he is awarded a certain number of points for each pass.

Besides the *écarteur*, there is also another person on the team called the *sauteur* or jumper. This person is normally a gymnast who jumps over the cow as she runs full speed across the plaza. There are four different jumps that are classified; they are the *saut de l'ange* (flying angel), *saut vrillé* (spinning jump), *saut périlleux* (perilous jump), and the *saut pieds-joints* (tied-leg jump).

Throughout the three-hour spectacle, each *écarteur* is judged by a jury, applauded by the public, rewarded with money given by village residents, fans, and local businesses, and given trophies by the *comité des fêtes*. Everybody on the team is paid differing amounts depending on their point total, but certainly not to the extent of a bullfighter. Because, unlike their Spanish counterparts, the money an *écarteur* earns from the *course* only *supplements* his regular income. All of these men work other jobs during the week, most usually related to agriculture.

During the four month summer season, there might be three or four competitions a week. With their other jobs, most *écarteurs* can earn five to ten thousand francs per month ($1,000-$2,000). The *best écarteurs* can earn 200,000 francs ($35,000) in a season, but very few do that.

Every year there is a championship where all the teams compete in the two major arenas of Les Landes, those of Mont-de-Marsan and Dax. It is during these competitions that the best men confront the best cows, and afterwards, the best men and the best cows are classified. Each spectacle brings with it folkloric music from the region—*pasodobles* similar to that of the corrida—as well as a sense of danger and excitement.

The *course Landaise* is extremely appreciated in the Armagnac region and has existed for a number of centuries. Certain *écarteurs* are legendary and still spoken of fondly (Coran, Suisse, Mazzantini, Meunier, Lalande, Forsans, the Gypsy brothers Ramunchito), while modern stars like Dusseau, Descazeaux, Laplace, Lalanne, Rachou, and Bergamo continue to improve upon the traditions set by their predecessors.

Rugby

Rugby is the major sport in the Southwest and by far the most popular sport in Armagnac. In fact, we could even call rugby the *official* sport of Armagnac. French rugby is divided into two categories, the national divisions for the city clubs and the regional divisions for the village clubs. Depending upon their play during the year, each team moves up or down a division the following season.

Kids begin to play rugby around the age of 8 and continue their career until they are 35 or 40-years-old. The greatest accomplishment one can hope to achieve is to be selected for the French National Team and play against the British or the teams from the Southern hemisphere.

In the countryside, most men breathe and eat rugby. Matches are on Sunday but on Thursday village residents begin to speak about their club's weekend activity.

The competition on the field is fierce but, once the match is over, the infamous *troisième mi-temps* or third-half begins. During this time, each team drinks at the bar, sings and has a lot of fun.

Both the mass and rugby match take place on Sunday: the latter undoubtedly draws the bigger crowd.

Pigeon Hunting

Wild pigeon hunting could be viewed as the other national sport of Armagnac and takes place during both the Spring and Autumn. These hunted pigeons (palombes) are light gray, and look somewhat similar to common street pigeons. They live in Scandinavia, Germany, Russia and Poland during the summer, but travel south to Spain and Northern Aftica for the winter. In the Spring, they migrate North again. During these migration periods, the pigeons fly at great heights and cover hundreds of miles a day. The Armagnac region is a natural stopping point before their long and arduous trek over the Pyrénée Mountains. Their preferred resting spots are within groves of trees—places they feel are safe and inconspicuous.

For weeks before the migration period, hunters have constructed intricate *palombières* or *hunting forts* beneath these trees. The *polombière* is normally constructed by three or four friends, one of who usually owns the property. These forts include a series of wire mesh and leaf-covered, camouflaged tunnels from which the hunters shoot.

In the main area, there are live pigeons called *les apaux* in cages. These cages are attached to small metal platforms and raised to the top of the trees. The live decoys have their eyes covered so that they are not excited by passing flights. They are strategically placed to make the grove of trees look occupied. Wires up to sixty feet in length are connected to the decoys; when a group of birds approaches overhead, they are pulled and the platform is tipped slightly; the decoy regains its balance by flapping its wings.

This gesture attracts the attention of the passing birds. When the other birds see these decoys, they come toward the trees to rest, figuring it to be a safe spot. Soon the treetops are filled with flapping wings.

At this moment, the hunters below are waiting patiently with their rifles, carefully taking aim.

Suddenly gunfire erupts! The birds move upward into the sky. Several, hit by well-placed shots, fall to the ground.

On a good day, three or four men might kill fifty birds. On a bad day, maybe only one or two. Almost more important than killing the birds, however, is the social element of the hunt, the camaraderie that goes on between the men in the *palombière*. This friendship is considered to be more important than having a table full of dead birds.

Because even when no birds pass, the hunters are sure to eat and drink well. Everybody brings something different; paté, charcuterie, *entrecôte*...there is even a barbecue and refrigerator in some of the elaborate *palombière*!

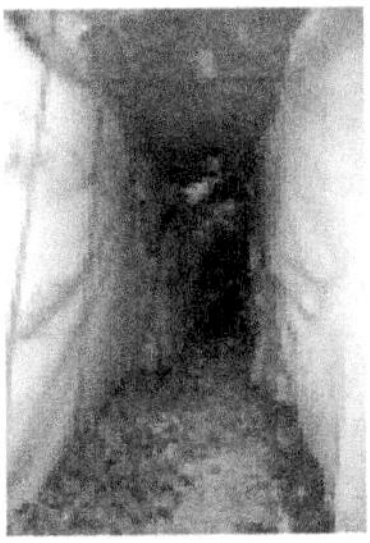

Hunters build elaborate forts with underground tunnels called palombieres (center) and fire at their unsuspecting prey through a camouflaged roof (right).

Famous Gascons Throughout History

Henry IV

Henry IV was born in 1553 in Pau, at the base of the Pyrénées. His father was Antoine de Bourbon, a Catholic. His mother, Jeanne d'Albret, was a Protestant and Queen of the Navarre territory, which is now the area that includes Gascony and the Pyrénée regions of Spain. In 1572, Henry IV married Marguerite de Valois, the sister of Henry III. When Henry IV became King of Navarre, he led the Hugenots (French Protestants) in numerous battles against the French Roman Catholics.

However, Henry IV was not a die-hard Protestant; in fact, he changed from the Protestant to Catholic religions six times during his life, normally for political reasons. One such change came shortly after becoming France's King in 1589 when, upon accepting Catholicism as his religion, he gradually gained favor of the large majority of French subjects.

This support was strengthened by his calm rule of the kingdom, peaceful resolution with King Philip II of Spain, and his love of life's simple pleasures. After all, instead of basing his political platform on military power, Henry IV promised that all families in his kingdom would have the financial means to put a chicken in their pot every Sunday!

In 1599, Henry IV also issued Europe's first long-lasting proclamation regarding religious tolerance. The Huguenots were granted certain freedoms that had previously been denied, thus ending France's numerous civil wars.

"One must drink before they have thirst."—Henry IV (above). The legendary d'Artagnan (below).

D'Artagnan

At the end of the first quarter of the 1600's, King Louis XIII created the Company of the King's Musketeers, an elite military regiment authorized to carry muskets. Having his roots in Armagnac and a chateau in Nérac, Louis added scores of *Armagnacais* to his regiments. Like this the *Armagnacais* became renowned for their bravery and patriotism. In fact, soldiers from the region accompanied every subsequent French king to battle after Henry IV's rule, heroically defending the French royalty while under constant fire.

D'Artagnan is without doubt the most famous musketeer from Gascony, immortalized by the author Alexander Dumas. D'Artagnan was born Charles de

Batz in 1615 at the Chateau de Castelmore, near the town of Lupiac at the base of the Ténarèze. He was the third of eight children and, not being the first-born male, destined to pursue his career away from his home. He set off for Paris where he served with the French guards. When he was 42, he became part of the King's Musketeers.

D'Artagnan gained his fame not only by accomplishing numerous dangerous missions, but also for his humanitarian relations with those who served under him. He led troops during the Fronde War, the siege of Dunkerque and, in 1659, accompanied the royal convoy to St. Jean-de-Luz for the marriage of Louis XIV to the Princess of Spain.

D'Artagnan continued serving his country until 1673 when he was killed in battle during a bloody conflict with Holland. Although destined to become the most celebrated hero of Gascony, d'Artagnan, at age 62, died a relatively poor man.

Jean Lannes

At the end of the 1700's, another military hero emerged; Jean Lannes, born in Lomagne, served under Napoleon Bonaparte during the first campaigns against Italy. "I took him as a little man, yet I lost a giant," Napoleon stated after Lannes lost his life in battle. "He had little education...nature made him. He was exceptionally brave. No other French general that served under me could equal his skill at maneuvering 25,000 infantry across the battlefield."

The People Today

In general, the typical *Armagnacais* has some shade of dark brown hair. They generally have pale skin highlighted by rosy red cheeks. As they age, both men and women tend to develop round shoulders. Many are slightly overweight and often walk with a rolling gait (lifelong diets of rich foods tend to encourage this). Even though they work hard when they're in the sun, they generally don't like the heat. From many spots in the Armagnac region, the snow-capped Pyrénées are clearly visible and the wonderful Atlantic beaches are less than two hours away. Despite their proximity, not many *Armagnacais* go to the beach or ski.

60% of their ancestry goes back several hundred years in France: however, 40% have immigrated to the country over the past seventy years, especially from Italy and Spain, which adds a Latin feel to the region. The population of Gascony has more in common with the natives of southern European countries than they do with those from Great Britain, Germany, Scandinavia or Paris even. Most inhabitants actually view those from *the North* as being somewhat cold and insular.

In comparison with other parts of France, there is a fairly low Arab population in the Armagnac region. Likewise, not many *Pieds Noirs* found the armagnac business lucrative enough to call the Gers or Les Landes their new home. Catholicism is by far and away the most popular religion.

Small towns within the Armagnac region lie about five miles apart, bound together by a patchwork of golden wheat, green corn, and yellow sunflowers that drape themselves across the gently rolling hills. Two-lane roads weave their way between these small hamlets. The Ténarèze tends to have houses made out of white stone, much of which comes from the area's limestone soil. The Bas-Armagnac region reflects the Landaise style—houses made of a mixture of dark wooden beams and tan-colored plaster made with the region's sand.

During the day, a typical armagnac producer is dressed in the common blue work overhauls. Grapes are but one of his concerns; others include the lack of moisture for his crops, his sick cow, repairs to his tractor, a loan from the bank...worse yet, his aging mother, cheating wife, wayward son or pregnant daughter...An armagnac producer always has something to worry about!

Few armagnac producers have ever been to the United States; not many have even been to Paris! They remain an isolated lot whose knowledge of the outside world has, for the most part, come through the excellent documentaries on French television or through the newspaper.

During an argument, whether it be about politics or sports, the typical *Armagnacais* will make a point and then repeat the statement repeatedly. Once they express an opinion, it will be hard to persuade an *Armagnacais* otherwise. It doesn't matter if your point of view makes more sense. Their opinion is *the* correct opinion!

Finally, the Southwestern accent, rather than being *pointed* like that of a Parisian, tends to be more elongated—somewhat like a southern drawl. It is recognized immediately by the French. Older natives roll their "r's" a little, a trait that stems from the dying *patois*—once the common language across the countryside.

Natives also tend to emphasize the last consonant of certain words, especially the "t". In Armagnac, people might say Bu-zette instead of Bu-zay or Tari-quette instead of Tari-quay. This pronunciation often makes non-natives laugh. However, pronouncing the word according to *correct* French rules certainly draws strange looks from the natives.

Scenes from the café: A modern muskateer parties into the wee hours at the village fête while two weathered veterans keep it going the next morning.

A typical landscape in the Gers

The Origin of the Armagnac People

Throughout the centuries, many nations have controlled Armagnac soil. Toulouse was once the capitol of the Visigoth empire, a territory that stretched from the Loire Valley to Southern Spain. The Moors, who conquered all of Northern Africa and Spain, likewise made their way across the Pyrénées and into Gascony. In addition, the Franks dominated the region for a brief period.

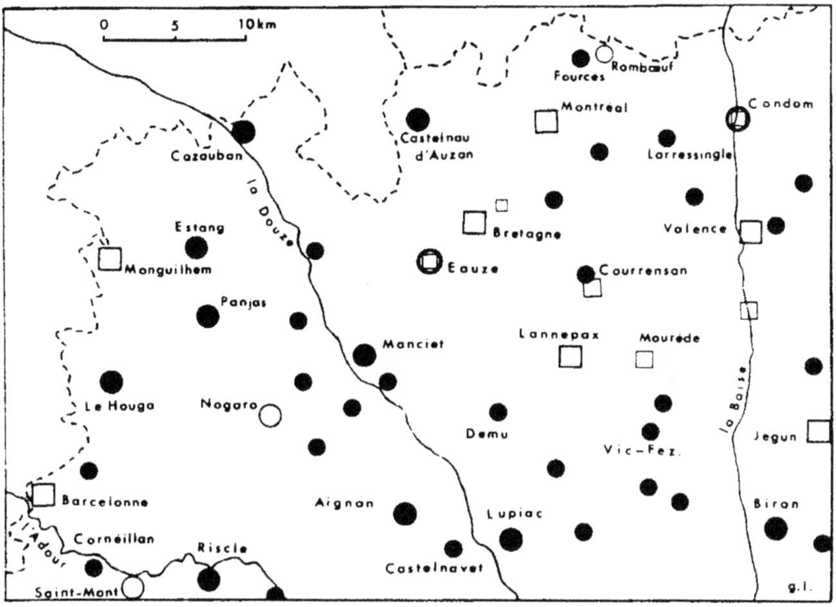

Eauze and Condom were two villages developed during the tenth century. The white circles represent villages developed in the eleventh century and the black circles represent castles built between the eleventh and thirteenth centuries.

From the time that Christ was born until the fifth century, the entire Aquitaine, also known as *Novempopulanie* or *land of the new people*, was part of the Roman empire. Some of its important towns included Eauze, Auch and Aire-sur-l'Adour.

Between the seventh and eleventh centuries, intermittent invasions by barbarians left some towns and villages devastated. Subsequent centuries saw a strong British/Acquitanian presence. To protect themselves from peasant upheavals, the British built walled villages or bastides. Many of these remain in the region to this day.

A town square served not only as a location for various shops but also as a gathering place. A church normally lay just off the square. These towns often took on prestigious names from cities in other countries: Fleurance (Florence), Mielan (Milan), Cologne, Barcelonne, or Bretagne.

Power struggles between the English and French continued off and on between the eleventh and sixteenth centuries. Perhaps the climax of the ongoing conflicts was during the Hundred-Year War of the fourteenth century. During their invasions, the English laid waste to countless vineyards, killed thousands of French peasants and raped countless French women. When the countries weren't battling, famine or disease ran rampant. Many villages were left to crumble.

The English were finally driven out in 1453, yet afterwards the French remained at war with themselves. This time, religious beliefs between Protestants and Catholics caused the bloody disagreements. It wasn't until the rule of Henry IV that this religious violence finally came to an end and the Gascony region of France as we know it today took form.

For nearly 2,000 years, wine has been depicted in the Armagnac region through mosaics and religious paintings. On the left, one of the beautiful mosaics found at Seviac; on the right, a painting in the Eauze Cathedral.

Armagnac: The Spirit Itself

Many factors play a role in the ultimate quality of an armagnac: the climate, soil, grapes, distillation, barrel-type, and the quality and length of aging. Like with wine, determining which is *the* most important factor (man or nature) is difficult.

Certain towns lie upon sandy soils that traditionally yield armagnacs that display tremendous finesse and class. Unfortunately many producers within these communes do not distill early or invest in new oak, which ultimately can lead to a mediocre spirit. On the other hand, some towns without the *correct* soil can have producers that make very good armagnac because they do everything else right.

Ultimately great armagnac is a synthesis of environmental factors (climatic conditions, *terroir*), materials (grapes, quality of barrels) and technique (storage conditions, racking, reduction). To understand armagnac, it is helpful to explore all of these facets in depth.

The Soil

Geographically, the Armagnac region was once part of a deep channel that flowed between the Pyrénées (along the Spanish border) and the *Massif Central* (a mountain range that begins in central France and descends nearly to the Mediterranean). These mountains formed over millions of years while the body of ocean that covered Southwestern France slowly relocated. Crevices developed as the currents of water shifted; submerged rubble was gradually transformed into layers of clay as bodies of water flowed through the valleys.

When the water level dropped, large amounts of sand and transient marine material like crushed mollusks, skeletons of fish, quartz sand, and crustaceans settled above the clay. The relatively flat area now known as the Bas-Armagnac (*Bas* as in *lower* altitude) remained covered with much of this sand and marine sediment which, even today, blows from the immense pine forests nearby.

As we move East across the Bas-Armagnac and into the Ténarèze, gentle hills begin to break up the flat expanses of land. The soil also becomes harder with layers of clay (minute particles of sand that have been compressed).

Further East in the Haut-Armagnac, we don't see much flat land at all. Parcels of sand are rare and the limestone content within the clay begins to rise.

The Relationship Between Soil And Vines And Its Effect On The Resultant Fruit

Soil is composed of different-sized grains of minerals and organic matter. In general, soil plays five roles for vines:

1. It provides support for the vine so that it can grow upwards.
2. It provides nutrients in the form of minerals (iron, zinc, copper, cobalt, potassium, magnesium, nickel, boron).
3. It allows for the drainage of water.
4. It provides reflection from the sun.
5. It holds heat at night.

Different soils have different structures that play an important role with planted vines. Sand is a large-grained soil through which water drains rapidly. Other soils are made of smaller material that has been compressed over the years into forms such as gravel, limestone or chalk. These materials tend to drain water slowly, allowing vines a steady water supply. Clay contains the most minute particles of all and allows little room for water to pass; consequently, clay tends to hoard water underground in stagnant pools.

While most vegetable plants and fruit trees thrive on this rich, clay-based soil, it rarely provides the raw ingredients for wines with any delicacy. Instead, vines tend to flourish on land rarely suitable for other plantings.

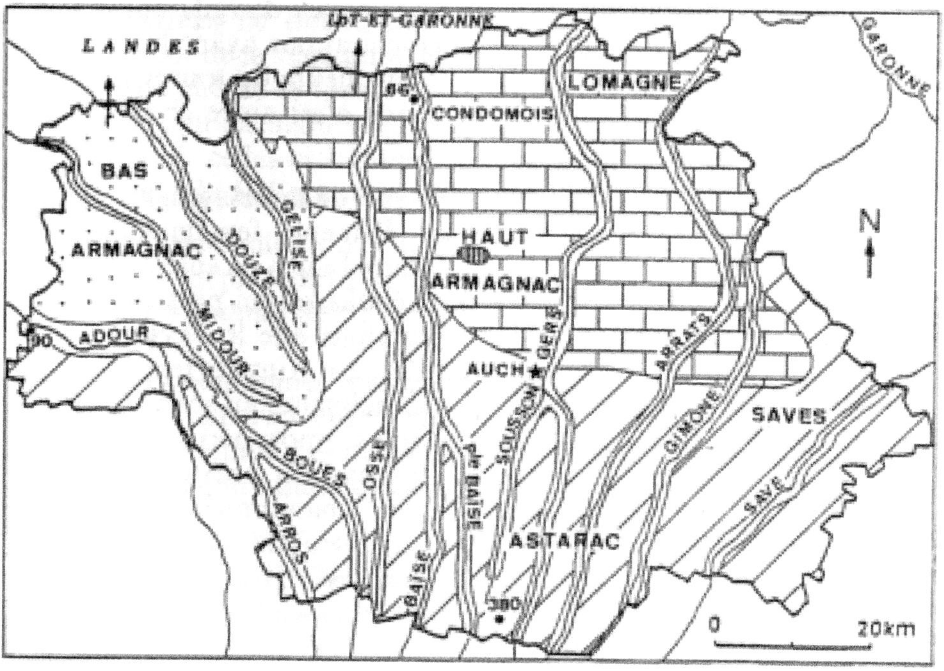

A generalized overview of the soil composition within the Armagnac region: The dots represent sand, the bricks a mixture of clay and limestone, and the diagonal lines, pure limestone.

Different soils also retain differing degrees of heat. Compressed soils like clay tend to stay cooler which, in turn, tends to produce late-ripening grapes. Conversely, sand tends to heat more quickly and provide roots with more growth potential. Consequently grapes grown on sand tend to ripen early. However, during cold weather, vines that grow on sand are much more susceptible to frosts. A point in case is the frost that arrived on April 23, 1997. Within the communes that contain high percentages of sand (Le Frêche, Lacquy, Hontanx, Perquie, Arthez), at least 60% of the year's harvest was lost.

The pH level of a soil measures its amounts of acidity and alkalinity. Grapes grown on sand tend to have higher acidity levels which lends itself to grapes with similarly high acid levels. As highly acidic wines tend to produce the most supple spirits, it follows suit that grapes grown in the regions with the most sand (like the western part of the Bas-Armagnac) offer the most potential for immediate quality.

As one moves from West to East through the Bas-Armagnac to the Ténarèze, the soil typically has lower levels of calcium and a lower pH levels that ultimately lead to less acidic grapes. These soils often produce armagnacs that are hard, flat, and relatively closed.

The soils typically found within the Armagnac region include:

Sablo-Limoneux (Sand): Technically, there are two types of sand; large sand measures between .2 and 2 mm in dimension and is commonly found on or near the beach. Fine sand measures between .05 and .2 mm in dimension and, unlike its larger counterpart, has the capability of providing stability for grapevines. Sand particles separate easily, allowing water to drain very rapidly. Sand is highly acidic and very susceptible to climatic change. Vines grown on sand tend to yield grapes with lots of acidity. The resultant spirit tends to be very round in its youth while also displaying plenty of finesse.

Sables Fauves (Iron-Rich Sand): Sand with a mixture of iron-rich quartz give this *terroir* its tawny or light brown color. The role of iron on the developing vine is uncertain; development of the fruit is similar to that grown on sand with less-iron—lots of suppleness in their youth along with admirable finesse.

Argilo-Sablonneux or Boulbènes (Sand with small pieces of clay): This soil is comprised of a mixture of sand and clay pieces. Grapes grown on this soil show good acidity levels. The traces of clay insure that the soil is slightly less susceptible to frost than straight sand. This soil stays slightly cooler than sand and moreover retains a bit more water. Armagnacs from vines grown on *boulbènes* tend to be excellent, and express themselves especially well after ten years of aging.

Argilo-Calcaire (Clay with small pieces of limestone): Grapes grown on this soil normally display lower acidity than those grown on sand and remain slightly firm in their youth. Because this soil tends to retain heat longer, the grapes also attain slightly higher alcohol levels. The porous nature of limestone stores rainwater and slowly releases it to surrounding vegetation, almost like a natural system of irrigation. Although spirits produced from grapes grown on this soil take a good fifteen years to develop, they decline very slowly as well.

The Armagnac Subsoil

Subsoil plays a tremendous role with regard to a grape's nutrient flow. The further down the vine has to search for nutrients normally means that the eventual quality of the harvested grapes is better.

Subsoil with gravel or limestone particles absorbs water which allows the vine to gradually gain nourishment. Most of the subsoil within the Bas-Armagnac and Ténarèze is composed of *terrebouc*, an hard iron-rich clay with limestone pieces. This subsoil generally lies several feet below the surface. The *terrebouc* tends to become waterlogged in the winter and lose its moisture in the summer. Therefore the best vines are generally found where the *terrebouc* lies the deepest.

The most common soils found in Armagnac include: quartz-rich sand (bottom left), iron-rich sand (center), sand with clay pieces (top left), clay (top right) and limestone (bottom right). The soil generally changes in this order as one moves across the region from West to East.

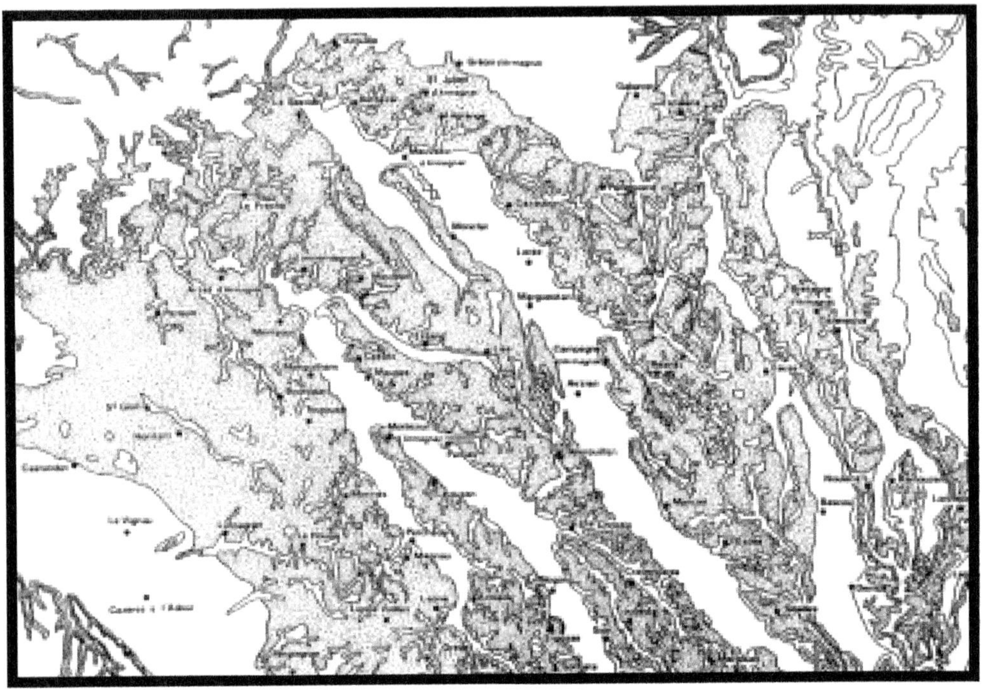

In this geological map of the Bas-Armagnac region, the shaded areas represent high contents of sand and marine-based sediment.

The Climate

The climate within the Armagnac region is influenced by two important geographical phenomena that surround it. Most significant is the Atlantic Ocean to the East; the ocean often attracts cool winds and rain that ensures temperate weather. Also important is the hot air mass that comes up from the Mediterranean Sea, hovers over the flat land near Toulouse and crosses Gascony.

The Bas-Armagnac tends to receive more rain than the rest of the region, mainly due to its proximity to the ocean. Producers in the western part of the Bas-Armagnac generally get more rain than those to the East. The majority of the time, however, it is hot, hazy, and humid. The Gers, on the other hand, receives less rain. The summer months are, however, sticky with humidity.

The region generally sees snow only a few times a decade; when it comes, it barely covers the ground. Rain is more common during the relatively short winter season, always accompanied by plenty of heavy fog. The average temperature during the winter is around 7° C (45° F). For the most part, the spring is long and humid, the summer hot and humid, autumn long and sunny, and the winter rainy yet short.

Armagnac producers get nervous during two seasons of the year; the spring and the summer. In April, prematurely warm conditions can cause grapes to bud. If a spring frost then occurs (like in 1991 and 1997), tremendous amounts of buds can be killed in their youth, prematurely freezing to death. Producers with sandy soil are especially susceptible to frosts, as roots growing in sand freeze more rapidly than roots growing in limestone.

During the late summer months, if the air masses from the East and West have a showdown, a beautiful yet potentially disastrous hail storm results that also puts ripening grapes in grave danger. Inch-wide hailstones falling for just ten minutes can rip entire clusters from the vine, demolish countless grapes, and drastically reduce the eventual yields for any particular year.

Whereas these devastating conditions normally occur only a few times a decade, most years see temperate weather throughout the Spring and summer with sunny conditions persisting into September. This insures plenty of sun—*the* most important ingredient for full maturation of armagnac's raw material.

The ability for grapes to consistently become ripe helps set it apart from other grape spirit-producing regions in France: fuller maturation leads to a *slightly* fatter wine and a slightly richer and more flavorful *eau de vie* when it exits the still.

Bad Moon Rising: Intense thunderstorms or "orages" strike often during the Gascon summer. They don't last very long, but often bring hailstones the size of golf balls that can partially destroy a producer's anticipated harvest.

The Grapes

The grapes grown on Armagnac's soil constitute one of the most important aspects of the spirit's character. Unlike in Cognac where the relatively neutral Ugni Blanc is irrefutably the boss, varietals that lead to tremendous variation in taste and texture are frequently distilled in Armagnac. The usage of these different grapes has evolved for more than four centuries and certainly helps give armagnac its unique character.

Around 1600, the vineyards were mainly planted with Piquepoult or, as we call it today, Folle Blanche. This remained the staple armagnac grape until the time of the phylloxera. When the huge replanting took place around the turn of the century, grapes less susceptible to gray rot and other maladies (Ugni Blanc, Colombard, Plainte de Grèce) took preference. When Bacco was introduced, a near revolution took place in the vineyards and made it the overwhelming favorite among farmers.

A well-tended Ugni Blanc vineyard near Eauze.

During the Sixties and Seventies, Ugni Blanc gained popularity. By the early 1980's, Ugni Blanc outweighed Bacco in the Armagnac vineyards for the first time. The reason was simple: it gained a much higher price from *négociants* because it could be used for both table wines and distillation, unlike Bacco which is rarely used for anything but distillation.

The grapes used for Armagnac tend to reach maturity at different times. Financial limitations compel the majority to pick and ferment the varietals together. Some producers, however, can afford to pick, ferment and distill their varietals separately.

For these producers, Folle Blanche is normally brought in first, around the second week of September. Bacco is typically picked around mid-month. The Ugni Blanc and Colombard are harvested last, customarily toward the end of September.

A healthy armagnac vine yields approximately 100-120 hectoliters/hectare, yet only 90 hectolitres are allowed to be distilled; everything above that quantity must be sold as grape juice or must. A few estates pick by hand, but the great majority harvest with machines.

Although not common, some vineyards, like this one in the Ténarèze, have highly-trellised vines.

Chaptilization is prohibited for wines to be distilled into armagnac—high alcohol is not what producers want anyway. The addition of any type of sulfur is also against the law, whether it be to stop fermentation or prevent the spread of bacteria. As long as careful measures have been taken to properly cleanse the fermentation vessels (normally stainless steel or concrete vats), the wine's strong acidity helps prevent the diffusion of unwanted microbes.

Although the grapes are not normally destalked, careful attention is paid to minimizing the amount of stalk and pit contact with the juice. The liquid is pumped and air contact is encouraged, which helps prepare the juice for fermentation. Very few people within the region add yeast strains to begin fermentation; generally the yeast is indigenous, coming from the skins of the grapes. Pumping over helps keep the liquid in the tanks homogenous.

Fermentation stops naturally; the wine then remains in closed tanks, aging *sur lie* and gradually taking on added complexity. The best armagnacs come from wine that have breathed through the lees. When young, these lees are full of ethyl esters and acids, which ultimately help produce floral and fruity aromas. If a wine remains too long on the lees, it becomes bitter and the resulting aromas become excessively herbaceous. A winemaker always has to retain the freshness of his wine and guard against oxidation; if oxidation occurs, the spirit will exit the still with off-aromas which will never be lost.

Armagnac's grapes produce wines that are tart, low in alcohol and high in acidity: Wines between 8° and 9° are considered ideal for continuous distillation. *Charentaise*-type pot stills and modern, large-scale alambics can distill wines with elevated alcohol levels without problem. Yet wines of more than 10° are problematic for the *traditional* alambic because they heat too quickly

The Armagnac Region Under Vine

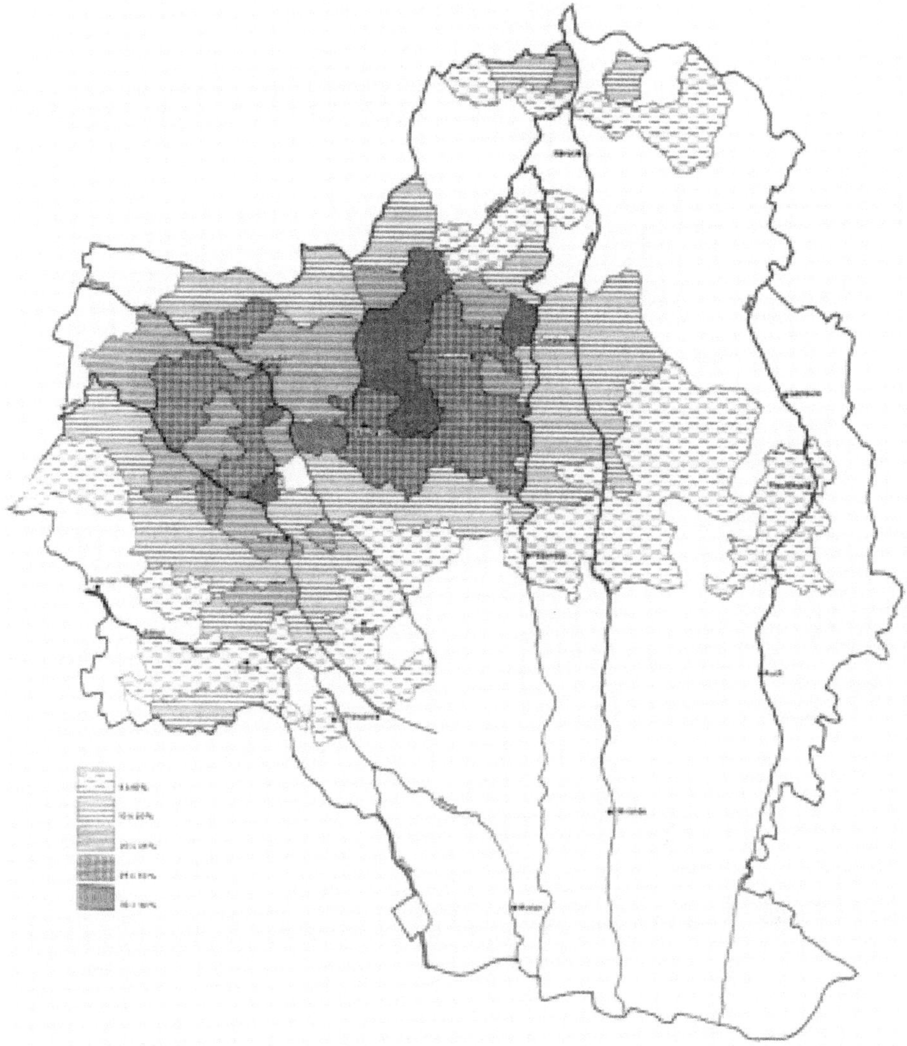

Statistics have not changed much in 15 years: The border between the Bas-Armagnac and the Ténarèze (the heavily-shaded areas) have the most acres under vine (30%-40%). Conversely, the Haut-Armagnac (the large white area) has very little area under vine.

and do not entirely condense as they leave the still. This causes flow problems—the spirit spurts out and part of the distillation ultimately is lost as a vapor.

Folle Blanche, Bacco, and Ugni Blanc normally arrive between 8° and 10°. Colombard, however, tends to reach 10½° or 11°, which might require the distiller to lessen the wine's degree by adding water—something that will certainly dilute some flavor but ultimately lead to a smoother distillation.

Currently nine grapes are permitted for the distillation of armagnac, although four are generally used. Apart from Colombard and Ugni Blanc, their wines are not very enjoyable at the table. For continuous distillation, however, they are ideal.

Folle Blanche

In pre-phylloxera days, the staple grape used to produce Armagnac was the Folle Blanche, known in Gascony as *Piquepoult* or *lip-stinger* because of its high acidity. It was also popular in other areas of France, like in the Languedoc where locals named it *Picpoul*, in the Aveyron where it was known as *Mendic*, and in the Loire where it's still called *Gros Plant*.

Folle Blanche produces a light to medium-bodied wine that is low in alcohol (7°-9°) high in acidity, and ideal for distillation into fine brandy. Unfortunately, the grapes form in compact clusters that, when mature, do not allow much air inside. Consequently, they are prone to mildew and rot and need to be treated extensively with costly chemicals, perhaps up to 12 times a year. Yields are also fairly low, meaning much less potential wine. *Precocious* is the word most commonly used by farmers to describe Folle Blanche.

Armagnacs made from a high percentage of Folle Blanche, however, offer seductive characteristics; they tend to be feminine and show especially well in their first fifteen years of life. They normally have a very fine texture and light, high-pitched, floral aromatics (including budding vine flowers, white peach, dried apricot and orange peel).

After fifteen years in cask they still retain lots of finesse, yet their primary aromatics begin to depart and their flavor characteristics begin to merge with that of other grapes.

Although Folle Blanche demonstrates tremendous aromatic and textural delicacy, it represents a mere 5% of the plantings throughout the region.

Bacco 22-A

Nearly all the vines in the Armagnac region were destroyed by the phylloxera that ravished French vineyards toward the end of last century. After the louse was conquered, French vines were grafted onto the phylloxera-resistant American rootstock and the vines budded again. Yet producers realized several things about their rejuvenated plants: Grafted Folle Blanche vines blossomed into even larger, tighter grape clusters than before, and the grafted plant was weaker *and* more susceptible to rot and disease.

Further studies showed that grafted Colombard was too high in alcohol and low in acidity to be distilled efficiently with a traditional alambic. The other grapes produced armagnacs that were not only coarse but also without character. Farmers, although excited at seeing grapes on the vine again, had arrived at a dead end concerning raw material for a good armagnac: Changes had to be made.

These changes started happening in the late-thirties when a Landais teacher named François Bacco developed a hybrid clone of the *vinifera* grape Folle Blanche and an American *labrusca* grape called Noah. This new grape, named Bacco 22 A, created sturdier wines than either of its parents while retaining some of Folle Blanche's aromatic charm. So good were the results with Bacco that it became the only *vinifera/labrusca* hybrid allowed in French AOC (*Appellation d'Origine Controlée*) vineyards.

Bacco's leaves are fairly round and its grapes develop in small, compact clusters, making them less susceptible to mildew and other maladies. The grape's tough skin prevents it from splitting during occasional hail storms. Bacco (occasionally spelled Baco) is strong, resistant to disease and, in comparison to other grapes, does not require much chemical treatment. Farmers in the region love it; they simply plant it and let it grow without tremendous attention.

Its wine normally does not reach higher than 10 degrees alcohol. It is medium-bodied, with a nuance that is normally combines lemon and green apple. After distillation, it gives a spirit lots of fat but does not offer very intense aromatics. After about a dozen years, however, it does yield an armagnac with a forward, full-blown bouquet that commonly evokes dried plum or *pruneau*, dried apricot and quince. While Bacco presently covers only 10% of the region's plantings, its grapes account for about 30% of the wine used for distillation.

Recently a law was brought into effect that stated that after the year 2010, no hybrid that crossed *vitus vinifera* and *vitus labrusca* grape types would be allowed in any AOC vineyard. Consequently, the future of Bacco does not look bright. This has, of course, created some controversy among armagnac producers, especially those located in Les Landes where the grape performs particularly well. Many hope for an impasse that will allow for ten or fifteen more harvests. Other producers have torn up their Bacco, replacing the vineyards with Ugni Blanc or Folle Blanche. Still others, disruntled with the entire controversy, have simply replaced their vineyards with corn.

To make matters even worse, recent tests done in Canada showed that Bacco, when consumed in extremely high doses (over one gallon a day for two years) can be carcinogenic.

Another unfortunate setback for the grape that has done so much to make armagnac the best *eau de vie* in the world.

Ugni Blanc

Whereas the grape is also planted in Provence, Ugni Blanc is most famous in the Charente where it is nearly the sole grape used for Cognac. Ugni Blanc is relatively easy to grow and gives high yields—in short, a big producer and wonderful investment. It has a neutral flavor, produces wines with elevated levels of acidity and low alcohol, and is clean and frank. Ugni Blanc now comprises about 55% of the grapes used for the distillation of armagnac.

Ugni Blanc is actually the Trebbiano from Tuscany, a grape that made its way to Gascony by way of Provence and the Languedoc. It buds late, making it less susceptible to late-spring frosts. It is also a late-ripener, which occasionally leaves it green at harvest time. Its leaves are more pointed than those of Folle Blanche or Bacco, and very large. Its grapes develop in long, narrow clusters.

At their best, armagnacs made with Ugni Blanc (pictured above) contain pleasing aromatics that tend to accentuate the spice notes from the oak in which they are aged. They are less powerful and less flamboyant than Bacco and, in comparison with Folle Blanche, less aromatic and less fine.

Colombard

Because of its high resistance to mildew, Colombard is widely planted within the vineyards of Gascony, although most of it goes into table wine. Almost cylindrical in shape, the grape produces fragrant, dry wines that include notes of apple blossom, pear drop, red grapefruit and herbs. They display lots of freshness in their youth, greatly helped by their higher alcohol level. Upon release, they often guard a slight spritz.

Although many producers still distill some Colombard, most put it at the bottom of their list of preferred varietals. After distillation its youthful aroma is slightly herbal and reminiscent of freshly mown hay. It never seems to develop the round flavors of Bacco or the delicate floral notes of Folle Blanche, nor does it provide the neutral foundation that Ugni Blanc offers. Although suitable in a blend, it rarely pulls things off on its own; its aromatic level simply remains fairly one-dimensional and flat (Domaine Boingnères is the great exception).

Colombard (on the right) is a late-harvester and currently makes up about 40% of the vines planted in the armagnac region, yet only 10% of its harvest is used for distillation. Instead, 20% is used for floc and the overwhelming majority is used for dry table wines. Excellent white wines thrive in the Armagnac region, especially the Ténarèze. In fact the *Vin de Pays de Côtes de Gascogne* has become one of the area's top exports.

Made mostly with Colombard and normally blended with Ugni Blanc or Gros Manseng, the wine is light, aromatic, and clean, provides an excellent accompaniment to seafood, flaky fish and poultry, and can also be served as a tasty apéritif. Long championed by American critic Robert Parker as being France's greatest white wine value, it is difficult to criticize armagnac growers for diverting some of their grape crops to something so pleasurable and refreshing.

The following varietals are not common in the region; the occasional producer, however, still has a small plot in their vineyard. Recent plantings of some of these have taken place at three domaines in the region (Chateau de Mons, Chateau de Laubade, and the Domaine de Paguy) as part of an ongoing experiment to determine if one of these indigenous grapes is suitable for the large-scale replacement of Bacco. These include:

Jurançon Blanc

Jurançon Blanc, sometimes known as *Quillard*, was popular before the phylloxera. This grape also turns up in the Charente and in the Lot et Garonne, where it is called *Dame Blanc*. Jurançon's grapes (which have nothing to do with those of the Jurançon region) are very compact and have a conical shape. A tasting of a two-year-old from barrel showed much promise. It had a fine texture and displayed elegant aromas of flowers and citrus fruit. Its character is most similar to that of Folle Blanche.

Mauzac

Mauzac was once common in Armagnac but now has more popularity in Gaillac, where it is made into the appellation's excellent white wines, and in Limoux, where the grape is the staple of their fine sparkling wines. Mauzac's grapes are compact, its pits round, and its skin thick. It is often susceptible to mildew and vine rot. To make matters worse, Mauzac has a slightly higher alcoholic potential and oxidizes very easily when it becomes over-ripe. Consequently, it is not the best grape for distillation and is now difficult to find in the region.

Clairette

Clairette is another varietal that was once distilled on a frequent basis. What remains today in the region produces a very neutral-flavored wine as well as a sweet smelling yet neutral-flavored spirit. It tends to absorb the aromas of new oak fairly quickly.

Plainte de Grèce

The Plainte de Grèce can still be found on some properties (notably *Domaine de la Boubée* in Montréal-du-Gers). A vigorous producer, its grapes produce fairly alcoholic wines that normally hit around 9° alcohol. Although not tremendously elegant with regard to texture, its distilled product tends to show good fat.

Meslier St. Francis

After the phylloxera, this grape was introduced to the Gers because of its resistance to black rot, a malady to which Folle Blanche was very susceptible. Also called *François Blanc*, its grapes are fairly small and its vines high yielding. Its wine is normally of neutral character; likewise is its *eau-de-vie*, although it does retain a certain elegance.

Vines near Labastide during winter.

Armagnac Distillation

"Distillation is a miraculous birth; into the world it brings a refined and subtle eau-de-vie that fills the room with perfume and the heart of the distiller with pride."—Léon Lafitte, Domaine Boingnères

How Does Wine Become A Spirit?

For the distillation of armagnac, the main objective is to heat wine until it boils, purely condense its flavorants, and finally reconvert its steam into liquid form again. Armagnac distillation always takes place in an alambic still. The still is made out of copper because of its resistance to corrosion.

Wines can be distilled either once or twice. Double-distillation, or *double-chauffe*, is performed in a pot still and typically is used to produce cognac, calvados and whiskey, as well as neutral spirits that go into port, liqueurs, and anis-based *apéritifs*. Double-distillation of armagnac, although trendy during the seventies and eighties, lost tremendous favor during the nineties and is currently popular with a handful of the large *négociant* houses. Those who double-distill generally use the result to complement their single-distilled products that are meant to be released at a young age. Others, Dartigalongue to name one, sell a great deal of double-distilled *eau-de-vie* to other countries that are then used in other brandies or to fortify liqueurs. Most of these foreign clients have no interest in single-distilled spirits because they are much more difficult to reduce and manipulate.

Traditionally the wine used to produce armagnac is distilled once in a continuous still known as an *alambic armagnacais*. The still is continuous because it does not have to be stopped after each distillation to empty out unwanted deposits. In French, the process is called *simple-chauffe, distillation armagnacaise*, or *distillation continue.* It is the single-distillation of armagnac that plays the biggest role in setting the spirit apart from other brandies.

In order for an armagnac to state an appellation on the label, the grapes must be grown and distilled in the same region. Whereas distillation was once permitted until the end of April, recent law changes have deemed that Armagnac must now pass through the alambic before the end of January. Many producers, however, begin to distill in late October or early November.

The History Of Distillation

Records show that distillation was practiced as early as the third century in Egypt. Mosaics found indicate that liquids were also distilled during the Greek dynasty. The *art* of distillation, however, was perfected in the Arab-speaking countries of Northern Africa during the XIth century. In fact, the word *alcohol* is derived from the Arabic *al kohl*, as is the distillation vessel used for traditional armagnac, the alambic (*al ambic*).

The Arabs obviously did not distill spirits to savor and consume; after all, the Muslim religion eschews alcohol. Instead, their distilled spirits made from fruits and flowers were mainly used for perfumes and medicines.

It wasn't until the thirteenth century that distillation was introduced to France. Records show that this took place during the various conferences between the Arab school in Salerne and the French school in Montpellier. Arnaud-de-Villeneuve, head of Pope Clement V's school of medicine, can perhaps be credited for compiling and releasing the first complete thesis on distillation in 1246.

Historians are unsure as to the exact date Gascony was exposed to distilled alcohol; most agree, however, that they were brought from Spain. Some believe this transfer first occurred during the religious wars between Spain and the African countries, when the army of Abd-el-Rhaman reached the foothills of the Pyrénées. Others feel that the first *eau de vie* was brought to Gascony by Pilgrims who regularly passed between the two countries.

Various texts document the first distillation in Gascony to be in 1348. The *eau de vie* was certainly not refined; like in the Arab countries, it was distilled by chemists and most probably used in medicines for the treatment of various ailments.

During the late fourteenth century, Charles the Bad, the King of Navarre, had a ritual of soaking his sheets in *eau de vie*, then wrapping his entire body with the moistened material. This, he claimed, soothed his body and relieved pain. Unfortunately, while entwined one night, a servant's candle set the sheets ablaze and the King was killed horrifically from the fiery blaze that resulted.

Fortunately, this unusual accident did not prevent the Gascons from additional distillations. Their first copper alambic was put into practice in 1480. Although wine was distilled, armagnac still had not become an enjoyable spirit. Progress had been made from earlier times, though, because besides medicines, locals now used the spirit to preserve fruits and fortify wines.

From 1500 onwards, the art of distillation exploded all over Europe. New, improved stills most often took on the name of their inventor: Brunswick, Berthelot, Chaptal, Fahrenheit. Medicines continued to be distilled, although spirits made for pleasure were also gaining favor.

Armagnac as a brandy, however, was barely known outside the region. Gascony's greatest export was sweet Jurançon, the exotic, honeyed wine from the foothills of the Pyrénées. This noble wine had a tremendous reputation that spread throughout France and as far as England.

In the 1700's, we have our first precise details concerning the operation of the copper distillation devices operating in Gascony. From various descriptions, we can assess that it was a portable unit that heated wine in successive stages, not unlike a down-scaled version of a *Charentaise* still today.

Unfortunately, this multiple distillation took a tremendous amount of energy and money to fuel, things obviously hard to come by for many poor and isolated Gascon farmers. Consequently, experiments were carried out to find a still that was more conducive to a farmer's needs.

In 1801, Edouard Adam, a scientist in Montpellier, helped provide the remedy when he came up with a primitive device that processed wine with a single distillation, an adjustment which greatly minimized fueling costs. As a bonus this distillation also allowed the alcoholic vapors to pass through the incoming wine before they condensed, thus collecting all the fragrance of the wine. This still was first used in Armagnac shortly thereafter by the innovative Antoine de Mellet at his Chateau de Bonas. So good were his results that a factory in Eauze began fabricating this still. Monsieur Verdier later perfected de Melet's still and, as decades passed, further adjustments were made to updated models.

During the mid-eighteenth century, distillation within the region became even more widespread. Monsieur Gier had seen de Melet's still in Eauze and Verdier's still in Montguilhem. He made a replica of the still in his hometown Estang, then made some minor revisions. After many months of trial and error, he came up with a structure that ultimately provided the model for the present armagnac alambic.

Gier's unit was relatively small and fueled with low-cost wood. Wheels could be connected to the still's base, making it easy for a team of oxen to transport it from one farm to another. With several of these portable units running around the countryside, each farmer with wine to distill could do so before oxidation took place *and* without a fortune.

During the days and nights spent at various farms across the region, the traveling distiller surveyed the heat source regularly to keep the flame at a consistent temperature which ensured an even distillation. The low strength at which the spirit exited the still helped retain more of the wine's primary aromas.

This richer spirit contained impurities that kept it raw for a longer time than those distilled twice at a higher temperature. After a decade of aging, however, complexity not experienced through double-distillation was clearly apparent. The aromatic, fruity elements transferred through Armagnac's sandy soil were brought into full bloom when its fatter wine dripped out between 52° and 55°.

Attempting to produce armagnac in this manner had its risks as well. It required more time, and more time always meant less payoff for the producer. Even today, very few independent producers survive on armagnac alone. Money is still sparse among those who raise armagnac; in fact, at times, the only reason for continuing seems to be to reward oneself for waking at sunrise, sweating all day under the scorching sun, and concluding the day's work in darkness.

The Distillation Process

To understand how stills work, we can look at both traditional Cognac and Armagnac models, charting the journey that wine takes before being transformed into a spirit.

Double-Distillation

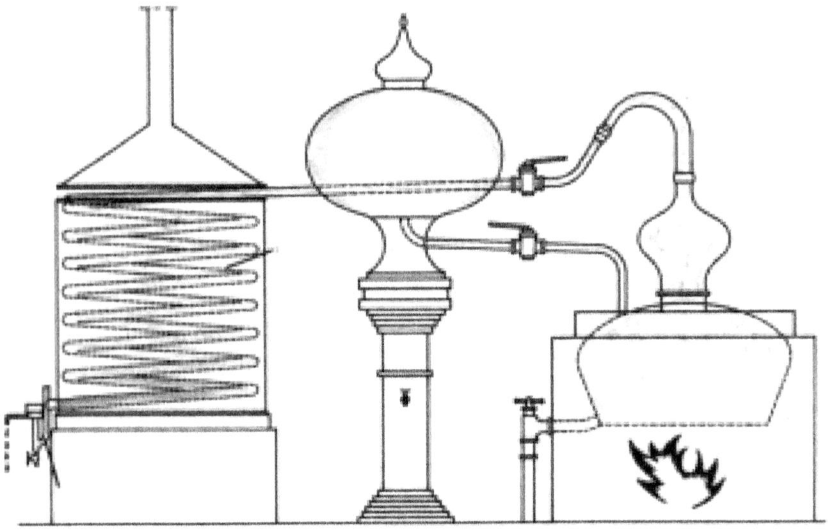

The alambic Charentaise, used to distill most of the world's brandies

The typical pot still used for double-distillation is often referred to as the *alambic Charentaise* because of its widespread use in Cognac. The still is comprised of several onion-shaped copper domes and holding tanks. The wine enters a central dome and gradually flows into a heating tank, under which a gas flame burns steadily. As the wine reaches the boiling point, a vapor begins to rise (just as it does with boiling water). This steam collects against the inside of the dome, then searches for a place to escape. Its only exiting point is a hole that leads to the curved pipe known as the swan's neck. Gravity then takes the vapor downward through a pipe coiled around a holding tank filled with cold water. From there it reconverts into liquid and exits the still with an alcohol level of around 28° or 56 proof.

A distiller carefully surveys the entire process. The first spirits to come out of the still, known as the *tetes* or heads, normally contain such high levels of impurities that they are discarded. The majority of the distillation, called the *brouillis*, is kept. The wine that takes the longest time to distill and remains at the end, called the *queues* or tails, is normally too weak and stripped of flavor to produce anything worth keeping. Consequently, like the heads, the tails are often discarded.

The useable material (*brouillis*) from the first distillation is collected and housed in holding tanks; afterwards, it is reinstated in the still and processed again. This time there is less waste material, and 99% is kept. The spirit exits at a higher strength the second time, normally somewhere between 67° and 72°. From there it goes straight into oak barrels.

Ironically, distillation in the pot still was widespread in Armagnac until the development of the continuous still in the early 1800's. Double-distillation was officially banned in 1936, only to be reinstated in 1972.

To distill one hectoliter (26 gallons) of pure alcohol, approximately 70 kilos (154 pounds) of propane gas is necessary. This energy expense warrants a distillation charge of anywhere from 1,400 to 1,600 francs (280 to 320 dollars) per 400 liter barrel.

Distillation Armagnacaise

Unlike cognac which is passed twice through a pot still, traditional armagnac is distilled once in a continuous still, a down-scaled, somewhat primitive version of the modern column still. Unlike industrial column stills—which can potentially heat to the same degree as a pot still—the traditional armagnac models often date to the beginning of the century and cannot heat the wine to above 120 proof. And while industrial models can distill up to 20 barrels a day, most traditional armagnac alambics produce three to four barrels in a 24-hour period and sometimes as little as one or two. Unlike with a pot still, the heads and tails are normally retained. Herein lies a tremendous difference with products like whiskey, vodka, gin and cognac that attempt to eliminate these *impurities* through multiple distillations.

This *alambic armagnacais* is squat and stable, and without the exotic domes present in stylish *Charentais* stills. In short, it looks smaller and more primitive than its cognac equivalent. And unlike the stationary *Charentais* still to which a producer must bring his wine, the *alambic*

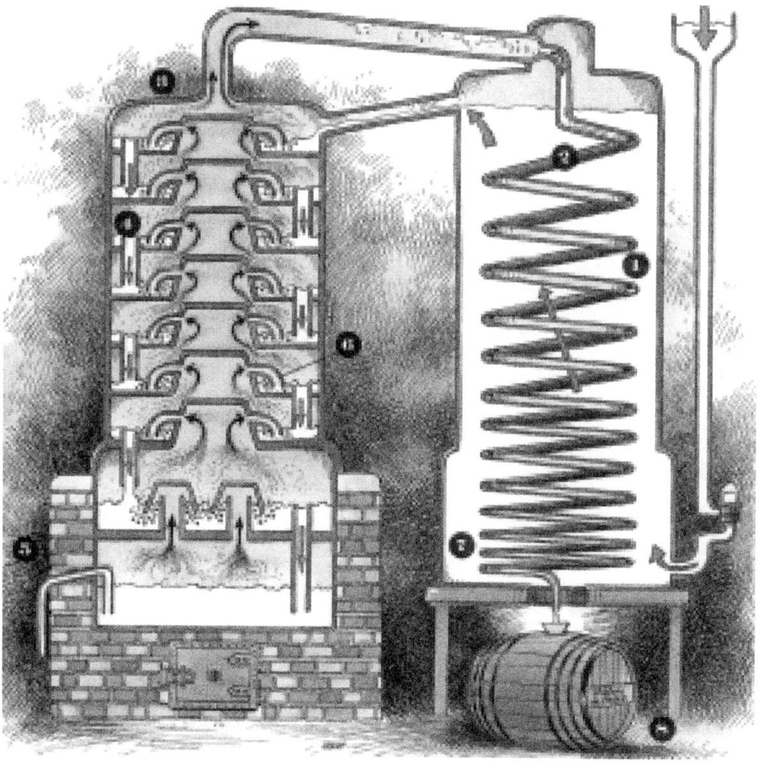

The alambic Armagnacais, used to produce the world's premier brandy

armagnacaise is normally portable which enables distillation to be performed right on each producer's property. 90% of the independent producers today are paid a visit by the traveling alambic each winter. Single-distillation remains their favored method by far.

The *alambic armagnacais* is either heated with wood or gas—which one is better is open to debate. Madame Dargelos uses only gas to fuel her alambics stating that the constant temperature leads to a more balanced spirit. Proponents of wood-fueled alambics, like Patrick Michalouski, claim that it is the slight variance in degree that leads to the extraction of differing esters which help create a more complex spirit. Both distill for between forty and fifty properties a year.

In any case, wine is gravity-fed into the wine-warmer (1) where it is heated by the hot upper part of the condensing coil (2). From there it flows into the main column (3) with its varying number of plates. The wine gets hotter and hotter as it flows over the copper plates (4). When it reaches the lower boiler, it finally begins to steam and evaporate (5). The alcoholic vapors rise back through the plates, continually being forced into contact with the incoming wine (6): like this, the vapor becomes saturated with the rich aromas of wine. The armagnac vapors exit through the top of the column and into the condensing coil (7), where they cool in the refrigerated lower portion and change from steam into liquid. The liquid eau-de-vie then flows into the wood cask (8).

One of the plates within an Armagnac alambic: The vapor exits through tubes called spider's legs and is forced into contact with the incoming wine, picking up additional flavorants before making its way up again.

If put under a microscope, one would see that the new armagnac was just over one-half pure alcohol, just under one-half water, and less than one percent non-alcohols. It is these last components, comprised of congeners, esters and acids, that give traditional armagnac its flavor. As these components age, they develop subtle, complex nuances that help set it apart from other spirits. Armagnac, with 4% of these non-alcohols, has tremendous potential for developing complexity. In comparison, cognac has 2.5%, whisky 1.5% and vodka .8%.

Madame Dargelos (left) runs a distilling firm as well as a ranch whose savage cows are used for the course Landaise: she sits amidst a few of the trophies her animals have won. Patrick Michalouski (right) owns three alambics which distill for most of the producers in the Ténarèze.

In their youth, these non-alcohols have a similar effect on the taster as high tannin and high acid levels have on a young wine. Yet one rarely criticizes an infant Bordeaux or Super Tuscan from a tremendous vintage because it is overly tannic—it is expected to be that way in order to evolve over 10 or 20 years.

Likewise, armagnacs that are single-distilled are meant to be drunk after 15 or 20 years of maturation. After that amount of time, the non-alcohols begin to oxidise and express themselves with an interesting nut-scented complexity known as *rancio*.

Unfortunately, the market is dominated by young armagnacs ranging from 3 to 5 years of age. With these, double-distillation *strips away* the esters and acids. This neutral base is then adjusted with permitted additives that help create its flavor (see Enologist section).

Back in the *chai*, distillation continues at a constant rate; the distiller surveys the alcohol gauge or *alcoolmètre* placed within the exiting spirit to make sure the desired alcohol degree is maintained. If levels begin to vary, adjustments concerning the pre-heater's temperature or wine flow must be made.

Each still has a particular capacity for the amount of spirit it can distill in a day, and most portable alambics can distill anywhere from 4 and 6 barrels a day. Not many distillers sleep next to the alambic anymore; nowadays, those who regulate the still normally work in 12 hour shifts.

Wines can be distilled so that they exit with an alcoholic degree that ranges from 52° to 60°. Much of this variance has to do with the initial alcoholic content of the wine. If the wine is relatively weak (8°-9°), the alcohol comes out at 53° or 54°. A wine of 9°-10° might produce an alcohol of 54° to 56°. If the wine is stronger in alcohol (like Colombard), the alcoholic degree might rise to 57° or 58°. According to Marc St. Martin, *eau de vie* that comes out at 52° has some off-aromas that include the copper scent of the alambic. Between 54° and 55° is ideal as it emphasizes the fruit aromas and minimizes the off-aromas. At 56° and 57°, the fruit aromas are preserved, but the texture is slightly drier because of the elevated alcohol level.

When one distills at a higher degree, less alcohol leaves the alambic, something which is advantageous for those who either lack the funds for barrels or lack space in their *chai*. Higher distillation degrees also tend to deliver a more neutral spirit, which is more *tolerant* to reduction. *Armagnacs distilled at 60° and above can be reduced with tremendous facility because they lack many of the volatile esters present in armagnacs distilled at a low degree.* A VSOP level armagnac distilled at a high degree always has a lighter mouthfeel than one distilled at a low degree.

Some producers distill at a higher degree because they also produce floc—grape must that is later fortified with young armagnac. Because the alcohol level of floc is normally around 18°, some producers prefer that some of their distillation comes out of the alambic around 60° to facilitate the fortification of this *aperitif.* Their armagnac meant to be aged, however, leaves the still at a much lower degree.

Although careful attention must be paid during the distillation, one can always find a moment to *faire la fête* or *party*. After all, it marks the end of another stage in the *vigneron's* season. To celebrate the event, friends are normally invited, the new spirit is shared, and meals are served around the still.

If heated by gas, only 17 kilos (37 pounds) of propane are needed, less than one-quarter the amount needed for the *double-chauffe*. In general, a traveling distiller charges between 300 and 400 francs (120 to 160 dollars) per 400 liter barrel of new alcohol. In addition, the producer normally supplies the meals for the distiller.

The final frontier between eau-de-vie and armagnac: as the clear eau-de-vie exits the still, it passes through a copper funnel before dripping into the barrel at which point it officially becomes known as armagnac.

Over the past century and a half, not much has changed with regards to the distillation device employed within the Armagnac region: Here one of the portable alambics of M.Roumat of Villeneuve-de-Marsan distills the 1997 harvest within the Château de Ravignan chai.

Barrels

After armagnac is distilled, it is placed in white oak barrels—the only type of oak that is completely water-tight. Barrels will be the armagnac's home for anywhere between a few years and several decades. Besides housing the spirit, barrels also provide a number of essential functions:

1. They give color to the spirit.
2. They provide tannin.
3. They offer flavoring components such as vanilla and spice.
4. They permit slow oxidation.
5. They provide storage space.

Oak grown in the region was traditionally employed for the aging of armagnac. Today, however, oak staves from many different forests are used. The trees within each forest have slightly different characteristics due to varying soil types and climates. Dry, poor soil allows for slow growth and therefore tight grain.

On the other hand, rich soil leads to fast growing trees with large grain. The wider the grain, the larger the potential to secrete tannin as well as flavoring material, like vanilla and spice. Wide grain also tends to promote fast oxidation, obviously important for armagnac. After all, to mature properly, the spirit must breathe through the wood.

The trees used for barrels are generally at least 100 years old, and often closer to 150. This age insures girth, something of utmost importance to the *tonnelier* because there is so much waste in the splitting process. Without the proper girth, the cooper ends up with extremely small pieces of wood that are of no use.

Only about 10% of a bought tree is normally used for the barrel: The bottom 6-8 feet (traditionally the most expensive part) goes to create veneers for furniture. The second tier, very straight, free of knots, and with no twisted grains, customarily is used for barrels. Generally two complete barrels can be made from one nicely-formed trunk. The top tier is the largest but also the least expensive part and goes to a variety of things, mostly furniture.

The Truth About Oak

Many armagnac producers, when asked what type of wood they use, will automatically say, "oak from the region". And although its usage was once widespread, nowadays very few barrels made by regional coopers employ regional oak. Since regional coopers buy wood from wood *négociants*, sometimes *they* don't even know which forest the wood comes from. What they will tell you, and with reason, is that ***the quality of grain found within any wood is more important than the name of the forest where the tree was grown***.

About 85% of armagnac *today* is raised in casks made of Limousin oak, while 10% is made from regional oak and 5% is made with oak from one of the other forests in France.

Here are some differences between those woods:

Gascon Oak

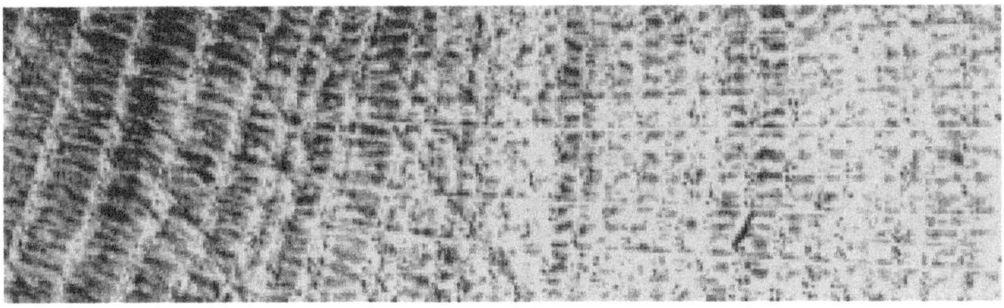

Gascon oak traditionally comes from the Monlezun and Monguilhem forests, near the center of the Armagnac region. Like oak from other forests in France, it is of the *quercus silicus* family and is often referred to as *black oak*. No one is exactly sure how this nickname originated (as the oak is certainly white), but several reasons are often cited for its nickname.

To begin, the soil upon which the trees grow is normally *sables fauves* or dark soil. Secondly, from the air neighboring pine trees have a green color, whereas the oak trees tend to be much darker (black) in color. Thirdly, the forests provide tremendous shade and block out most of the light even during the daytime. Finally, the outside of the trees, often covered with ivy and moss, are dark (black).

Whereas it was once common to age a spirit in wood that was cut from a tree in the region, today there are very few hectares of *black oak* left in the forests of Armagnac. In fact, most independent armagnac producers have more corn planted on their property than the entire surface of trees contained within the Monlezun Forest!

Nowadays, some producers look to regional forests in the Gers, Dordogne, or the Pyrénées that have similar soil and moisture conditions found within Armagnac. As was the case in the past, these trees do not grow as straight as those from the central forests; therefore, instead of the nine yards of wood normally available for the cooper in Limousin, only four yards of useable wood are available in Gascony.

True Gascon oak tends to have wide grain (about 8-9 per inch), yields lots of tannin (slightly more than Tronçais and about 25% more than Limousin) and secretes a generous dose of flavorants that include vanilla and spice. Its strong tannin content makes a good match for the thick, rich *eau de vie* coming from a single distillation.

Limousin

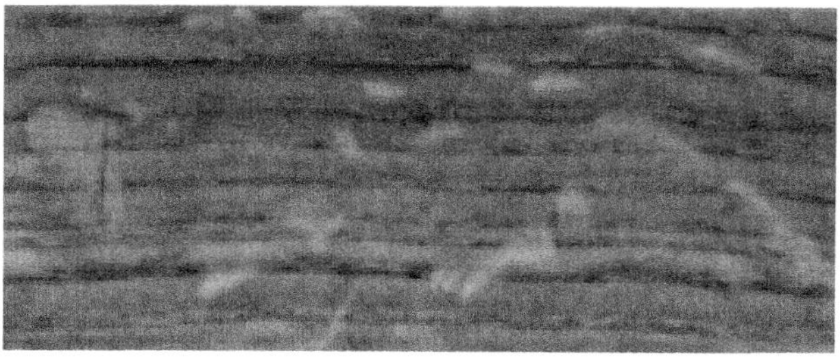

The Limousin forest is located about a hundred miles east of the Cognac region. Limousin has the widest grain (about 8 grains per inch) because it is the fastest growing oak, due to richer soils and higher rainfall within the forest. The limited amount of Gascon oak has now made Limousin the primary wood used for aging armagnac. Its loose pores allow the spirit to oxidize at a fast rate, helping to concentrate, gain a deeper color, and allow for greater extraction of flavorants contained in the wood.

Limousin oak has fat grains similar to those of Gascon oak; but whereas Gascon oak traditionally gives *slightly* higher levels of tannin, Limousin gives *slightly* higher levels of vanilla. According to armagnac folklore, there is a tremendous difference between Limousin oak and Gascon oak. According to about every *tonnelier* in the Armagnac region, however, the physiological differences are minimal. Today adjustments can be made with regards to toast levels and initial aging periods which helps draw the effects of Limousin and Gascon oak closer and closer together.

Allier and Tronçais

The Allier forest, located in central France between Limousin and Bourgogne, produces tight-grained wood that contains about 17 grains per inch. A subforest within Allier is called Tronçais and produces more expensive oak that also grows more slowly, thereby giving a tighter grain—about 18 per inch. In comparison with Limousin or Gascon oak, this tight-grained wood gives less vanilla nuance to the developing armagnac and slightly less tannin. Its high pricetag makes it a rare choice for armagnac producers.

Producers who use Tronçais to house their armagnac often make quality wine as well, and originally used the barrels to age their best wines. Additionally their smaller size allows them to be stacked in a *chai* with a low ceiling where two 420 liter barrels might not fit.

The Making Of A Barrel

Once the middle piece has been cut from a log, the outer cambium is removed so that the heartwood is exposed.Wood of the *quercus silicus* family has transformation cells that, under a microscope, look like straws packed together. Because of this tight grain composition, it is essential to split the trunk into staves rather than cut it with a saw. This was once performed with a sledgehammer and a wedge but nowadays is performed with a pneumatic wedge. After the staves have been split, they are roughly planed until they are of uniform width.

Chemical reactions occur both in the air drying of the staves and during the aging of a wine or spirit that lead to the accumulation of differing tannins.The goal of a cooper is to allow the wood time to dehydrate its liquid from 90% all the way down to between 12-14%. To accomplish this, the staves are placed outside in a criss-cross pattern that allows for wind flow as well as exposure to moisture and snow that allows for full *seasoning*. This slow airing process brings out the polysaccharides in the wood and depletes its astringent bitters and tannins. The staves are always air-dried for at least three and often five or six years.

One always gets a higher level of perceived sweetness in a barrel that has been properly dried. Water helps force tannins from the wood while the cellular structure is open in the stave. Tannin still remains in the wood, but it helps build structure to the finished spirit rather than to mask fruit or delicacy. It takes a minimum of 18 months to grow the positive effects of mold on the developing stave, which is why the staves in a woodyard often look gray or black. Industrial methods include drying the staves in a large oven; while certainly less expensive and less time consuming, the tannin remains somewhat astringent and imparts the spirit with slightly green flavors.

Some producers, like Claude Lacourtoisie from Labastide, will not lodge an armagnac in barrel unless its staves have air-dried for at least ten years. He feels that this elongated aging period minimizes the amount of tannic elements that often cause an armagnac to be over-oaked. It still gains its color, yet simply over a longer time. Unlike with new oak, Lacourtoisie claims, one can keep an armagnac in a barrel made with well-aged planks for its entire life.

Once the staves are dry, they are planed again to remove their gray color and make them more aesthetically pleasing. The barrel is then assembled: The cut pieces are arranged by staggering wide and narrow staves in a loose barrel form. A cable then cinches the base of the barrel and a hoop is slipped around the wood to hold it in place. The oak is gently heated over a fire so that it bends more easily. Finally its curves are made with the aid of a hydraulic hoop press while further truss hoops are put around the barrel. No nails or glues are used during the entire process.

Toasting

After the barrel has been put together, the cooper stimulates the sweet components in the wood by *toasting* the inside of the barrel.

This is accomplished by rocking the barrel over a slow burning fire. This step is of critical importance to a developing armagnac for several reasons: It helps give color to the spirit, it activates the vanilla scents contained in the wood, and it allows the tertiary elements within the oak (licorice, spice, coffee, cocoa) to be more easily diffused within the spirit.

Several levels of toasting are often employed, depending upon the effects a producer desires. These include:

Medium toast: A gentle heating and light char of the barrel that helps release light vanilla elements contained within the wood without giving tremendous color.

Medium + Toast: Fully releases vanilla flavors and heightens the amount of colorant material from the wood.

Heavy Toast: Cuts some of the potential vanilla flavors while increasing caramel, licorice, coffee and chocolate nuances. Delivers color rapidly.

Ideally barrels are toasted with their scrapwood so that the smoke flavors are clean and delicate. Most armagnac coopers rock the barrel over the fire for forty-five to fifty minutes. Gilles Bartholomo, the expert cooper for most producers in Les Landes, tends to give the barrels a medium + toast, then finishes with four minutes of stronger heat so that a slightly higher toast level is achieved. This will help to give the spirit more color and also hold back some of its vanilla flavorants; at the same time it will caramelize the natural wood-sugars which impart an impression of sweetness.

After the toasting is complete, a bung hole is drilled in center of the barrel and seized with a hot poker. Its ends are planed and made even. The heads and tails are made with staves held together with wooden dowels. These are cut into circular forms and inserted into each end of the barrel. Further truss hoops are added. The barrel is tested for airtightness, then sanded so it is clean. Finally it is topped with a plastic or rubber cork.

The typical 420 liter armagnac barrel, known as a *pièce,* will cost about 4,200 francs or $840.00, including tax.

The barrels for most top quality Landais armagnacs are constructed by Gilles Bartholomo (left) at his humble cooperage in Le Frêche (right).

Every top armagnac producer will let their spirits see the effects of some new oak. This exposure allows the armagnac to receive heightened levels of flavoring components. Little by little, the air passes through the wood, interacts with the armagnac and carries with it wood secretions that include tannin, vanilla and spice.

Producers must always make sure, however, that their armagnacs don't swallow too much tannin or get too dark—two traits difficult to lessen once present. As years pass by, tannin becomes extremely important within a spirit; ideally it provides a delicate structure that also allows the armagnac's fruit to shine. If not carefully monitored, however, it can outweigh the fruit and become very dry.

A new barrel can normally give adequate flavoring substances to three vintages; for example, a 1982 vintage might rest for between 18 months and two years in a new barrel. The 1984 might have to rest for 3 or 4 years in the same barrel to receive comparable substances. Finally, the 1988 might have to rest 7 years in the same barrel to receive similar levels of tannin, color, and vanilla that the 1982 derived. In 1995, this barrel would then become a housing vessel rather than a substance provider.

Why Don't All Producers Use New Oak?

In short, the price of a new barrel is simply too expensive for many producers. This might sound crazy considering all the oak used for inexpensive table wines nowadays. But remember, a *typical* Gascon farmer might make anywhere from $1,000 to $1,500 dollars a month (of which 10% is related directly to armagnac). If he has a *chai* with plenty of stock and is only selling a couple hundred bottles a year, $800 for a new barrel becomes a real difficult investment.

The heads of most armagnac barrels, like this one at Domaine Laffitte in Montlezun, are covered in chalk scrawl: the information might include vintage, alcohol degree, contents in liters and/or grape blend.

As an alternative, *tonneliers* also refurbish used barrels, adding new tops and bottoms or replacing damaged staves. At a reduced price, this at least allows for some flavoring material to be transferred between the barrel and the new spirit. Still, this four or five-hundred dollar investment is often diverted to pay-off a bank loan instead.

A few other methods can also be employed which, at a lessened price, allows for some *natural* wood influence. These include:

1. *Wood Chips*: These range anywhere from one-inch, mechanically cut nuggets to six-inch, roughly hewn pieces of oak. Wood chips will give color, tannin and some vanilla and toast flavors. However, their tannin is normally green, which ultimately gives the spirit a slightly bitter taste.

2. *Wood Planks*: These are longer pieces of oak that can be inserted into the bunghole of a barrel or the top of a vat to provide some effects of new oak without the expense of refurbishing a barrel.

Overall a purer flavor than woodchips, but not as rapid in achieving their effect.

Of course another inexpensive method is always available to producers, that being boisé. For more information on this unfortunately *permitted* additive, see the enologist section.

Wood chips serve a variety of purposes by certain "eleveurs" of brandy. They can be added to the barrel to give some effects of new oak, or their extract can be poured into the spirit in the form of boisé.

A few of the remaining "black oaks" in the Monlezun forest.

The Evolution Of Armagnac In Oak

After receiving the initial benefits of new oak, an armagnac is normally transferred to older barrels where it peacefully breathes and mellows through the oak. Its fiery quality begins to wear off and the armagnac begins to develop at a leisurely pace, becoming more concentrated and at the same time slightly less alcoholic.

A producer's *chai* (a French term for an above-ground *cellar*) will largely determine the type of evolution his armagnac will take. *Chais* vary greatly from property to property. The *négociant* firms have large *chais* that are like miniature replicas of the warehouses in the Charente; others, like Chateau de Pellehaut, have several well-organized *chais* with cement floors lit by fluorescent light. The majority, however, are located in a dimly lit side of a barn, kept moist with a beaten dirt floor and illuminated by several dim light bulbs.

Because wood is porous and alcohol and water reduce gradually when exposed to air, a certain amount of armagnac is lost each year through evaporation. This loss is known as *the angel's share*, because it is those lucky ones above that supposedly claim this loss in quantity. A black fungus called *torula compniacensus* thrives on the alcoholic fumes and covers the roof tiles of many *chais*. Because of their presence, it is fairly easy to recognize which building on a property holds the maturing spirits.

When a cask is full, it tends to lose less quantity through evaporation. Therefore topping up the casks *with the same vintage* is common in the Armagnac region because it allows for slower evaporation. If a producer does not top up, evaporation is accelerated and his armagnac will become more concentrated at a younger age because it will contain less water.

The chai at Domaine Boingnères (left) is very dry which leads to an extremely slow reduction of alcohol. One of the chais at Domaine de la Boubée (right) is extremely rustic: its dirt floors retain moisture and promote alcohol reduction.

Dry conditions tend to promote quantity loss while minimally affecting the alcohol level. On the other hand, the amount of humidity within a *chai* helps determine the amount of alcohol that will be lost each year. *In general*, 1-2% of the quantity is lost annually, and anywhere from 1/10 of a degree to 1/2 a degree is naturally lost in alcohol per year. With rates like these, one might expect to lose anywhere from 20-25% in quantity after fifteen years of aging and anywhere between three and eight degrees (6 to 16 proof) of alcohol over the same period.

If it is humid, like at the Domaine de Nautina, alcohol levels diminish at a faster rate while quantity evaporates less slowly. In a dry *chai*, like at the Domaine de Martin, the alcohol reduces at a much slower rate while the quantity evaporates quicker. This helps account for their 49° alcohol levels even after 15 years of aging.

Some producers or *négociants*, like Bernard l'Huillier at Château La Béroje in Hontanx or Darroze in Roquefort, keep various barrels at different heights in an attempt to better control the amount of evaporation and development at various stages of the spirit's life. The angel's claim a larger share when the top row of stacked barrels rest near the hotter confines of a low hanging roof of the *chai*. At the cooler floor level, degree loss takes place at a more rapid rate while the liquid content remains more constant.

Ideally, this reduction takes place naturally. However, the lessening of alcoholic strength can be tightly controlled; when performed vigorously, racking can also promote natural alcoholic and volume loss by giving the armagnac added contact with the air. Racking is normally done by conscientious producers perhaps once every year or year-and-a-half; one barrel is usually pumped into another, which allows additional oxygen to encounter the spirit. This method, which basically gives the armagnac a breath of fresh air, is the most common form of aeration. Another common form takes place when barrels from the same vintage are pumped into a larger vat to *marry* for a few days, then rediffused into different barrels.

The most modern method of aeration sees more of the producer's intervention, and is performed in a special holding tank that mechanically circulates the spirit. This encourages tremendous oxygen contact that promotes volume and alcoholic evaporation as well as the loss of certain volatile acids. When performed occasionally, aeration is certainly beneficial: However, overworking armagnacs can unfortunately strip many spirits of their rich esters that would ultimately be responsible for giving a complex bouquet.

Like with wine, some aeration is necessary, yet *minimal* intervention is best. Although painstakingly long and costly (because of loss through evaporation) a pure form of armagnac is realized. Natural reduction, however, poses several problems for every member of the commercial chain:

For the producer...

The turn-around time of the product is very slow, as it takes several decades before the product is ready for the market. Taxes are also higher. And there is the possibility that the spirit will become over-oaked if left too long in cask.

For the négociant...

Reducing a spirit gives the négociant more product to sell. If a spirit is reduced from 48° to 40°, a quantity gain of 17% is made. Reducing also allows many more possibilities for the house enologist who can reduce different armagnacs to different levels for his house blend.

For the importer...

Higher alcohol levels mean higher taxes, which ultimately lead to higher prices. High alcohol levels can also scare consumers. 96 proof sounds a hell of a lot stronger than 80 proof.

For the consumer...

Price often dictates choice. Many times one will choose an 80 proof item because it is less expensive. High alcohol levels also tend to intimidate consumers, especially to end a meal where wine consumption has been involved.

Intricate armagnac nuances begin to surface around their tenth birthday. After about 12 years, the spirit itself reaches a stage where the interaction of fruit and the vanilla/caramel nuances of the oak begin to harmonize. Most traditional armagnacs can strut their stuff at this point. They are fiery, yet not threatening: Their rich, friendly qualities help balance their power.

Armagnac As It Matures

From the time an armagnac comes out of the alambic until it is bottled, it undergoes many changes. The normal evolution of a good, traditional armagnac distilled at 52° and raised under optimum conditions (healthy wine, non-problematic distillation, aging in new oak) normally follows this course of progression:

Upon exiting the still

The color is clear. Lots of aromas that evoke the budding vine, some herbaceousness, and a hint of spice. Texture is usually viscous and slightly oily, and the spirit is sweet. Lots of fruit in the mouth, albeit difficult to pinpoint. Alcohol, normally between 104 and 120 proof, is hidden in the mouth by the fruit yet becomes increasingly noticeable on the finish.

The first year in barrel

A light golden hue begins to color the spirit. Tannin begins to make its presence known. Approximately one degree of alcoholic strength is lost. Lots of sweet, vinous flavors still remain.

Years one, two and three in barrel

The wood begins to have tremendous influence upon the maturing spirit. The tannin leaves the oak and immerses itself with the armagnac, creating color while at the same time injecting tannin. When smelling armagnacs at this age, the primary fruit aromas are overwhelmed by aromas of moist wood. We say that the spirit has the *maladie du bois* or the wood disease. It is not tremendously enjoyable to consume. Extreme caution must be taken by the producer so as not to allow too much tannin to be swallowed by the spirit. If too much tannin is consumed, the resultant spirit will never be balanced and will always finish with an excessively dry, bitter aftertaste. Alcohol, although beginning to slowly diminish, is omnipresent.

Years Four Through Eight In Barrel

Most producers have invariably transferred their spirits to barrels that have previously been used by this point. Like this, they promote oxidation while limiting the amount of tannin and color sucked in by the spirit. In ideal storage conditions, the spirit will continue to reduce in alcohol at the rate of 2/10 to 1/2 a degree per year. The color continues to gain in hue, and the aromatic substances derived from the wood (vanilla, chocolate, pepper, clove) begin to integrate themselves with the fruit, still locked beneath a layer of alcohol. Aromas of melted caramel, milk chocolate and nougat begin to express themselves. The evaporation of some of volume leads to a slightly more concentrated spirit.

Between 9 and 15 years

Color is an attractive deep amber. Fruit aromas are heightened and often show hints of quince, apricot, and melted toffee. Natural sweetness becomes evident, and alcohol helps the fruit to penetrate and stay on the palate. Vanilla aromas become more concentrated, occasionally showing themselves with flattering nuances that include coconut cream and milk chocolate. *Rancio* begins to arrive and express itself as an aroma of blanched almond. The spirit gains viscosity and shows attractive legs. Alcohol level continues to slowly descend, perhaps reaching 47°-48° naturally.

Between 16 and 25 years

Color remains an attractive amber. Deeper, preserved fruit notes arrive, often displayed as prune, apricot and grilled almond. The spirit is rich and viscous while the alcohol dances across the honeyed-fruit on the palate. The finish is long and shows well-integrated wood notes. Alcohol level is now between 46-47°. The fruit still covers the tannin. *Perhaps the optimum consumption stage.*

The storage conditions within the chai at the Chateau de Castandet (above) are extremely rustic. The cardboard boxes on top of the barrels help prevent mice from eating the barrel corks!

Between 26 and 35 years

In an ideal world, we take the previous stage and shift it into high gear. Color continues to deepen. In addition, a hint of smoky oak begins to weave its way into the aromas. A walnut nuance surfaces. Palate is thick and sweet, and the alcohol level is diminishing. Oak notes and tannin creep in on the finish. In a more realistic world, the wood begins to dominate dry fruit. Its appeal is that it is old rather than good.

Between 36 and 40 years

Color deepens to mahogany, and the highlights become dull. Secondary aromas (wood, developed vanilla, rancio) completely dominate the fruit that, if nothing else, gives birth to an extremely interesting nose. Dry notes of polished, antique oak is about all one perceives in the mouth, while the finish is painfully dry. In short, the spirit has reached the end of its life and has more interest in being something old than being something good.

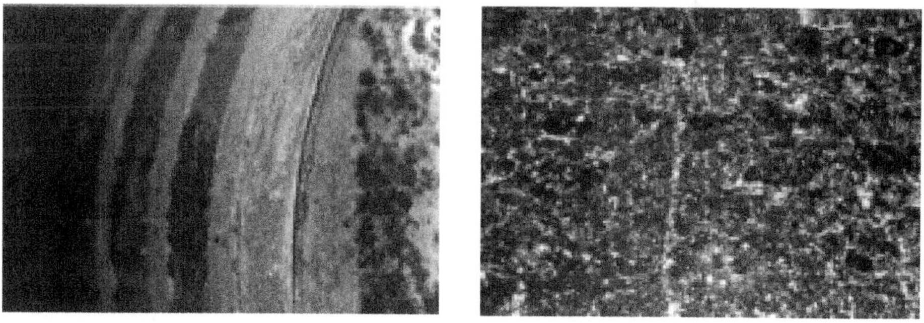

Various forms of mushrooms grow on both the barrels (left) and the chai walls (right). The former, if not monitored carefully, can produce off-aromas.

Additional Aging in Tonneaux

When an armagnac begins to take on too much oak or begins to descend below a desired alcohol level, it is often shifted into larger containers called *tonneau*. These *tonneaux* or vats might hold anywhere from 4000 to 10,000 liters, and their thick, weathered oak staves do not normally allow for much air contact or wood influence. Consequently, the spirit evolves much slower than in a normal-sized *pièce*, which helps allow certain producers to better control alcohol and wood levels for an extended period.

Vats serve a number of purposes during the production of armagnac: they can be used to blend a number of barrels together, to create a blend using the permitted additives, or to simply slow evaporation, alcohol loss and the accumulation of tannin.

The Role Of The Enologist

An enologist is a person who has studied the chemistry of wine and spirits and is technically qualified to oversee its production and adjust various factors that might lead to a smoother *fermentation*, *élevage*, and *assemblage*.

Enologists often make their presence felt during three important phases of an armagnac's life. The first is during the fermentation of wine when scientific measures, far from a farmer's knowledge, are necessary to create a correct, healthy base material for distillation. The second is during the *élevage* when a producer desires advice on barrel rotation or aeration. It is normally the third, however—during the blend or *coup*—when the skills of an enologist are utilized the most.

Ideally, the enologist's influence is minimal; he combines various barrels together and comes up with a great, natural blend. Realistically, the enologist plays a role that includes an increasing amount of intervention. During this time, the enologist normally uses his stable of *permitted* additives to *correct* a blend. Within armagnac, there are four groups of additives permitted. These are:

1. Water

Water is introduced to reduce a spirit's alcoholic degree. *Lessening the final alcoholic degree can be performed in a number of artificial ways and, like every phase of production, can be done with expertise or negligence. These include:* ***Distilled water***: Water, passed through an alambic and therefore extremely pure, is added to the spirit. This process quickly lessens the alcoholic degree while increasing the volume. ***Demineralized water***: Water that has been filtered so that its minerals are removed, consequently making it softer. Less expensive than distilled water. ***Petites eaux*** **or** ***little brandies***: Brandy mixed with distilled or demineralized water and aged in barrel. This liquid is normally between 20° and 30° which lessens the alcoholic degree while increasing the liquid volume. Obviously the most fluid form of reduction, as the armagnac has already had the time to blend with the water.

Ideally those producers that reduce will do so either immediately after distillation or very gradually over the course of several years. If done in one shot, a proper blend does not take place and the resultant spirit seems dilute—watery even. When done correctly, an armagnac might get a dose of *petites eaux* or distilled water fairly early on, another perhaps two years later, and a final reduction a year or so before bottling takes place. This slow reduction, at three to five degrees a shot, ensures proper harmony within the final spirit and is more difficult to detect. Ultimately this lessened strength permits a more supple spirit that can allow certain aromas to surface above the alcoholic heat.

It is undeniable that even when reduced properly, the spirit is tremendously altered. It loses purity and is therefore less concentrated. It is like the difference between *perfume* and *eau de toilette*. Quality wine made with a harvest of 50 hl/ha and one made with 100 hl/ha. Simply a question of pure material related to final volume.

Some producers will reduce to 45° or 46°, which perhaps gives them the best of both worlds. Concentration is not terrifically lost, the palate is not overwhelmed with alcohol, the volume is boosted, taxes are lowered somewhat, and the spirit is ready for the market sooner.

An *unofficial* test often used to see if reduction has taken place entails shaking the bottle and watching the formation of bubbles along the surface of the spirit. If bubbles barely form and disappear almost instantly, chances are the spirit has been reduced. If, however, the bubbles form a higher layer and take several seconds to vanish, chances are the spirit is near its natural degree.

The degrees of the spirit to be reduced	To obtain 46°		To obtain 45°	
	Brandy	Water	Brandy	Water
75°	60.31	39.69	58.99	41.01
74°	61.77	38.23	59.80	40.20
73°	62.03	37.97	60.68	39.32
72°	62.92	37.08	61.53	28.47
71°	63.85	36.15	62.46	37.54
70°	64.80	35.20	63.37	36.63
69°	65.78	34.22	64.35	35.65
68°	66.80	33.20	65.31	34.69
67°	67.84	32.16	66.31	33.69
66°	68.44	31.56	67.38	32.62
65°	69.97	30.03	68.44	31.56
64°	71.12	28.28	69.51	30.49
63°	72.30	27.70	70.72	29.28
62°	73.52	26.48	72.60	27.40
61°	74.73	25.27	73.09	26.91
60°	76.04	23.96	74.34	25.66
59°	77.39	22.61	75.70	24.30
58°	78.80	21.20	77.04	22.96
57°	80.19	19.81	78.43	21.57
56°	81.69	18.31	79.79	20.21
55°	83.19	16.21	81.36	18.64
54°	84.81	15.19	82.91	17.09
53°	86.43	13.57	84.56	15.47
52°	88.18	11.82	86.20	13.80
51°	89.72	10.08	87.95	12.05
50°	91.82	8.18	89.76	10.24

A great deal of water must be added to a brandy to reduce its alcoholic volume from 72% to 45%. Nearly one third of a double- distilled product released at 80 proof is ultimately water. In contrast, traditional armagnacs have no water added: these highly concentrated spirits are released at cask strength.

2. Caramel

Caramel is a liquid made from burned sugar. It is very dark in color and, rather than being sweet, is slightly bitter. Because of this it is not used to sweeten armagnac, but only to adjust color. The colors of *non-vintage* armagnacs are just about always adjusted in some way. There are a couple of reasons for this:

a) A darker spirit gives the impression of having been aged longer. As a three-year-old spirit (minimum age for *3 Étoiles*) has little color and therefore appears raw, added caramel gives it the impression of being older and therefore smoother.

b) When a brand releases 100,000 bottles of a *VSOP* or *Napoléon* spirit, it is important to have a consistent color. As every oak barrel will give differing levels of coloring material, the ultimate blended release must look the same. Imagine if each bottle of *Chateau du Tariquet VSOP Armagnac* at Southdown Wines and Spirits had a different color! Customers would certainly ask questions and become suspect. A consistent color makes it look as if each bottle came from the same barrel. This consistency is something of utmost importance to *negociants*.

Caramel is normally added after various barrels have been emptied into a larger blending tank. As an artist would reproduce a color on his palate, or as a paint store would reproduce Benjamin Moore's *Royal Blue* as color scheme 4210, so Marquis de Caussade or Clés des Ducs works out the color of their *VSOP*'s and *Napoléon*s.

Colorant, finally, has the same affect on armagnac that a military uniform has on a soldier: close-up or from a distance, the troops in line look exactly the same.

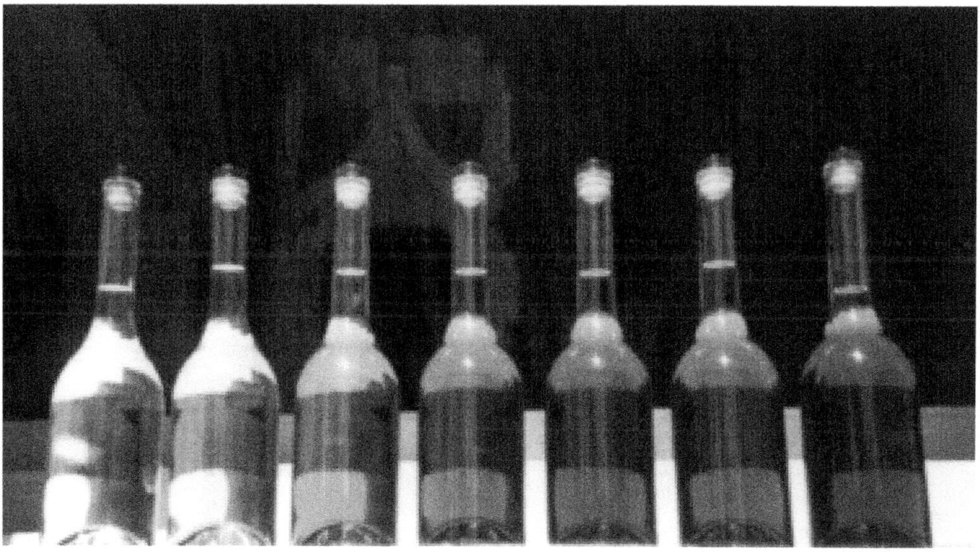

Wood is what gives an armagnac its color: above, the effects of a new barrel on the housed spirit (from left to right): eau-de-vie, 6 months, 1, 2, 3, 4 and 5 years.

3. Boisé

Boisé is created by boiling wood chips in water for several hours, then removing the wood chips and slowly reducing the remaining liquid. What one is left with is a dark brown liquid that is replete with wood flavor and tannin. When tasted alone it is, as one might expect, extremely dry and bitter.

The reasons for using boisé are simple; it basically gives the impression of oak aging to a final spirit. This is important, especially when a producer cannot afford to buy new barrels or ages his spirit in vats, which normally give very little colorant and tannic material. Most boisé that is used in the armagnac region has its origins in the Charente, where its use is widespread. Most cognac producers have warehouses filled with barrels of boisé that, when blended with spirit, evolve gradually and provide a economic shortcut to long-term aging.

For boisé to be well-integrated, it should be added to a cask early in the spirit's life. In this way, it matures along with the spirit. If this is not possible, an aged-boisé, aptly called Rancio®, is also available to the enologist. It is less bitter than straight boisé, and offers secondary wood aromas like vanilla and grilled nuts. Rancio® helps give an *impression* of age to a spirit.

4. Sugar

The type of sugar used to add sweetness to armagnacs is sugarcane syrup. It is viscous, and can either be dark or light. Legally, 2% of an armagnac's content can be sugar. It is normally added if the armagnac is too tannic, or to remove any rough edges it might contain.

Certain countries, like Japan, China, and Spain, tend to like spirits that have lots of sweetness. The maximum legal limit is therefore always employed in blends destined for these countries, not necessarily as a corrector, but simply to add sweetness and pander to the market.

Cognac has long relied on its enologists or blenders to continue an established *house* style. They have always been aware that no two individual barrels are alike and that a blend—rather than individual vintage—is essential to establish a consistent product. Double-distilled Ugni Blanc creates an extremely neutral brandy that is remarkably easy to manipulate with the permitted additives.

Every *négociant* house in armagnac has their enologist whose influence, like in Cognac, is enormous; in addition, an increasing number independent producers regularly solicit the advice of freelance enologists.

Single-distilled armagnacs display too much personality in their youth to be easily adjusted and do not cut as well with water. It is for this reason that many commercial armagnac houses use some double-distillation in their youngest blends; it simply makes their alteration that much easier.

Methods Of An Enologist

For a commercial *Hors d'Age* blend (minimum age 10 years), the enologist might taste his way through all the barrels in a *chai* and come up with some notes. These might include:

1986: 49°. Light amber, too light. Not much wood influence. Still showing lots of alcohol. Lacks some structure.

1984: 48°. Deep amber. Lots of fruit showing above alcohol. Well-integrated wood notes ride just below apricot-scented fruit. Hints of pepper on the finish.

1983: 47°. Deep amber. Tannin leaves palate extremely dry.

1982: 48°. Amber. Deep fruit is balanced wonderfully by spicy oak and well-integrated tannin. Long, pure finish.

1981: 48°. Amber. Some accumulating fruit fat but lacking some oak. Finish is long but slightly hot.

In this case, the enologist might feel that the 1986, 1983, and 1981 should be blended into an *Hors d'Age*, that 1982 is released as a vintage, and that 1984 continues to age for a future vintage release.

He then produces a trial blend of those three vintages. With this trial blend, he begins experimenting with the permitted additives. The tannin from the 1983 did not sufficiently cover the lack of tannin with the 1986 and 1981. Therefore, some boisé will be needed. He adds some distilled water to bring the degree down to 45°. Some sugar syrup is added to make the mouthfeel slightly more round. Finally, a little Rancio® is added to give that *nutty* taste.

To the 1982 vintage, he might add just a touch of Rancio® and an extremely small dose of sugar, while leaving it at its natural degree.

If a enologist is good at his job, his work should not be obvious and conceivably could be passed off as being natural. That, of course, is the goal of all enologists.

Fortunately, it is still possible to obtain armagnacs that have not in any way been influenced by the tools of an enologist. Unfortunately, these natural spirits are becoming harder and harder to find.

The laboratory at a typical armagnac négociant: always plenty of sample bottles from potential sources as well as test blends using the "permitted" additives.

The Age Game Of Non-Vintage Blends

How old is a non-vintage spirit? This question has plagued true spirit connoisseurs for ages, mostly because they remain completely in the dark concerning the *true* age of a non-vintage armagnac or cognac. Sure, one can attempt to recognize certain characteristics of a well-aged brandy but, as we've observed, it is fairly easy to give a young spirit the impression of being something much older with the addition of a few chemicals.

It is not surprising that publicity often states that this *Réserve de la Famille* is 20 years old, or that this *Très Vieille Réserve* has 60-year-old cognac in it, or that this *Réserve Personelle* has armagnacs that average 30 years. There are no actual records to document these ages: In fact, *all it takes is a press release to determine this spirit's age*; then a sales manager and sales reps to repeat or exaggerate it.

Of course, houses that release these products are thrilled when the true age of their products becomes inflated, because older, in the eyes of the public, means smoother, more mellow and, ultimately, better and more expensive.

Most cognac houses have a small area in one of their many stadium-sized warehouses called *Paradis*. It is where their oldest stocks lie, mostly in dusty glass demi-johns, streamed with cobwebs and covered in dust. The fact is that much of the spirit in *Paradis* has not developed in decades. Some was distilled in 1948, then put in a glass demi-john in 1974. In 1998 it is used as one of the spirits in a blend. The resultant blend *technically* contains 50 year old spirits. Realistically, the "50 year old" spirit is simply 26 years old, as sprits do not mature once in glass.

But *50*-year-old spirit sounds a hell of a lot more impressive than 26, doesn't it?

The Making of an Adulterated Armagnac or Cognac

We know that there are many fine brandies from many regions in the world. Some of these are made traditionally with strict attention to detail. Unfortunately, there are also many brandies on the market—be it in Armagnac or Cognac—that are not traditional and are made in bulk without nearly as much care. Yet because of their known appellation, they have an immediate market and normally sell well.

The motive for launching such a mediocre product is simple: profit. Such producers and *négociants* are jaded and completely disrespectful to the heritage of fine brandy. They have absolutely no respect for the consumer and are content to conquer them with various methods of tomfoolery.

But how does a producer put together such a product? What steps does he take? How does such a commonplace product manage to comply with appellation requirements and reach the market?

Nine Steps to Fool The Undiscriminating Customer

1. Buy cheap wine from vines that originate on soils not tremendously conducive to brandy distillation.

2. If one is to put XO on the label, the spirit must be 6 years old. Yet XO does not signify in what type of barrel the spirit is housed. Therefore, age the spirit in large vats rather than small barrels. Even though 5 years aging in a vat signifies one or one-and-a-half years in barrel, the aging

requirement is being met. Other effects will be used to *simulate* true aging.

3. Use oak chips to give the impression that the spirit was aged in small barrels. Also add boisé to imitate long contact with wood.

4. Attempt to slow evaporation by topping up the vats with water as often as possible. This will reduce the alcohol at a faster rate while keeping the maximum product.

5. Tame the fiery nature of the brandy and smooth out its rough edges with sugar syrup. It is legal to use up to 2% of syrup in one's final product. Its sweetness also gives an impression of concentration and full-body. Most undiscriminating customers feel that a spirit's quality is to be judged by its level of *smoothness*; foreign substances such as syrup help give this final impression. Add every ounce of the allowed percentage.

6. Dump a few liters of thirty-year-old spirit into one of the vats. Its qualitative effect will be minimal, but its advertising possibilities are important; after all, one will be able to say that the final product contains brandies that are "thirty years old".

7. Liberally add caramel to deepen the color of the spirit. Make it *real dark* so that it looks *real old*.

8. Package the product in an odd-shaped, expensive looking bottle.

9. Through market research and consultation with advertisers, have a label designed that will appeal to customers. Make it resemble a label that is already popular. Make sure XO is highly visible and add some meaningless yet eye-catching terms like *Trés Vieille Réserve* or *Réserve Familiale*. Make sure to place on the back label that brandies up to 30 years old are used in the blend.

There will always be sleazeballs who show no respect for the consumer and offer them an inferior product at an inflated price. It is only through the efforts of discriminating spirits retailers and restaurateurs that demanding customers are given *the real thing*.

An orage moves over the vineyards in St. Vidou, Les Landes.

Armagnac and Cognac Over The Centuries

Being France's two finest grape brandies, it is only natural to mention armagnac and cognac in the same phrase. Historically, however, cognac has always stood in the spotlight, with armagnac playing the understudy, waiting in the wings for its big chance. How did this situation develop?

In the 1600's, Bordeaux was the major shipping point for products like salt and wine. The most important destinations for boats were England and Holland, where trendy societies eagerly consumed goods from abroad. One of these was wine, which tended to oxidize during long sea voyages. Fortifying a wine with a brandy protected the wine from spoilage and left it drinkable once in a foreign land. The distillers in Cognac—being closely connected to Bordeaux by the well-traveled Garonne and Charente Rivers—became the obvious place for the Dutch and British to quickly seek fortification material.

Henceforth, because of its proximity, Cognac's *brandewijn* (burnt wine) or *brandy* had an immediate outlet. When determined that Cognac also produced a spirit that was finer than other boat-accessible cities like Nantes and La Rochelle, its demand rose. When discovered that the spirit was fine enough to be consumed on its own, investment besieged the Cognac region. With this money came increased production *and* increased prosperity.

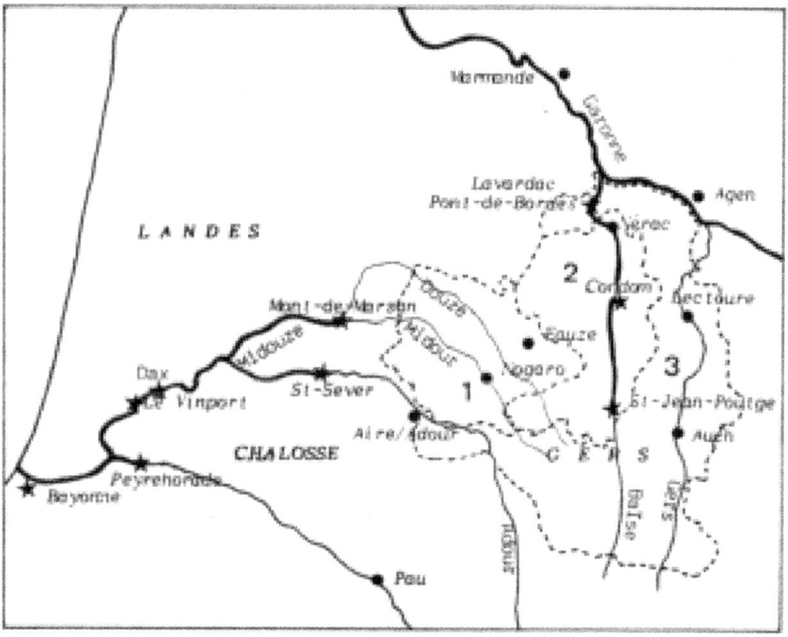

The complicated water routes from the isolated armagnac region to a major portduring the eighteenth and early-nineteenth centuries.

At the same time, traders in Armagnac were *geographically* caught in a trap: transporting their distilled spirits to Bordeaux was problematic: First the spirit had to cross uneven terrain by oxen until it reached Lavardac, a shipping town along the Baïse River. From there it slowly headed to Bordeaux along an unpredictable waterway, which at times did not even have enough water for boats to pass.

The only alternative was to transport the armagnac to Bayonne, a port located between Bordeaux and the Spanish border. This route was considerably longer and required the casks to reach Mont-de-Marsan by cart, then descend the complicated Midouze River which, because it was nearly unnavigable in places, took some three days to cover the first twenty-five miles.

Conditions like this made the transport of spirits impossible from the deep countryside. In short, the Armagnac region was isolated from the lucrative, aggressive and well-connected British and Dutch markets flourishing in the Charente. So while investors in Cognac watched their gold coins mount, producers in Armagnac were forced to enjoy their spirit at home after a hard day in the fields.

Fortunately, the nineteenth century brought with it a few major developments that laid the foundation for the commercial future of Armagnac. The first was the new still that was not only economically efficient but also portable. The second was a lowered tariff barrier, which permitted the export of goods without excessive charges. The third was a canal that finally connected the center of the region to the Baïse River, allowing direct access to Bordeaux. At last, armagnac could reach a distribution point within a reasonable time and for a reasonable price.

These changes inspired farmers in the region to expand their vineyards. Excitement swept through Les Landes and the Gers. *Négociant* firms suddenly arose. Like in Cognac, brand names were established that sold casks with their names on the barrel. Castarède, then known as Nismes-Delclou, established a small *chai* or *warehouse* in Point-de-Bordes. Larresingle soon began buying barrels from local growers and marketing them under their name. Janneau set up shop in Condom in 1851, and Gelas in Vic-Fezansac shortly thereafter.

Even with such rapid progress, the brandy trade centered in Cognac had a jump of over 150 years and had *already* flourished into a booming commercial center. The foreign firms of Hennessey, Martell, and Courvoisier were firmly established. Export consumers had become accustomed to a product that was supposedly the best brandy to be found. It was a difficult market in which to compete.

Still, word slowly spread. Not only did people within France see a gradual infusion of armagnac, but so did certain markets abroad. Foreign clients, previously unheard from, began placing orders.

At last, with an outlet for their goods, armagnac production took a dramatic upswing. Corn crops were ripped up and more grapes were grown. In 1804, the Gers (the predominant *département* or county of armagnac production) was covered with 72,000 hectares of vines and distilled just less than 50,000 hectoliters of pure alcohol. By 1853, 96,000 hectares (or 15% of the land) were covered by vine. And by 1872, the amount of land under vine was one of the largest in France; most of the resultant wine was used for distillation, and production reached 100,000 hectoliters of pure alcohol.

Consumers from outside the region were finally beginning to notice—and speak about—the brandy from Armagnac. It was different than what they were used to: Cognac displayed a lovely balance between delicate alcohol and the spicy oak it was matured in, while armagnac presented a spirit with earthier qualities that were more profound. The richness of fruit and haunting plummy depth of this previously unknown spirit were two things that cognac *couldn't* derive from its chalky soil.

Soon, connoisseurs began shaking their heads while tasting. Armagnac was not only an interesting brandy, but a worthy *competitor* to cognac. There was something to this *rustic* brandy. This...armagnac.

And then, as smiling eyes seemed to look down on the Gascon farmers, fate reared its ugly head.

In late 1878, grape-growing regions all over France were plagued by a tremendously humid summer. Vines began to mature, then grew heavy with mildew before ripening. Spores of bacteria, driven on by the moist conditions, formed on these damp vines and caused them to rot. A louse, known as phylloxera, thrived on these weakened plants.

It started its destruction with one plant, then a row of vines. Soon it was an entire field. Before the Autumn arrived, many of the wine-regions of France were completely infested. By mid-September, the entire country was under siege. By the end of the year, most grape vines in France were dead.

At first, partly because the phylloxera did not thrive on sandy soil, the Armagnac region remained an isolated enclave seemingly immune to its onslaught. But by 1893, rapidly multiplying bugs attacked the damp, disease-prone plants in droves, not only destroying the season's harvest but any expectations for future crops as well.

For the Armagnac region, as well as all the other established and renowned wine regions in France, the result of the phylloxera was the complete annihilation of grape vines and, therefore, of wine.

At the beginning of the 1900's the *Armagnacais* began pulling themselves back together. Dead vines were ripped up and intensive studies done regarding the soil within the region. In 1909, based on the results of these studies, the government divided Armagnac into three regulated appellations.

Their decision drew heavily from two sources. The first was a written work published in 1854 called *Ampelographie*, in which the author Rendu established six *cantons* concerning high quality. He cited Maupas, Panjas and Estang as being the best, followed by Labastide, Parleboscq and Castelnau d'Auzan.

The second was a book published in 1859 by Jules Seillan entitled *Topographie des Vignobles du Gers et de l'Armagnac*. In the book, Seillan included a map in which he drew up three Armagnac regions: Bas-Armagnac, Ténarèze and Haut-Armagnac.

The appellation board decided to retain these three regions, yet made some adjustments to Sellian's map. The most notable was that Eauze and Lannepax, part of the Ténarèze according to Sellian, became part of the Bas-Armagnac, while Condom and Nerac, part of the Haut-Armagnac, became part of the Ténarèze.

Folle Blanche dominated the new plantings and the distilling of armagnac was slowly restored. The tight clusters of Folle Blanche, however, were extremely susceptible to black rot and mildew. This created extremely unprofitable yields.

Scientists began experimenting with various hybrids that would give better yields and be resistant to disease. François Bacco, a teacher in Les Landes, came up with a cross between Folle Blanche and the American grape Noah. Its initial experiments were encouraging. This new grape, Bacco 22-A, soon became the favored grape throughout the region.

During the first World War, very little armagnac was distilled. However, when the war ended, Armagnac experienced a boom. Prices soared from 400 francs a barrel to 3,600 francs a barrel.

In the 1920's, prohibition in the United States hit the armagnac market hard. Again, the spirit's value was reduced, this time to 900 francs a barrel.

Many farmers, depressed and miserable because of financial losses, replanted their fields with corn or invested in cows. These crops earned them less money than grapes, but at least insured money and guaranteed food on the table. In 1937, the region produced a mere 22,000 hectoliters of spirit, less than a quarter of the pre-phylloxera volume.

By 1940, armagnac production slumped even further. The problem seemed to be the *Amagnacais'* difficulty in promoting their product outside the region. A few decent-sized firms existed, but they failed to create much impact abroad.

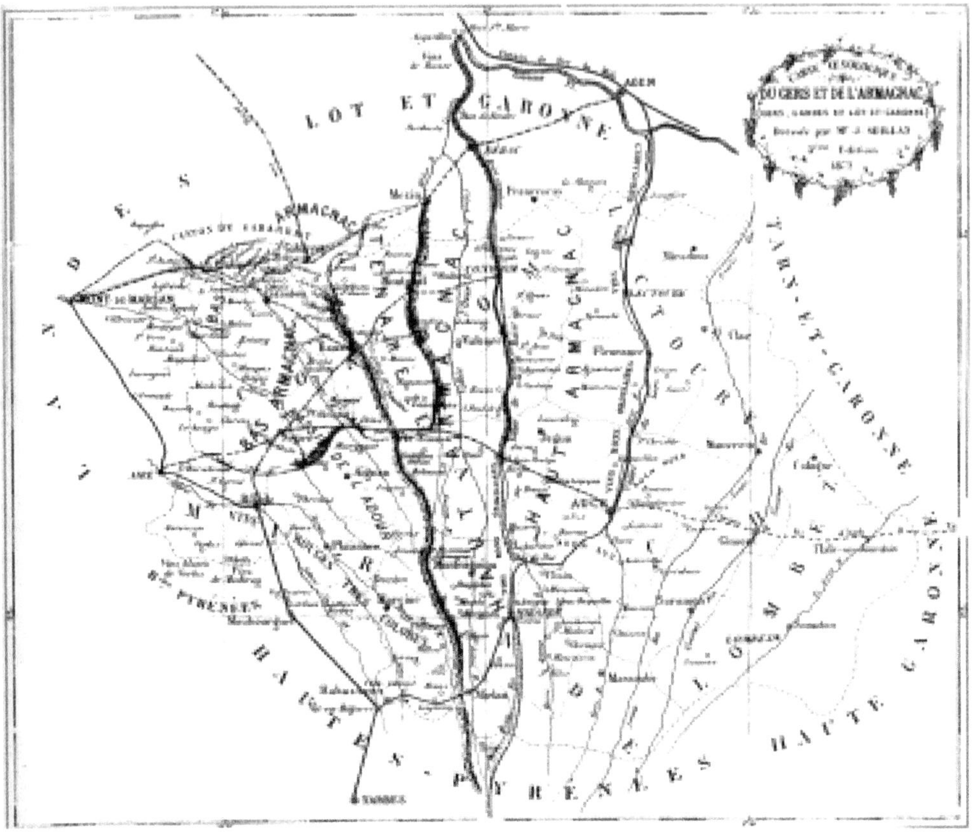

The 1857 map of Jacques Seillan

In Cognac, the situation was in complete contrast. The rapid replanting of grapevines after the phylloxera got production back to what it had been before the disease struck. Many foreign-owned firms merged with large firms and rode a larger promotional wave.

Business was lucrative in Cognac and most of the major houses had multiple stills of their own built into immense warehouses along the Charente. Concerning international relations, those of Cognac were in tailored three-piece suits, while those in Armagnac were still in dusty overhauls.

Armagnac After World War II

In 1941, the BNIA (Bureau National Interprofessional d'Armagnac) was established to control the quality of Armagnac before it reached the market. During the German occupation, armagnac distillation experienced a boom and surpassed pre-war levels. The existing *négociants* continued to purchase quality raw material from local farmers, which they later blended and sold.

Very few producers bottled their own product. They sold their stock to *négociants* whose market, although faithful, remained small. Vintages arrived slowly. Armagnac was relatively costly in comparison with other brandies. And the Cognac publicity machine continued to persuade the public that cognac was *the* finest brandy and that all others were inferior.

Like this, Armagnac wallowed in the spirit mire.

A Break From Tradition

During the Fifties and Sixties, armagnac receded into the navel of France's underbelly. The spirit's image existed like an antique postcard yellowing on the mantel of an abandoned farmhouse.

The BNIA studied the marketing problems that faced armagnac. They knew the cognac consumer demanded lighter spirits that were ready for the market after only three or four years. This was difficult with a single-distilled product—the raw esters and congeners took a decade or more to express themselves in a pleasing manner. As it cost too much to wait this long, a business decision had to be made that would possibly save Armagnac.

In 1972, the BNIA decided to amend their regulations. These included allowances for double-distillation in pot stills—commonly practiced throughout the Charente for centuries—which helped *cleanse* the young spirit. Ironically, this method had been the most common form of distillation in Armagnac until the point the more efficient and less costly continuous still was developed in the early-1800's.

They also permitted the spirit's reduction in alcohol to 40° with the addition of distilled water (like in Cognac) which took away some of its alcoholic fire. As with commercially produced cognacs, the Bureau also allowed the use of sugar and other additives.

Between the mid-seventies and early-nineties, this form of production became widespread at the *négociant* houses. Ironically, some of the money (and power) was pumped in by Cognac firms who also bought large stocks of armagnac and took control of distribution for several houses. Whether all of this stock was released as armagnac or made its way to enrich the stock in the Charente is a topic still debated in the region.

Major Differences Between Armagnac And Cognac

There are a number of major differences between *traditional* armagnac and *traditional* cognac. These include:

Traditional Armagnac	*Traditional Cognac*
1. Armagnac's grapes are split between Bacco, Folle Blanche, Ugni Blanc and Colombard.	1. Cognac's grapes are comprised of 98% Ugni Blanc.
2. Armagnac's best grapes are grown on sandy soil with predominantly warm temperatures.	2. Cognac's best grapes are grown on chalky soil with predominantly mild temperatures.
3. Traditional armagnac is single-distilled at a low degree (52°-55°).	3. Cognac is double-distilled, first to between 26° and 32°, then to 72°-78°.
4. Armagnac is generally aged in Limousin or local Gascon oak.	4. Cognac is aged in oak from the Limousin and Tronçais forests.
5. Traditional armagnac has an alcoholic content that is normally between 46° and 48°.	5. Cognac is reduced with *petites eaux* or distilled water to 40°.
6. Traditional armagnac is given a vintage date.	6. Vintages are extremely rare in Cognac. Instead, cognac is nearly always a blend of various vintages.
7. Single-varietal armagnac is common, especially Folle Blanche.	7. One rarely sees a varietal printed on a cognac label.
8. A large Armagnac *négociant* like Larresingle bottles 25,000 cases of armagnac a year.	8. A Cognac *négociant* like Hennessey releases some 2.5 million cases of cognac per year.
9. Top independent armagnac producers often sell less than 200 cases per year.	9. A *small* cognac *négociant* like Delamain releases 40,000 cases per year.

General Taste Differences Between Armagnac and Cognac

With regard to grapes, distillation type and politics of reduction, consumers and especially connoisseurs should become aware that armagnac and cognac are distinctively different products. Knowledgeable consumers do not ask, "What is better, a Rioja or a Ribeira del Duero?" Both are great wines when released by top-notch producers and must be regarded as separate entities.

As armagnac and cognac represent the two finest brandies in the world, connoisseurs should have several selections of each within their collections, just as they would have various wines from California, the Rhone or Champagne. We have already gone over the differences between the spirits regarding production. So what are the *generalized* taste differences between armagnac and cognac?

The Most Basic Taste Differences Between Armagnac and Cognac
(or how to tell an armagnac from a cognac in a blind tasting)

1. Armagnac, when single-distilled, has a fatter texture than the double-distilled cognac.
2. The fruit of Armagnac typically shows notes of plum, apricot and orange. Cognac's fruit is normally lighter and more floral.
3. The reaction with armagnac and the oak often yields notes of toffee, bourbon, caramel and pepper. Cognac's interaction with oak normally delivers plenty of spice, but frequently herbal, steamed and resinous notes as well.
4. Cognac's aromas are subtle yet not always forthcoming. Its concentration has, after all, been diluted. Traditional armagnac is normally more aromatic: heightened alcohol helps push aromas from the glass.
5. Armagnacs often contain intriguing earth and smoke aromas. Cognac's alliance with wood is often more in balance: yet rarely does it give the complexity that armagnac offers.
6. Armagnacs hit their peak between 20 and 30 years of age: Perhaps due to their higher alcohol, cognac's evolution curve is slower and often peaks around the 40 or 50 year mark..

Reduced Armagnacs And Cognacs Less Than Ten Years Old

These highly commercialized products are certainly *not* the examples by which one should judge either cognac or armagnac as a whole. Their adulteration (see chapter on Enologists) is widespread, and their reduction tremendously cuts their concentration. Many producers and *négociants*, realizing that they are not "serious" products, will not even taste journalists or connoisseurs on these releases.

Even so, armagnacs and cognacs under 10 years old comprise over 90% of the entire market. With the skill of those in the blending laboratory, it is often difficult to determine what flavors are pure and which simulate flavors that would normally arise after a much longer aging period.

But, if we must...

Single-distilled armagnacs have a fairly rich-mouthfeel. Nuances that commonly arise are orange peel, hard caramel and licorice. Its esters and acids can give it slightly earthy and rustic character.

Double-distilled armagnacs usually retain less concentrated flavor and a thinner texture than their single-distilled counterparts, making them lighter on the palate. The nose is more reticent, although hints of orange, hard caramel and young vanilla are normally somewhere to be found.

Cognacs of this age often display a medium-bodied palate, with nuances that include young vanilla, hard caramel and a slight herbaceous/floral note that is at times reminiscent of steamed wood.

Armagnacs And Cognacs Around 10 Years Old

Ten years of age is normally the minimum that one must have to determine the pure differences in taste between an armagnac and a cognac. One must remember that grapes also play a tremendously important role with regard to a brandy's ultimate texture and taste; armagnacs made from Bacco tend to be richer on the palate than those made from Ugni Blanc, while those made from Folle Blanche tend to demonstrate the most finesse. In short, it is difficult to generalize the taste of armagnacs when one is made from pure Bacco and the other is made from pure Folle Blanche. Cognacs, being made nearly entirely from Ugni Blanc, are slightly easier to characterize.

To make it more difficult, soil also plays a role with some armagnacs and cognacs, as does the quality of oak in which the spirit was raised.

But, if we must...

Traditionally distilled armagnacs will have naturally lost between 3 and 9 degrees of alcohol, yielding a spirit with good concentration of flavor, a rich mouthfeel and plenty of natural sweetness. Typical flavors might include melted toffee, quince, prune, chocolate, almond, vanilla, pepper, orange and peach. The 46°-50° alcohol level adds more heat on the nose; however, it also helps lift aromas and increase length on the palate.

Cognacs of this age will have been reduced by at least 50 proof; therefore, nearly one third of their contents is added water. Because of this the spirit is not tremendously concentrated on the nose or palate and comes across as having less body. The flavors are fairly high-pitched and evoke bright fruit, vanilla, cut flowers and wood spice. They possess some finesse and finish moderately long.

Armagnacs and Cognacs 18-25 Years Old

Most armagnacs and cognacs, if raised properly, are in their prime at this age. Evaporation has caused the spirit to concentrate and become more viscous, and alcoholic loss has provided a rounder, softer mouthfeel. The fruit has condensed and certain acids have oxidized, lending the complex nutty notes known as *rancio*. Both the armagnac and cognac should be outstanding.

As you know, it is difficult to generalize tastes. But...

Traditionally-distilled armagnacs tend to exhibit aromas and flavors of preserved fruit that is rich and dark; prune, fig, walnut, cocoa, coffee. The texture of the spirit is fat, creamy and full-bodied. Spiced-wood notes with hints of vanilla cream, *rancio*—even butter, weave their way through the fruit. The alcohol is between 45°-48°, which tends to drive the flavors into the palate. The finish is long and repeats itself in waves.

Cognacs of this age show much better natural concentration than their younger siblings. Aromas include brighter preserved fruits; preserved apple, pear, quality English toffee and wonderfully-integrated spice, vanilla notes. On the palate, the spirit is medium-bodied, although it might exhibit budding viscosity. Some fine *rancio* notes should be present, and it should finish with lovely, sublime length.

Armagnac Today

Since the early 1990's, a financial crisis has besieged the Armagnac region. Sales have plummeted. Major upheavals have taken place with two of the region's leading *négociant* houses: In 1996 one of the region's most visible brands, Sempé, closed its doors amidst a state of financial ruin. The following year it was bought for an embarrassingly low sum. Likewise, the Janneau family definitively severed their ties with the firm they established a century-and-a-half before when they sold the company to an Italian businessman in early 1997.

Whereas a healthy stock once meant two years of sales in inventory, stocks for many *négociant* houses now equal five, ten, even fifteen years. Unfortunately, sales continue to decline and show little sign of recovery. Producers and *négociants* cite several reasons for this recession:

General Changes In Consumption

Alcohol control by the police on the roads in France has caused people to drink less at restaurants, traditionally a showplace for armagnacs. Nowadays, an *aperitif* and a glass or two of wine over the course of several hours normally puts consumers near their limit. With people afraid of breathalyzer tests, the drink they are likely to avoid is the *digestif.*

In addition, heightened tax laws for distilled spirits has made armagnac an even more expensive product than before. Nearly a third the price of a bottle of armagnac goes toward taxes of various sorts, putting many bottles in a different price category than they should be found.

Finally, an unstable economy has left the French with less money than before, making the purchase of luxury items like vintage armagnacs more difficult for the typical consumer.

In an effort to combat the decline, the BNIA regularly discusses new market strategies and thinks of ways to adapt armagnac to a changing public's demands. Unfortunately, and perhaps due to inverted snobbism, whiskey has become the beverage of choice for patrons of cafés. Even in the small Landais village Le Vignau, whiskey comprises 80% of their alcohol sales. It is not quality whiskey, mind you, but run of the mill, unaged, young whiskey, certainly of lesser quality than *Dewars* or *Johnnie Walker Red.* The French are keen to mix it with orange juice or soda.

This whiskey consumer is the one the BNIA would like to recapture. Over the past few years, new ideas have surfaced with regards to armagnac-based *apéritifs*. Drinks have been invented that feature various recipes for mixed drinks and cocktails designed to be consumed before the meal. *Armagnac Blanc* and armagnacs less than 3 years old are the basis for these drinks. Some of these cocktails are nothing short of delicious; success within the marketplace, however—although on the upswing—has not been as promising as expected.

On a more positive note, the *apéritif* Floc—the regional version of *Pineau des Charentes*—has provided a viable alternative to armagnac from the cask and now sells about a million bottles a year.

The Lack Of A Powerful Marketing System

Armagnac has never established a true identity abroad with the spirits consumer. Over the decades, the general public has learned exactly what cognac is. They might not like it, but they know *what it is*; Cognac does not need to be explained. On the other hand, ask one hundred people on the street what an armagnac is and chances are you'll have a 5% success rate—at best! Whereas it's common in some bars to order a cognac and Coke, few customers in the same bar would request an armagnac and Coke. Unfortunately, even many sommeliers or buyers in wine stores haven't had the opportunity to taste great armagnac. It still needs to be explained to them. One can only *imagine* the work that needs to be done with the mainstream.

Certainly the reasons for such widespread international sales differences has to do with the strength of the Cognac marketing machine that has developed over decades in hundreds of foreign markets. Magazine ads are frequent for cognacs, yet extremely rare for armagnacs. Billboards advertising cognac are often seen throughout inner cities. It is common for retailers to buy five or ten case drops of cognac, yet not many exist who buy more than a few bottles of armagnac at a time. In short, cognac is a household word—for God's sake, the Spanish even call *their* brandy coñac! Meanwhile, armagnac remains unknown to a tremendous amount of spirit consumers throughout the world.

Why hasn't the armagnac business succeeded like that of cognac? Historically we can cite difficulties with transportation because of the region's remote location and lack of contact with important foreign outlets. But nowadays all that has changed—the entire world is well-connected.

So what exactly *is* armagnac's problem?

Lack of advertising

The Armagnac region has never had the capital to advertise on a grand scale. While flipping through an issue of *Cigar Aficionado* magazine, one passes at least half-a-dozen full page ads for various cognac brands. Armagnac publicity, however, is just nowhere to be found.

Lack of consumer knowledge

Unfortunately outside of France, armagnac is still considered to be an esoteric item, which gives it very little clout with importers and distributors. It simply is not a commodity for many of the large distributors who have the ability to shift thousands of cases of another spirit. Some armagnac *négociants* have managed to become part of huge distribution chains (Janneau with Seagrams and Sempé with Brown-Foreman). Yet because these armagnacs sell fairly small quantities next to cognac, vodka, or rum, they are considered *low priority* items. Therefore they get very little push from the heads of these multi-nationals *or* their salespeople.

Lack of press coverage

One rarely reads about armagnac in the press. In 1996, *The Wine Spectator* did a large article on brandy. They spoke plenty about cognac, but nowhere in the substantial spread was armagnac even mentioned. Likewise is the case with *The Wine Enthusiast* and *Wines and Spirits*. Even Robert Parker made the nearly inexcusable *faux pas* in his otherwise excellent *Wine Advocate* when he wrote that more than their wines, the Côtes de Gascogne region of southern France was far better known for its foie gras and *cognac*! When critics with tremendous influence are misinformed about the product, how can one expect a large public to discover it?

Lack of stylistic consistency with the independent producers

Armagnac is a spirit whose ultimate taste depends on a number of factors including soil, grapes, distillation degree, quality of oak, aging time, storage conditions, etc. Because weather conditions vary, the base material for armagnac is not the same year after year. Many producers do not buy new barrels every year, which leads to differing amounts of vanilla and spice infused in the spirit. Good distillation material along with new oak leads to one spirit, while weak distillation material with old oak leads to another. *Consequently, it becomes difficult to pinpoint a stylistic consistency even at one particular domaine!* Most spirits (because they are blends) display consistent character (light, sweet, smokey, etc.) which make them easier to understand. The stylistic inconsistency with armagnac, however, makes it an extremely difficult entity to market.

Lack of investment money

Cognac's success, of course, did not happen overnight. It was built, year after year, and foreign markets were slowly nurtured. Sales were of a sufficient nature that money was readily obtained from banks to increase future profits. In Armagnac, however, banks have never been as willing to invest in a product that did not at least have a foot in the door of important foreign markets. With the value of armagnac stock continuing to plummet, there is even less potential for investment nowadays.

Price

Blended armagnacs such as those released by *négociants* strive for consistency every year—the VSOP from Domaine "Z" released in 1995 tastes the same as their VSOP released in 1998. Armagnacs with similar ages are blended in similar proportions, which also keeps the price relatively consistent.

Vintage armagnac,on the other hand, matures with each passing year. Because of this continuous development, it is generally more expensive than blended armagnacs which ultimately makes them more difficult to sell. Unlike at a blending house or with the *solera* system, a producer cannot top up barrels with other vintages to keep consistent stock and price. Therefore, assuming that the producer has kept the spirit in barrel until bottling time, a 1980 vintage released in 1995 and a 1980 vintage released in 1998 will not taste the same; the 1998 version will have three further years of maturation which, hopefully, has created a more developed and complex release. This extra development and rarity—as is the case with Port or any fine wine—understandably moves them into a higher price category every year. Unfortunately this often puzzles buyers of fine spirits who are accustomed to the consistent prices of blended products.

Excess Stock

Another huge problem that exists in Armagnac (and Cognac for that matter) is the excess of stock or stored spirit; this means the product is not selling at its expected rate and ultimately creates a backlog. Whereas it is financially healthy to have two years of stock in inventory, many *négociants* now have five years of stock in inventory. They simply do not need anymore stock because they do not have an outlet for their goods. Marquis de Montesquieu, a large *négociant* house and once a tremendous buyer of wines from the area, can now rely on their own vineyards near Eauze for all of their distillation needs. With sales down, they simply cannot use the wine of others.

If new stock is to be purchased, low market prices have made it more advantageous for *négociants* to purchase existing stock from the various cooperatives. Nowadays they can purchase a two or three year old armagnac *along with* the barrel for approximately the same price that a new spirit alone would have cost them 10 years ago. In short, the overabundance of stock in the region has driven prices down. Way down.

Fifteen or twenty years ago, cask purchases of older vintages were common. Not now; many vintages are bought to order—twenty or thirty liters at a time. In fact, vintage armagnacs now comprise less than three percent of the armagnac market

In Armagnac, the forecast is not entirely opimistic: A former locomotive within the region, the Chateau de Lacaze chai (left) now rusts while awaiting a new owner. On the right, another abandoned vineyard in Les Landes.

Internal Strife

Even though the BNIA provides some direction for the entire armagnac market through blanket publicity, nearly all *Landais* producers feel that governing body greatly favors the *négociants* located in the Gers. The dislike (to use the most *polite* term) between the independent *Landais* producers and the BNIA is not often publicized but becomes evident after speaking with only a few people close to the source.

To begin, producers in Les Landes (pictured at right) unequivocally feel that they produce a spirit that carries the name armagnac with pride. They believe that they rest with tradition; unblended, unreduced vintages from a single property and single year. Yet statistics show that armagnacs less than five years old (3 *Étoiles*, VSOP) comprise 85% of worldwide armagnac sales. To a *négociant* house (and the BNIA), these

releases are worthy of attention. To a *Landais* producer, however, this product is *not even* an armagnac, it is a brandy *barely worthy* of the name armagnac.

The BNIA and most *négociants* are keen to point out that the consumer dictates the future of the armagnac market and that today the consumer wants something that doesn't exhibit tremendous personality. Like this many *négociant* houses tailor their older blends to a commercially-minded consumer's palate; they are reduced with water to 40°, rounded with a bit of sugar and enhanced with *rancio* liquid. When one becomes accustomed to tasting these adulterated products, it follows that unreduced, natural armagnacs often show a fiesty, rambunctious character. So much, in fact, that the BNIA might even view them as faulty; too much attack, too much fruit, too much heat on the finish. When viewed in this light, an extremely well-made, traditional Landais product is suddenly viewed as defective by their own governing bureau!

The use of Bacco is a final sticky point between the Landais producers and the rest. Bacco is, by far, the most widely planted grape in Les Landes. And while Bacco, a hybrid, will be eliminated by the year 2010, a recent promotional page published by the BNIA did not even mention Bacco as being one of Armagnac's current *authorized* grapes. Almost as if saying that someone making armagnac with Bacco is producing an *unauthorized* product.

The Financial Burdens Of An Independent Producer

Tradition is one thing, survival is another. With the market in turmoil, armagnac is becoming a depressing subject for many farmers to talk about. For the majority of producers, armagnac now costs more than it pays.

How so? In short, the financial compensations for products of the vine are extremely unpredictable. While loss through hailstorms is partially insured, loss through frosts are not. 1991 and 1997 both saw tremendous losses through frost in many parts of the Bas-Armagnac. For many producers, those years display financial catastrophe. Anything gained in good years is virtually nullified by the bad years.

The vine also requires a tremendous amount of work. Nearly every month demands some form of attention. Costly chemicals and machinery are required to raise healthy grapes. On average, one person is required to work every ten hectares of vineyard. A farmer with a good-sized vineyard is therefore obliged to hire others whom he must pay.

Corn is big business within the Armagnac region: Many farmers have opted to rip up their unpredictable vines and plant safe crops like corn instead. (Left) An experimental field with no less than a dozen different types of corn. (Right) The great majority of corn is grown for the consumption of ducks and geese rather than humans. Most farmers have wire storage cages on their property to supply their birds all year long.

With Bacco to be outlawed by the year 2010, many farmers will need to replant other grapes, another costly procedure. In addition, they will have to wait four years before they can harvest grapes of fermentable quality. This financial burden is certainly too heavy for many farmers to deal with, especially those approaching retirement age and without a successor to take over the business. *Replanting with crops other than grapes is their only viable option.*

Corn, soy beans, sunflowers, wheat, and barley, on the other hand, are predictable crops. They don't pay as well as grapes, but they require much less effort. Not surprisingly, many farmers have uprooting their vines and replanted with less temperamental crops.

Higher education and increased exposure to the outside world has also changed the mentality of many would-be successors to a farm. In general, the younger generation wants to work less and gain more, a very difficult concept to understand to those accustomed to *working* the land. Unlike in the past, young people nowadays *do not* want to emulate the life of their parents and now have the choice to do something different.

Between 1945 and 1955, the sale of five *pièces* of armagnac could buy a house. The sale of eight barrels could buy the same house on 50 acres of property. One once hoped that if they were in need of something (a tractor, a car, a marriage, a home improvement), they could call a *négociant* who came and bought a portion of their product which gave them the money to accomplish their goal. The rest would be sold to a foreign agent perhaps. To the Gascon *paisan*, a *chai* full of armagnac was like a bank full of money, a fund that would enable the family to exist comfortably in the future.

Today, phone calls are made to *négociants* and letters are sent, but there is no response. On the rare occasion a *négoce* offers to buy, the price is so low it is almost insulting. Most producers still have plenty of armagnac; the problem is that no one wants to buy it in sufficient quantity to make it a worthwhile venture.

Still, someone stops at their farm once and a while to purchase a bottle or two. Like this, at least *some* revenue from their armagnac arrives.

Le Frêche: A soon to be ripped-up Bacco vineyard displays an uncanny resemblance to a cemetery of war dead.

Vintage Armagnac

Vintages are an important element that set armagnac apart from cognac because it is common for armagnac, unlike its *Charentais* relative, to be marketed by the year in which it was distilled. Vintage cognacs do exist, normally under the banner of Early Landed Cognacs. These have been distilled in the Charente and reduced by about 25° in their first two years of life, then transferred to strictly controlled storage warehouses (often in England) for the remainder of their lives. They normally are released around their twentieth birthday. These, however, make up about 1/100th *of a percent* of overall cognac production—virtually nothing.

The *Charentais* have never been keen on vintages because it allows for much less play when blending. Vintages, according to those in the Charente, are never perfect and always contain some type of defect. Blending helps *correct* these defects and allow for a consistent, *uniform* taste—which ultimately is their goal.

Laws state that an armagnac marketed with a vintage date must come solely from wine distilled in the given year *and* must be at least ten-years-old. But how can the consumer be sure that a vintage is, in fact, authentic?

A carbon-14 test once was used to determine an armagnac's age. However, this method was shown later as being inconclusive.

Today, authenticating a vintage is done through records of actual stock that a producer or *negociant* maintains, along with a taste test. Once a year, every producer's stock is controlled; the quantities of each vintage, measured in pure alcohol, are reported to the BNIA which also updates their sales records every quarter.

In addition, every time a blend or vintage is to be marketed, a sample must be submitted to the BNIA for approval. First, records are checked to make sure that the producer has stock of that particular vintage. Then, the sample is tasted blind by a panel to see if it corresponds to an armagnac of that age. If so, it is permitted. If not, it is not allowed to reach the market.

Afterwards, another specially tagged sample must remain within the producer's *chai*. This may, at any time, be compared with the original sample to make sure that the marketed product is the same as the sample that was submitted and approved.

But can we really say that a 1939 vintage is authentic?

Like with an aged bottle of Chateau Yquem, Lafite-Rothschild, Petrus, Springbank, Dom Perignon, Romanée-Conti, , Fonseca, or Vega Sicilia...

Not really.

It ultimately comes down to one's judgment and trust.

Is There Any Such Thing As A Great Vintage Year?

It is fairly easy to determine good vintage years when speaking generally about wine. Before the grapes are even picked from the vine, one can look at the overall weather, ripeness levels achieved, and the quality of tannin and get a pretty good impression of what the vintage will be like. Predicting the specific quality of the final wine is slightly more complicated; we need to consider the soil, the quality of the grapes, quality of vinification, and the quality of aging vessels to be employed.

It is even more difficult to make sweeping generalizations about armagnac vintages. First we speak about the wine; we consider the soil, the quality of the grapes, and the quality of vinification. Then we consider the type of distillation, the degree of distillation, the quality of oak, the age of the oak, the time the armagnac spends in new oak, the dry or humid conditions of the *chai*, and finally the time the spirit spends in cask before bottling. In short, there are more variables involved with the production of armagnac than with the production of wine.

The most important variables, however, are:

1. the soil base
2. the quality of the wine
3. the distillation degree
4. initial aging in new, quality oak
5. subsequent aging in used, quality oak
6. occasional aeration of the barrels
7. storage conditions that allow for the passage of air
8. occasional observation of the barrels

The soil base or *terroir* normally plays an important role concerning the texture of a spirit. Sandy soils tend to give supple armagnacs, while harder, limestone-based soils yield armagnacs that are firmer.

The quality of wine is determined largely by the climatic conditions of a particular year. Many people claim that strong wine years, like 1989 and 1990, produce armagnacs of lesser quality while typically bad wine years, like 1987 and 1991, produce armagnacs of excellent quality. How can this be?

As stated before, the best wine for armagnac is high in acid and low in alcohol. Ripe years tend to produce wines with lower acidity and higher alcohol. A portable armagnac alambic has difficulty distilling wines higher than 10°; if the wine is stronger than this, water will occasionally be added to the wine to make the distillation smoother. This obviously cuts some of the wine's concentration, leading to a spirit with less overwhelming fruit and inherent aromatics.

On the other hand, wines that are *slightly* green due to inclimate weather will retain high levels of acid and low levels of alcohol as well as plenty of pure flavorants. These qualities provide base material that passes through the alambic with tremendous facility and does not need to be diluted.

Like that, good wine years can produce mediocre armagnacs and mediocre wine years can produce excellent armagnacs.

Apart from the soil and quality of wine, all the other variables are largely within the control of the producer. His personal finances, energy, and skill will determine whether he can make the most of his base product.

One cannot place enough emphasis on the quality of oak that is used from the outset; if the oak has been dried properly (4-6 years), it will complement the armagnac with lovely notes of vanilla and spice. If it has not been dried properly (less than 4 years), it will yield green, steamed notes. Without the influence of some new oak, an armagnac will never naturally achieve the necessary tannin and color that might ultimately make it outstanding. Likewise, if it is kept in the same barrel for too long, it is in danger of becoming too dry—once again diminishing its potential for greatness.

The barrels also need to be racked occasionally, then rediffused into other barrels. This lets them breath temporarily and lessens the chance that they will pick up off-aromas from one barrel in particular, like damp mushrooms. This, of course, takes a producer's time and effort. Without the effort, however, one will most likely have to call in an enologist and rely on his *tricks of the trade* to make their product acceptable.

Getting back to the original question: Is there such a thing as a great Armagnac vintage?

Not really. Vintages over the past twenty-five years that have produced *many* great armagnacs include 1970, 1972, 1973, 1974, 1979, 1980, 1982, 1985 and 1986. Part of this has to do with relatively high yields during those years that were often accompanied by high acid levels.

Ultimately, however, there are so many factors involved besides weather and ripeness of grapes that determine an armagnac's ultimate quality; the ten, twenty, thirty or forty years a spirit spends in oak is so crucial to its eventual quality that one really has to look at the producer and his production methods before looking at a vintage date.

To conclude, there are many great armagnacs from *just* about any mediocre year, and a plethora of mediocre armagnacs from years that were supposedly *great.*

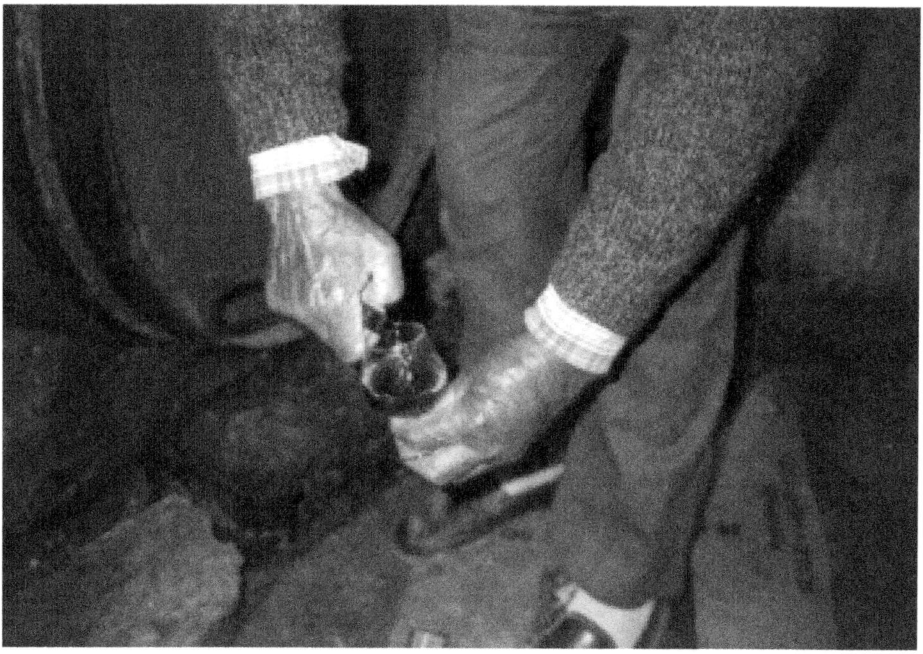

Is An Older Vintage Better Than A Younger Vintage?

One of the biggest myths among spirit consumers is that something older is automatically better. It happens with Scotch—yet seldom have I met a true Macallan fan who preferred the 25-year-old to the 18-year-old. It happens with cognac; "Pssst, this XO contains 60 year old cognacs in the blend"—said with the implication that because it is old, it is great. And it happens with armagnac: one often assumes that the 1950 is better than the 1978.

The fact is that most armagnacs peak, with regard to their fruit, alcohol and tannin balance, between their 18th and 30th birthdays. It is *possible* to obtain outstanding armagnacs distilled 30, 40, or 50 years ago; yet if they have remained in wood until their bottling date and have not been tampered with, chances are that they will be excessively dry, tannic and will have lost most of their fruit.

What many people do not realize is that many of the older vintages have been in glass *bonbonnes* for decades and, because armagnac does not age in glass, have not changed since leaving the barrel. Bottling dates must be put on vintage armagnacs; yet one cannot assume that the bottling was done directly from barrel. Therefore, that 1947 armagnac may have been put in glass in 1975, truly making it a 28-year-old armagnac. Consequently, an armagnac distilled in 1970 and bottled in 1998 has the same amount of maturity.

Because the *Armagnacais* have the right to put a vintage date on their bottle, the spirit retains a large market of people who want to buy a gift for someone who was born in a particular year, or those who have an anniversary in a particular year. Yet ultimately, a fifty-year-old armagnac is not automatically better than one with half or even a third its age. Ideally people should buy armagnacs from various properties and various vintages, having confidence in the quality of the producer rather than relying on a specific year.

One closing note; consumers should not be afraid of finishing the bottle just because it is from a particular date that holds a specific memory. Instead they should simply decide to finish the bottle and replace it with another that will certainly provide a new and exciting tasting experience!

Tasting Armagnac

How Does One Properly Taste An Armagnac?

The brandy snifter (bottom left) is the most common and traditional form or glassware used, and is certainly the most common in Armagnac. This snifter should have a bowl with a 8 to 20 ounce capacity and ideally taper as much as possible toward the top. When the glass is too small, it is difficult to concentrate the aromas, while too large a snifter sends the aromas in too many directions.

Three glasses by Riedel perhaps work better: the Gourmet Glass (second from left), Spirits Glass (third from left) and Brandy Glass (right) all tend to focus the fruit rather than accentuating the alcohol.

Always wash the glass carefully before a tasting, rinsing it under hot water and wiping it clean with a dry cloth. You don't want dirty glassware impeding your impressions of a complex armagnac.

One should be able to properly make an assessment of an armagnac with about 15 ml (or the equivalent of a third of a mini-bottle) in the glass.

Before putting the spirit in one's mouth, a number of visual and olfactory examinations take place—in other words, you check out the color and nose the glass.

Color

The first impression of an armagnac is its color. When a spirit exits the still, it is clear. It begins to take on color when placed in oak barrels to age. This coloring is largely derived from the tannin and other chemical components that gradually secrete from the wood and infuse themselves within the spirit. A deep color is not only attractive in a spirit, but it also gives the impression that it has mellowed over dozens of years.

It is therefore understandable that an armagnac aged for 16 years has a deep amber hue. Or that an armagnac aged 40 years in oak has a mahogany hue. These are colors that have developed naturally, deepening with each passing winter, with each passing decade. These are true colors, completely natural tones.

The most important thing with color, however, is its aesthetic nature. Who wants a coffee that looks watered down or a tea that is over-brewed and almost painful to look at? Likewise with armagnac, one should look for a beautiful color that is pleasing to the eye.

When looking at an armagnac, one should ask themselves: Does it look natural? Does it hint at what the nose might offer? Does it hint at what texture might come across in the mouth?

To complicate things slightly, one must also remember that new oak gives off more coloring material than used oak. Because of this, a 1960 vintage placed in new oak at the beginning of its life could consequently be darker than a 1942 vintage aged for its entire life in a barrel that was not initially new.

Normally a base color will exude additional hues that seem to dance along its surface. These bands of color or *highlights* often add additional depth and aesthetic beauty to the base tone, in the same way that filtered rays of sun electrify an otherwise normal sky. Highlights, although not always present or essential, normally give an added impression of vibrancy to the spirit.

These are the colors most often used to describe armagnac: clear, pine, straw, gold, amber, deep amber, chestnut, mahogany.

Likewise, these are the normal highlights used to describe armagnac: green, gold, amber, auburn, red, mahogany.

One also notes the intensity of the color: cloudy, clear, bright.

Traditional armagnacs rely on the time spent in wood barrels for their color and nothing else.

Aromas

Within a glass of armagnac, one can sense a tremendous array of aromas. However, when one speaks with an armagnac producer and asks how they might describe their armagnac, their response, seven times out of ten, will be, "It smells like *pruneau*". Two out of ten will say, "It smells like violet." And one out of ten will say, "It smells like *pruneau* and violet!"

In general, armagnac producers are *not* trained tasters. When one tastes with a producer and mentions various aromas found in the glass, one often receives a look of bewilderment or a nervous smile. Many of them, retired now for quite some time, do not even drink anymore. At times the connoisseur must ask themselves how these producers make such tremendous product!

For the sommelier and the connoisseur, however, there is a huge array of aromas to be found, perhaps more than in any available spirit. Many of these aromas have a direct relationship with the amount of time the spirit has spent in wood. After all, an armagnac is the synthesis of an intensely concentrated grape spirit and flavor-rich wood, which over time begins to mesh into a harmonious whole.

Pruneau is a common scent in armagnac that normally begins to arrive after ten or fifteen years of aging. Its English translation—*prune*—unfortunately brings back memories of a type of juice most commonly used among the aged to relieve constipation. The *pruneau*, however, is but one of over ten types of prunes found in France, and the one that is considered a delicacy in the Southwestern part of the country. It is often consumed on its own or used to make tarts, duck *terrines* or to stuff pork roast. It has a wonderful scent that bears little relation to that jar found in your grandparent's refrigerator.

All said, sandy soil, which tends to produce sweeter, more supple spirits that develop rapidly, is obviously more prone to develop this preserved scent of *pruneau* at a younger age. This aroma is evident in many, but not all, armagnacs that are between six and ten years old.

Although it is often cited as being a typical armagnac aroma, violet is hardly ever encountered. During my extensive tastings, I came across the scent only once. When I asked Marie-Claude Segur, the enologist from the BNIA, if she had ever come across the scent, she paused, smiled, then said, "Yes. Once." Interesting to note that we both lost this olfactory virginity with a Ténarèze, whose harder soil is certainly more apt to produce armagnacs that emphasize lighter, floral notes.

With a traditional armagnac, aromas are tremendously concentrated and can be divided into various groups. These include:

Herbal aromas: Often relating to either grass, fresh leaves or dried leaves. These include fern, hay, mint, jasmine, and tea.
Floral aromas: Often evoking fresh or, more commonly, dried flowers. These include iris, rose, geranium, chrysanthemum and violet.
Ripe fruit aromas: Related to the pulp of fresh fruit. These include apple, pear, prune, quince, white peach, banana, apricot, and mango.
Dried fruit aromas: Normally recalls the scents of fruit-based jam. These commonly include prune, fig, and apple.
Preserved fruit aromas: Evocative of the scents of fruit zest. These commonly include orange peel, lemon peel, and ginger.
Candied aromas: Often include nougat, butterscotch, toffee, white chocolate, dark chocolate, coconut milk.
Spice-related aromas: Include vanilla, cinnamon, licorice, mint, black pepper, white pepper.
Toasted aromas: Include toast, coffee, toasted coconut, tobacco, leather, truffles.
Wood-related aromas: Young oak, old oak, cedar, acacia, hickory, resin, pine.
Rancio-related aromas: Blanched almond, toasted almond, hazelnut, walnut.

Normally one begins the nosing by tilting the glass and placing the nose about one inch above the rim of the glass. One will notice various aromas begin to surface. The armagnac is then lightly swirled in the glass and the nose is taken again from an inch above the rim of the glass. Similar aromas should arrive with slightly more force. The nose is then placed into the glass and the aromas are inhaled from this proximity. Through these three steps, one should certainly be able to note the intensity of the aromas (reticent, forward, or intense) as well as particular, individual scents.

It is commonly said that one should warm the snifter in the palm of one's hand in order to release its bouquet. While it is pleasant to partake in this form of ritual, it normally releases aromas of alcohol more readily than those of fruit and is therefore not the best method for serious assessments of a spirit.

One should never, of course, heat an armagnac glass with a candle.

Connoisseurs normally grip the base of the glass between the forefinger and the thumb and swirl its contents gradually before moving it to the nose. As the spirit airs, it will climb in temperature gradually and release its full range of flavors naturally.

Texture or Mouthfeel

Armagnacs display different weights. Some will come across as being very light or delicate in the mouth, others show lots of character yet remain medium-bodied. Spirits whose components are extremely concentrated can be described as full-bodied.

Full-bodied armagnacs are certainly the most flattering but not necessarily the best. These spirits can give lots in the mouth but fail to deliver either on the nose or the finish. Likewise, medium-bodied armagnacs might not be as viscous on the palate but offer much longer length. Light-bodied spirits also have their place, perhaps with a before-dinner cocktail or as a mellow nightcap.

An ideal armagnac is one that displays finesse, or one which tends to deliver as much as possible with the least amount of overt weight. This is not easy with a spirit that has been distilled only once—a good portion of armagnacs are rich yet flabby. When these are adjusted with additives, they can even be viewed as crude or vulgar.

Finesse is seen with the finest armagnacs—these are intensely aromatic, delicate on the palate, and tremendously long and complex.

Balance

One should never judge an armagnac by its body alone. More important than body is the relationship between the *fruit*, *alcohol* and *tannin* of the spirit. One should always attempt to regard these parts as comprising a whole, always bearing in mind the subtle tension between these elements.

Flavors

The French do not have a separate word for the flavors one senses on the nose and what one tastes in the mouth. Aroma is the word normally employed to encompass both of these terms and it comprises the third and most enjoyable part of the armagnac tasting trilogy. There are primary aromas, normally related to fruit flavors and young oak, and secondary aromas, normally related to maturing fruit and tertiary aromas coming from slow oxidation.

The primary aromas one notices on the nose can be even more intense on the palate. When combined with wood secretions like vanilla, it lends a natural sweetness to the armagnac that leaves us with a most impressive memory.

Sweetness can come from the authorized addition of sugar. However, when added discreetly and professionally, it is often difficult to detect sweetness of artificial means. Even so, when tasting, one should question whether the sweet fruit has the sensation of being natural or artificial.

Secondary aromas normally begin surfacing around an armagnac's tenth birthday. The fruit often loses its youthfulness and becomes more jammy, almost like marmalade. *Rancio* begins to express itself in the form of nutty aromas, starting with almond, then moving toward walnut and hazelnut. *Rancio* occurs when esters of fatty acids slowly oxidize while gradually breathing through the barrel. It is most obvious in tawny port, aged amontillado sherries, Madeira and *vin jaune*, and its aromas tend to multiply with time and become more present.

Rancio adds a profound aromatic complexity to the armagnac. Some spirits take decades to develop this, but because more fatty acids tend to be present in spirits distilled at a lower degree, *rancio* tends to expose itself within a traditional armagnac at a younger age.

With a commercialized armagnac that has been reduced, one systematically loses some of the *pure* nose. This is normal, as water has diluted the raw material. One wouldn't expect the same concentration or intensity of aromas with a glass of Château Margaux that has been diluted with water, would they?

Alcohol

Armagnacs are normally distilled between 52° and 60°. They lose a small amount of alcohol each year, greatly depending on the humidity of the *chai* and the amount of aeration a cask sees. With time (normally between 15 and 20 years), the alcohol, fruit and tannin begins to arrive at a harmonious state of development. The alcohol is not aggressive on the nose or on the palate, nor does it burn on the finish.

Young armagnacs, in the 50° territory, are often aggressive on the nose. Likewise, older armagnacs, between 40° and 43°, are often top-heavy with sweetness and consequently lack some structure. Reduced armagnacs are rudely shaken out of balance. This balance can be partially regained by artificial means or through a complex blend.

A tremendous misconception amongst consumers is that a spirit at 40° is automatically *smoother* than one at 47°. The truth is that the alcohol of 40° armagnac is often younger, cruder and more brute, while the alcohol of the 47° armagnac is more integrated with rich fruit and therefore less noticeable.

Tannin

When an armagnac exits the still, it does not contain tannin. Tannin enters the spirit via the barrel in which it is aged. New barrels have lots of tannin to offer. With each succeeding year, a barrel loses its potential to offer this tannic material. After eight years, very little tannin remains within the wood.

Not all tannin is the same. There is round tannin, dry tannin, green tannin and astringent tannin. Round tannin tends to give structure to the alcoholic component, while the other tannins can often be distracting. Armagnacs need to be carefully monitored when placed in new barrels because they can become overly tannic after several years. Likewise, older oak may not give sufficient tannin to a spirit and consequently throw the armagnac completely out of balance.

The most important aspect of tannin is its integration with the fruit. The firm aspect of tannin should always compliment the fruit rather than overwhelm it with bitter, dry notes.

The Finish

Many connoisseurs will tell you that what an armagnac delivers on the nose and in the mouth is important, but the length is the factor by which one truly assesses a great armagnac. It is, so to speak, something that separates the men from the boys. Ideally one smells certain aromas which continue to gain importance in the mouth. The finish tells a taster much about the purity of the armagnac, as well as the concentration of its most important components *and* their balance. The finish often gives the impression that the armagnac is still on the palate. It is, in fact, a lingering crescendo, an extended curtain call, a long fade. It is one's ultimate impression of an armagnac.

The finish begins after one has swallowed the armagnac. At this point, there is normally a quick burst of heat from the alcohol which gracefully meshes with the fruit and wood elements after several seconds. Then one normally recalls the trinity of tasting elements; subtle fruit notes may surface along with chocolate, cinnamon and pepper-scented oak notes. The alcohol tends to carry and extend these.

If an armagnac has been reduced with water, its finish is almost always shorter. There is no secret in the fact that dilution reduces concentration, purity and, therefore, length. Likewise, an armagnac that emphasizes fruit and is excessively sweet does not have the structure to continue in the mouth. Its length, therefore, is bound to be short.

With older armagnacs, tannin often creeps in on the finish, making the final memory of a spirit somewhat disagreeable. An extremely dry finish could be due to an exceedingly high alcohol level that also lacks fruit, but is most normally due to too much oak at some stage in the armagnac's life. One should expect a dry finish if something has been in oak for several decades, but there should also be a certain amount of fruit that balances this oak influence. What sometimes happens with older armagnacs is that the oak overtakes the fruit and therefore dominates any evidence of pure sweetness that might remain. The spirit ends up severely tannic and is almost painful to drink.

Armagnacs of grand class should always have an extended finish. Short finishes normally drop off before the thirty-second mark. Moderate length normally entails something that remains on the palate for up to a minute. And excellent length normally extends for over a minute.

Overall Assessment

All of these aforementioned factors must be considered when ultimately assessing the quality of an armagnac. Balance is, of course, the key. If the aromatics are focused, the fruit, alcohol and tannin in balance, the mouthfeel fine, and the finish long, one can say that the armagnac is outstanding. Depending upon which elements are lacking, we can then rate in the descending order:

Excellent, Very Good, Good, Average, Poor, Unacceptable

The last category would be reserved for a spirit that bore little resemblance to armagnac at all and, consequently, should be rare.

Fond de Verre

The *fond de verre*, literally *bottom of the glass*, is the smell that remains in the glass after the armagnac is no longer there. Obviously a highly-concentrated armagnac will leave a more concentrated flavor in the glass. An armagnac that has been diluted leaves a scent that is much less strong.

If one has drunk a highly concentrated armagnac and smells the snifter the next day, they can still detect aromas of spicy-oak, preserved fruit, and flowers. These scents should be a pleasant reminder of the spirit that was savored the night before.

Armagnac Tasting Chart

Taster________________________ Town________________________
Degree________________________ Tasting date________________________
Armagnac________________________ Appellation________________________
Bottling Date________________________ Location________________________

Visual Appearance

Color

☐clear
☐pine
☐straw
☐golden
☐amber
☐chestnut
☐mahogany

Highlights

☐green
☐gold
☐amber
☐red
☐mahogany

Primary Aromas

Intensity:

☐retiscent ☐forward ☐intense

Herbal Aromas

☐fern
☐hay
☐mint
☐peppermint
☐tea

Floral Aromas

☐violet
☐iris
☐rose
☐geranium
☐dried Flowers
☐honey

Fruit Aromas

Ripe Fruit

☐apple
☐pear
☐prune
☐quince
☐white peach
☐banana
☐apricot
☐mango

Preserved Fruits

☐orange peel
☐lemon peel
☐ginger
☐coconut

Dried Fruits

☐prune
☐fig
☐apple

Candied Aromas

☐nougat
☐butterscotch
☐caramel
☐toffee
☐white chocolate
☐dark chocolate
☐coconut cream

Wood

☐young oak
☐old oak
☐damp oak
☐mushrooms
☐acacia
☐hickory
☐resin
☐pine

Spice

☐vanilla
☐cinnamon
☐licorice
☐mint
☐black pepper
☐white pepper

Toasted/roasted aromas

☐toast
☐coffee
☐toasted coconut
☐tobacco
☐leather
☐truffle

Secondary Aromas

Rancio:

☐almond
☐walnut

Relation with Primary Aromas

☐Balanced
☐Dominant

Mouthfeel

Weight

☐delicate
☐medium-bodied
☐rich

Alcohol

☐lacking
☐well-integrated
☐hot

Tannin

☐lacking oak
☐well-integrated oak
☐over-oaked

Perceived sweetness

☐natural
☐artificial

Alcohol-Tannin-Fruit Balance

1 2 3 4 5 6 7 8 9 10

Finish

Balance

☐well-balanced
☐wood out of proportion (dry)
☐alcohol out of proportion (hot)
☐fruit out of proportion (sweet)

Persistence

☐short
☐moderate
☐long

Overall impression

☐ unacceptable
☐ mediocre
☐ good
☐ very good
☐ excellent

Armagnac Bottles

Although there are laws concerning the volume contained within a bottle of armagnac, there is no set law as to what shape bottle may be used in the marketplace.

Traditionally, the round bottle or *Bâsquaise flacon* (pronounced flack-cone) has been employed for armagnac. While rustic and quaint, the *Bâsquaise* bottle provides some problems for both the retailer and the restaurateur—it takes the place of two bottles on the shelf and simply lacks *class*.

Consequently, many armagnacs are marketed in the clear, smooth-shouldered *Cognacaise* bottle. This not only allows consumers to see the spirit's beautiful color but also makes the bottle more homogenous with the other packages on the market. The *Pichet Gascon*, a 2.5 liter version of the *Cognacaise*, is often seen in restaurants.

Several firms have their own special bottles, like Samalens (in the shape of a shell), Sempé (in the form of a Musketeer and with hand-blown snifters inside), or Larressingle (a variation on the *Basquaise*). Others, like Louis Oreja, use a Normand-shaped bottle. Intricately-designed porcelain or ceramic decanters are popular with Asian markets, and new designs—in forms ranging from d'Artagnan to a goose—hit the market in those countries each year.

Which bottle is best?

The one *you* prefer, of course.

(Three bottles, left to right): The Cognacaise, Bâsquaise and the Normand.

Labeling Information

Consumers are often confused by the age of a blended armagnac. What exactly does *VSOP* imply? *Napoléon*? *Hors d'Age*? Exactly how old are these releases?

The BNIA has established a minimum age *count* that helps simplify labeling information. This count system, unfortunately, is slightly confusing because of its awkward numbering. It is explained with more clarity here:

Count 00: This first year is known as count 00 and runs from the harvest date until the last permitted date of distillation, now January 31. These spirits may not be marketed as Armagnac.
Count 0: This period runs from January 31 to the following January 31. These spirits, between 4 and 12 months old, do not have the right to be marketed as Armagnac.
Count 1: Armagnacs that have achieved their first birthday. Likewise, these cannot be marketed as Armagnac.
Count 2: 2 years old. Allowed the *VS* or *3 Étoiles* titles.
Count 3: 3 years old. Allowed the *VS* or *3 Étoiles* titles.
Count 4: 4 years old. Permitted the *VS* or *3 Étoiles* titles.
Count 5: 5 years old. *5 Étoiles*, *VSOP*, *VO*, *Réserve* or *Réserve Spéciale* titles.
Count 6: 6 years old. Allowed the *Extra*, *Napoléon*, *Vieille Réserve*, or *XO* title.
Count 7: 7 years old
Count 8: 8 years old
Count 9: 9 years old
Count 10: 10 years old. Permitted the *Hors d'age* title.

Or, in other words:
VS* or *3 Étoiles: Must be two years old.
5 Étoiles, VSOP, VO, Réserve* or *Réserve Spéciale: Must be five years old.
Extra, Napoleon* or *XO: Must be six years old.
Hors d'Age: Must be ten years old

Occasionally these blends contain armagnacs that are older than the minimums, but they do not normally differ from their minimum requirements by more than a few years.

Vintage armagnacs can come solely from the vintage listed on the label.

Bas-Armagnac: Must contain spirit made from grapes grown *and* distilled in the Bas-Armagnac region.

Ténarèze: Must contain spirit made from grapes grown *and* distilled in the Ténarèze region.

Haut-Armagnac: Must contain spirit made from grapes grown *and* distilled in the Haut-Armagnac region.

Armagnac: Can contain blends of distillates from the various regions. Most *négociant* labels are marked solely Armagnac because they normally blend Armagnacs from the Bas-Armagnac and Ténarèze.

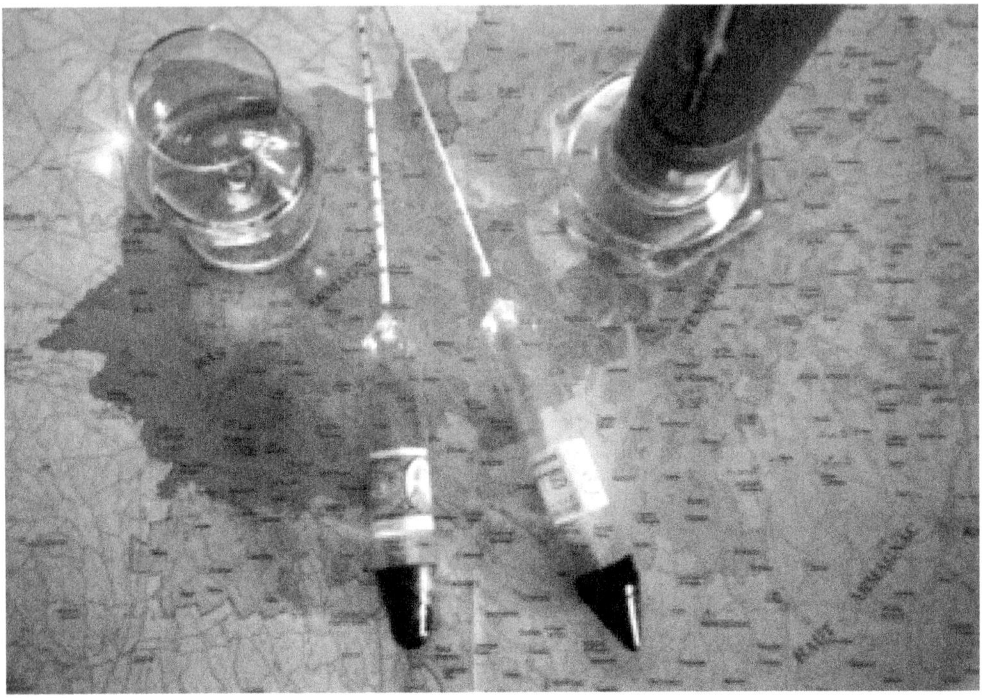

Along with a cylander and a thermometer, the buoyant alcoolmetre (center) is a tool used to guage a spirit's alcoholic strength.

The Tale Of The Tape

There is a tremendous difference concerning domestic and international sales of Armagnac and Cognac. And while these sales have nothing to do with quality, they do make for entertaining observation!

Alcohol sales have generally decreased over the past decade and, within France, Armagnac and Cognac now account for just under two percent of total spirit sales. On the other hand, anise-based alcohols, like Ricard and Pernod, control 38.1% of the French market while Whiskey, Gin and Vodka take up 21.2%.

Within France, for every 3 bottles of Cognac sold, 1 bottle of Armagnac is sold. Cognac has a 1.3% share of the French *spirits* market, while Armagnac controls just under .5% of the country's alcohol consumption.

Internationally, however, the figures are staggeringly different between Cognac and Armagnac. A few facts:

1. Cognac sales to Scandinavia are greater than Armagnac sales around the world!
2. Over three times as much Cognac is sold in the United States than Armagnac worldwide!
3. Cognac's contents in their yearly production of *Pineau des Charentes* outweighs Armagnac's annual production at a rate of 3 to 1!
4. Cognac's losses through evaporation are nearly 4 times greater than Armagnac's production per year!

Shocking, isn't it? Yet that's not all. Observe the following and get the big picture!

1996 STATISTICS
Based upon information supplied by the BNIC and BNIA

(1 hl a.p. equals approximately 250 bottles at 100 proof or 300 bottles at 80 proof)

Regional size (under vine or not)
Cognac: 82,000 ha (202,540 acres)
Armagnac: 15,000 ha (37,050 acres)
Difference: 5.5:1

Distillation (the following spirits may be used to fortify liquers, wine, etc.)
Cognac Distillation: 534,801 hl a.p. (160,440,000 bottles)
Armagnac Distillation: 18,083 hl a.p. (5,412,900 bottles)
Difference: 30:1

The following figures refer to bottled Cognac and Armagnac and do not include their bulk sales or usage in products like Pineau, Floc, Grand Marnier, Cointreau, etc.

Worldwide Total Sales
Total Cognac Sales: 354,281 hl a.p. (106,284,300 bottles)
Total Armagnac Sales: 13,380 hl a.p. (4,014,000 bottles)
Difference: 26:1

(Sales in France)
Cognac Sales in France: 20,138 hl a.p. (6,041,400 bottles)
Armagnac Sales in France: 6,696 hl a.p. (2,008, 800 bottles)
Difference: 3:1

(Sales Abroad)
Cognac Sales Abroad: 334,143 hl a.p. (100,242,900 bottles)
Armagnac Sales Abroad: 6,684 hl a.p. (2,005,200 bottles)
Difference: 50:1

Stock (in hl a.p.)
Cognac Stocks: 3,551,733 hl a.p. (1,065,519,900 bottles)
Armagnac Stocks: 210,619 hl a.p. (63,185,700 bottles)
Difference: 17:1

Leading Export Countries for Cognac (in hl a.p.)

United States	77,554	(23,266,200 bottles)
Japan	50,861	(15,258,300 bottles)
Great Britain	33,831	(10,149,300 bottles)
Hong Kong	31,300	(9,390,000 bottles)

Leading Export Countries for Armagnac (in hl a.p.)

Japan	1,244	(373,200 bottles)
Great Britain	936	(280,800 bottles)
United States	649	(194,700 bottles)
Germany	622	(186,600 bottles)

Differences (Cognac:Armagnac)

United States 120:1
Japan: 41:1
Great Britain: 36:1
Germany: 38:1
France: 1.75:1

Cognac Sales Leaders
1. Hennessey (30.7 million bottles, 99% exported)
2. Martell (24 million bottles, 88% exported)
3. Remy Martin (22 million bottles, 95% exported)
4. Courvoisier (16 million bottles, 98% exported)
5. Louis Royer (2.3 million bottles, 96% exported)
6. Otard (1.8 million bottles, 94% exported)

Armagnac Sales Leaders

1. Clés des Ducs (571,000 bottles, 45% exported)
2. Ducastaing-St. Vivant (500,000 bottles, 20% exported)
3. Marquis de Caussade (450,000 bottles, 60% exported)
4. Janneau (360,000 bottles, 77% exported)
5. Larressingle (350,000 bottles, 55% exported)
6. Château de Laubade (310,000 bottles, 35% exported)

Armagnac and Cognac Consumption By The French And Those From Abroad

Armagnac in France
VS or 3 Etoiles: 61%
VSOP: 23%
Seven years and older: 17%

Cognac in France
VS or 3 Etoiles: 75.4%
VSOP: 17%
Seven years and older: 7.6%

Armagnac Abroad
VS or 3 Etoiles: 23%
VSOP: 63%
Seven years and older: 14%

Cognac Abroad
VS or 3 Etoiles: 51%
VSOP: 45%
Seven years and older: 4%

1997 statistical differences between cognac and armagnac remained constant, although both categories were down about 5% from the previous year.

With regards to the top four armagnac markets, the Japanese bought about 8% less than in 1996 and the Germans about 15% less. The British market remained relatively stable, while the only market that showed growth was the United States.

Distillation within the Armagnac region dropped by nearly 15%, to 15,500 hl a.p. (4,650,000 bottles). 7,414 hl a.p. were from the Bas-Armagnac, 960 hl a.p. from the Ténarèze, 66 hl a.p. from the Haut-Armagnac, while 7,045 hl a.p. were blends of these regions.

Of the 15,550 hl a.p. that were distilled, 14,455 were from the Gers, 737 from Les Landes, and 293 from the Lot-et-Garonne.

The amount of aged stock (7 years or older) rose by about 12%. This aged stock category was the only one that showed sales growth both in France and abroad when compared with the statistics from the year before.

Like with most spirits, the public is drinking less but they're also drinking better.

Products Based On Armagnac

Armagnac is generally consumed on its own. However, several delicious products made with armagnac can also be found on the market. These include:

Eau de Vie

Eau de vie is the spirit as it exits the still: only after it is aged in oak barrels can it be called armagnac. The clear *eau de vie*, known as *la blanche*, is usually made with Folle Blanche (which provides lots of aromatics), Ugni Blanc or Colombard. It should be served ice cold and is most commonly consumed between courses of an especially rich meal. When the stomach can seem to handle no more *magret* or *confit*, a shot of chilled *eau de vie* creates *le trou Gascon* (the Gascon hole) which suddenly makes room for the cheese and dessert plates on the menu.

Various food matches have also proved to be successful with chilled *eau de vie*. These include: smoked salmon, delicate charcuterie and caviar.

Top *eau de vie* producers include: Domaine de Bordeneuve, Château de Briat, Château de Pellehaut, Château de Tariquet, Domaine Boingnères.

Floc de Gascogne

One of the more popular aperitifs in Gascony is called Floc de Gascogne. This comes in both red (legally referred to as rosé although it remains ruby in color) and white versions, and is produced by both established domaines and in the homes of most grape growers.

Floc is made by combining three parts unfermented grape juice with one part armagnac that has been aged a minimum of one year. The addition of the armagnac prevents the grape juice from fermenting, yet raises the mixture's alcohol level to around 18°. Occasionally it is aged in wood; normally, however, it is aged in plastic or stainless steel vats for between six months and a year.

Pineau des Charentes is the version of floc in the Cognac region. In fact, for over one hundred years, most Gascons called their aperitif *pineau*. The name floc—meaning bouquet of flowers in *patois*—did not actually become popular until around 1970.

Floc de Gascogne gained official recognition with the French ministry in 1977, when it was classified as a V.D.L.Q. P. R. D. *(vin de liqueur de qualité produit dans une région déterminée)*. At that time, official production was only 4,000 bottles. This figure skyrocketed in 1984, when more than 1,000,000 bottles were produced. In 1990, Floc de Gascogne was finally granted AOC status.

White floc, most commonly made with Colombard, Ugni Blanc, and Gros Manseng, is normally served chilled and makes a refreshing aperitif. Wonderful with nuts, one might also choose to serve white floc with foie gras or, after a meal, with fruit salad. Rosé floc, made with Tannat, Merlot, Cabernet Sauvignon, Cabernet Franc and/or Gamay, is normally served at room temperature, but at times slightly chilled or with an ice cube. It can also be served inside a melon in place of port, with cheeses (especially *brebis* from the Pyrénées or Roquefort) and as a dessert wine.

Top floc producers are all located in the Ténarèze. They include the Domaine de Cassagnoles, Domaine de Chiroulet, Domaine de Bordeneuve-Entras, Domaine de la Lartigue, Château Millet, Château de Tariquet, Domaine de Gagnet, Domaine de Cazeaux.and Domaine des Roches Freres.

Floc de l'été

In 1997, ideas for new cocktails were launched by the Floc promotional bureau under the banner *floc de l'été* (*summer floc*):

2/3 White Floc de Gascogne
1/3 Perrier water
Slice of lemon
1 or 2 ice cubes

2/3 Red Floc de Gascogne
1/3 Schweppes
Slice of lemon
1 or 2 ice cubes

Pousse-Rapière

Pousse-Rapière or *sword-thrust* is the brand name of a champagne cocktail made with an armagnac-based liqueur and sparkling wine. It was invented by the Lassus family at their Château Monluc in the Gers. The liqueur is made with a *secret* mixture of armagnac, orange peel, herbs and sugar. It is not usually drunk on its own, but takes the place of the crème de cassis traditionally used for a *kir royal*. Champagne, regional *vin mousseux* or homemade *vin mousseux* fills the glass and a slice of orange is added as an attractive garnish.

Fruits Macerated In Armagnac

Nearly every home in the armagnac region will have a jar of fruit that has been preserved in armagnac. The most typical is the *pruneau d'Agen* (whose flavor has a tremendous rapport with armagnac). But the possibilities are endless: cherries, raspberries, oranges, pears, mandarins, figs, dates, nuts. When added to ice cream, these make for a spectacular treat!

The *négociant* firm Prince de Gascogne specialize in preserved fruits, and their range of excellent products includes raspberries, cherries, blackberries, plums, clementines and *pruneau*.

La Grande Passion

Invented by the Bordeaux *négociant* Michel Roux, *La Grande Passion* surfaced in the early 1980's and was marketed heavily in the United States. At just under 50 proof, it competed with Cointreau and Grand Marnier as a perfumed liqueur and had very brief success. Although armagnac was its alcoholic base (bought from the Condom and Nogaro coopératives), its flavor was much more reminiscent of peach. When sales began to dwindle, the product was marketed in a heart-shaped, metal canister. When that marketing attempt failed, production of *La Grande Passion* was discontinued.

La Belle Sandrine

Created by Cognac-owned firm Gerland in Villeneuve-de-Marsan, this 32 proof product is a mixture of passion fruit juice and armagnac, and not dissimilar in taste to Alizé.

Bagheera

Created by the Sempé firm, this was another blend of armagnac and passion fruit juice, somewhat similar to a tropical punch.

Crèmes a l'Armagnac

The *négociant* Aurian, located in Condom, makes tremendous *crème de cassis* and *crème de mûres* (blackberry) using *eau de vie d'armagnac* as his alcohol base. A lovely addition to white wine and sparkling wine, and delicious on sorbet.

Vin de Pêche

This local *aperitif* can still be found on many farms in the armagnac region. It is always homemade and normally stored in leftover bottles. Its slightly bitter taste makes it ideal before a meal. Its recipe is as follows:

20 leaves from a peach tree
22 large sugar cubes
750 ml of red wine
1 cup of *eau de vie d'armagnac* or *3 étoiles* armagnac

Steep the fresh peach leaves in the armagnac for a week. Strain the armagnac off the leaves, place the ingredients together and mix well. Pour it into clean bottles and leave them corked in a cool spot. Leave for a week or two before serving.

A delicious vin de noix (walnut-leaf wine) can also be made by substituting the peach leaves for walnut leaves.

Mixed Drinks

In an attempt to draw consumers away from Scotch-based cocktails *and* turn over young stock, mixed drinks using armagnac are now widely promoted. These include:

Armagnac and Soda
1/3 VSOP level armagnac
2/3 club soda
Serve with an ice cube

Armagnac Sour
1/4 VSOP level armagnac
Juice of half a lemon
Two dashes of sugar syrup
3/4 Club Soda
Ice

Armagnac With Blood Orange Juice
20% VSOP level Armagnac
20% Club Soda
60% blood orange juice
Serve chilled, with several ice cubes

These two following tropical cocktails use armagnac blanc whose scent of alcohol is not as pronounced as that of rum.

Plantignac
5 cl lemon juice
5 cl strawberry syrup
40 cl guava juice
20 cl pineapple juice
10 cl of armagnac blanc
20 cl Floc de Gascogne (red or white)
pinch of cinnamon
Served with ice and a slice of fruit

Tignac
5 cl Armagnac Blanc (50-55°)
15% sugar syrup
Dash of lime juice
2 ice cubes

Armagnac and Cigars

Whereas cigars were once the mainstay prop of circus barkers, porn producers, and bullfight fans, they have now become a symbol of success among both males and females. Advertisements in *Cigar Aficionado* are not directed at the common man, but at those who have achieved a certain social stature or at least dream about achieving such a position in the financial world. Nowadays, cigars are not only chic but increasingly expensive. And what could accompany that cigar better than something more chic and more expensive?

Something Great + Something Great = Something Tremendous

Or synergy, the goal of wine and food matching. Foie gras and Jurançon, oysters and Chablis, Chocolate and Maury all reach new heights when *combined* on the palate.

We can attempt to create the same experience through fine spirit and cigar matching. But how do we determine the perfect Armagnac/Cigar match?

Before answering, we have to examine a few factors: Cigar producers tend to produce their smokes to a certain house style. Some examples:

Mild: Macanudo, La Flor Domenicana, Royal Jamaican, Majestic
Medium-bodied: Hamilton, Gloria Cubana, Davidoff, Romeo y Julieta
Powerful: Partagas, Montecristo, Cohiba, Punch

Likewise, armagnacs can be divided into several categories. Some examples:

High-pitched (floral): Château de Briat 1982 Folle Blanche, Domaine Boingnères 1980 Cépages Nobles, Domaine d'Ognoas 1985, Château de Laubade Hors d'Age, Tariquet Folle Blanche

Medium-pitched (bright fruits): Domaine Boingnères 1974 Pur Colombard, Domaine d'Ognoas 1982, Domaine de Baraillon 1985, Laberdolive 1979, Château de Tariquet 1975, Larressingle XO, Dartigalongue Hors d'age, Château de Martet 1977

Low-pitched (preserved fruits): Château de Ravignan 1973, Domaine de Jouanda 1971, Domaine de Jean du Haut 1983, Domaine de St. Aubin 1968, Domaine de Rieston 1975, Samalens Relique d'age Inconnu, Janneau *Réserve de la Maison,* Clos de Moutouguet 1968

Delicate armagnacs, for the most part, are lost with full-bodied cigars. Armagnacs with some alcoholic kick do not pair well with spicy cigars. Rich armagnacs run the risk of drowning out subtly spiced cigars. Balance should always be of utmost importance.

One should also play with flavors. Many nuances can surface while aged tobacco slowly burns, while myriad nuances also surface with a great vintage armagnac. It is always fun to see how notes of one complement the other. Listed beside are some flavors commonly found in cigars. Highlighted are the most common-crossovers with armagnac.

Nutty Notes: **Roasted Nuts**, Chestnuts, **Hazelnuts**
Fruity Notes: Ripe Berries, **Orange Peel**
Spicy Notes: Nutmeg, **Pepper**, **Anise**, Mint, Cinnamon, Curry
Roasted Notes: **Cocoa**, Coffee Beans, Toast, Leather
Floral Notes: Vegetal, Grassy, Herbal, **Woody**

So, how do we determine the perfect Armagnac/Cigar match? Sweetness and smoke usually blend well, which is one reason cigars seem to harmonize best with spirits that contain a hint of sweetness. Rich, full-bodied armagnacs that lack finesse could become a wonderful companion to a powerful cigar. With drier armagnacs or those with elevated alcohol levels, one would be safer with a more mild cigar. The subtle intricacies of each will be allowed to play off one another and bring each medium to a new and exciting level.

In general, mild cigars like *Macanudo, Partagas or Don Tomas* tend to pair well with most armagnacs, while stronger cigars like *La Gloria Cubana* or *Montecristo* run the risk of masking the more subtle nuances of a truly sublime armagnac.

21 Final Guidelines

1. Traditional armagnac is distilled once. Single distillation yields a thicker spirit as well as one rich in esters and acids. These latter elements do not flatter the consumer much during their first ten years of life, which is why traditional armagnac is *not* meant to be drunk young. When the esters and acids oxidize during their teenage years, however, they add tremendous aromatic complexity to the spirit.

2. Four grapes are commonly used for armagnac (Bacco, Ugni Blanc, Colombard, Folle Blanche). The resultant spirit from these grapes (like with wine) are different, both in their flavors and textures.

3. There are tremendous differences between blended armagnacs and traditional armagnacs. If the bottle bears the words *VS*, *3 Étoiles*, *VSOP*, *Napoléon*, *XO*, or *Hors d'age*, it is a blended armagnac that is probably single-distilled but might also include some double-distillation. It will surely be reduced with water and normally have a touch of sugar and boisé. It will certainly be a good *brandy*, but without overwhelming or memorable *armagnac* character.

4. Armagnacs released as *VSOP*, *Réserve*, *Napoléon*, *XO* or *Hors d'Age* are *not* the spirits by which armagnac should be judged. In most cases, they do *not* have tremendous interest to connoisseurs.

5. The ideal alcohol content for a traditional armagnac is between 45% and 48%. Many are reduced to 40% because their quantity automatically rises, their tax is reduced and their alcoholic contents (80 proof) are easily understood by the mass market.

6. If the label bears a vintage date *and* has an alcohol degree between 44° and 49° (depending on its age), chances are the armagnac is *traditional*. Therefore it has been single-distilled, reduced only by nature, and untouched with additives. These factors do not automatically make it great; in comparison with reduced armagnacs, however, the nose should be more profound, the palate fatter, and the finish longer.

7. Just because the armagnac has a vintage date does *not* mean that it is great or even good.

8. Rather than seeking one particular vintage for gift or sentimental reasons (which can be hit or miss), buy a *great* armagnac on the reputation of the domaine and the advice of your trusted wine merchant or sommelier.

9. Most estate-bottled armagnacs have an extremely limited production: an average year might see the equivalent of 6,000 bottles produced. That's not 6,000 bottles for the California market or 6,000 bottles for the United States. That's 6,000 bottles for the world!

10. Armagnac *producers* are not *négociants* and cannot increase their production by simply buying from other growers. Their production is limited to their small vineyards.

11. The production of armagnac is expensive: first there is the expense of growing grapes and sanitary winemaking. It takes ten liters of wine to make one liter of armagnac. Tremendous

evaporation occurs during aging. After 15 years, one might expect to lose 30% of their initial quantity. Twelve barrels gradually become eight. 6,000 bottles slowly diminish to 4,000.

12. Armagnacs that undergo a painstakingly slow evolution understandably carry a higher price tag than mass-produced, commercially-oriented products.

13. The production scale between armagnac and cognac is astronomical. An armagnac *négociant* like Darroze has about 400 barrels of stock. Remy Martin has 240,000 barrels of stock.

14. Nowadays, very little armagnac is aged in wood from Gascon forests. The great majority is aged in wood from Limousin.

15. Just because an armagnac says Bas-Armagnac does not mean that it is good. There are many armagnacs from the Ténarèze that outshine the quality of many Bas-Armagnacs.

16. As with wine where the trinity is fruit, tannin, and acidity, armagnac has a trinity that includes alcohol, tannin, and fruit. One is no more important than the other, and an excellent armagnac must have good balance between all three components.

17. Knowledgeable wine consumers don't use the word *smooth* to describe a wine. Nor do knowledgeable spirit connoisseurs when describing a fine spirit.

18. Words that have traditionally been used to describe armagnac include rustic and earthy—adjectives that do not necessarily sound positive or inviting. There are other descriptors that are more appropriate, including aromatic, exotic, long, rich, complex and refined.

19. There are many styles of armagnac: some are floral, others show lots of bright fruit, others emphasize preserved fruit, others are dominated by secondary aromas.

20. Do not overlook the importance of glassware when tasting fine spirits. Small snifters or snifters with thick glass are not necessarily appropriate when *seriously* tasting an armagnac. Opt for a snifter with thin glass, a tulip glass or a specially designed brandy glass such as those made by Riedel (see page 91).

21. Don't limit armagnac consumption until after plates have been cleared away. Many armagnacs work well with desserts including chocolate, toffee or walnuts.

The Producers

A producer is one who grows his own grapes, makes his own wine, oversees distillation of his spirit, and ages his armagnac on the property. In this way, producers differ from *négociants* in that they give birth and *produce* an armagnac from start to finish, rather than simply being responsible for its upbringing and/or sale.

There are some 800 producers in the region yet most, like Alain Dupuy of Montréal-du-Gers, do not bottle their product. Instead, they bargain through *courtiers* or agents who, in turn, sell to *négociants*. Even though many of Dupuy's armagnacs are excellent, he has no interest in bottling and creating a market for them. Armagnac is a small part of his farm's income, and bottling leads to more complications than he wants. Even though he makes less selling his stock in bulk, it is much easier than bottling, advertising, and receiving potential clients on his farm (especially if the visit interrupts a rugby match).

About 200 producers now bottle their product, yet they account for less than 10% of the Armagnac market. A handful manage to make a *comfortable* living from sales (Laberdolive, Château de Lacquy, Domaine Boingnères, Chateau de Lacquy, Château de Ravignan); these are the grand old names in Armagnac whose products have been enjoyed in fine restaurants for decades. An exceptional product and steady clientele has enabled them to invest money in their production every year instead of diverting their funds toward more pressing necessities. While not in business suits, they are not in overhauls either. They normally run the business side of things (paperwork, taxes, distribution deals, etc.) from small home offices and have one or two people who work in the vineyard and the *chai*.

The great majority of producers (who *are* normally in overhauls) sell less than 500 bottles a year. Armagnac is but one of the things they raise along with corn, cows and other crops. In fact, most distill only about 10-15% of their grape crop and sell off the rest in bulk. Consequently, the majority of revenue that comes from their vineyards is not from distilled wine but from table wine destined for the center of France or Eastern Europe.

It is possible to find extraordinary armagnacs at the homes of these producers; when one does, the excitement is unsurpassed; after all, we know that Boingnères makes fabulous armagnac...but Dr. Gabriel's quality is unexpected. When approaching a property, one often feels the aniticipation of discovery.

Most armagnac producers live in extremely humble domaines: Grapes are but one portion of their annual income, the rest normally comes from sunflowers, corn, soy beans and perhaps the odd animal.

The *typical* armagnac producer lives on a farm that was owned by his grandparents or perhaps the grandparents of his wife. The house itself is normally a few centuries old but, like many houses in Europe, one does not necessarily sense its age. Some chickens or ducks often waddle nearby. Around the house are normally vineyards or corn fields. Usually a few barns or storage buildings surround the house, in which are located the vinification equipment, tractors and farm machinery. Inside one of these barns also lies the *chai.*

The size and state of the *chai* varies greatly from farm to farm. Most are cool and dark and normally lit by a series of dim light bulbs. Many have dirt floors, which helps keep the area humid. Other floors are covered with cement, which at times is watered to add humidity. Others built specifically to house armagnac might have floors covered in cement with portions under the barrels exposed to the earth. This gives a *chai* lots of humidity while making its surface much more practical for work.

Most producers have a sign near the road that marks their sale of armagnac, and those who sell wine or floc often have a small tasting room connected to their house. These tasting rooms are certainly not elaborate or modern, normally just a simple bar with a few small snifters. They neither hold nor see tremendous amounts of people. During my visits, we were rarely interrupted by someone wanting to taste or make a purchase.

60% of the producers I saw had retired from their normal duties and had either sold a good percentage of their land or passed it on to a child. Not many producers speak English, although some of the children or grandchildren can *communicate* in English. Visitors can normally taste various releases at no charge. A purchase of some sort, although not mandatory, is always appreciated.

The Bas-Armagnac

The Bas-Armagnac is certainly the best known armagnac sub-region and the one with the highest concentration of producers. It spans two *départements*, Les Landes and the Gers, and incorporates a number of different soil types and microclimates. Nearly everything that has been written about armagnac has stated that the best armagnac comes from the Bas-Armagnac. That phrase would best be changed to, "The best armagnac comes from *certain parts* of the Bas-Armagnac," as not every part of the Bas-Armagnac has soil conducive to producing great *eau de vie*. Certain vines planted on sandy soils in the Ténarèze produce better armagnac that vines planted on harder clay soil in the Bas-Armagnac. So one shouldn't assume that just because Bas-Armagnac is on the label that the spirit is automatically great.

The Bas-Armagnac can really be divided into two *unofficial* sections, that being the *Armagnac Landais* (or from the department of Les Landes) and the *Armagnac Gersois* (or from the *departement* of the Gers). Most connoisseurs will tell you that *the best* Bas-Armagnac comes from the Landes/Gers border, a region unofficially known as the *Grand Bas-Armagnac*.

Even though many producers in Les Landes and the Gers are part of the Bas-Armagnac, certain differences remain between them. These include:

1. *The soil.* The grand percentage of soil within Les Landes is sand-based. The sand tends to yield a spirit with tremendous suppleness in its youth.

Much of the soil in the Gers has a high percentage of limestone and a low percentage of sand. Vines grown on limestone tend to produce armagnacs that are fairly hard in their youth and that take many years to soften. In short, they are generally not *showy* in their youth.

2. *Bacco.* 80% of the armagnac region within Les Landes is planted with Bacco, a grape that performs extremely well on sandy soil.

Although Bacco was once widely planted in the Gers, the favored varietal today tends to be Ugni Blanc, which grows well on limestone and chalk-based soil and gives a low alcohol wine ideal for distillation.

3. *Distillation degree.* Grapes grown on the sandy soil of Les Landes tend to express themselves best when distilled at a low degree, normally around 52°. Most producers in the Gers tend to distill between 54° and 56°.

Most producers in the eastern part of the Bas-Armagnac also make floc, and normally distill spirits destined for this *aperitif* at 60° or 62°. Those wanting to simplify things might distill all their wine at this higher degree.

4. The crops most often seen in Les Landes are corn, grapes and pine trees. In short, the landscape is very green. So green, in fact, that one often has the impression that they are watching a green and white movie! Les Landes tends to have slightly more rainfall than the rest of Armagnac which, of course, helps nourish all the green foliage. In addition, the landscape of Les Landes tends to be flat and the roads that cross its expansive surfaces tend to be straight.

In comparison with Les Landes, the Gers part of the Bas-Armagnac is visually more interesting. Rolling hills are covered with colorful sunflower, corn, wheat and grape fields. Unpredictable roads twist along its surface. It doesn't rain as much here, and the sun always seems to shine a little bit brighter.

5. The people from the armagnac-producing region of Les Landes have not seen as much *outside* influence as others within the Armagnac region. Small hamlets have remained small, immigration and emigration has been fairly rare, and the region has remained fairly pure. Likewise, traditions and customs continue to be carried on.

In contrast, the Gers has seen a tremendous amount of cultural interaction over the past fifty years. Whether it be from Spanish and Italian immigrants who were avoiding the fascistic conditions from their homelands during the Second World War, the *pieds noirs* who returned from Algeria after that country's uprising, or from English and Dutch residents now residing in the area, one senses a more cosmopolitan nature across the land.

6. Most of the wine produced in Les Landes is either used for distillation or sold in bulk to *négociants* who haul it to the center of France and blend it with other wines to produce a generic table wine. Some *quality wine* is bottled in the region, but not in tremendous quantities. Likewise, some excellent Floc de Gascogne is produced in Les Landes but not with the consistency that one finds in the Gers part of the Bas-Armagnac.

Because of slightly higher temperatures and soil more adapted to quality wine, the Gers has an abundance of excellent wine. Many producers bottle their own wine, and a handful sell over a half-million bottles per year. The same grapes that produce this wine also gives a grape juice that produces deeply colored, fresh and flavorful floc. This success of these two exports has helped lead to a more positive commercial mentality that is rarely seen in the Landes *département.*

7. The majority of armagnac producers within Les Landes have now retired yet continue to distill some armagnac every year. Most of these continue doing things as they were taught, relying on time to reduce alcoholic degree and waiting for either *négociants* to buy their spirit in bulk or the occasional passerby who will perhaps buy a bottle or two.

Armagnac producers within the Gers are more apt to tailor their products to a commercial market. ie. reduce to a lower degree or call in an enologist to construct a viable blend. VSOP and Napoléon are common releases for many producers, and vintages comprise a very low percentage of their sales.

In addition to being divided between two *départements*, the Bas-Armagnac, like the Ténarèze and the Haut-Armagnac, is also separated into a number of communes or *cantons*. Although certain communes do tend to produce better spirit than others, their groupings are for political rather than qualitative reasons.

Bas-Armagnac Producers

Author's Notes: A typical armagnac barrel is called a *pièce*, and holds between 400 and 420 liters, making it nearly twice the size of an ordinary wine barrel from Bordeaux. A hectolitre is 100 liters. *Hectolitre d'alcool pur* is a French term for 100 liters of pure alcohol, or 200 liters of alcohol at 50% volume or 100 proof. Therefore your standard armagnac *pièce* holds, approximately, 2 hectoliters of pure alcohol or 4 hectoliters (400 liters) of spirit at 50°.

When referring to production per year or stock, it is most common to use the term *hectos d'alcool pur* (hectoliters of pure alcohol). Whereas this measurement has been left intact, I have also given an approximation in terms of barrels so as to give a more concrete impression to unfamiliar terminology. Simply be aware that these barrels mentioned are actually those of between 400 and 420 liters.

Due to climatic variations, production varies greatly from year to year. The figure given for production per year refers to an average over five years.

Arthez d'Armagnac (Landes), population 93

Tiny community between Le Frêche, Perquie and Villeneuve-de-Marsan. A church at the small crossroads is interesting, although a visit to the following 14th Century domaine is certainly more entertaining.

Proprietor: Conseil Général des Landes ***Name of Property***: Domaine d'Ognoas ***Vineyard size***: 25 ha (61.75 acres) ***Other production***: Corn, Wood, Cows, Floc, White wine ***Percent of production used for distillation***: 60% ***Grapes used for armagnac***: Bacco (30-40%), Ugni Blanc (60-70%), Folle Blanche (1969 and 1973 vintages used up to 80% ***Soil***: *Sables Fauves* (Iron-rich sand) ***Production of armagnac per year***: 120 hl a.p. (60 barrels) ***Distiller***: Domaine d'Ognoas ***Distillation***: *Armagnacaise* ***Alcohol degree when leaving the still***: 52° ***Barrels***: Oak from the property ***Stock***: 850 hl a.p. (425 barrels) ***Chai***: Several well-ventilated barns, with both cement and dirt floors ***Oldest spirit still in cask***: 1958 ***Blended armagnacs available***: XO (8 years old) ***Vintages available***: All between 1958 and 1986 except 1975 ***Reduction with vintages***: No

Domaine d'Ognoas is an experimental estate owned by the *Conseil General de Les Landes* (the region's governing body). Each year, students from around France come to learn the traditions of the *Landais* countryside, including agriculture and viticulture.

For their armagnacs, three vineyards from three villages are employed; Arthez, Perquie and Le

Frêche. Distillation is done in the region's oldest alambic, which was made in 1804. From this dependable relic, the spirit drips out at a low 52° which helps emphasize its rich fruit. The varietals are aged separately for 9 to 15 months in plenty of new oak coming from trees cut on the property. They are later transferred to older oak where they continue to develop.

The XO is the domaine's commercial armagnac, reduced to 42°. It is a wonderful blend of three vintages; 60% 1986, 10% 1987, and 30% 1982. In contrast to the XO, none of the vintages are reduced with water and all are marketed at 45° or 46°.

Managing Director Patrick Arnaud is running the domaine with both enthusiasm and intelligence and, regarding armagnac, perhaps *the* most knowledgeable within the region. He works hard on packaging and finding outside markets, as well as keeping prices down. Domaine d'Ognoas eschews additives like boisé and, apart from the XO, reduction or sugar syrup. Their armagnacs are traditional, of excellent quality and show good value; they are always rich in aromas of prune and apricot along with vanilla and spice.

Patrick Arnaud of the Domaine d'Ognoas

XO: Deep amber. Rich nose hints at apricot and prune; lots of fruit. Notes of vanilla, licorice and pepper on the palate. Lush texture and good balance. Lots of pepper on the finish. One of the better blended armagnacs on the market.

1985 (60% Ugni Blanc, 40% Bacco): Amber. Rich nose hints at prune, vanilla, and spice. Fat mouth with a hint of chocolate, orange, and vanilla. Lots of spicy wood on the finish and with a pleasing *fond du verre*.

1982: Lots of fruit including notes of prune, quince and apricot, along with lots of oak—spice, vanilla, pepper. Full-bodied. Extremely expressive for its age and with a degree of finesse. Moderately long finish. Excellent price/quality rapport.

1981 (60% Ugni Blanc, 40% Bacco, 46°): Ugni Blanc seems slightly more dominant, leading to slightly flatter aromas. Hint of butterscotch. Good attack with lots of spice and pepper notes. Very good length.

1969 (60% Folle Blanche, 40% Ugni Blanc): Lighter color. Almond, vanilla on nose. Slightly floral hint in the mouth and with nice structure. Admirable finesse.

1965 (100% Bacco): Deep aromas include ripe apple, prune, licorice and almond. Very complex, still in evolution. Well-integrated wood with excellent length.

Proprietor: The de Poyferré Family ***Name of Property***: Domaine de Jouanda ***Vineyard size***: 8.5 ha (21 acres) ***Other production***: Trees, wheat ***Percent of production used for distillation***: 75% ***Grapes used for armagnac***: Ugni Blanc (100%). Vintages prior to 1976 were made with at least 35% Bacco ***Soil***: *Sables fauves* (iron-rich sand) ***Production of armagnac per year***: 6-20 hl a.p. (3-10 barrels) ***Distiller***: Formerly Broustet of Labastide. Since 1993, Dargelos of Eauze ***Distillation***: *Armagnacaise* ***Alcohol degree when leaving the alambic***: 52°-53° ***Barrels***: From the property and Limousin ***Stock***: 200 hl a.p. (100 barrels) ***Chai***: Two: a well-aired barn *and* a humid cellar under the house ***Oldest spirit still in cask***: 1966 ***Blended armagnacs available***: None ***Vintages available***: 1966, 1975, 1976, 1977 ***Reduction with vintages***: No

The de Poyferré family has lived in Arthez since 1880. In addition to owning Jouanda, they also own the Domaine de Jean du Haut in nearby Gaube and, until 1980, were part owners of the deuxième cru classé Léoville-Poyferré in St. Julien. Baron Jacques de Poyferré, a retired salesman for IBM, also has a house in Paris where he spends about half his time.

The Jouanda estate lies atop the crest of a small hill; two-thirds of the property is in Les Landes, while one-third lies in the department of the Gers. There is an extreme adherence to tradition at the estate, with the possible exception that the armagnacs are now made with Ugni Blanc alone, a rather odd concept in the *Grand Bas*. Mr. de Poyferré defends Ugni Blanc, however, by claiming that after 10-15 years of aging, differentiating the spirits made from different grapes is nearly impossible. "There is good Bacco and bad Bacco," he states. "Good Ugni Blanc and bad Ugni Blanc." His is good Ugni Blanc.

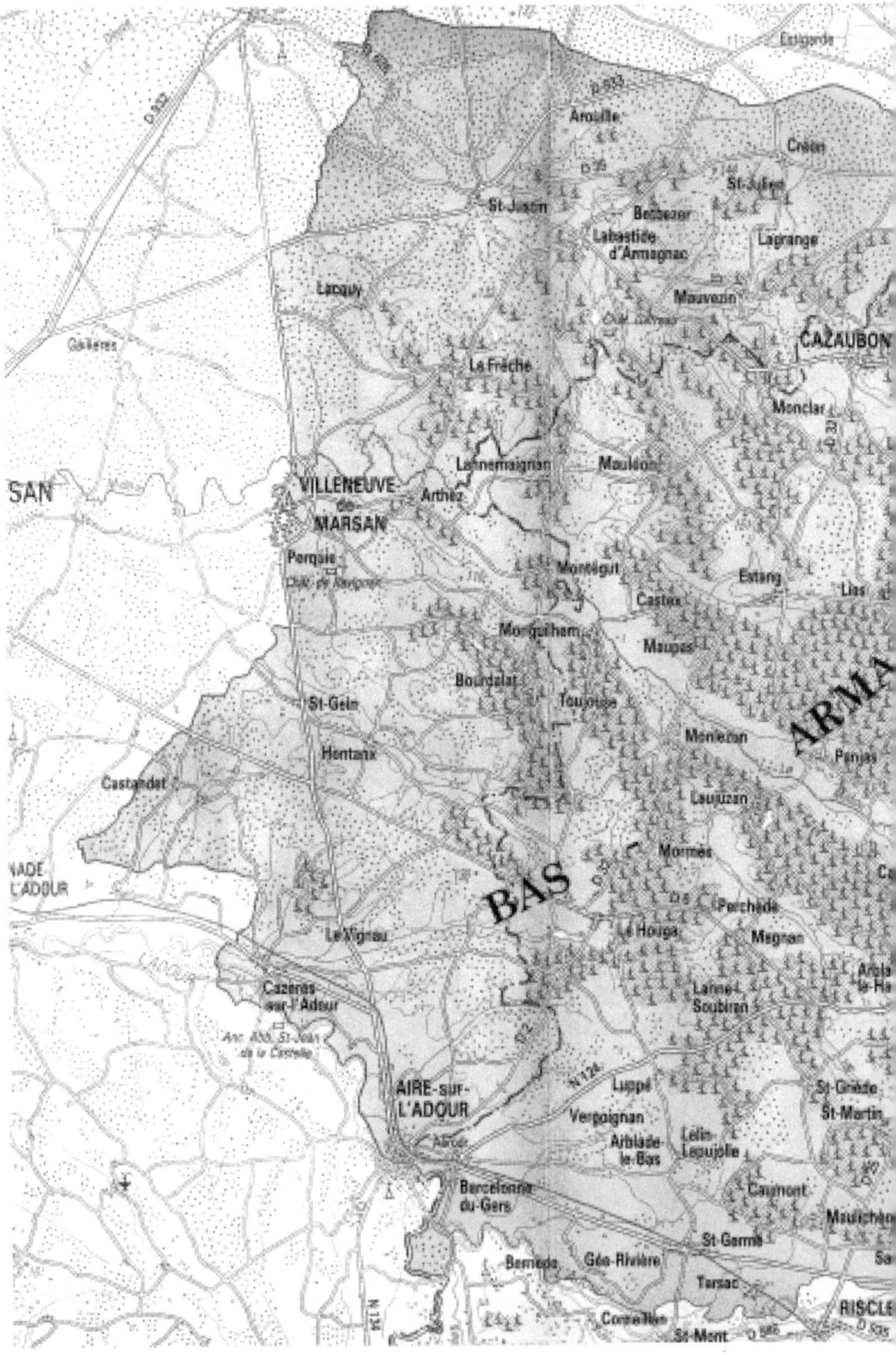

The Bas-Armagnac

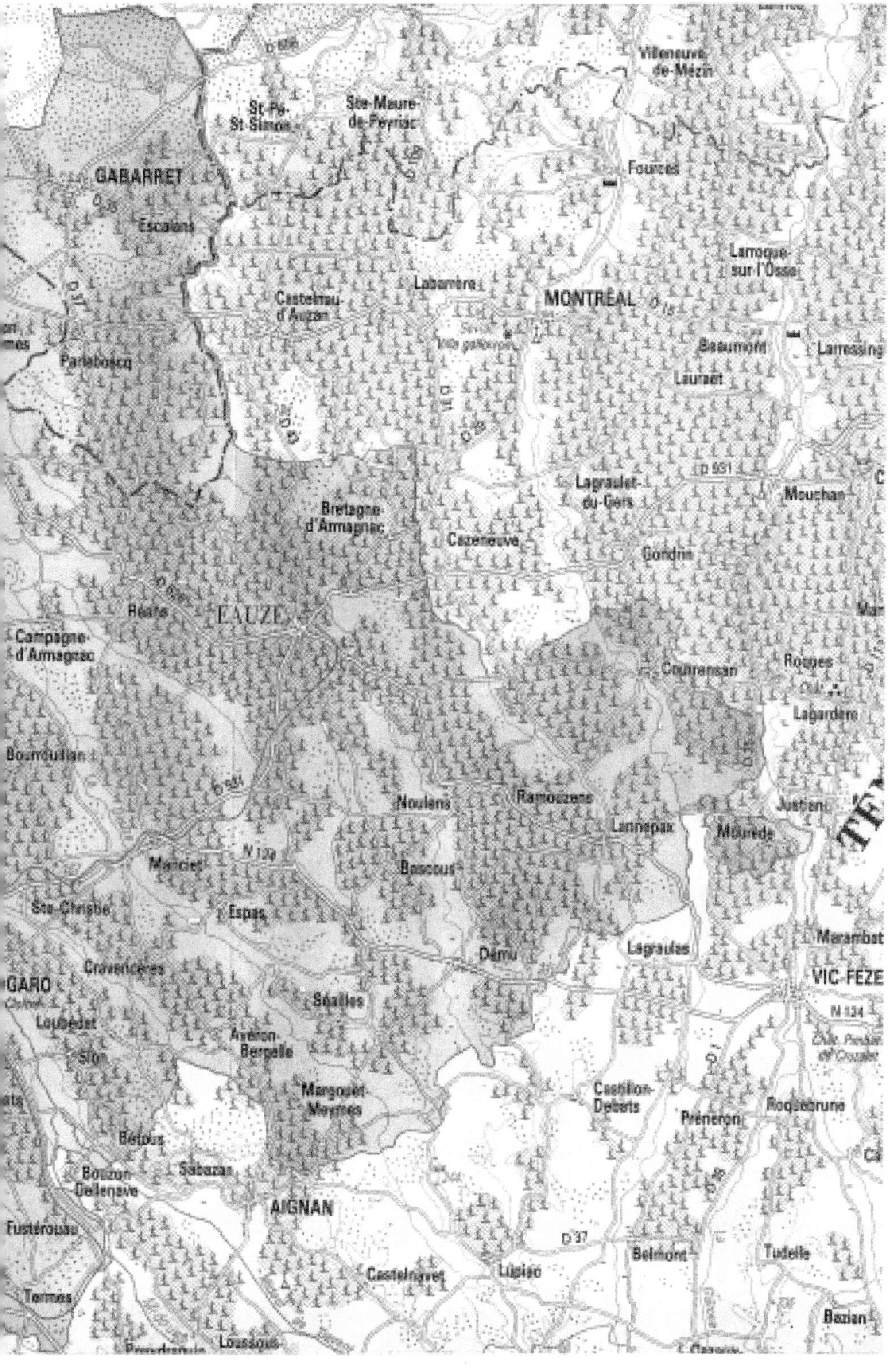
Villeneuve-de-Mézin
St-Pé-St-Simon
Ste-Maure-de-Peyriac
GABARRET
Fources
Escalans
Larroque-sur-l'Osse
Labarrère
Castelnau-d'Auzan
MONTRÉAL
Parleboscq
Beaumont
Larressingle
Lauraet
D 931
Lagraulet-du-Gers
Mouchan
Bretagne-d'Armagnac
Cazeneuve
Gondrin
Réans
EAUZE
Campagne-d'Armagnac
Courrensan
Roques
Lagardère
Bourrouillan
D 931
Noulens
Ramouzens
Lannepax
Justian
Mourède
N 124
Manciet
Bascous
Espas
Dému
Lagraulas
Marambat
Cravencères
Séailles
Loubédat
Sion
Avéron-Bergelle
Margouët-Meymes
Castillon-Debats
Préneron
Roquebrune
Bétous
Bouzon-Gellenave
Sabazan
AIGNAN
Fustérouau
D 37
Belmont
Tudelle
Castelnavet
Lupiac
Termes
Bazian

Barrels come from trees grown on the property. The staves are air-dried for 7-8 years. Before accepting a spirit, they are rinsed intensely to remove bitter tannins and then filled. Distillation is at a low temperature and the armagnac is left in new wood for as long as possible, sometimes up to 20 years. No reduction takes place and the alcohol degree is normally around 47° or 48°.

Armagnacs from Jouanda show lots of class and, understandably, are available in many of France's fine restaurants. They normally display a fine, expansive mouthfeel along with a wonderful balance of fruit, alcohol and subtle oak notes.

1978: Deep amber. Pronounced oak notes on the palate, along with prune, chocolate and spice. Hint of resin on the finish.

1977: Notes of damp, smoky oak on the nose. Some fat on the palate, and with a fine texture.

1976: Hints of *rancio* on the nose, along with some aged oak notes. Fine texture with hints of prune and some accumulating fat. Long.

1975: Lots of fat on the palate with extremely well-integrated alcohol. Spicy, peppery notes add a youthful note. Very supple, and with a smooth, expansive finish.

1966: Fat, rich and buttery nose. Fine, elegant texture. Well-integrated oak. Superb armagnac.

1927 (made with Folle Blanche and bottled in 1985): Rich butterscotch aromas. Fine texture with hints of antique wood outweighed by viscous prune and vanilla-scented fruit. Still retains alcohol which perfectly balances this dazzling spirit.

Proprietor: Guy Duhurc ***Name of Property***: Le Béroy ***Vineyard size***: 5 ha (12.35 acres) ***Other production***: corn ***Percent of production used for distillation***: 5% ***Grapes used for armagnac***: Bacco (100%) ***Soil***: *Sables fauves* (Iron-rich sand) ***Production of armagnac per year***: 2-4 hl a.p. (1-2 barrels) ***Distillation***: *Armagnacaise* ***Distiller***: Yvan Auban of Estang ***Alcohol degree when leaving the alambic***: 52° ***Barrels***: Limousin ***Oldest spirit still in cask***: 1976 ***Stock***: 40 hl a.p. (20 barrels) ***Chai***: Garage attached to the house, cement floor, organized ***Blended armagnacs available***: No ***Vintages available***: 1976, 1978, 1982, 1983, 1985, 1986, 1987 ***Reduction with vintages***: No

I met Guy Duhurc in 1995 when I asked him for directions to the nearest gas station. Noticing a sign on his property advertising the sale of armagnac, I decided to stop by after fueling up in nearby Villeneuve-de-Marsan.

Duhurc stopped distilling in 1989 when he retired. Unfortunately his son has shown no interest in continuing production, so the grapes are now sold to a *négociant* and Guy sells what remains of his small stock to the occasional passing tourist.

Duhurc's Bacco was distilled with Yvan Auban's alambics in Estang. His barrels are kept in his garage, under the cans of preserves, rifles and Bayonne hams. Duhurc's armagnacs are medium-bodied, possess a fine texture and contain well-integrated wood notes.

1987: Notes of quince and sweet plum, along with hints of spice. Great potential.

1976: Deep amber. Notes of quality toffee and toasted almond. Good sweetness and a fine texture.

Averon-Bergelle (Gers), population 174

Tiny village located between Cravencères and Aignan. Once the site of a medieval château and now the home to a lovely chapel with an octagonal bell-tower. Michel Dupont, tonnelier for many producers in the region, has his workshop just outside of town.

Proprietor: Pierre Lartigolle and sons ***Name of Property***: A Parot ***Vineyard size***: 32 ha (79 acres) ***Other production***: corn, sunflowers, soy beans ***Grapes used for armagnac***: Bacco (45%), Ugni Blanc (45%), Colombard (10%) ***Percent of production used for distillation***: 10 % ***Production of armagnac per year***: 40 hl a.p. (20 barrels) ***Soil***: *Boulbènes* (Sand with clay pieces) with *sables fauves* (Iron-rich sand) ***Distiller***: The Lartigolles themselves ***Distillation***: *Armagnacaise* ***Alcohol degree when leaving the alambic***: 54°-55° ***Barrels***: Gascon ***Oldest spirit still in cask***: 1960 ***Stock***: 145 hl a.p. (73 barrels) ***Chai:*** a large barn with a dirt floor ***Blended armagnacs available***: 8, 15, and 20-year-olds ***Vintages available***: 1961 ***Reduction***: All armagnacs reduced to 43°

Pierre Lartigolle has been the mayor of the tiny town of Aveyron-Bergelle for over four decades. He has now officially retired from his agricultural duties, having turned over the business to his sons.

The armagnac market depresses the sixty-four-year-old Lartigolle. In the past, he sold to Janneau and other *négociants*. Now, sales from the domaine are minimal and *négociants* are not buying. Stock once put away from his retirement presently sits unwanted in his two rustic *chai*. He did not even illuminate the property's wood-driven alambic in 1996: it just didn't seem worth it.

Despite commercial hardships, Lartigolle is the first to admit that they are not very organized to sell their product—there is not even a sign with the property name in front of the house (as is the case with many producers). Lartigolle currently offers 8, 15, and 20-year-old armagnacs. They are naturally made and show light color for their age. The oak, which is not normally new, is never intrusive. Medium-bodied, balanced, and showing hints of vanilla and orange, the 15 and 20-year-olds also show decent depth.

1961 (43°): Amber with gold highlights. Buttery nose with creamy nut notes. Well-integrated, spicy oak in the mouth with just a hint of dryness. Full yet supple mouthfeel. Very good length. Still finishes with a decent kick of alcohol.

Ayzieu (Gers), population 141

Remnants of the Roman occupation are to be found surrounding this small town about 6 miles outside Eauze. Two churches can be visited in the small town, as well as the remains of an old windmill. Its high location allows for a wonderful view of the Pyrénées.

Proprietor: Raymonde de Mandelaëre ***Name of Property***: Domaine de Saoubis ***Vineyard size***: 10 ha (24.7 acres) ***Other production***: Corn ***Grapes used for armagnac***: Bacco (50%), Ugni Blanc (50%) ***Percent of production used for distillation***: 60% ***Soil***: Boulbènes (Sand with clay pieces), *sables* (sand) ***Production of armagnac per year***: 50-60 hl a.p. (25-30 barrels) ***Distiller***: St. Martin of Réans ***Distillation***: *Armagnacaise* ***Alcohol degree when leaving the alambic***: 54°-55° ***Barrels***: Gascon ***Time in new oak***: 12-18 months ***Oldest spirit still in cask***: 1952 ***Stock***: 330 hl a.p. (165 barrels) ***Chai***: converted barn with a dirt floor ***Blended armagnacs available***: *Extra Vieux (8 years old)* ***Vintages available***: 1956, 1966, 1975, 1984 ***Reduction***: To 45° with distilled water.

Maurice de Mandelaëre enjoying a sample from a barrel made from wood air-dried for 50 years.

Following the death of his father, Maurice de Mandelaëre took over the production at the Domaine de Saoubis located on the route between Eauze and Estang just outside the tiny town of Ayzieu. Much of Maurice's time, however, is spent in Germany where he runs a successful *négociant* business specializing in the top wines from Southwestern France. Of course, the major export country for the Domaine de Saoubis is Germany.

The property's armagnacs already have a good reputation in France. *Négociants* such as Trépout occasionally buy vintages here, as do some of the country's top restaurants. The reasons are obvious; generous amounts of new oak every year, a healthy percentage of Bacco and careful surveillance of each barrel's progress.

Grapes are distilled separately and then aged apart. The dirt and cement floors of the *chai* combine the old with the new; recently, Maurice found some 50-year-old staves and had them fabricated into a barrel. The results have been intriguing; less tannin given to the spirit which ultimately makes it less aggressive. Less vanilla yet better oxidation. A rare kickback to times gone by.

De Mandelaëre also packages some vintages in a special bottle: Ten years ago, the Dutch government discovered one of the country's nineteenth century ships submerged off the coast of England. When they brought it to shore, they discovered a number of bottles of Montbazillac in a curious *flacon*.They bought 30,000 reproductions of this bottle to sell as souvenirs of the find; several years later, they still rested with thousands. In stepped de Mandelaëre. Like this, original packaging ideas surface.

The armagnacs of the Domaine de Saoubis tend to offer good attack in their youth and accumulate fat around their 15th birthday. A nuance reminiscent of cocoa is present with many of their vintages, and the balance between fruit and wood is superb.

Most of the domaine's armagnacs are reduced to between 42° and 45°. The unreduced vintages tasted from barrel, however, offered more concentrated aromas and deeper flavors than their reduced versions already on the market. The 1991 Folle Blanche, not yet available, displayed excellent potential.

Extra Vieux (1989): Moderate fruit on nose with a hint of caramel. Smooth texture with a pleasing, licorice-scented finish.

1984: Somewhat closed on the nose. Good attack, but remains somewhat one dimensional in the mouth.

1976: Good attack, with some notes of butterscotch and orange. Nice length.

1966: Hint of chocolate on the nose along with prune. Rich, supple texture, with excellent persistence.

1956: Lots of almond *rancio*, along with a note of cinnamon. Fat mouthfeel, and a touch of dry oak on the finish.

1979 (from 50 year old barrel, 47°): Chocolate on the nose, with a medium to full-bodied mouthfeel. Lots of penetration on the palate. A note of orange surfaces on the long finish.

Betbezer (Landes), population 135

Tiny village centered around the Château de Juliac, in existence in one form or another for more than 1,000 years.

Proprietor: Pierre Cassagne ***Name of Property***: Château de Juliac ***Vineyard size***: 35 ha (86.45 acres) ***Other production***: Corn, floc ***Grapes used for armagnac***: Ugni Blanc (50%), Colombard (50%). Early vintages include a higher percentage of Bacco ***Percent of production used for distillation***: 33 % ***Soil***: *Sables, boulbènes* (Sand and sand with clay pieces) ***Production of armagnac per year***: 100 hl a.p. (20 barrels) ***Distiller***: Lamothe ***Distillation***: *Armagnacaise* ***Alcohol degree when leaving the alambic***: 55° ***Barrels***: Limousin ***Time in new oak***: 10 years ***Chai***: Part of the château, cement floor ***Oldest spirit still in cask***: 1964 ***Stock***: 190 hl a.p. (95 barrels) ***Blended armagnacs available***: Napoléon (5 years), *Hors d'age* (10 years) ***Vintages available***: 1967, 1972, 1978 ***Reduction***: No

The Château de Juliac, centerpiece for the tiny town of Betbezer, dates back to the 9th century. Since the late 1950's, this actual castle has been owned by the Cassagne family, *pieds noirs* who were forced to leave Algeria.

Much of Juliac's stock was bought by Francis Darroze, who now markets many excellent vintages from the Fifties. Vineyards have been replanted with Ugni Blanc and Colombard, and several commercial armagnacs are now available at the property. A good deal of new oak is used to age the young spirit and Pierre Cassagne plans to buy his retiring distiller's alambic in the near future.

The armagnacs from the Sixties and early Seventies at the Château de Juliac offer tremendous purity and richness of flavor. The *chai*, with lots of air flow, permits fairly rapid evaporation and concentration of aromas. The domaine also produces a lovely red and white floc.

1976 (45°): Rich amber. Not necessarily flattering, and with lots of attack. Hint of almond and nougat on the nose. Pure depth. Hint of apricot and quince in the mouth, with some developing fat and good integration of wood. Very well made.

1972: Deep amber. Round nose with lots of attack on the palate. Notes of vanilla and oak in the mouth. Slightly dry oak continues on the finish.

1968 (44°): Deep amber. Hint of nuts, with lots of fruit and plum jam nuance. Hints of oak help give this soft armagnac structure. Lots of round, natural fat. Lovely.

Proprietor: Albert Darzacq ***Name of Property***: Domaine de Paguy ***Vineyard size***: 11 ha (24.17 acres) ***Other production***: *ferme-auberge*, restaurant, conserves, corn, floc ***Grapes used for armagnac***: Bacco (50%), Ugni Blanc (25%), Folle Blanche (25%) ***Percent of production used for distillation***: 35 % ***Soil***: *Sables fauves* (Iron-rich sand) ***Production of armagnac per year***: 30 hl a.p. (15 barrels) ***Distiller***: Was Lamothe, now Dargelos ***Distillation***: *Armagnacaise* ***Alcohol degree when leaving the alambic***: 54-56° ***Barrels***: Tronçais ***Chai***: Barn attached to the gîte, cement floor, organized ***Oldest spirit still in cask***: 1957 ***Stock***: 120 hl a.p. (60 barrels) ***Blended armagnacs available***: 5, 8, 10, 15, 20, 25, 30, 40 year olds ***Vintages available***: No ***Reduction***: With *petites eaux* to 45°

Albert Darzacq runs a successful hotel/*ferme auberge* located on the route between Betbezer and St. Justin. From a distance, the domaine is impressive; on the ground floor one even finds a restaurant overlooking a swimming pool! Towards the back, however, one enters the dark chamber known as the *chai*.

About 50 barrels are housed inside; Darzacq claims he doesn't have the stock to market vintages, so he blends various years together and releases his armagnacs at five year intervals. Ugni Blanc, he claims, performs well the first 15 years and then begins to decline. Bacco, on the other hand, is his staple grape and certainly the backbone of his prize-winning releases.

In order to promote alcohol loss, Darzacq racks his armagnacs two or three times a year. His spirits are left at their natural degree until about a year before release. At this time, he reduces to 45° with *petites eaux*. Below this, he feels, too much aroma is lost.

The armagnacs of Paguy offer rich fruit even after five years of aging and continue to age gracefully for several decades.

5 Year Old: Deep color. Fairly supple with some tannin and well-integrated alcohol.

10 Year Old: More supple, round in the mouth. Good depth of flavor for its age.

15 Year Old: Decent depth of flavor with some cinnamon and vanilla notes. Finishes with slightly bitter tannin.

20 Year Old: Nice aromatics hint at almond and prune. Medium-bodied, with some prune and nut in the mouth along with well-integrated alcohol.

30 Year Old: Rich mouthfeel with good attack. Hint of smoke in the mouth with additional notes of antique oak. Long finish.

40 Year Old: Deep aromas include prune, vanilla, antique oak and walnut. Flavors continue in the mouth, while the finish is in balance.

Proprietor: Michel Plouvier ***Name of Property***: Château Joutan ***Vineyard size***: 10 ha (24.7 acres) ***Other production***: Corn ***Grapes used for armagnac***: Bacco (80%), Colombard (10%), Ugni Blanc (10%) ***Percent of production used for distillation***: 20% ***Soil***: *Sables fauves* (Iron-rich sand) ***Production of armagnac per year***: 8-10 hl a.p. (4-5 barrels) ***Distiller***: Lamothe, Loubère ***Distillation***: *Armagnacaise* ***Alcohol degree when leaving the alambic***: 52°-55° ***Barrels***: Gascon ***Oldest spirit still in cask***: 1962 ***Stock***: 60 hl a.p. (30 barrels) ***Chai***: In a barn next to the house ***Blended armagnacs available***: 5 year, 10 year, 15 year, 20 year ***Vintages available***: No ***Reduction***: To 44° with *petites eaux*

Michel Plouvier left his native Belgium in 1959 to manage the crops surrounding the Château de Juliac in Betbezer, located a few kilometers north of Labastide. In 1964, after some family disputes, the Juliac property was divided into parcels, some of which were sold. Plouvier was one of the lucky buyers, and soon became proprietor of his own small château. He admits that he is still kidded by the natives because his accent is not from the area, but he has had no problem adapting—he's even the President of the local Pétanque club.

Bacco is the predominant grape on the Joutan property which, coupled with sandy soil, helps give lots of suppleness to its product. Vintages are not offered because they involve too much paperwork and too much space. Overoaked releases, therefore, are rarely a problem at Joutan, as their rough edges can always be rounded out with younger armagnacs. Plouvier's armagnacs are reduced a year or two before being put on the market.

Foie gras and other regional specialties are also available at the château.

10 Year Old: Light color. Soft texture hints at dried plum and brown sugar. Good balance in mouth.

20 Year Old: Deep nose with a hint of almond. Rich yet soft on the palate, with some good natural sweetness. Pleasingly long finish.

Bourrouillan (Gers), Population 167

Located between Panjas and Manciet, this small community, like most in the region, has a church but no stores or café. It does, however, produce some of the best armagnacs in the Nogaro canton.

Name of Proprietor: André Dando ***Name of Property***: Larriou ***Vineyard size***: 18 ha (44.5 acres) ***Other production***: Corn ***Grapes used for armagnac***: 8 ha Bacco (40-50 years of age) ***Percent of production used for distillation***: 45% ***Soil***: *Boulbènes* (Sand with clay pieces) ***Production of armagnac per year***: 40 hl a.p. (20 barrels) ***Distillation***: *Armagnacaise* ***Distiller***: Lestage of Manciet ***Alcohol degree when leaving the alambic***: 53° ***Barrels***: Gascon, Limousin ***Time in new oak***: 12 months, depending on the color and flavor ***Chai***: Rustic, dirt floors, humid ***Oldest spirit still in cask***: 1967 ***Stock***: 220 hl a.p. (110 barrels) ***Blended armagnacs available***: VSOP, *Hors d'age* ***Vintages available***: 1969, 1970, 1971, 1972, 1973, 1974, 1975, 1977, 1978, 1979, 1980, 1981, 1982, 1983, 1984, 1985, 1986, 1987, 1988 ***Reduction***: Very gradually, with distilled water.

Seventy-one-year-old André Dando is the third generation to raise armagnac on the Larriou property. He is also the last, as no child wants to continue the business. In 1993, Dando sold all but two of his 18 hectares of vines to his neighbors, *les* Dufrechou, and quit distilling. Today, he farms the remaining land and, more importantly, looks after his wonderful collection of armagnacs.

Dando sells two commercial armagnacs, a VSOP and an *Hors d'age*. He does not blend various vintages together; he simply feels he doesn't have the skill. Instead, he offers a product which is a blend of barrels from the same vintage, reduced very slowly with aged *petites eaux*. Dando's armagnacs have tremendous respect within the region, and his *chai* contains many hidden treasures.

1985 (Hors d'age): Hint of *rancio* on the nose. Rich caramel, licorice and vanilla on the palate. Slightly high alcohol on the finish but with good length.

1978: Prune jam with slight hints of orange and quince that have not yet fully developed. Creamy licorice notes brood below the surface. Well-integrated wood with a slightly elevated level of alcohol. Not ready yet, but with great potential. To follow with pleasure.

1977 (46°): Slightly exotic nose includes coconut, vanilla, white chocolate and marzipan! Good fat in the mouth with hints of pepper on the long finish. Delicious armagnac!

1976 (from a 500 liter barrel): Pleasing nose but slightly over-oaked in the mouth. A Castarède favorite.

1975 (40°): Moderate depth of fruit. Orange marmalade and floral nuance along with some caramel. A little disappointing.

1973 (42°): Prune and apricot on the nose with lots of richness and depth. Lovely hint of *rancio*. Extremely well-integrated wood. Wonderful armagnac.

1972 (51°, an experiment with double distillation from the first year it was authorized): Rich nose, with prune and a hint of *rancio*. Lots of oak on the palate. In fact, too much oak leads to an overly dry and spicy finish. The nose promised but the palate delivered the wrong goods.

1924 (bottled 1991 after 66 years): Deep amber with red highlights. Profound notes of prune. Well-integrated oak and alcohol. Lots of black pepper notes on the finish. Long.

1893: Deep amber with orange highlights. Hints of prune but without the roundness or fat of the former. Slight floral hint along with some spiciness. Licorice picks up on the finish.

Proprietor: Pierre Dufréchou ***Name of Property***: Domaine de Péré ***Vineyard size***: 50 ha (123.5 acres) ***Other production***: Corn ***Grapes used for armagnac***: Bacco (50%), Ugni Blanc (50%) ***Percent of production used for distillation***: 5% ***Soil***: *Boulbènes* (Sand with clay pieces) ***Production of armagnac per year***: 30 hl a.p. (15 barrels) ***Distiller***: Punsola of Cravencères ***Distillation***: *Armagnacaise* ***Alcohol degree when leaving the alambic***: 53°-57° ***Barrels***: Gascon ***Time in new oak***: 1-2 years ***Oldest spirit still in cask***: 1958 ***Chai***: In a barn, cement floor, dry ***Stock***: 400 hl a.p. (200 barrels) ***Blended armagnacs available***: No ***Vintages available***: 1986, 1956 ***Reduction***: No

Today the Domaine de Péré, located next to André Dando's property, makes much more money from the sale of white wine and corn than armagnac. In fact, very few armagnacs are for sale at the domaine. When Henri Dufréchou died in 1993, most of his stock, apart from several barrels, were either sold or split between his son and son-in-law.

The Domaine de Péré is now run by Henri's son, Pierre. Nearly all of his wine produced at his computer-run, outdoor facility is sold *en vrac* to the *coopérative* in Panjas (the equivalent of 500,000 bottles). A small percentage, half Bacco, half Ugni Blanc, is passed through the alambic. Afterwards it is placed in relatively new oak. Once every couple of years the *pièces*, resting in a well-aired *chai* next to the attractive house, are aired.

When he started distilling in 1978, Pierre was able to sell his armagnac in bulk. Nowadays he doesn't sell much in such a fashion—*négociants* are not buying. Yet thanks to his 110 hectares of corn and tremendous wine production, he can afford to stock armagnac for future sale. His brother-in-law, located about a mile away, blends his portion of stock for a more commercial market, releasing his armagnacs as Domaine de le Greau.

The current armagnacs at the Domaine de Péré are mostly young. The 1986 showed tremendous promise. The 1958, still in barrel, was fortunately not over-oaked and still showed lots of life on the palate.

1986 (47°): Deep licorice notes on the nose, along with a hint of mint. Decent depth of fruit, just beginning to gain fat. Medium to full-bodied, with very good, spicy length.

1958 (45°): Lovely amber color. Lots of wood spice on the nose. Medium to full-body with some remaining attack. Some notes of antique, polished wood in the mouth, yet covered by prune-scented fruit. Excellent balance and with a sense of finesse. Very long and spicy finish. Excellent armagnac.

Proprietor: Jean-Paul Sempé ***Name of Property***: Domaine de l'Herité ***Vineyard size***: 46 ha (113.62 acres) ***Other production***: Corn ***Percent of production used for distillation***: 10-20% ***Grapes used for armagnac***: Ugni Blanc 95%, Bacco 5% ***Soil***: *Sablo-limoneux, boulbènes* (Sand, sand with clay pieces) ***Production of armagnac per year***: 15-40 hl a.p. (8-20 barrels) ***Percentage of the production sold to negociants***: 95% (after 3-5 years) ***Distillation***: *Armagnacaise* ***Distiller***: Punsola of Cravenceres ***Alcohol degree when leaving the alambic***: 55° ***Barrels***: Gascon ***Chai***: In a barn, rustic, dirt floor ***Time in new oak***: 6 months to 1 year, although not systematic ***Oldest spirit still in cask***: 1960 ***Blended armagnacs available***: No ***Vintages available***: 1986, 1979, 1976, 1975, 1973, 1970, 1964, 1962, 1960, 1949, 1924 ***Stock***: 400 hl a.p. (200 barrels) ***Reduction***: *petites eaux* to 43-45°

Jean-Paul Sempé (no relation to the ex-senator and *négociant*) is a 50-year-old farmer whose family has resided in the region for several hundred years. A busy man, Sempé is not only the mayor of Bourrouillan but also President of the *Cave* in Nogaro.

Understandably, much of his production is sold to the *coopérative* or *négociants*. The armagnacs that he retains, however, are aged for at least ten years and released only as vintages. His armagnacs are reduced with *petites eaux* to between 43° and 45°.

The armagnacs of l'Herité are very good and reinforce Bourrouillan's position as the best armagnac-producing town in the Nogaro canton. Sempé regards the property's 1924 as being like a symphony; starting slow, building through various intricate movements and finally ending with a crescendo.

1986 (43°): Lightly floral nose with fruit that hasn't yet condensed. Hint of burnt sugar and heat on the finish.

1975 (43°): Amber with red highlights. Hints of prune, vanilla and pepper on the nose, along with a faint hint of almond. Medium-body, with fairly well-integrated alcohol. Moderate oak in the mouth and with good balance.

1979 (43°): Deeper aroma than 1975, and with rich, fatter fruit. *Rancio* beginning to surface on the nose. Vanilla and a hint of almond in the mouth. Good length.

1962 (42°): Creamy, nutty nose with good depth of fruit. Sexy mouthfeel; real fat with notes of creamy vanilla. Good length.

1924 (42°): Deep amber with red highlights. Prune, butterscotch and walnut on the nose. Hints of polished oak. Medium to full-bodied and with a classy mouthfeel. Well-integrated oak. Carries its age well.

Bretagne d'Armagnac (Gers), population 345
Bretagne is located four miles outside of Eauze on the route to Montréal. Its church lies opposite the town square. Speed bumps let you know that you are both arriving and leaving the town. Not far away is the region's golf course Guinlet—18 holes built into the Gers countryside.

Proprietor: Francis Lacave ***Name of Property***: Domaine de la Lartigue ***Vineyard size***: 40 ha (99 acres) ***Other production***: VDP de Côtes de Gascogne, white and red floc, vine stock ***Percent of production used for distillation***: 20% ***Grapes used for armagnac***: Ugni Blanc (50%), Folle Blanche (50%). Grapes are distilled, aged and marketed separately. ***Soil***: *Boulbènes* (Sand with clay pieces) ***Production of armagnac per year***: 80-100 hl of a.p. ***Distillation***: *Armagnacaise* ***Distiller***: St. Martin of Réans ***Alcohol degree when leaving the alambic***: 55° ***Barrels***: 75% from Limousin, 25% Allier ***Time in new oak***: 12-14 months ***Oldest spirit still in cask***: 1975 ***Chai***: Modern, organized, cement floor ***Reduction***: *petites eaux* to 45° (less than 10 years), 42° (vintages) ***Stock***: 340 hl a.p. (170 barrels) ***Blended armagnacs available***: 5 years, 9 years ***Vintages available***: 1986, 1973

Francis Lacave remembers when he helped his father pick grapes during the horrendous 1962 vintage—he was just a kid, cold and covered in mud and rain. Everybody told his father that distillation that year was a waste. But he distilled nonetheless.

Then waited.

During the 1980, Lacave finished off what bottles remained of his father's stock and recalls it as being the best armagnac he's ever had. Perhaps hoping to create something that will surpass that memory, he still distills nearly every year. Like many producers in the Côtes de Gascogne, however, Lacave has seen much more recent financial success with his wines than with his armagnac.

Lacave is interested in grape varietals; as a side business, he has a commercial nursery specializing in young vines. In addition to the typical Gascon varietals, he also vinifies chardonnay and will soon plant viognier. The Ugni Blanc used for his armagnac was planted nearly 25 years ago; a decade ago, he planted a parcel with Folle Blanche. These grapes are distilled separately and aged apart.

Lacave's wine is one of the first to be distilled each year by St. Martin. This insures lots of freshness in his wine and resultant spirit. The new distillation is placed in a large vat for about 12 months. Afterwards, a percentage of the spirit is removed for floc (which wins awards) while the rest is placed in *pièces*, both from the region and from Allier. He tries to expose most of the armagnacs to new oak for at least 10 months.

Lacave tops up regularly, replacing what remains in 220 liter barrels near the top of his *chai*, this ensuring a higher rate of oxidation. His armagnacs display profound amber hues.

In 1998, the Folle Blanche will replace Ugni Blanc in Lacave's armagnac production. He likes its suppleness and aroma, and feels it is well-adapted to his soil. His armagnacs currently available, however, are made with Ugni Blanc and generally show good weight and decent fruit in the mouth.

1996 Folle Blanche: Aromas include vine flowers and melon. Lots of sweetness in the mouth that completely covers the alcohol. Very well-made *eau-de-vie*.

1986 Ugni Blanc: Deep amber. Hints of orange and toffee on the nose. Medium-bodied. Pleasing finish.

1973: Toffee with a hint of prune and almond-*rancio* on the nose. Fine texture, medium to full-body, and with good balance. Supple finish with surprising length.

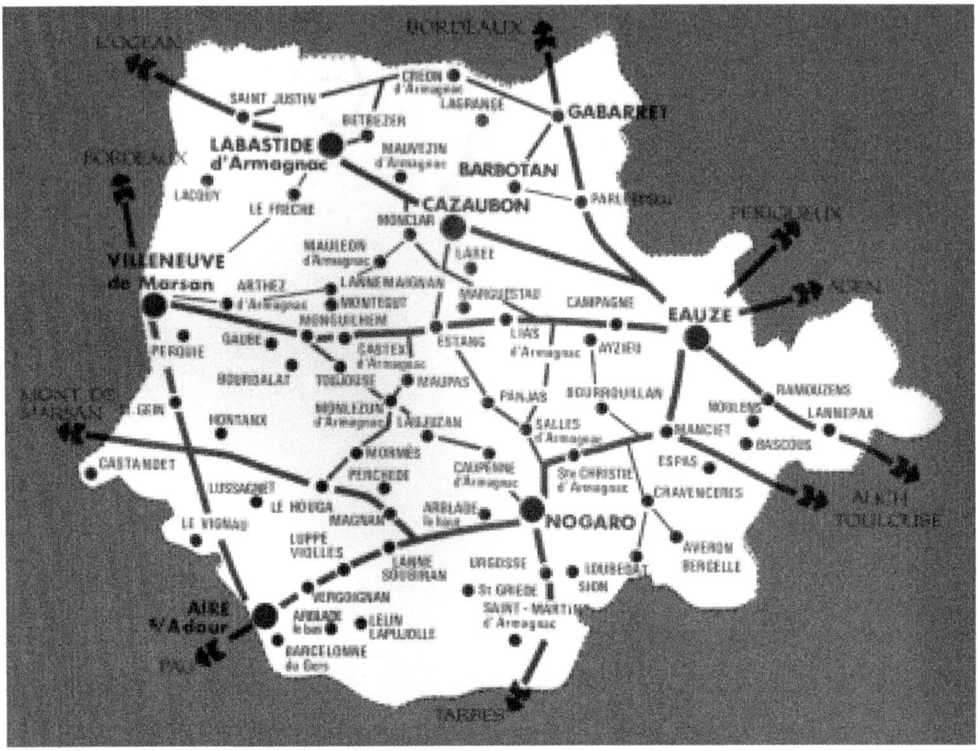

The major villages within the Bas-Armagnac

Castandet (Landes), population 375

Western-most town in the Bas-Armagnac, located between Villeneuve-de-Marsan and Aire-sur-Adour.

Proprietor: Francis de Coutard ***Name of Property***: Château de Castandet ***Vineyard size***: 8.5 ha (21 acres) ***Other production***: corn, wood, cows ***Grapes used for armagnac***: Bacco (100%) ***Soil***: *Boulbènes* (Sand with clay pieces) ***Production of armagnac per year***: 4-6 hl a.p. (2-3 barrels) ***Distillation***: *Armagnacaise* ***Distiller***: Formerly Cournet of Panjas. Now Regert of Villeneuve ***Alcohol degree upon exiting the still***: 53° ***Barrels***: Gascon ***Chai***: In an old barn, dirt floor, extremely rustic ***Stock***: 64 hl a.p. (32 barrels) ***Time in new oak***: 17 years minimum ***Oldest spirit still in cask***: 1974 ***Blended armagnacs available***: *Hors d'age* (17 years old, 44°) ***Vintages available***: 1974, 1975, 1976, 1977, 1978, 1979 ***Reduction***: No

The Château de Castandet has been part of the de Coutard family for generations. Its current owner, Francis de Coutard, is a retired electronics engineer. In 1980, his father died suddenly, leaving Francis in control of the property. He directed its business from his home in Paris and, over the years, cut down its vineyards by nearly 75%.

Once a month or so, he would come to the impressive château to pass the weekend and make sure things were in order. Of course, he continued the family tradition of distillation, if only three barrels per year. One or two new barrels were bought every year; in these vessels the spirit stayed for four to five years; from there the spirit was transferred to another *pièce* where it rests for over a decade more.

Now retired, de Coutard spends about a third of his time in Les Landes. He grows some red grapes for his own wine, although the yields are often lowered by the area's abundant deer. A good portion of de Coutard's white harvest is purchased every year by large *négociant* houses in the Gers.

His *chai* lies within an old barn. It is certainly rustic; dirt floor, stained walls, lots of mushrooms and spider webs. The humid conditions allow him to lose important levels of alcohol. De Coutard has only one release—an armagnac whose minimum age is 17 years. It is a natural blend, including the lot-ends from older vintages with no reduction or additives.

Castandet's armagnacs, which feature an extremely attractive label, show rich aromas of caramel and prune, lots of oak and a slightly dry finish.

17 Year Old: Amber. Prune and vanilla on the nose without aggressiveness. Some mushroomed-oak notes in the mouth which are covered by some dark, preserved fruits. Light notes of dry oak on the finish.

1978: Notes of nougat in the mouth. Supple texture. Hint of chocolate. Medium-body. Some alcohol showing. Good length.

Castex d'Armagnac (Gers), population 121

Sleepy village best known for the grand Château de Castex, in existence for more than 500 years. Two churches also exist, one of which dates to the 12th Century.

Proprietor: The St. Pastou Family ***Name of Property***: Château de Castex d'Armagnac ***Vineyard size***: 15 ha (37 acres) ***Other production***: Corn, sunflowers, cows ***Grapes used for armagnac***: Ugni Blanc (100%) ***Percent of production used for distillation***: 15 % ***Soil***: *Boulbènes, sables fauves* (Sand with clay pieces, iron-rich sand) ***Production of armagnac per year***: 8-10 hl a.p. (4-5 barrels)***Distiller***: Alambic of the property ***Distillation***: *Armagnacaise* ***Alcohol degree when leaving the alambic***: 54° ***Barrels:*** Regional oak. Some from the property ***Time in new oak***: 5 years ***Oldest spirit still in cask***: 1936 ***Chai***: Part of the château. Cement and sand floor. Organized and attractive. ***Stock***: 300 hl a.p. (150 barrels) ***Blended armagnacs available***: No ***Vintages available***: 1984, 1979, 1978, 1976, 1975, 1972, 1971, 1969, 1968, 1967, 1966, 1963, 1960, 1959, 1952, 1944, 1936 ***Reduction***: 42° to 45°

The Château de Castex (above) has existed in one form or another for more than 500 years. It was devastated in 1610 and reconstructed to its present, wonderful circular form in 1814. Today it rests hidden by trees just off the route between Estang and Montguilhem. Much of what remains of the surrounding forest of Montguillem belongs to the domaine's owners, the St. Pastou family. A good chunk of the wood that has gone into their barrels over the past 100 years has come from the trees surrounding the domaine.

Distillation takes place with the property's own alambic. Vintages before 1975 were made with mostly Bacco. Since that time, however, only Ugni Blanc has been distilled. In the past, many vintages were bought by *négociants*. Consequently, ruptures in stock exist between the two epochs; after all, *négociants* are not stupid—they buy the best things available.

The *chai* is impressive; one side has been refurbished and houses the younger vintages, housed in lots of new oak. The other side curves along a semi-circle and contains the older vintages lodged in older wood. While the majority of the Bacco vintages are undoubtedly mature, the younger spirits show lots of muscle, new oak and tremendous potential. It will be extremely interesting to see how this Ugni Blanc develops over the next few years.

The Baron de St. Pastou, a well-known personality within the region, died in 1985; his wife, shortly thereafter. Today, the property is run by four of the five St. Pastou children, two of whom live full-time at the property. Most of the sales are either to selective stores and restaurants around France or to the occasional tourist who stops to look at the château.

A tremendous amount of top-notch armagnacs still remain at the Château de Castex. Unfortunately the château has adopted a policy of reducing a portion of their vintages to 42° which, although pleasing to a certain segment of the market, emasculates the product for the true connoisseurs.

Fortunately, they only cut the alcohol level with one barrel of each vintage, leaving the others at their natural state. And it is with these vintages that one begins to see the quality within the armagnacs of the château; the medium-bodied texture shows lots of attack, nice depth of prune and walnut flavors, medium-body, and a dry, slightly oaky finish. In short, well-made, traditional armagnacs that carry lots of history within the glass.

1985: Amber. Nice sweetness on the palate. Lovely notes of wood spice. Oak beginning to deepen. Lots of finesse. Excellent potential.

1979: Nose beginning to gain depth. Rich fruit on palate with lots of wood spice and an overall impression of warmth. Medium-bodied, yet with attractive length.

1973: Lots of rich fruit on the nose. Medium to full-bodied texture with notes that include chocolate and spice. Still in development.

1966: Lots of walnut and vanilla on the nose. Mouth shows deep notes of prune with a lingering nuance of walnut. Still medium-bodied, but with good length and a sense of class.

1952: Rich nose with exotic hints of mango and walnut. Nice fat, well-integrated notes of antique oak and a slightly dry finish.

Proprietor: Madame Jeanne d'Agrain ***Name of Property***: Château de Monbel ***Vineyard size***: 29 ha (72 acres) ***Other production***: Bulk wine ***Grapes used for armagnac***: Bacco (33%), Ugni Blanc (33%), Colombard (34%) ***Percent of production used for distillation***: 5% ***Soil***: *Sablo-limoneux, sables fauves* (Sand and iron-rich sand) ***Production of armagnac per year***: 60 hl a.p. (30 barrels) ***Distiller***: Olivier d'Agrain ***Distillation***: *Armagnacaise* ***Alcohol degree upon exiting the still***: 55° ***Barrels***: From all over France ***Oldest spirit still in cask***: 1950 ***Chai***: In a nearby barn. Dirt floor, semi-organized ***Stock***: 300 hl a.p. (150 barrels) ***Blended armagnacs available***: VS (2.5 years), VSOP (4 years), *Hors d'age* (10 years) ***Vintages available***: 1975, 1972, 1968, 1963, 1959, 1950, 1947 ***Reduction***: With *petites eaux* to 42°

Outside of the virtually non-existent town of Castex sits an actual château, the kind one dreams of, the kind one sees in the movies.

When entering the grounds of the Château de Monbel, however, one is reminded of the classic film *The Swimmer*, in which Burt Lancaster returns home to find his family gone and his mansion deserted.

Around the turn of the century, the house belonged to Raymond de Monbel, French ambassador to China and Japan. His home reflected some of his influences from abroad; a stable was constructed in the form of a pagoda, the gardens after a Tuscan park.

Today, one detects a sense of decay around the property. The tower crumbles. Fountains are full of stagnant water. Swings with broken ropes hang from the trees. Half the castle is boarded up. This once manicured yard now looks like an overgrown wheat field.

If one listens closely, they can almost hear the sounds of days gone past; parties on the lawn, visitors from abroad, the sounds of children playing. Forty servants once looked after this majestic property. Only three workers remain and the sounds are those of insects buzzing around the two-foot grass.

One cannot blame the d'Agrain family for the complete devastation of their property; over the past ten years father Robert has died and son Olivier has received three kidney transplants. Such hardships had left the family in fairly difficult financial straits. Still Olivier, healthier and more mobile, has continued to press on.

Vines have recently been replanted and distillation—in two wood-fueled alambics co-owned with Michel Lamothe of Lannemaingnan—takes place on the property. Very little new wood is used—instead, wood chips are placed in some barrels while others contain boisé aged over several decades.

At the end of the Eighties, Monbel exported armagnacs to 15 countries. Today, like with just about every producer in armagnac, sales are down. Still, the US remains an important market, and Monbel's armagnacs are available on both the East and West Coasts. All those tasted were of sound commercial quality.

Outside the *chai*, however, the grass gets a little bit longer, the insects snap a little bit faster, and a dog barks in the far away distance.

Cazaubon (Gers), population 1,605

Cazaubon is perhaps best-known for the spas of healing waters at nearby Barbotan-les-Thermes. With its 1,628 inhabitants, the town also boasts a XII century church with a gothic portal.

Proprietor: SA C.T.S. Thermes de Barbotan ***Name of Property***: Château de Sandemaignan ***Vineyard size***: 50 ha (124 acres) ***Other production***: Sunflowers, floc, wheat, red and white wine ***Grapes used for armagnac***: Ugni Blanc (70%), Folle Blanche (20%), Colombard (10%) ***Percent of production used for distillation***: 20% ***Soil***: *Argilo-sablonneux, boulbènes* (Sand, sand with clay pieces) ***Distiller***: With the property's alambic ***Distillation***: *Armagnacaise* ***Alcohol degree when leaving the alambic***: 55-56° ***Barrels***: Limousin and Tronçais ***Time in new oak***: 2 Years ***Oldest spirit still in cask***: 1966 ***Chai***: In a barn next to the château. Well-organized, impressive. ***Blended armagnacs available***: *Hors d'age* (a blend of the 1975 and 1976 vintages)***Vintages available***:No ***Reduction***: To 41° with *petites eaux*

An old property once belonging to the Caffin family and purchased in the Seventies by Michel Guérard, one of France's great chefs. The château, while attractive from the outside, is in complete and utter decay within. Next-door, however, rest nearly 500 barrels of aging spirit, an impressive stock for an independent producer.

Many are filled with unreduced spirit whose aromas leap from the glass. However, the only product currently on the market is a well-aged yet reduced *Hors d'age*.

Hors d'age: Deep amber. Some toffee and vanilla on the nose but not as forward as expected. Rich mouthfeel, yet lacks some finesse. Decent length. Well-made commercial style.

Proprietor: Pierre Donnefoi ***Name of Property***: Le Canteloup ***Vineyard size***: 11 ha (27 acres) ***Other production***: Corn ***Grapes used for armagnac***: Bacco (100%) ***Percent of production used for distillation***: 8 % ***Soil:*** *Sablo-limoneux, boulbènes* (Sand, sand with clay pieces) ***Production of armagnac per year***: 4 hl a.p. (2 barrels) ***Distiller***: Cave Coopérative de Cazaubon ***Distillation***: *Armagnacaise* ***Alcohol degree when leaving the alambic***: 60° ***Barrels***: Oak from the property ***Time in new oak***: 18-24 months ***Oldest spirit still in cask***: 1960 ***Chai***: At the cave coopérative ***Stock***: 62 hl a.p. (31 barrels) ***Blended armagnacs available***: No ***Vintages available***: 1950, 1960, 1970, 1975, 1979, 1987 ***Reduction***: No

After one passes the spa town of Barbotan and approaches the route that runs from Eauze to Cazaubon, one sees the humble orange sign of Pierre Donnefoi, marking his domaine *Le Canteloup (call of the wolves).* In addition to being a farmer of the region's traditional grapes and corn, Pierre was also the director of the Cave Coopérative in Cazaubon between 1980 and 1993. According to him, armagnac has experienced a decline for two specific reasons; 1) the rapid turnover of young armagnacs sold in bulk has inhibited the region from creating a sufficient stock to create a large market and 2) the banks have not had sufficient confidence in armagnac to provide loans needed to successfully build various brands.

Like most armagnac producers, Donnefoi is now retired. He last distilled in 1991 but still has about 24 barrels of stock most of which is lodged at the coopérative. The majority of his vintages were distilled to a relatively high 60°. They contain no additives and were bottled at their natural degree.

The armagnacs of Canteloup are made from pure Bacco. Rather than containing the softness and depth of flavor found in the *Grand Bas*, however, they retain lots of attack, medium-body, and show good length. In short, more typical of a good traditional Ténarèze than a Bas-Armagnac.

1970 (46°): Rich nose shows good balance between alcohol and fruit. Some fat in the mouth, although finishes somewhat dry. Treads the fine line between soft and hard.

1960 (45°): Aromas somewhat closed. Vanilla and spice on the nose. Good attack on the palate. Medium-bodied, with a spicy, slightly peppery finish.

1950 (44°): Lots of aroma with some notes of *rancio.* Fat in mouth with some spicy fruit and and some antique wood notes on the palate. Medium-body. Lots of wood notes on the dry finish.

Cravencères (Gers), population 112

Tiny village where one can find the chapel of the neighboring St. Christie Hospital, a charming example of architecture between Roman and Gothic times.

Proprietor: Jean-Louis Dubuc ***Name of Property***: Boutille ***Vineyard size***: 10.5 ha (26 acres) ***Other production***: Corn ***Grapes used for armagnac***: Bacco (50%), Ugni Blanc (50%) ***Percent of production used for distillation***: 15% ***Soil:*** *Sables fauves* (Iron-rich sand) ***Production of armagnac per year***: 15 hl a.p. (7-8 barrels) ***Distiller***: M. Punsola of Cravencères ***Distillation***: *Armagnacaise* ***Alcohol degree when leaving the alambic***: 54° ***Barrels***: Gascon ***Oldest spirit still in cask***: 1953 (from his father), 1980 (his own) ***Chai:*** In two barns, both with dirt floors and both rustic ***Stock***: 200 hl a.p. (100 barrels) ***Blended armagnacs available***: 10-Year-Old, 15-Year-Old ***Reduction***: With *petites eaux* to 42°

Although he has 25 hectares of corn planted, Jean-Louis Dubuc will quickly tell you that grapes are the crop that pay. Most of his grapes are sold to the *coopérative* in Nogaro where they turn it into wine; 15%, however, comes back to the property where his neighbor/distiller Punsola lets it drip out of his alambic at 54°

Dubuc isn't interested in marketing vintages because the years vary too much, making it difficult for a small producer like himself to sell. Instead, he makes about six or seven barrels a year and offers the consumer a 10-year-old (actually made with the 1986 vintage) and a 15-year-old (made with a blend of the 1981, 1982 and 1983 vintages). Both are reduced with *petites eaux* to 42° and enhanced slightly with boisé.

Dubuc's modest stock is kept in three small *chai*, two of which lie next to the rabbit and chicken cages. His commercial armagnacs tend to have decent depth and, like many from the canton of Nogaro, a fairly strong presence of alcohol and lightly spicy finish.

Proprietor: Robert Chevalley ***Name of Property***: Domaine de Guechet ***Vineyard size***: 12 ha (30 acres) ***Other production***: Cows, horses, red and white floc ***Grapes used for armagnac***: Bacco (50%), Colombard (25%), Ugni Blanc (25%) ***Percent of production used for distillation***: 10 % ***Soil***: *argilo-sablonneux, sables fauves* (sand and iron-rich sand) ***Production of armagnac per year***: 10 hl a.p. (5 barrels) ***Distiller***: Punsola of Cravencères ***Distillation***: *Armagnacaise* ***Alcohol degree when leaving the alambic***: 52-54° ***Barrels***: Some from the property, others from Limousin ***Oldest spirit still in cask***: 1944 ***Chai:*** In a barn, with dirt floor. Rustic. ***Stock***: 140 hl a.p. (70 barrels) ***Blended armagnacs available***: *Hors d'age* (11 years old) ***Vintages available***: 1986, 1980, 1975, 1963 ***Reduction***: To 45° with *petites eaux*

Robert Chevalley moved from Switzerland to this modest farm near Cravencères in 1950. At the time his grandparents were the owners of the property, which had fallen into disrepair. As Chevalley's Italian-born wife recalls, "There were fig trees between vines and cows grazing near the front door. The place was a mess."

Little by little, they rebuilt the farm until it was manageable. Mr. Chevalley later became one of the founding members of the Nogaro Coopérative.

Now in their 70's, one would be hard-pressed to differentiate the Chevalley's from any of their other Gascon neighbors: one needs to sit no more than five minutes before being offered a home-made *Pousse-Rapière*.

The domaine's armagnacs tend to be softer than some of the others in the Nogaro canton, less marked by alcohol and with a good deal of sweetness. They reduce as little as possible, but generally bring down the alcohol level to 45° with *petites eaux*.

Their vintages heavily outsell their *Hors d'age*. "One can't rush an armagnac," says Chevalley with a sigh. "One just has to wait."

1980: Round nose that shows lots of brown sugar. Good attack, with spice notes and hints of chocolate and vanilla. Moderately long finish.

1975: Slightly deeper nose, with a hint of chocolate, coffee and nougat. Good weight in the mouth. Soft texture, subtle fruit, and with a lovely note of orange on the finish. Slightly dry aftertaste.

1963: Hint of walnut-scented *rancio* on the nose. Very pleasant note of cinnamon in the mouth. Medium-fat texture and a moderately long finish.

1944: Nice deep aromas shows lots of *rancio* notes. Good fat, but the mouth is extremely out of balance. Some heat, followed by lots of mouth-drying oak. Too long in the damn barrel!

Eauze (Gers), population 4,137

Eauze (pronounced ay-owz) has a rich history that dates back to the 3rd century BC, at which time it was known as Elusa. Around the birth of Christ, it was considered the capital of Gascony and in 300 AD, the capital of the Roman colony. Today it is the capital of Armagnac, and is also home to the BNIA (Bureau National Interprofessional d'Armagnac). This administrative bureau regulates the appellation standards of Armagnac.

Up until 1975, armagnac trading was common near the arcade of the house of Jeanne d'Albret during the market on Thursday. At this time, producers would meet with négociants and agents and arrange for the sale and purchase of armagnacs.

The town's population of 4,137 makes it the largest in the Bas-Armagnac. Its cathedral dates to the XVth century.

Proprietor: Francis Dèche ***Name of Property***: Château Millet ***Vineyard size***: 60 ha (148 acres) ***Other production***: Cows, Corn, Wheat, Côtes de Gascogne, Floc ***Grapes used for armagnac***: 50% Bacco, 50% Ugni Blanc ***Percent of production used for distillation***: 15% ***Soil:*** *Boulbènes, sablo-limoneux* (Sand with clay pieces and sand) ***Production of armagnac per year***: 60 hl a.p. (30 barrels) ***Distillation***: *Armagnacaise* ***Distiller***: St. Martin of Réans ***Alcohol degree when leaving the alambic***: 56° ***Barrels***: 60% Limousin, 40% Gascon ***Chai***: In a barn, cement floor, well-organized ***Oldest spirit still in cask***: 1958 ***Stock***: 400 hl a.p. (200 barrels) ***Blended armagnacs available***: 2 year old, 5 year old, ***Vintages available***: 1984, 1979, 1974, 1965, 1958 ***Reduction***: All armagnacs reduced to 42° with *petites eaux*

Francis Dèche is a jovial man in his fifties who owns one of the more picturesque properties in the Eauze canton. Much of his production now goes to his floc, for which he consistently wins awards. He also makes excellent red and white Côtes de Gascogne which is produced with modern, temperature-controlled equipment.

In the late fall, St. Martin brings his alambic to the property for the distillation. Armagnacs destined to be aged normally drip out at 56°. In years when the grapes are very ripe, Dèche will search for a parcel that has slightly lower sugar levels. "A wine with too much alcohol causes one to distill at a higher temperature" says Dèche. "Consequently some flavorants are lost and the spirit tends to be dryer."

Dèche feels that his armagnacs develop the scent of *pruneau* faster than other properties, after five years even. He normally keeps his spirit in new oak for one year, then transfers it to old barrels for four years. After that, the spirit is transferred to 3000 liter vats where it continues to age without accumulating more tannin.

Dèche reduces his armagnacs with *petites eaux* to 42°. Although once against any sort of reduction, he has come to believe that more aromas are released at a lower proof and that the spirit is much more accessible to a grand public.

1984: Light amber. Some vanilla on the nose along with some brandy notes. Balanced and made in a feminine style.

1974: Light amber. Hint of almond on the nose. Weight beginning to pick up on the palate, although the armagnac remains feminine. Prune and licorice on the palate, with spice, white pepper and orange on the finish. Nicely made.

1979: Deep amber. Lots of almond-scented *rancio* on the nose. Fairly aggressive in the mouth, with some scents of antique wood. Somewhat rustic overall, yet with a pleasant *fond du verre* that shows some *pruneau* and orange.

1965: Nice walnut *rancio* on the nose. Antique wood notes leave the palate dry. Lighter than the 1979 and with a bit more elegance.

1958: Deep mahogany color. Nice walnut tones on the nose. Medium-bodied, but with well-integrated wood. Very long in the mouth.

Proprietor: Constantin Georgacaracos ***Name of Property***: Lagajan ***Vineyard size***: 33 ha (82 acres) ***Other production***: milk cows, floc, white wine, *eau de vie* ***Grapes used for armagnac***: 50% Ugni Blanc, 50% Bacco ***Percent of production used for distillation***: 15% ***Soil***: *Boulbènes* (Sand with clay pieces) ***Production of armagnac per year***: 35 hl a.p. (16 barrels) ***Distillation***: *Armagnacaise* ***Distiller***: Mr. Georgacaracos himself ***Alcohol degree when leaving the alambic***: 55° ***Barrels***: Gascon and Limousin ***Oldest spirit still in cask***: 1980 ***Stock***: 120 hl a.p. (60 barrels) ***Blended armagnacs available***: VSOP (6-7 years old, 47°), *Hors d'age* (12-20 years old, 47°) ***Vintages available***: 1990, 1984, 1980 ***Reduction***: Vintages reduced to 47° with *petites eaux*

Constantin Georgacaracos was born in Greece but moved to Paris as a young boy. Several years later, his family moved to Southwestern France. Taking George out of Greece certainly took Greece out of the boy, and he no longer speaks the language or knows the country's customs. He is now a true Gascon who tends his cows and works the land.

His wife comes from a family that has made armagnac for generations. In fact, Eauze distiller Madame Dargelos grew up on the farm where Georgacaracos now lives. Today, Constantin uses the property's alambic for his own wines. It has 11 heating plates which makes it slightly taller than most alambics and has its pre-heater and condenser housed separately which, he feels, leads to a slightly cleaner distillation.

Next to the small tasting room is a museum that houses old farming tools, barrels and winemaking apparatus Through this one reaches a small *chai* that houses a few wooden vats for floc and about 50 barrels of aging armagnac.

Georgacaracos markets his armagnacs under the *Gentilhomme de Gascogne* label, mainly because his own name is too damn hard to pronounce—by any of his potential market! Likewise he has given a name to his three releases: *Jouvenceau* or VSOP is his youthful boy, *Damoiseau* or *Hors d'age* is his middle-aged man and *Chevalier, t*he 1981 vintage, his most mature and valiant armagnac.

Eau de Vie (made from the 1.5 hectares of Folle Blanche on the property, 50°): Hints of prune and herbs. Clean, fresh and invigorating.

VSOP: Light caramel notes hide the elevated level of alcohol. Pleasant.

Hors d'age: Deeper fruit than the VSOP with additional hints of licorice. Good length.

1981 (bottled 1997): Amber with gold highlights. Nose offers scents of prune, orange peel and toffee along with a hint of almond. Medium-bodied, with a good balance between alcohol, tannin and fruit. Hint of cinnamon on the moderately long finish. Well-made.

Proprietor: The Grassa family ***Name of Property***: Château de Tariquet ***Vineyard size***: 330 ha (815 acres) ***Other production***: VDP, varietal wines, floc ***Grapes used for armagnac***: Bacco (40%), Folle Blanche (33%), Ugni Blanc (27%) ***Percent of production used for distillation***: 20-30 % ***Soil***: *Boulbènes* ***Production of armagnac per year***: 400-600 hl a.p. (300 barrels) ***Distiller***: The Grassa family ***Distillation***: *Armagnacaise* ***Alcohol degree when leaving the alambic***: 56-60° ***Barrels***: Allier and Limousin ***Time in new oak***: 6-8 months ***Oldest spirit still in cask***: 1972 ***Stock***: 3,200 hl a.p. (1,600 barrels) ***Blended armagnacs available***: 3 Étoilles, VSOP, *Hors d'age*, Folle Blanche. All reduced with *petites eaux* ***Vintages available***: 1975, 1972 ***Reduction***: No

The Château du Tariquet, located in the small hamlet of St. Amand about five kilometers outside Eauze, is owned and operated by the Grassa family. Their dry white wines made with Ugni Blanc and Colombard are among the finest in the region, as are their rather untraditional whites made with Sauvignon Blanc, Chardonnay and Gros Manseng.

Like in most of Southwestern France, the phylloxera crisis of the late 1800's completely destroyed the vineyards of Gascony. Most grape growers turned to safer ways of using their land to make money, notably grains, sunflowers and as pasture for cattle. In 1912, the Grassa family acquired the splendid 17th century château and dedicated itself to restoring the property's vines which lay on sand and clay-based soil. Throughout the 1950's and 60's, Pierre Grassa replanted the vineyards with Ugni Blanc, Colombard, and Folle Blanche. He sold most of the wine to the *coopèrative* in Eauze. Like any Gascon farmer, however, he distilled every year, building stock while also selling occasional casks to *négociants*.

The domaine took tremendous strides forward when Pierre's son Yves took over wine and spirit production and his daughter Maïté began running the administrative end of the business. During the 1980's, the Grassa's invested heavily in modern winemaking equipment, like temperature-controlled vats which helped extract all the wonderful aromatic charms of the Colombard grape. Just as Brumont became the reference for Madiran, so Tariquet became the reference for Côtes de Gascogne wines.

A property was bought in Mauléon and planted with Chardonnay, never seen before in the area, while another parcel near Tariquet was planted with Sauvignon Blanc. Yves, constantly seeking ways to better his already excellent product, began intense studies into the use of oak barrels. Soon experiments were taking place: the first to reach the market created some stir among locals; *Cuvée Bois* combined Colombard and Ugni Blanc with Chardonnay, Sauvignon Blanc and Gros Manseng. Aged in new oak, it enveloped an inner core of ripe fruit with complex vanilla and spice scents. It held tremendous appeal for the international palate and fueled Grassa's creativity.

Since that time Tariquet has released pure chardonnays, sauvingnon blancs, and late-harvest gros mansengs. Their properties now total over ten, most of which are released under their own names, including Domaine de Jalousie, Domaine de Pouy and Domaine de Rieux. Their white Côtes de Gascogne, their first success, is still their top seller.

Their most recent creation is an oak-aged blend of Sauvignon Blanc and Chardonnay—a wine not only delicious but unmistakably Grassa.

Their grapes for armagnac include Ugni Blanc, Bacco, and Folle Blanche, all grown on property surrounding the château. The varietals are distilled separately with the family's wood-fueled alambic, then kept in new Limousin and Allier oak for between 6 and 8 months. The young armagnacs are aired twice a year and the older armagnacs once a year. Their consumption of oak is carefully monitored. A year before bottling, the armagnacs are assembled and reduced to 40° with aged *petites eaux*.

Recently their Folle Blanche production has picked up, and several different bottlings are now on the market. The US version, released at 6 years of age, shows outstanding value. Fortunately much more Folle Blanche from Tariquet will reach the market in the near future; the Grassa's terrain is much more suited to Folle Blanche than to Bacco, and Folle Blanche always shows more character than Ugni Blanc.

The young, blended armagnacs of Tariquet are among the best on the market. They display pleasing depth of fruit and a sense of natural sweetness. Small quantities of vintage armagnacs, bottled close to their natural degree, are also available, although they account for only 2% of their spirit sales. Based around Bacco, they show nice fat along with a hint of *rancio*.

An *eau de vie* made from Folle Blanche is also released every year in small quantities.

With over 800 acres covered by vine, the Grassa's holdings are among the largest in Gascony.

Eau de Vie de Folle Blanche: Lots of aroma. Sweet in the mouth yet with a fine texture. Hint of vine flowers and white pepper. Pleasing length.

3 Star (4 years old): Discreet nose, yet enticing flavors in the mouth include orange and anise.

VSOP (7 years old): Pleasing primary fruit aromas along with a hint of sweetness and spice.

Hors d'age (10 years old): Deep amber. Slightly deeper aromas include hints of almond, vanilla and anis. Well-crafted, yet finishes somewhat short.

Folle Blanche (Six Years Old): Aromatic, with hints of oak, white pepper and orange. Soft palate feel, with lots of pepper and spice. Impressively long finish for its age.

10 Year Old Folle Blanche: Lovely amber. Lovely primary fruit aromas. Fine texture. Notes of well-integrated, spicy oak. Very good length.

Yves Grassa, the driving force behind Côtes de Gascogne wines, changes hats and draws an aged Folle Blanche from cask.

1975 (47°): Deep amber. Forthcoming nose offers aromas of quince and almond brittle. Lacks some finesse but shows decent depth of flavor and a pleasingly long finish.

1972 (47°): Deep amber. Melted toffee and orange on the nose along with tantalizing almond-scented *rancio*. Heavy, Bacco-dominated notes. Rich mouthfeel lacks some depth. Well-hidden alcohol. Decent length with a recurring note of orange peel.

Proprietor: Jean-Claude Guasch ***Name of Property***: Château de Bordeneuve ***Vineyard size***: 10 ha (24.7 acres) ***Other production***: kiwi trees ***Percent of production used for distillation***: 100% ***Grapes used for armagnac***: Ugni Blanc (100%) ***Soil***: *Sables fauves* (Iron-rich sand) ***Production of armagnac per year***: 70-80 hl a.p. (35-40 barrels) ***Percentage of the production sold to négociants***: 50% ***Distillation***: *Armagnacaise* ***Distiller***: Mr. Guasch himself ***Alcohol degree when leaving the alambic***: 57-58° for *3 Étoiles*, 55° for armagnacs to be aged longer. ***Barrels***: From many forests in France ***Chai***: In a barn, cement floor, well-organized ***Stock***: 200 hl a.p. (100 barrels) ***Time in new oak***: 2-3 years ***Oldest spirit still in cask***: 1981 ***Blended armagnacs available***: VS (3 years), VSOP (6-7 years), *Hors d'Age* (10-12 years) ***Reduction***: To 41° with *petites eaux* ***Vintages available***: 1981, 1982, 1985, 1986, 1987

Jean-Claude Guasch was born in Algeria and, like many other *pieds noirs*, came to France during the Algerian revolution. Afterwards he flew to New York and hitchhiked with his wife to Acupulco, Mexico. They eventually went to Guadeloupe where they stayed for seven years.

Guasch ended up outside Eauze and bought the Château de Bordeneuve in 1974. After restoring the house and planting vines, he bought an alambic built around the turn of the century and began distilling his harvest. Although he also has a few hectares of kiwi plants, he does not consider himself to be a farmer; most of the money he makes comes from his work as a *courtier* or agent for brandy firms. In fact, he is the president of the *courtier's* union.

Because of his work, Jean-Claude is an expert taster. After working through his armagnacs, we tasted some of the samples he had been sent by producers; within five minutes these included, amongst others, a Folle Blanche from de Maillac up for resale by Coirvoisier, a fifty-year-old blended by Darroze and marketed by Lafite-Rothschild, and a 1942 from Le Frêche.

His own armagnacs show lots of fruit and are quite supple in their youth. Being in the "business", he has learned a few tricks of the trade from cognac domaines which he, like a tremendous amount of armagnac producers, employs with his own releases. Some of the things he finds go to Vaghi, the *négociant* firm where his son works. In fact, the VSOP from their *Baron de Sigognac* was bought entirely from Guasch's stock.

His *eau de vie* is luscious; extremely supple, round and showing very pleasing floral notes.

1993: Young and unevolved on the nose; some floral hints and spice in the mouth.

1991: Hints of vanilla, round in the mouth, and with good fat starting to develop.

1985 (47°): Deep amber. Lots of fat on the nose with a slight hint of almond on the finish. Good length.

Proprietor: The Tastet Family ***Name of Property***: Domaine de Larroude ***Vineyard size***: 32 ha (79 acres) ***Other production***: Corn, cows ***Grapes used for armagnac***: Bacco (60%), Ugni Blanc (40%) ***Percent of production used for distillation***: 10-30 % ***Soil***: *Boulbènes* (Sand with clay pieces) ***Production of armagnac per year***: 20-30 hl a.p. (10-15 barrels) ***Distiller***: Dargelos ***Distillation***: *Armagnacaise* ***Alcohol degree when leaving the alambic***: 54-55° ***Barrels***: Gascon ***Oldest spirit still in cask***: 1961 ***Chai***: Garage adjoining house. Cement floor, lots of vats and barrels ***Stock***: 300 hl a.p. (150 barrels) ***Blended armagnacs available***: *Hors d'age* (from 1983) ***Vintages available***: 1972, 1961 ***Reduction***: Minimal

Since his father Georges died in 1991, Alain Tastet has been running this small property located on the route between Eauze and Cazaubon. The vines slightly favor Bacco over Ugni Blanc, and the vineyards are located in nearby Réans. Distillation is by Georges' aunt, Madame Dargelos, at 54°. They are normally lodged in used *pièces* for up to ten years before being transferred to larger vats where they continue to mature for thirty-five or more years. The *chai* is located in the garage adjoining the house.

In years gone by, Tastet's armagnacs were bought by a number of negociants, including Laubade, Trepout and Samalens. Nowadays, all sales take place at the domaine.

In comparison with some of the other armagnacs from the Eauze canton, Tastet's tend to be more supple and offer slightly more depth of flavor than many of their neighbors. The 1983 and 1972 vintages have been reduced slightly to 45° while the excellent 1961 is sold at its natural strength.

1983: Bright amber. Lots of rich caramel notes on the nose. Good depth of aroma. Supple texture in the mouth with pure sweetness. Good penetration on the palate.

1972: Hint of nougat and walnut on the nose along with some alcohol showing. Nice sweetness in the mouth with lots of fat. Moderately long finish.

1961 (47°): Lots of *rancio* on the nose. Exotic nuances on the nose include coconut and mango. Additional notes of chocolate and cocoa. Hints of oak-scented *rancio* play harmoniously with nuances of prune and vanilla. Very good balance. Very long finish. Impressive armagnac.

Le Frêche (Landes) Population 392

Rumor has it that Francois I was married in the village church. Apart from that, there is not much to say about this tiny town apart from the fact that its fine sandy soil produces some of the finest armagnacs in the region..

Proprietor: Jean-Jacques Cazenave ***Name of Property***: Domaine de Guillemouta ***Vineyard size***: 15 ha (37 acres) ***Other production***: cows, corn, sweet corn ***Grapes used for armagnac***: Bacco (50%), Ugni Blanc (50%) ***Percent of production used for distillation***: 10% ***Soil***: *Argilo-Sablonneux* (Sand with clay pieces) ***Production of armagnac per year***: 10 hl a.p. (5 barrels) ***Distiller***: Roumat ***Distillation***: *Armagnacaise* ***Alcohol degree when leaving the alambic***: 52° ***Barrels***: Gascon, Limousin ***Chai***: In a barn connected to the house. Dry, and with a cement floor ***Time in new oak***: 3 Years ***Oldest spirit still in cask***: 1979 ***Stock***: 40 hl a.p. (20 barrels) ***Blended armagnacs available***: No ***Vintages available***: 1980, 1986 ***Reduction***: No

In 1982, Jean-Jacques Cazenave (right) took over his father's production on the family's small farm located between Le Frêche and Arthez. His father went out in a fashion that most producers can now only dream; in one fell swoop, he sold his entire stock to Francis Darroze.

Today, Jean-Jacques continues to sell part of his production to Darroze while also cultivating corn and raising cows. He distills between 3 and 5 barrels a year, depending on his finances. In 1997 he will not distill, as nearly all of his crop, like others in Le Frêche, was completely destroyed by the Spring frosts. His *eau de vie* leaves the alambic at a low 52° and is aged in barrels of which 50% are new.

Cazenave airs his armagnacs once or twice a year to promote some oxidation, yet often laments the fact that his *chai* is dry and therefore retains its high alcohol level. However, even with a degree of 48° to 50°, the fruit of Guillemouta sings above the alcohol. In the mouth, the alcohol is streamlined along a wonderfully fine texture. The wood is incredibly well-integrated and provides lovely hints of spice. Notes of almond-scented *rancio* begin to arrive after ten years. The finish is always fine and long.

The few armagnacs in the Cazenave *chai* are nothing short of excellent.

1986: Deep amber. Lots of fruit on the nose hides alcohol. Hint of almond, melted toffee and caramel notes in the mouth, along with some accumulating fat. Slight note of alcohol on the finish along with a touch of orange.

1980: Lovely amber. Lots of oak on the nose and with good weight in the mouth. Profound vanilla on the palate along with toasted almonds. Slightly tannic finish ends with a toasty note.

1979: Deep amber. Lots of nose and lovely integration of vanilla aromas. Almond notes glide along a medium-full-bodied, fine texture. Wonderful mouthfeel. Excellent length. Extraordinary armagnac!

Proprietor: Roger and Bernard Lacave ***Name of Property***: Jouatmaou ***Vineyard size***: 9 ha (22 acres) ***Other production***: corn, wheat, cows ***Grapes used for armagnac***: Bacco (40%), Folle Blanche (30%), Ugni Blanc (30%) ***Percent of production used for distillation***: 5% ***Soil***: *Sablo-Limoneux* (Sand) ***Production of armagnac per year***: 6 hl a.p. (3 barrels) ***Distiller***: Duffau of Ayzieu ***Distillation***: *Armagnacaise* ***Alcohol degree when leaving the alambic***: 52° ***Barrels***: Regional ***Chai***: Under the house, rustic, dirt floor ***Oldest spirit still in cask***: 1948 ***Stock***: 200 hl a.p. (100 barrels) ***Vintages available***: 1962, 1974, 1982 ***Reduction***: No

Roger Lacave and a friend pose for the camera in the unique chai under Jouatmaou.

Jouatmaou is a small domaine located at the end of a dirt drive, behind corn stalks, grape vines, cows grazing in a pasture, and rickety, mesh-covered structure half-filled with corn.

Roger Lacave has been making armagnac since before World War II, and has a rather unique *chai* located underneath his house. Its height is under six feet tall. The walls are covered with green and black spores of fungus. The floor consists of layers of packed mud covered in places with old newspaper and budding potatoes. Resting on its uneven surface are the house's treasures: barrel after barrel of non-reduced pure armagnac dating back to 1934.

Much of the Lacave's stock from the Seventies and Eighties was sold to Francis Darroze, and they have not distilled any armagnac since 1994. What spirit remains is sold to the occasional passerby. The *chai* under the house is certainly worth a visit, and their younger vintages offer excellent value.

1982 (49°): Lots of aromatics (toffee, quince) with some slightly dry tannin in the mouth. Finishes with some heat.

1974: Notes of dried apricot and quince on the nose. Nice balance of oak and fruit on the palate, yet the spirit still finishes slightly dry.

1944: Caramelized raisins, prune and nut on the nose. Viscous texture, with just a hint of dry oak on the finish.

1934 (42°): Walnuts, toffee, prune and a hint of mushroom on the nose. Thick texture, with little sign of alcohol. Drying oak builds on the relatively long finish. Very impressive for its age.

Proprietor: The Lafitte Family ***Name of Property***: Domaine Boingnères ***Vineyard size***: 22 ha (55 acres) ***Other production***: None ***Wine production***: 1800 hl ***Percent of production used for distillation***: 50% ***Grapes used for armagnac***: Folle Blanche (50%), Ugni Blanc (25%), Colombard (25%). All vines average 30 years. ***Soil***: *Sables fauves* (Iron-rich sand) ***Production of armagnac per year***: 60-80 hl a.p. (30-40 barrels) ***Distillation***: *Armagnacaise* **Alcohol degree when leaving the alambic**: 52° ***Distiller***: With the alambic of the property ***Barrels***: Gascon ***Time in new oak***: One year ***Oldest spirit still in cask***: 1959 ***Chai***: One in St. Vidou, one in Le Frêche. Both spacious and dry ***Stock***: 1,150 hl a.p. (575 barrels) ***Blended armagnacs available***: *Réserve Spéciale* (5 year old at 48°) ***Vintages available***: Many between 1959 and 1985, including pure Folle Blanche, Colombard, Bacco and Ugni Blanc ***Reduction***: No

Léon Lafitte tastes his beloved Folle Blanche from the still during the 1986 distillation.

During the distillation of the 1994 vintage, Armagnac lost one of its prominent producers, Léon Lafitte. Lafitte, son a local merchant, was also an army officer and Mayor of Labastide for 18 years, taking over the Domaine Boingnères when his father passed away in 1953. That same year, he purchased another parcel of land lying adjacent to an existent parcel in Le Frêche.

With the encouragement of Raymond Baudoin, founder of the *Revue des Vins de France*, Lafitte began bottling his armagnacs in the early 50's and selling them from the domaine. Soon every major restaurant in Paris carried his vintages. Several years later, however, he fell ill and was bedridden for nearly half a decade. Understandably, he could not give his armagnacs the attention they deserved.

At the end of the Fifties, cured of his illness and with newfound life, Lafitte returned his attention to his armagnac. He began removing the Bacco and replanting the vineyards with what he considered to be armagnac's noble grapes (Folle Blanche, Colombard and Ugni Blanc). He constructed a new *chai* with two horizontal presses so that he could better control the vinification of his base matter. In 1975, a gas-fueled alambic was built for the domaine. Its plates each contain ten exiting pipes which gives the spirit greater contact with the incoming wine and, along with a low-distillation temperature, ensures lots of potential flavorants.

Now Marguerite Lafitte and her daughter Martine run the domaine. After the deaths of several other family members and the burden of financial paperwork, the future looks bright for Boingnères. All of the Bacco is now gone and the one remaining hectare of Mauzac has been ripped up and replanted with more Folle Blanche. "Without question, this grape produces the best armagnac," claims Martine. "It's fine, elegant and very complex. Bacco, on the other hand, is rich and deep, but somewhat one-dimensional. Commendable attributes on one hand, yet not very refined."

The dry conditions in the Lafitte *chais* allow for very slow alcoholic reduction. Consequently, the armagnacs of Boingnères normally reach the market at between 96 and 100 proof.

The Lafitte's use a good deal of new oak. They purchase between 10 and 15 new barrels per year; 50% rests for twelve months, then the other 50% spends the second year in this same oak. This ensures good color and integrated vanilla extraction which is always present in their armagnacs. They eschew boisé and caramel additives.

They have one armagnac which they consider to be *commercial.* This *Réserve Spéciale* (currently from the 1990 and 1991 vintages) is *reduced* to 96 proof with distilled water.

The armagnacs of Boingnères invariably display high-pitched aromatics, a lovely chocolate note, wonderful depth of fruit and plenty of finesse. They are rarely heavy, yet intense and bursting with character. Their vintages are always bottled in their most natural state.

In short, refined armagnacs of premier class and an undeniable reference for the region.

Réserve Spéciale: Amber. Hints of nougat, chocolate, coffee with a touch of almond. Lots of aroma despite its alcohol and relatively young age. Pure, and with good length.

1985 Folle Blanche: Light, fresh fruit on nose with just a hint of almond. Very well balanced. Touches of coffee and cocoa. Elegant and very long.

1984 Cépages Nobles: Hint of orange and a burnt sugar note on nose. Lots of vanilla-scented oak not quite integrated with fruit. Excellent potential but needs some time to express itself.

1980 Cépages Nobles: Deeper nose. Hint of peppermint and toffee on the nose along with a touch of almond and orange peel. Excellent penetration on the palate and with lovely medium-bodied weight. Subtle vanilla notes arise on the long, pure finish.

1979 Folle Blanche: Almond on the nose. Fine, soft palate with excellent depth. Very elegant. Hint of orange peel, clove and chocolate.

1978 Folle Blanche: Refined aromas of dried apricot, almond, and cocoa. Plenty of finesse on the palate. Finishes with well-integrated white pepper and spice notes.

1977 Cépages Nobles: Deep amber. Notes of orange, almond and spice on the nose. Medium-bodied with pleasing natural sweetness on the palate. Vanilla notes pick up on the finish, along with recurring peppery notes.

1976 Bacco: Heavier nose that hints at prune and apricot jam. Lots of depth with notes of creamy vanilla.

1976 Ugni Blanc: Deep amber. Light, floral notes on nose combine with complex aromas of cocoa, herb and pepper. Medium-bodied mouth with budding viscosity. Pure, refined finish.

1974 Pur Colombard: Lots of almond-scented *rancio* with notes of apricot dancing below. Rich yet refined texture with plenty of attack and a hint of buttered rum. Additional notes of coffee, mocha, nougat, herbs and orange. Very long finish. Simply outstanding.

1968 Cépages Nobles: Deep prune nuance with almond covering the surface. Additional floral and orange notes. Medium-body, lots of attack, with a long, dry finish.

1964 Bacco: Deep amber. Profound nose includes *pruneau*, coffee, butterscotch, *rancio* and well-integrated oak. Lots of finesse on the palate, and still with plenty of alcohol. Extremely long, expansive finish doesn't know when to stop.

1959 Bacco: Deeper *rancio* hinting at walnut. Round and fat prune notes in the mouth with lots of developed vanilla and some smoke.

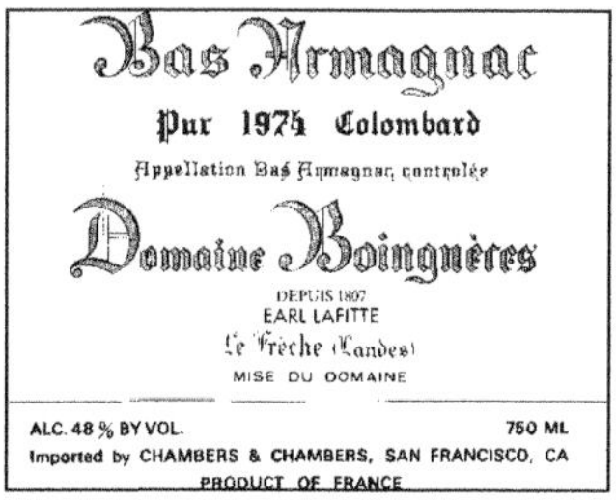

(Top) Léon Lafitte and his wife Marguerite stand in front of their alambic at the end of the Seventies. (Bottom) Martine and Marguerite, summer 1997. The armagnacs of Boingnères are arguably the region's best.

Proprietor: Jean-Claude Lasseignou ***Name of Property***: Domaine de Maouhum ***Vineyard size***: 15 ha (37 acres) ***Other production***: corn, sweet corn, floc ***Grapes used for armagnac***: Bacco (50%), Ugni Blanc (50%) ***Percent of production used for distillation***: 35% ***Soil***: *Sables fauves* (Iron-rich sand) ***Production of armagnac per year***: 33 hl a.p. (16 barrels) ***Distiller***: Roumat ***Distillation***: *Armagnacaise* ***Alcohol degree when leaving the alambic***: 52° ***Barrels***: Limousin and Gascon ***Time in new oak***: Varies ***Oldest spirit still in cask***: 1978 ***Stock***: 203 hl a.p. (101 barrels) ***Blended armagnacs available***: XO ***Vintages available***: 1978, 1979, 1980, 1982, 1984, 1985 ***Reduction***: No

One finds the Domaine de Maouhum just below the town of Le Frêche. A couple of kilometers away rests the *chai* surrounded by fields of grapes and corn. Jean-Claude Lasseignou's Bacco vines are planted on *sables fauves*, historically the two most important building blocks of *Grand Bas Armagnac*. This combination, in addition to sufficient new oak, allows for lots of suppleness early on in life. Production is completely traditional; distillation is at a low degree and the spirit is left to reduce naturally (normally to 46° and 48°). Recently he has made, with the assistance of Patrick Arnaud of the Domaine d'Ognoas, an XO which averages 9 years of age. Very supple and round, it is devoid of any hard edges and offers excellent value.

The domaine has two outlets for their sales; from the property or at the Landais beach town of Vielle-Saint-Girons. It is at this Atlantic resort that the Lasseignou's share a boutique called *La Maison des Paysans* with four other producers; Jean-Claude sells his armagnac and floc, while the rest sell their products; asparagus, foie gras, confits and honey. In this way, they are able to reach a large foreign market who vacation at the beach and who would never have made it to Le Frêche.

Lasseignou sells about 600 bottles a year and remains optimistic about the future. He became the third generation to run the property in the early 80's, and the armagnacs since then have been a bit more restrained with tannin while showing more supple fruit. Normally they display medium-body, good attack, a fine texture, notes of almond brittle and a very dry finish.

XO (42°, from 1987): Almond brittle aromas move into a lush mouthfeel that shows notes of vanilla. Nice round feel. A little hint of dry heat on the finish along with an additional note of vanilla.

1985: Round, full nose. Flattering in the mouth with good fat and vanilla. Slightly hot finish. Wonderful to see down the road with one or two degrees less.

1984: Flattering nose with lots of vanilla. Note of cream. Generous in the mouth with some alcoholic heat on the finish. Very dry.

1982: Lots of almond on the nose, with some orange. Fine texture. Medium-body, beginning to gain fat. Dry, alcohol-charged finish.

1980: Nice nutty *rancio* with hints of orange. Good balance in the mouth with some dry oak on the finish. Fine texture, nice sweetness in the mouth. Good length.

1979: Nice almond *rancio* on the nose. Medium-bodied, lots of attack and plenty of oak on the dry finish.

1978: Deep amber. Walnut note on nose. Lots of oak in the mouth. Unappealingly dry finish.

1976 (Ugni Blanc experiment): Slightly dry and one dimensional in the mouth with a dry, woody finish.

Gaube (Landes), population 258

This tiny hamlet is actually part of Perquie, yet because of its rich armagnac heritage, it has been included in its own right. For centuries, the Château de Gaube was the center of activity. It still remains but no longer bottles armagnac. Apart from the château, there is not much to see except plenty of corn fields and grape vines.

Proprietor: Jacqueline Lafargue ***Name of Property***: Domaine de Pariot ***Vineyard size***: 12 ha (30 acres) ***Other production***: Corn ***Grapes used for armagnac***: Bacco (80%), Folle Blanche (20%) ***Percent of production used for distillation***: 30 % ***Soil***: *Sablo-limoneux* (Sand) ***Production of armagnac per year***: 4 hl a.p. (2 barrels) ***Distiller***: Regert ***Distillation***: *Armagnacaise* ***Alcohol degree when leaving the alambic***: 52°-53° ***Oldest spirit still in cask***: 1940 ***Stock***: 60 hl a.p. (30 barrels) ***Vintages available***: 1974, 1970, 1968, 1966, 1965, 1961, 1955, 1949, 1943, 1940 ***Reduction***: No

The Domaine de Pariot once encompassed 20 hectares. In 1978, Claudine Lafargue, the daughter of owner Jacqueline, married Michel Ponge, and the property was divided in two sections. Ponge continues to distill next door with his own alambic while the majority of Jacqueline's stock was sold following the death of her husband.

Today her son Bernard continues to distill, and either sells his product *en vrac* or adds it to his mounting stock. An impressive selection of old vintages still exist, some of which are still in barrel, others of which are in larger *tonneaux*.

1955 (43°): Deep amber. Walnut, prune and orange peel on the nose. Medium-body. Soft penetration on the palate with just a hint of old oak in the mouth. Touch of tannin on the pleasingly long finish.

1949 (44°): Slightly lighter color than the 1955. Maple, walnut and a hint of melted toffee on the nose. Moderately fat in the mouth while retaining a sense of finesse. Well-integrated old oak notes, with a touch of vanilla. Dry finish, but not over-oaked considering its age. Excellent length.

Proprietor: Claudine and Michel Ponge ***Name of Property***: Coutchot ***Vineyard size***: 8 ha (20 acres) ***Other production***: Corn ***Grapes used for armagnac***: Folle Blanche (50%), Bacco (25%), Ugni Blanc (25%) ***Percent of production used for distillation***: 33% ***Soil***: *Sablo-Limoneux* (Sand) ***Production of armagnac per year***: 10-15 hl a.p. (5-8 barrels) ***Distiller***: Mr Ponge himself ***Distillation***: *Armagnacaise* ***Alcohol degree when leaving the alambic***: 52-53° ***Barrels***: Gascon, Limousin ***Time in new oak***: 3-4 Years ***Oldest spirit still in cask***: 1978 ***Chai***: In a barn, dirt floor, extremely rustic ***Stock***: 106 hl a.p. (53 barrels) ***Blended armagnacs available***: No ***Vintages available***: 1986, 1985, 1981, 1980, 1979, 1978 ***Reduction***: No

Michel Ponge has been distilling armagnacs for many years, but it wasn't until he bought his own alambic in 1986 that he decided to bottle and commercialize his product. He still doesn't sell many bottles, but continues to raise his armagnac in a traditional manner; low distillation degree, no reduction. According to him, he'd much prefer to sell fewer bottles of very good quality armagnac than many bottles with inferior quality. He, like so many other Landais producers, feels the BNIA does not share the same philosophy.

The sandy soils of Gaube lend an admirable finesse to his spirit. A high percentage of Folle Blanche also adds elegance. With time, some fat develops which never becomes heavy on the palate.

Michel Ponge has also helped develop several delicious cocktails based around armagnac. The first, the *Plantignac*, is a blend of various red fruits and a young armagnac. The second, the *Tignac*, is made with armagnac blanc, sugar syrup, lime and ice.

Michel Ponge in front of his humble domaine in Gaube.

1986 (47°): Light amber. Slightly green oak notes along with a hint of cocoa. Fine texture. Pleasing spice and a natural note of sweetness. Hint of chocolate on finish. Good length.

1985 (47°): Hints of cocoa on the nose, with a tad more oak. Attractive vanilla and chocolate notes in the mouth. Lots of attack. Slightly hot finish. An armagnac to follow.

1981: Slightly floral and without as much depth. Less sweet, yet beginning to gain some fat. Hint of almond in the mouth. Good length.

1980 (45°): Very rich nose with lots of fat. Full-body and with lots of chocolate. Supple in the mouth. New oak still evident. Excellent length.

1979 (45°): Amber. Less oak notes on nose, yet with some moderate tannin. Additional aroma includes orange peel. Fairly supple, although without tremendous complexity.

1978 (44°): Rich aromas shows more depth, with vanilla, oak and spice notes. Lots of oak in the mouth; Well-integrated alcohol and plenty of natural sweetness. Long finish.

Proprietor: Indivision Corderoy/Debains ***Name of Property***: Chai de Muret ***Vineyard size***: 7.5 ha (18.5 acres) ***Other production***: Corn, Cows ***Grapes used for armagnac***: Bacco (80%), Ugni Blanc (20%) ***Percent of production used for distillation***: 33 % ***Soil***: *Sables Fauves* (Iron-rich sand) ***Production of armagnac per year***: 8 hl a.p. (4 barrels) ***Distiller***: Charles Garreau of Labastide ***Distillation***: *Armagnacaise* ***Alcohol degree when leaving the alambic***: 52°-53° ***Barrels***: Regional oak. 50% new each year ***Time in new oak***: 2-3 years ***Oldest spirit still in cask***: 1973 ***Chai***: In a barn, cement floor, well-organized. ***Stock***: 120 hl a.p. (60 barrels) ***Blended armagnacs available***: No ***Vintages available***: 1985, 1984, 1983, 1982, 1981, 1979, 1973 ***Reduction***: No

At the beginning of the 1950's, Mademoiselle de Muret sold the Château de Gaube, located midway between Montguillem and Perquie. She retained, however, the majority of the property surrounding the château, including its prized vineyards. Following her death in 1970, the property was divided between her two nieces. Today their husbands, Mousieurs Corderoy and Debains, control the property, although both live in Paris.

Their armagnacs are made from Bacco and Ugni Blanc, then aged in a good percentage of new oak. While always retaining tremendous fruit, it isn't until their 10th birthday that some of their new oak aromas begin to dissolve into the spirit. It is at this point that the domaine's armagnacs really begin to strut their stuff.

The Corderoy/Debains armagnacs are released as *Chais de Muret*. They are *Grand Bas Armagnacs* of extremely high caliber that always show tremendous depth of nuance, lovely balance and excellent length.

1996: Lots of fat, beginning to develop color, rich mouthfeel still marked slightly by the copper scents of the alambic.

1985: Amber. Classy, young wood notes on nose (chocolate, vanilla) not quite integrated. Fine texture. Great potential but still very young.

1981: Amber. Wood becoming submerged. Some *rancio* in mouth (grilled almond). Slight menthol note. Medium-body, good attack, very good length with notes of spice. Still young but with great potential.

1973: Hints of prune, chocolate and almond on nose. Extremely well-integrated notes of antique oak. Medium to full-body, with lots of attack and accumulating fat. Notes of smoky oak on the finish. Excellent length.

Proprietor: Jean-Pierre Serres ***Name of Property***: Domaine de Gaube ***Vineyard size***: 8.5 ha (21 acres) ***Other production***: Corn, cows ***Grapes used for armagnac***: Bacco (80%), Ugni Blanc (20%) ***Percent of production used for distillation***: 33 % ***Soil***: *Sables Fauves* (Iron-rich sand) ***Production of armagnac per year***: 8 hl a.p. (4 barrels) ***Distiller***: Garreau of Labastide ***Distillation***: *Armagnacaise* ***Alcohol degree when leaving the alambic***: 52-53° ***Barrels***: Regional oak. 20% new each year ***Time in new oak***: 2-3 years ***Oldest spirit still in cask***: 1962 ***Chai:*** In a barn, cement floor, well-organized ***Stock***: 70 hl a.p. (35 barrels) ***Blended armagnacs available***: No ***Vintages available***: 1985, 1979, 1984, 1983, 1982, 1981, 1979 ***Reduction***: No

Jean-Pierre Serres lives next to the Corderoy/Debains property and is in charge of their vineyards, crops and armagnac production. Included with his salary is the right to distill 50% of the vintage, which he ages in the same *chai* as his patrons, located just across from the Château de Gaube. The sole difference between his armagnacs, released as the Domaine de Gaube, and those of de Muret is that Serres uses slightly less quantities of new oak, normally about 20% each year, and also reduces by one or two degrees very early in the spirit's life. Because of this, his armagnacs tend to trail just slightly behind the others with regards to aromatic complexity and length.

Like the armagnacs of his bosses, however, those of Gaube display lots of body and sweetness in their youth, and normally begin to come into their own around their tenth birthday.

Over the course of 15 years, approximately one-third of the contents of these barrels is lost through evaporation, the so-called "part-des-anges".

1985: Deep amber. Lots of chocolate notes, along with deep prune-scented fruit. Sweet in the mouth, with lots of wood still not completely integrated. Lovely medium to full-bodied mouthfeel and very good length.

1982: Deep amber. Lots of aroma includes chocolate and vanilla notes. Lacks some attack in mouth and shows lots of oak. Still young. Finishes with moderate length.

1981: Amber. Hint of almond *rancio* on nose. Medium to full body. Lots of sweet fruit (prune, apricot, quince) covers 47° alcohol. Relatively long, yet without tremendous finesse.

1979: Hint of almond-scented *rancio* on nose. Fat in the mouth, with lots of sweet fruit. Lots of material that will fully bloom in the near future. Very good length.

1962 (47°): Deep amber. Lovely, deep nose includes deep, creamy vanilla notes and hints of polished antique oak. Fat prune fruit in the mouth with attractive and complex spicy notes. Lots of class. Extraordinary length with notes of walnut. Superb armagnac.

Hontanx (Landes), population 513

Small village near the border of Les Landes and the Gers. A church built in 1870 stands in the center of town. The town's most memorable piece of architecture, however, is a 13th Century tower through which one direction of traffic must drive. The community is a hotbed for armagnac, with a handful of producers continuing to distill every year.

Proprietor: Francis Blondeau ***Name of Property***: Domaine de Lassabatju ***Vineyard size***: 15 ha (37 acres) ***Other production***: Corn, wheat, aperitif with red fruit juice and armagnac ***Grapes used for armagnac***: Bacco (40%), Folle Blanche (25%), Ugni Blanc (20%), Colombard (15%) ***Percent of production used for Distillation***: 90% ***Soil***: *Boulbènes* (Sand with clay pieces) ***Production of armagnac per year***: 35 hl a.p. (18 barrels) ***Distiller***: Dargelos ***Distillation***: *Armagnacaise* ***Alcohol degree when leaving the alambic***: 52°-53° ***Barrels***: Gascon, Allier ***Oldest spirit still in cask***: 1970 ***Chai***: Next to the house, cement floor, well-organized ***Stock***: 220 hl a.p. (110 barrels) ***Blended armagnacs available***: Napoléon (7 years), *Hors d'age* (11 Years) ***Vintages available***: 1986, 1983, 1982, 1981, 1975, 1973, 1970 ***Reduction***: With demineralized water to between 43° and 45°

Francis Blondeau is not very happy; Bacco's demise is imminent, armagnac consumption is down, and the *syndicat du floc*, of which he is a member, turned down *his* samples.

What's worse, an aperitif he recently invented, blending red fruit juice and armagnac, was forced off the market because its name infringed the copyright law of a published song (*Brin d'Amour*). Begrudgingly, Blondeau will change its name to *Fruit d'Amour.*

Despite his anguish, Blondeau's armagnac releases are of excellent quality, always displaying a fine texture, lovely integration of oak, and an accessible, soave character. Distillation is at a low degree, and aging takes place in a mixture of Gascon and Allier oak. Careful reduction with demineralized water certainly takes away some alcoholic heat while preserving subtle aromas, and the varied grape blend helps account for the armagnac's balance and delicacy.

Hors d'age (actually the 1985 vintage): Fine texture, with plenty of natural caramel notes. Hint of orange and heat on the finish, but with good, pure length.

1986: Amber. Admirable sweetness on palate, along with good integration of oak. Better depth than most ten-year-olds, and with a smooth finish.

1982: Almond on the nose. Fine texture, yet lacks some intensity. Almond brittle notes on palate. Medium-bodied; pleasing armagnac with a sense of style and grace.

1981: Almond notes on the nose. Good attack, but with a fine texture. Light to medium-bodied, and with a polished and subtle finish.

1975: Good attack. Some growing fat in the mouth. Nice wood integration. Supple, yet with some alcoholic kick.

1970: Almond on nose along with some alcohol. Hints of walnut and orange on the palate. Medium-bodied, yet with good penetration. Long, fine finish.

Proprietor: Bernard L'Huillier ***Name of Property***: Le Béroje ***Vineyard size***: 15 ha (37 acres) ***Other production***: Corn, cows, wheat, cereal ***Grapes used for armagnac***: Ugni Blanc (80%), Bacco (20%) ***Percent of production used for distillation***: 50 % ***Soil***: *Sablo-Limoneux* (Sand) ***Production of armagnac per year***: 120 hl a.p. (60 barrels) ***Distiller***: Dargelos ***Distillation***: *Armagnacaise* ***Alcohol degree when leaving the alambic***: 54° ***Barrels***: Gascon ***Oldest spirit still in cask***: 1951 ***Chai***: Three-leveled, rustic, with a dirt floor ***Stock***: 600 hl a.p. (300 barrels) ***Blended armagnacs available***: No ***Vintages available***: 1986, 1983, 1979, 1976, 1975, 1974, 1966, 1963 ***Reduction***: With distilled water to 45°

The 73-year-old Bernard L'Huillier runs this grand property located between Le Houga and Hontanx. When arriving on the small, curvy lanes that weave through the countryside, one doesn't expect to find this 19th century mansion. Yet among the corn and wheat fields between Hontanx and Le Houga, there it is; the stately yet somewhat neglected Le Béroje.

Bernard L'Huillier on the top floor of his impressive chai at Le Béroje.

The L'Huillier family once owned over 300 hectares (740 acres) of land in the Champagne region. Nearly two-hundred years ago, it was sold to Möet, who continues to use the *cru* as the backbone of their Dom Perignon blend. At Le Béroje, L'Huillier recalls that until the turn of the century, 10% of the property's production went to Cognac to help add body and perfume to their brandy. Over the years, L'Huillier, a former corn speculator and merchant, has sold armagnacs to nearly every major *négociant* in the region—Janneau, Gelas, de Malliac, Samalens, Delord, Dartigalongue...Currently, Auxil markets one of his vintages.

The *chai* has the grandeur of the accompanying mansion (600 hl of stock) yet is extremely rustic (dirt floor, lots of mushrooms, lots of must, and a ceiling made of roughly-hewn wooden planks). A second level is reached by a suspect, handmade ladder. L'Huillier normally lets his spirit age for 7 or 8 years after distillation, then blends the same vintage in a *tonneau* to assure some continuity between the 30 or 40 barrels he distills each year.

Afterwards, he reduces by a few degrees, then lets them rest without any topping up. He knows more evaporation takes place this way, but is convinced that the ultimate product is more concentrated; in short, he sacrifices quantity for quality.

The armagnacs from Le Béroje always display lots of fat and a full-bodied mouthfeel. Although not necessarily elegant, they are soft on the palate and offer excellent value.

1988: Deep amber. Rich chocolate notes, supple texture, with a hint of nougat. Seems less than its 49°. Nice sweetness and with good length.

1979: Amber. Soft mouthfeel contains flavors that are not fully-developed. Still charged with alcohol and without too much oak. Displays good potential.

1975: Nice sweetness on palate with a hint of almond and chocolate. Currently lacks some oak but developing very nicely.

1966: Deep amber. Vanilla, walnut and prune on the nose. Fat in the mouth, with excellent balance. Additional notes of toasted coconut in mouth, along with well-integrated oak. Full-bodied. Long, balanced finish that has plenty of dimension.

Proprietor: Mr. and Mrs. Guy Deyres ***Name of Property***: Domaine du Martin ***Vineyard size***: 5 ha (12 acres) ***Other production***: ducks, sweet corn, corn ***Grapes used for armagnac***: Bacco (50%), Ugni Blanc (33%), Colombard (17%) ***Soil***: *argilo-sablonneux, sables fauves* (sand, iron-rich sand) ***Production of armagnac per year***: 45 hl a.p. (22 barrels) ***Distillation***: *Armagnacaise* ***Distiller***: Mr. Deyres himself, with the alambic of Mr. Roumat of Villeneuve-de-Marsan ***Alcohol degree when leaving the alambic***: 52° ***Barrels***: Gascon, Limousin ***Time in new oak***: 3-5 years, depending on the color and tannin level. ***Oldest spirit still in cask***: 1978 ***Chai:*** Recently reconstructed, cement and stone floor, well-organized. ***Stock***: 110 ha a.p. (55 barrels) ***Blended armagnacs available***: No ***Vintages available***: Every vintage from 1978 onwards ***Reduction***: No

Guy Deyres stands upon the Martin property. His son's Domaine de Rieston lies behind the trees in the distance.

Guy Deyres has been blessed with some luck; since taking over his father-in-law's farm in 1973, he has sold 80% of his spirit production to the Darroze firm. Darroze brings empty barrels and returns to Roquefort with plenty of fresh stock.

The reasons for Darroze's interest is obvious; lots of Bacco planted on *sables fauves*, distilled at a low degree. Mr. Deyres, once an member of neighbor Paul Lasserre's distillation team, now distills his own spirit with one of Roumat's alambics. He normally keeps two or three barrels a year and sells bottles to individual clients.

A steady cashflow has enabled Deyres to renovate his *chai*, construct iron barrel rails and lay partial cement/earth floors. The farm itself is clean and neat; an optimistic air permeates the room. In short, Guy Deyres is one of the few armagnac producers who consistently turn over products and make money.

Deyres' son, Jean-Luc, bought the neighboring Domaine de Rieston in 1983. This domaine is, as well, a Darroze vehicle. 90 % of each vintage is purchased by the *négociant* in Roquefort. The 1 or 2 barrels that remain are aged in the same *chai* as those of Martin.

Martin's armagnacs show lots of fruit as well as high levels of alcohol. Sales from the domaine have been good for Deyres; so good, in fact, that his oldest spirit in barrel is from 1978. Somewhat unfortunate because these armagnacs are certainly still in evolution and not yet in their prime.

1982: Amber with gold highlights. Rich nose shows good depth and color. Hint of almond in the mouth. Very well-integrated wood and alcohol. Nice vintage.

1981: Buttery, rich oak on the nose. A tad over-oaked in the mouth, however, with some dry wood notes on the finish.

1979: Rich aromatics, fine texture, well-integrated wood. Expansive on palate, with an attractively long finish.

1978: Hint of almond on the nose with good balance between fruit and tannin. Slightly hot finish.

Proprietor: Claude and Josette Lacoste ***Name of Property***: Domaine de Laubesse ***Vineyard size***: 10 ha (24.7 acres) ***Other production***: Chickens ***Grapes used for armagnac***: Bacco(50%), Folle Blanche (50%). Varietals are aged and bottled separately ***Percent of production used for distillation***: 25 % ***Soil***: *Sables fauves, boulbènes* (Iron-rich sand, sand with clay pieces) ***Production of armagnac per year***: 25 hl a.p. (12 barrels) ***Distiller***: Duffau of Ayzieu ***Distillation***: *Armagnacaise* ***Alcohol degree when leaving the alambic***: 54° ***Barrels***: Gascon ***Time in new oak***: All armagnacs see some new oak ***Oldest spirit still in cask***: 1980 ***Chai***: Two, both humid and rustic, one with cement and one with dirt floor ***Stock***: 200 hl a.p. (100 barrels) ***Blended armagnacs available***: Reserve (6 years old), Napoléon (10 Years Old) ***Vintages available***: 1980 Bacco, 1984 Folle Blanche ***Reduction***: No

Josette and Claude Lacoste, natives of the Chalosse, bought the 10 hectare Domaine de Laubesse in 1960. They expanded the vineyards with large parcels of Folle Blanche, and distilled for the first time in 1970. Today the quality of spirit produced at the property is admired by the heavy-hitting *négociants*; Gelas and Veuve Goudoulin have frequently bought stock. The majority, however, is sold either from the domaine or from the shop the family shares with other regional producers in Capbreton, near the Atlantic coast.

Madame Lacoste is the first to tell you that armagnac does not sell itself—it must be sold. Consequently, she has taken charge of sales and public relations, while her husband Claude works their stock. This means plenty of racking, as in a high 3 or 4 times per year. This intensive aeration helps their armagnacs lose volatile acids and lessen their degree so that they can reach the market at a relatively young age without being reduced with water. The constant rotation of new and old oak ensures that every vintage gets plenty of color.

Their releases are split between two varietals, both aged and bottled separately. So passionate of Bacco is Madame Lacoste that she has aged a floc made with Bacco juice and armagnac from the 1983 vintage. The bottle she pulled from her cellar had certainly defied those who might say that floc is simply for short term drinking; at age 14, it combined youthfulness with minor notes of *rancio*, which lent a tremendous nutty complexity. The *Réserve* and *Hors d'age* armagnacs are made with 100% Bacco and show plenty of the grape's characteristic weight.

The *Napoléon* and 1984 Vintage are made with only Folle Blanche. At over ten years of age and with plenty of new oak influence, both were somewhat difficult to pin down as being made solely with *the crazy white*.

In general, the armagnacs of Laubesse deliver plenty of flavor and an extremely rich mouthfeel, yet tend to lack some finesse and length. One gets the impression that the armagnacs are overworked, causing certain subtleties to literally dissolve into the air.

Even so, if one seeks a full-bodied, rich, and round spirit that naturally delivers plenty of sweetness on the palate, the armagnacs from this welcoming domaine are sure to please.

Reserve: Deep amber. Nutty, rich, chocolate flavors with a hint of licorice. Fairly sweet palate shows some developing fat.

Napoléon: Heavy, nutty aromas with good attack. Oak influence covers some of the Folle Blanche aromatics. Nougat note on the palate, with a touch of orange peel on the finish.

1984 Folle Blanche (46°): Almond and vanilla note on the nose. Rich mouthfeel with some spicy aromas. Nice balance of fat and alcohol. Round in the mouth and with moderate length.

Hors d'age: Nose smells rich but lacks definition. Fat texture contains notes of prune and coconut.

Proprietor: Paul Lasserre ***Name of Property***: Le Miquer ***Vineyard size***: 9.5 ha (23.5 acres) ***Other production***: Corn ***Grapes used for armagnac***: Folle Blanche (60-70%), Ugni Blanc (30-40%) ***Percent of production used for distillation***: 20 % ***Soil***: *Boulbènes* (Sand with clay pieces) ***Production of armagnac per year***: 20 hl a.p. (10 barrels) ***Distiller***: Mr. Lasserre himself ***Distillation***: *Armagnacaise* ***Alcohol degree when leaving the alambic***: 53° ***Barrels***: 50% new/ year (Gascon and Limousin) ***Time in new oak***: 2-3 years ***Oldest spirit still in cask***: 1975 ***Chai:*** Well-organized, modern, and with cement floor. ***Stock***: 250 hl a.p. (125 barrels) ***Commercialized armagnac available***: VSOP (4 years old, reduced to 42°) ***Vintages available***: 1983, 1982, 1980, 1979, 1977, 1976, 1975 ***Reduction***: No

The 77-year-old Paul Lasserre is a well-known distiller in Les Landes who once performed the alcoholic alchemy for over 40 clients a year. Since he retired in 1986, however, the only wine his alambics have distilled have been those of his sons, Patrick and Jacques, who now look after Le Miquer's production.

The armagnacs of Le Miquer are excellent, showing lots of finesse, wonderfully-integrated hints of wood spice and notes of playful, medium-bodied fruit. They are one of the few domaines who truly succeed with the capricious Folle Blanche; in fact, this grape normally comprises at least 60% of their blend.

Why do the Lasserre's succeed with Folle Blanche when the others do not? Careful surveillance and minimal intervention are the most obvious reasons. Sand with chunks of limestone in the vineyard is another. And finally, simple *savoir-faire*.

The family's 100 or so barrels rest on iron rails in a fairly dry *chai* next to the house. They are racked once a year which helps allow for the evaporation of unwanted esters. No reduction takes place, apart from a VSOP level armagnac made for the English market.

Over the past 20 years, the vineyard has been reduced from 25 ha to 9½ hectares. Paul Lasserre sells his stock little by little (occasionally several barrels a year are bought by Gelas) while his sons continue to build their stock. Jacques and Patrick still distill about ten barrels a year, although the former will admit that corn brings them slightly more money when the accounts are finally tallied at the end of the year.

Although many fine armagnacs are produced in the town of Hontanx, the quality of the Lasserre's spirit seems to rise slightly above the rest.

Jacques Lasserre draws a work in progress from one of Le Miquer's many fine barrels.

1983: Fine texture, still marked by notes of wood. Even so, lots of fruit shows, along with attractive spice. Excellent potential.

1979: Amber. Lovely, jovial aromatics. Lots of spice. Fine on the palate. Decent length. Medium-body with nice attack. Hint of orange on the finish.

1977: Amber. Lots of aroma. Fat in the mouth. Wonderful balance. Lovely armagnac with an attractive almond finishing note.

1975: Displays lots of fat in the mouth yet manages to retain a sense of finesse. Note of almond in the mouth, and with excellent length.

Name of Proprietor: André Labarbe ***Name of Property***: Bacoge ***Vineyard size***: 6 ha (15 acres) ***Other production***: Sweet corn, corn, duck conserves, gîte ***Grapes used for armagnac***: Bacco (100%) ***Percent of production used for distillation***: 12 % ***Soil***: *Boulbènes* (Sand with clay pieces) ***Production of armagnac per year***: 6 hl a.p. (3 barrels) ***Distiller***: Was Lasserre, then Roumat ***Distillation***: *Armagnacaise* ***Alcohol degree when leaving the alambic***: 52° ***Barrels***: Gascon and Limousin ***Time in new oak***: All of their life ***Oldest spirit still in cask***: 1975 ***Chai:*** Attached to the house. Well-organized, cement floor ***Stock***: 80 hl a.p. (40 barrels) ***Blended armagnacs available***: No ***Vintages available***: Between 1975 and 1991, most are available ***Reduction***: No

André Labarbe once worked for Francis Blondeau. In 1970, he began distilling his own wine at his small property located about a mile outside Hontanx. During the 1980's, Labarbe sold a percentage of his production to the *négociant* Gerland in Villeneuve-de-Marsan. After his retirement in 1991, however, he stopped distilling. Today, one can stay in the *gîte* on his property, or pass by to sample his armagnacs and purchase products made from the 600 or so ducks that call Bacoge home.

Labarbe distilled his wine at a low degree and most of his spirits started their lives in new wood where they have stayed, without being aired, for their entire lives.

Because of this, Labarbe's armagnacs are extremely marked by wood, whether it be by young chocolate and vanilla notes or dry tannin.

The property itself is interesting; littered with disused equipment, a broken down automobile still rests in the middle of the duck pen. Kind of like a cross between backwoods Landes and backwoods Kentucky.

1986: Hints of new wood include chocolate and spice. Nice depth of fruit with a sweet note. Hint of alcohol surfaces on the finish.

1979: Lots of flattering oak notes on the nose. Medium-bodied in the mouth, with plenty of alcoholic kick. Slightly dry, oaky finish.

1970: Complex, smoky aromas. Old oak, *rancio* and wax notes in the mouth. Remaining fruit barely covers antique oak notes on the finish.

Labastide d'Armagnac (Landes), population 731

Charming village with a picturesque plaza and bastide constructed in 1291. The town was often visited by Henri de Navarre, who later went on to become Henri IV, King of France.

Proprietor: The Clavé Family ***Name of Property***: La Bouc ***Vineyard size***: 12 ha (30 acres) ***Other production***: cows, corn, floc, white wine ***Grapes used for armagnac***: Bacco (80%), Folle Blanche (10%), Ugni Blanc (10%) ***Percent of production used for distillation***: 15% ***Soil***: *Boulbènes* (sand with clay pieces) ***Production of armagnac per year***: 20 hl a.p. (10 barrels) ***Distiller***: Mr. Clavé himself ***Distillation***: *Armagnacaise* ***Alcohol degree when leaving the still***: 55° ***Barrels***: Normally uses second-hand barrels ***Oldest spirit still in cask***: 1964 ***Chai:*** In a barn, organized, cement floor ***Stock***: 120 hl a.p. (60 barrels) ***Blended armagnacs available***: VSOP (7 years old) ***Vintages available***: 1982, 1974, 1965 ***Reduction***: Minimal, with demineralized water

When Michel Clavé decided to buy an alambic in 1993, he realized a dream that most armagnac producers secretly nurture; to distill his own wine and see his production through from start to finish. At the time his wife called him crazy; nowadays, he secretly wonders if she wasn't right. After all, the armagnac market, according to him, cannot sink any lower. It just doesn't pay to distill nowadays; Sempé and other *négociants* who bought from him before are not interested anymore. They've got too much stock of their own. And if Sempé can't sell their own stock, how can one expect a small producer to keep afloat?

Even so, distilling his own product gives him pleasure, and each year he fills between eight and ten barrels with *eau de vie* made from nearly all Bacco. Not much new wood is employed—it's just too expensive nowadays; however, he does look for used barrels, and his most recent purchase was from the coopérative in Aignan. Once a year, the barrels are aired in an effort to reduce the alcohol slightly. One of Clavé's sons is employed at the cave in Cazaubon and undoubtedly has some influence within his father's small, relatively neat *chai*.

Le Bouc's armagnacs show typical Bacco suppleness in their youth, and a tendency to consume copious amounts of tannin after their twentieth birthday. The 1974 and 1982 have been frequent medal winners.

A light, dry white wine is also available at the property as well as an aromatic *eau de vie* made with Folle Blanche.

1990: Light, straw color. Chocolate notes in the mouth with a fairly supple texture along with some heat on the finish.

1982: Amber. Hint of oak in the mouth with elevated level of tannin. Notes of preserved fruit and licorice. Dry oak on the relatively long finish.

1974: Amber. Rich nose includes hints of prune, orange peel, vanilla and aged oak. Lively on the palate. Polished antique wood notes in the mouth. Moderately fat mouthfeel. Dry, somewhat tannic finish. Rustic and traditional armagnac.

1965: Amber with gold highlights. Lots of aroma (vanilla, walnut, oak). Dry, oaky finish. Lovely nose but exceedingly dry on the palate.

Proprietor: Michel Couerbe ***Name of Property***: Domaine de Mahu ***Vineyard size***: 8 ha (20 acres) ***Other production***: Corn ***Grapes used for armagnac***: Bacco (70%), Folle Blanche (30%) ***Percent of production used for distillation***: 50% ***Soil***: *Boulbènes* (Sand with clay pieces) ***Production of armagnac per year***: 30 hl a.p. (15 barrels) ***Distiller***: Loubère ***Distillation***: *Armagnacaise* ***Alcohol degree when leaving the still***: 52° ***Barrels***: Gascon and Limousin ***Time in new oak***: 6 months ***Oldest spirit still in cask***: 1966 ***Chai:*** Rustic barn attached to the house, dirt floor, lots of puddles ***Stock***: 120 hl a.p. (60 barrels) ***Blended armagnacs available***: *Hors d'age* ***Vintages available***: 1984, 1982, 1979, 1971, 1966 ***Reduction***: With demineralized water to 42°

The Domaine de Mahu sporadically produced armagnac between 1900 and 1936. It was at that point that Raoul Dupont took over, distilled the entirety of his 12 hectares of old-vine Bacco every year, and elevated the Domaine de Mahu to one of the most reputable domaines in the Grand Bas-Armagnac.

The domaine was later passed on to his son, Jacques Dupont (also the owner of Domaine de Jouanchicot in Mauléon). In the mid-Eighties he sold the property, located on the route between Cazaubon and Labastide, to one of his long-time employees, Michel Couerbe (pictured at left), who had overseen the production of Mahu's armagnacs since 1964. Whereas all of Dupont's stock was sold to Francis Darroze, Couerbe continued production on his own.

Today Couerbe's wine is distilled at Loubère's distillery to a low 52°. The spirit then rests in barrels that are normally bought after several years of use. Most recently he purchased used barrels from the Camus cognac firm, where one of his sons is employed. He reduces the alcohol level slightly after distillation, then lets them reduce naturally to around 42°.

Couerbe's *chai* is one of the more rustic aging areas within the region; water leaking from the roof fills potholes on the dirt floor. Old farm machinery hangs on the walls. Inside one becomes unaware of the time of day. Its humidity allows for faster alcohol loss than volume loss (something which obviously doesn't bother Couerbe!)

Couerbe is well-liked within the region. His wife was born at the Château Monbel in Castex while her parents were employed there. He is the cousin of Claude Escoubets in St. Justin and the President of the Hunting Committee in Labastide. His armagnacs tend to show good color and lots of aromas and a masculine character reminiscent of Labastide.

Hors d'age: Amber. Hint of almond-scented oak on the nose. Supple texture includes a hint of orange. Well-made.

1984: Amber. Deeper fruit note include prune along with some nut. Tastes slightly reduced, although with good length.

1982: Deeper nose, with a walnut note. More fat in the mouth along with additional oak. Finishes with a touch of dryness yet possesses excellent length.

1979: Walnut note on the nose. Nice fat in the mouth with some noticeable alcohol and wood. Somewhat out of balance. Slightly dry finish. Too much oak.

1971: Deep nose includes prune and apricot along with walnut. Lots of fat in the mouth covers the elevated tannin level. This masculine, even macho, armagnac also has a very long finish.

1966: Nice nutty nose with well-integrated oak notes. Good overall length. Easy to enjoy yet not incredibly complex for its age.

Proprietor: Philippe de Bouglon ***Name of Property***: Château du Prada ***Vineyard size***: 2.5 ha (6 acres) ***Other production***: None ***Grapes used for armagnac***: 50% Colombard, 50% Folle Blanche ***Percent of production used for distillation***: 100% ***Soil***: *argilo-sablonneux* (sand with clay pieces) ***Production of armagnac per year***: 4 hl a.p. (2 barrels) ***Distillation***: *Armagnacaise* ***Alcohol degree when leaving the still***: 55° ***Distiller***: Broustet and Loubère ***Barrels***: Limousin and Gascon ***Chai:*** Part of the château, dirt floor, humid ***Time in new oak***: 5 years ***Oldest spirit still in cask***: 1978 ***Stock***: 80 hl a.p. (40 barrels) ***Blended armagnacs available***: No ***Vintages available***: 1978, 1979, 1981, 1982, 1983, 1984 ***Reduction***: No

In 1974, Philippe de Bouglon moved into the grandiose Château du Prada, located just in front of the center of Labastide. The huge mansion was an inheritance of sorts, and de Bouglon decided continue his father's tradition of raising armagnac while continuing his own work as a wine distributor. His catalogue contains numerous small domaines in Bordeaux.

The jovial, mustached de Bouglon produces only one or two barrels per year, and each vintage gets to see new oak. His *chai* is below ground and at a cool temperature. The damp dirt floor is covered with fungus. Small windows at each side of the *chai* allow for constant air movement.

De Bouglon realizes the obstacles that prevents armagnac from gaining a larger market share and is perplexed that many French people don't even know what armagnac is. He wishes his armagnacs could reach the market sooner, if only to help pay for its costs. He refuses, however, to reduce or traffic his product in any way so that it is artificially more approachable.

Château de Prada's armagnacs are highly impressive—not surprising since de Bouglon distills at a low temperature, ages in new oak, and airs his armagnacs frequently. Varietals are aged separately and each *pièce* is worked separately. The man does all the right things, and his product is always replete with deep fruit, lots of vanilla and spice, as well as tannin and alcohol. They almost appear like top domaine releases from Bordeaux's 1990 vintage; full-bodied, structured, yet still in their infancy. A domaine that one can look forward to tasting from barrel over the next decade.

1984 Folle Blanche: Exotic coconut and vanilla on the nose. Lots of fat in the mouth helps hide the alcohol. Additional notes of apricot, ginger and prune. When the wood becomes better integrated, this will offer great potential.

1983: Hints of roasted almonds. Nice fat and sweetness, with better-integrated wood. Dry, spicy finish.

1982: Lovely amber color. Wood very evident on the nose. Rich fruit in the mouth with impressive attack. Slightly dry, tannic finish.

Proprietor: Charles Garreau ***Name of Property***: Château Garreau ***Vineyard size***: 29 ha (72 acres) ***Other production***: Floc, white wine, liqueur, fruits a l'armagnac ***Grapes used for armagnac***: Bacco (60%), Ugni Blanc (20%), Colombard (20%) ***Percent of production used for distillation***: 50% ***Soil***: *Argilo-sablonneux, sables fauves, boulbènes* (Sand, iron-rich sand, clay pieces) ***Production of armagnac per year***: 130 hl a.p. (65 barrels) ***Distiller***: Mr. Garreau himself ***Distillation***: 30% *Armagnacaise*, 70% *double-chauffe* ***Alcohol degree when leaving the still***: Varies greatly ***Barrels***: Oak from the property ***Stock***: 300 hl a.p. (150 barrels) ***Blended armagnacs available***: 3 Étoiles, Napoléon, Cuvée Royale ***Vintages available***: 1975, 1951 ***Reduction***: With *petites eaux* to 40°

Charles Garreau is a medical doctor with an office in Barbotan-les-Thermes. In addition, he is a local experimenter specializing in distillation technique. In his alambic museum, he has a total of eleven stills, four of which he uses each year to distill his harvest. He is a proponent of double-distillation, and is one of the few independent producers who prefers this method to the *armagnacaise*. Not surprisingly, his commercial blends make up 90% of his sales.

In 1974, Garreau brought the local aperitif floc to national prominence and was instrumental in its achieving appellation status. Today he continues his pioneering work with one hectare of experimental vines, whose results will certainly aid the search for a suitable replacement for Bacco.

Proprietor: Pierre Laberdolive ***Names of Properties***: Jaurrey and Pillon ***Vineyard size***: 42 ha (104 acres) ***Other production***: None ***Grapes used for armagnac***: *Jaurrey*: Folle Blanche (50%), Ugni Blanc (50%), *Pillon*: Bacco (80%), Colombard (20%) ***Percent of production used for distillation***: Very dependent on the vintage ***Soil***: *Sables limoneux, Sables fauves* (Sand and iron-rich sand) ***Production of armagnac per year***: Very dependent on vintage ***Distiller***: Mr. Laberdolive himself ***Distillation***: *Armagnacaise* ***Alcohol degree when leaving the still***: 53° ***Barrels***: Oak from the property and Limousin made by a cooper in Bordeaux ***Time in new oak***: 3 years ***Oldest spirit still in cask***: 1965 ***Stock***: 1,600 hl a.p. (800 barrels) ***Blended armagnacs available***: *Les Sables Fauves* (10 year old, reduced to 42°) ***Vintages available***: Most since 1965 and several dating back to 1935 ***Reduction***: No

Laberdolive. The very name carries with it an aura. With regards to *reputation*, the family firm sits upon France's upper eschalon alongside Mouton, Romanée-Conti, Petrus, Roederer, Guigal, Yquem; Laberdolive's armagnacs are the ones that get the most press, the ones once bought by Onassis and Fernandel, and the ones whom locals regard with critical envy.

Laberdolive was founded in 1866 by Joseph Laberdolive, whose property, the Domaine d'Escoubes, was in Larée, a tiny village near Cazaubon. In 1893, he bought the Domaine de Jaurrey, located between Labastide and Mauvezin. In 1956, Gerard Laberdolive bought the Domaine de Pillon, located across the main road. The Domaine de Labrune, next to Jaurrey, was purchased in 1963 and shortly afterwards the two properties were coupled.

When Gerard Laberdolive died, the family's properties were divided between his children; Pierre took Jaurrey and Pillon, while his sister (now married to Yvan Auban of Estang) took d'Escoubes. Several years later, amidst a family dispute, she sold the legendary property and put its ownership outside of the illustrious Laberdolive name.

Today the 57-year-old Pierre Laberdolive looks after Jaurrey and Pillon, located just next to and across from the family house. They are located on soils comprised of iron-rich sand and clay pieces along the Landes/Gers border.

Today, the Domaine d'Escoubes (left) is in a state of disrepair. On the other hand, the vines planted at the Domaine de Jaurrey (right) produce some of the finest armagnacs in the region.

Laberdolive has the four traditional varietals planted, and the blend varies with the vineyard. Jaurrey produces Folle Blanche and Ugni Blanc, Pillon is planted mostly with Bacco. The grapes are fermented on the property and then distilled in the one of two alambics the family owns. The newer alambic has intricate mushroom caps that force the spirit into contact with the incoming wine when exiting through the plates. In general, the *eau de vie* exits the still at 53°.

"Many people say it's the vineyard that creates the concentration within a final spirit," Pierre states. "Yet I don't think so. It's the alambic that creates the concentration. One can never discount its importance."

Aging takes place in new 430 liter casks which come from wood made by a Bordeaux *tonnelier*. There the spirit rests for three years. This armagnac is then transferred to older barrels or *tonneaux* where it stays until deemed ready for the market. Barrels are topped up with armagnac from the same property and vintage and released in their natural state.

Recently Pierre built the first completely underground *chai* in the region, running between the distillation room and his office. It currently houses 85 of his 650 barrels. He is unsure of the effect the lack of air will have on his spirit but nonetheless pleased with his originality. "In any event," he says with a smile, "it's something else for people to talk about."

Laberdolive's armagnacs always display a fine texture, well-integrated alcohol, subtle fruit and a long finish. In short, they are excellent spirits. When asked what he looked for in an armagnac, Pierre responded, "Its liveliness, the display of power without noticeable burn, the harmony between the oak and tannin, and length. The aromas are secondary," he adds, "yet those are the things that give pleasure when one sits with the glass in hand."

Laberdolive remains a reference in the region and a name that is associated with armagnac of grand class: Whether Laberdolive's armagnacs are the best the region has to offer, however, is debateable: Like with all legends, one sometimes gets the feeling that the elevated pricetags simply *act* to perpetuate the belief that the product is rarer, more exclusive, and one step above the rest.

Les Sables Fauves (10 year old armagnac reduced to 42°. Laberdolive, a staunch traditionalist, did not seem overly enthused with this reduced spirit, but conceded that tremendous demand with oversees markets made its production viable): Deep amber color. Hints of chocolate and toffee. Fairly one-dimensional. Moderately long.

Domaine de Jaurrey 1979 (46°): Amber. Fine aromatics with nice integration of alcohol. Polished. Fine texture, with lots of class. Hint of natural sweetness on palate. In no way heavy or fat, but delicate and very pure. Extremely long and balanced.

Domaine de Jaurrey 1976 (46°): Richer nose with a deeper sense of fruit. Young, almost grape-like fruit gives lots of aroma. Fatter in the mouth but with lots of penetration on the palate. Hint of almond. Fine texture, with lots of length and class.

Pierre Laberdolive

Domaine de Pillon 1970 (46°): Deep amber. Rich, more flattering style with lots of vanilla and melted caramel notes on the nose. Fat mouthfeel with a slight nutty hint. More rustic and traditional style, less fine than Jaurrey. However, a fine expression of the Bacco grape.

Domaine de Pillon 1962 (44°, made with 90% Bacco): Amber color. High aromatic notes hint at pine and vanilla. Extremely soft in the mouth, with fine integration of oak. Slight hint of *rancio*. Tremendous finesse and very long.

Domaine de Jaurrey 1954 (last vintage of Folle Blanche that had resisted the phylloxera): Amber. Highly aromatic, with hints of spice. Excellent balance between alcohol and aromas, very fine in the mouth and with a long finish that hints at white peach.

Domaine de Jaurrey 1946 (44°): Perfect amber color. Highly aromatic nose. Soave, seductive mouth with everything in balance. Hints of pine, with lots of finesse. Very long. A real gentleman.

Proprietor: Claude Lacourtoisie ***Name of Property***: Domaine de la Coste ***Vineyard size***: Originally 10 ha (24.7 acres). Now being reduced ***Other production***: None ***Grapes used for armagnac***: Bacco (50 years old), Colombard (10 years old), Ugni Blanc (30 years old). The Folle Blanche was recently ripped up. Blends vary from year to year ***Percent of production used for distillation***: 100% ***Soil***: *Sables fauves* (Iron-rich sand) ***Production of armagnac per year***: Varies greatly ***Distillation***: *Armagnacaise* ***Alcohol degree when leaving the still***: 52° ***Distiller***: Lamothe of Betbezer ***Barrels***: Gascon ***Time in new oak***: 3 to 10 years ***Oldest spirit still in cask***: 1967 ***Chai:*** In a rustic, humid and dark barn ***Stock***: 300 hl a.p. (150 barrels) ***Blended armagnacs available***: Upon demand ***Vintages available***: Most from 1977 onwards ***Reduction***: No

When one meets Claude Lacourtoisie, one is impressed with his gentlemanly demeanor. His Victorian house sits just outside Labastide, on the route to St. Justin. His living room is attractively furnished with plush, comfortable chairs, while books dealing with classical music and literature adorn the walls. Colorful rugs decorate the polished wood floors. His armagnacs are served in suitable glassware. He is an educated man.

At 84 years of age, Lacourtoisie (pictured at right) still has lots of spunk. It doesn't take much to get him into his *chai* to pull samples from barrels with extreme speed. He is excited by his life's work; the single varietal studies, experimentation with the *double chauffe*, the differences in barrels among the same vintage...

Wood should be of great interest to Lacourtoisie, as he made his money as a wood merchant. He firmly believes that wood should be aged for an extended period before being used; Wood seasoned for three years just doesn't cut it; too much color and harsh tannin is extracted. Six years drying time, according to him, is the minimum, 10-12 is the ideal. This ensures a nice, gradual coloring and extraction of soft tannin.

Lacourtoisie's *chai* is extremely humid. Mushrooms and mold are rampant. Consequently, lots of alcohol is lost while the volume is kept. He attempts to aerate the barrels a couple of times a year to keep the life blood flowing within the spirit.

Between 1975 and 1979, Lacourtoisie experimented with double-distillation. Some of these studies have been allowed to reduce naturally so that they now fall between 50 and 55 degrees alcohol. While still powerful, they do sport some fat along with vanilla and chocolate notes on the finish. Perhaps because of their non-interventionist upbringing, they remain some of the best *Charentais* works-in-progress around.

The traditional, non-reduced armagnacs from Domaine de la Coste always display a fine texture and develop nicely over the years. Whereas most 40-year-old spirits have eaten too much wood, many of Lacourtoisie's carried lovely wood spice without being too dry.

1981: Nose hints at spice. Fine texture with medium-body. Not real fat and with a hint of alcohol on the finish. Pleasant *fond du verre*.

1981 (from barrel): Hint of almond on the nose. Fine texture but with more kick. Good pure length.

1978: Almond on the nose. Nice fat texture. Hint of brown sugar on the palate. Good sweetness in mouth, yet retains a fine texture. Impressive length.

1977 (test with double-chauffe, 100% Bacco, 55°): Lots of vanilla-scented oak on nose. Nice note of almond *rancio* on nose. Decent fat in the mouth with good attack, but without much developed fat underneath. Good length.

1964: Buttery, rich nose. Some hints of antique oak in the mouth although not overly dry. Long finish.

1962: Nutty nougat on nose. Marzipan, butter and cream in the mouth. Very well integrated oak on the finish. Excellent armagnac.

40 Year Old Assemblage: Creamy vanilla and butter on the nose with light, lively spice. Extremely well-integrated wood. Lush texture, viscous on the palate. Very long. Simply outstanding.

Another 40 Year Old Assemblage: Cashew nut, mushrooms and spicy oak on the nose. Not quite as fat in the mouth, but with an expansive texture. Creamy butter notes surface on the finish.

Proprietor: Marthe Tarbe ***Name of Property***: Hourtica ***Vineyard size***: 18 ha (44.5 acres) ***Other production***: Corn ***Grapes used for armagnac***: Bacco (34%), Ugni Blanc (33%), Colombard (33%) ***Percent of production used for distillation***: 10-15 % ***Soil***: *Sables, boulbènes* (Sand, sand with clay pieces) ***Production of armagnac per year***: 10-12 hl a.p. (5-6 barrels) ***Distiller***: Roumat of Villeneuve-de-Marsan ***Distillation***: *Armagnacaise* ***Alcohol degree when leaving the still***: 52-53° ***Chai***: Large, dark barn with cement floor ***Stock***: 67 hl a.p. (34 barrels) ***Oldest spirit still in cask***: 1969 ***Blended armagnacs available***: No ***Vintages available***: 1939, 1942, 1962, 1969 and most until the present ***Reduction***: No

Domaine de Hourtica was run by Hubert Tarbe until his death in the mid-Nineties. Now his widow Marthe looks after his stock and sells bottles to individual clients. Next to their 25 barrels in the dirt-paved *chai* lies the same quantity of stock distilled by their son. For the moment, his younger vintages are not for sale.

Madame Tarbe recalls that one of the reasons for producing armagnac was to have some security in the future; before, a retired couple could sell a few barrels of aged stock a year and pay for their necessities—it was like money in the bank. They did so on more than one occasion to Francis Darroze. Now, no *négociants* are interested in older stock anymore—they have enough of their own.

The domaine lies on the lonely road between Labastide and Lannemaignan. Next door is Michel Lamothe's *Le Basque*. Unlike their neighbor's consistent sales, however, it is only the occasional tourist who stops and buys a bottle or two of armagnac at Hortica. It's a pity, because the Tarbe's armagnacs are extremely traditional, show admirable finesse and wonderfully pure length.

1984 (48°): Light amber. Nose closed because of alcohol. Nice sweetness on palate, however, and with slightly hot, yet pleasing length.

Madame Tarbe and her sister-in-law at Hourtica

1976 (46°): Deep amber. Hint of almond on the nose. Rich flavor in the mouth with hints of apricot and quince. Some heat on the finish.

1970 (47°): Rich, creamy nose with hints of coconut in the mouth. Slightly exotic in the mouth, with hints of cinnamon and toasted coconut. Excellent length.

1962 (40°): Deep amber. Deep nose hints at ginger, spice, prune and vanilla. Antique wood in the mouth outweighs the fruit. Dry finish.

Lacquy (Landes), population 193

A number of small lakes often collect around the low groves of pine trees throughout this community, giving it an eerie resemblence to Southern Louisiana. There are no cafés or stores in the village, although a church can be visited. Its most famous monument is the Château de Lacquy, built in the style of Louis XIII.

Proprietor: The de Boisseson family ***Name of Property***: Château de Lacquy ***Vineyard size***: 15 ha (37 acres) ***Other production***: Pine trees, corn, sweet corn, *vin de pays de Terroir Landais* ***Grapes used for armagnac***: Bacco (50%), Ugni Blanc (50%) ***Soil***: *Sables-limoneux, sables fauves* (Sand and iron-rich sand, with some ocean sediment) ***Production of armagnac per year***: 30-40 hl a.p. (15-20 barrels) ***Percent of production used for distillation***: 30-40% ***Distillation***: *Armagnacaise* ***Alcohol degree when leaving the still***: 52° ***Chai***: Well-organized, in a humid barn with a dirt floor. ***Distiller***: Roumat ***Barrels***: Gascon and Limousin ***Stock***: 400 hl a.p. (200 barrels) ***Blended armagnacs available***: VSOP, Hors d'Age, Référence, Réserve Exceptionelle ***Vintages available***: 1972-1985 ***Reduction***: No

Owned by the de Boisseson family since 1711, the Lacquy estate covers 400 hectares, yet only 15 are devoted to vines. In contrast to some of the other producers in the *Grand Bas Armagnac*, Lacquy is completely surrounded by the pine trees so famous to Les Landes. Understandably, 270 hectares of land are devoted to their growth, while the remaining 110 hectares are devoted to various other crops like corn and sweet corn.

Lacquy rests only a couple of miles from the edge of the Armagnac region. The soil contains an extremely high percentage of marine sediment and *sables fauves*.

Swampland near the Domaine de Lacquy

An excellent dry white table wine is made at the property with Colombard, Ugni Blanc and Gros Manseng. The only grapes used for their armagnacs, however, are Bacco and Ugni Blanc, normally split evenly, although at times in favor of Bacco. They are single-distilled in the traditional manner by the visiting distiller Roumat; the armagnac drips from his wood-fueled alambic at 52°.

Mr. de Boisseson is a strict believer in minimal intervention. After gaining enough tannin and color in newer oak, the spirit is transferred to older oak where it rests for perhaps 10 years. The casks are not topped up nor are they aired; their quality is monitored but, in general, they are left to mature on their own.

In the château, de Boisseson has handwritten records of the property's armagnac production that dates back several centuries. The present *chai* is well over a hundred- years-old. Its stone walls insure lots of humidity, which promotes consistent evaporation of alcoholic degree without the loss of volume.

Several commercial armagnacs are also available at the domaine, including a *VSOP* (5-years-old, 40°), *Hors d'age* (12-years-old, 40°), and *Référence* (15-years-old, 42°). The *Réserve Exceptionelle* (20-25-years-old, 44°) is a blend of various lot ends that have been carefully composed without being reduced. It is an exceptional blend that is a must try for armagnac connoisseurs.

Mr. de Boisseson is one of the few producers who remain optimistic about the future of armagnac. His product is represented in most of France's finest restaurants, and his clientele has remained faithful. His sales average between five and six thousand bottles per year.

Behind Laberdolive, the armagnacs from Lacquy are the highest priced in the Armagnac region; what one gets, however, is an armagnac with tremendous finesse and elegance coupled with deep, complex fruit and subtle notes of chocolate and *rancio*.

VSOP: Light amber. Hint of vanilla on nose, mixing with caramel in the mouth. Supple finish.

Hors d'age: Amber. Hint of chocolate in the mouth. Soft texture with a slight note of burnt sugar in the mouth. Nicely balanced *Hors d'age* with a soave, natural mouthfeel.

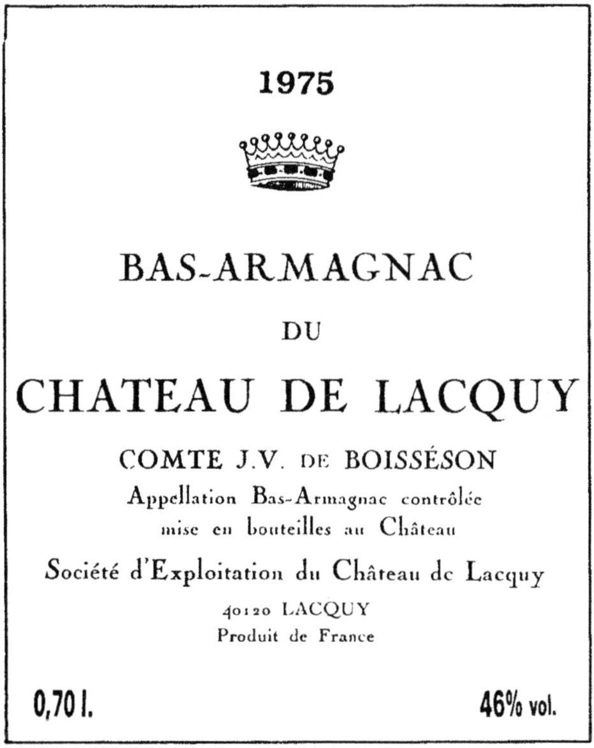

Référence: Slightly lighter, more floral nose. Soft texture is replete with notes of almond. Additional hints of orange and rich caramel. Good persistence.

Réserve Exceptionelle (100% Bacco, approximate 20 years blend, 44°): Deep amber. Wonderful blend of almond and prune, along with hints of cinnamon. Soft and round in the mouth, with additional notes of licorice and chocolate. Excellent integration of wood and very long.

1985: Deep amber. Hints of burnt sugar, cocoa and cinnamon. Good balance of wood and alcohol.

1984: Amber with gold highlights. Aromas of preserved apricot and prune. Full-bodied and vigorous, with a wide range of flavors in the mouth that include apricot, quince and prune.

1983: Bright amber. Lots of finesse on the nose, with spicy hints including pepper and spice. Medium-bodied in the mouth, with lots of finesse. Subtle touch of grilled almonds and chocolate on the finish. Very smooth for its age and agreeably long.

1982: Golden amber. Aromas include cinnamon, pepper, tobacco, almond and toffee. Very round, and not aggressive. Apricot, chocolate and dried raisins continue in the mouth. Dry finish has good length.

1981 (48°): Light amber color. Profound nose that hints at peach and apricot. Nicely integrated wood shows hints of spice (pepper, cinnamon) and a touch of licorice. Generous fruit nearly covers the alcohol. Long finish.

1980: Beautiful amber color. Pleasing wood notes on the nose that also includes pepper and cinnamon. Fruit in the mouth seems slightly one-dimensional, although subtle hints of cinnamon and pepper sneak through. Lots of spice on the finish.

1979 (48°, 50% Bacco, 50% Ugni Blanc): Deep amber with red highlights. Fat in mouth, with prune, licorice and chocolate flavors. Finishes with slightly aggressive tannin.

1978: Golden amber. Fine, floral nose includes lots of wood spice. Smooth mouth shows good depth. Flavors include cocoa, vanilla, cinnamon and prunes. Pleasing, feminine-styled armagnac.

1977: Deep amber. Delicate yet frank nose shows nuances of cinnamon and pepper. Round, fat and smooth. Chocolate and vanilla in the mouth. Very long.

1976 (2/3 Bacco, 1/3 Ugni Blanc): Deep amber. Sweet nose with lots of vanilla and jammy fruit. Round, feminine and with flavors of prune and vanilla. Slight hints of pepper on the finish. Unfortunately finishes slightly shorter than one might expect.

1975 (2/3 Bacco, 1/3 Ugni Blanc): Deep amber. Very aromatic, with lots of *pruneau* and spice. Very forceful on the palate, with additional hints of pear. Extremely long. Superb.

1974 (2/3 Bacco, 1/3 Ugni Blanc): Light amber. Very fine nose hints at spice. All finesse in the mouth, with a finishing floral note.

1973 (47°, 2/3 Bacco, 1/3 Ugni Blanc): Toffee and prune on the nose with a touch of almond. Fine, expansive style of armagnac that isn't heavy, but which delicately fills the mouth with flavor. Lots of finesse. Hints of orange and peach in the mouth along with delicately-spiced oak. Spirit caresses the palate with expansive flavor. Very long and very good.

1972 (2/3 Bacco, 1/3 Ugni Blanc): Pleasing aromatics with lots of finesse. Rich, fruity mouth with intriguing hints of chocolate and pear. Very smooth, yet only moderately long.

Lagrange (Landes), population 171
Tiny village about 8 kilometers north of Cazaubon. A small, picturesque church, built in 1091 and occupied by Benedictines until 1227, has been wonderfully restored and is worth a visit.

Proprietor: Dr. André Pitous ***Name of Property***: Domaine de Cavaillon ***Vineyard size***: 28 ha (69 acres) ***Other production***: Corn ***Grapes used for armagnac***: Bacco (50%), Folle Blanche (50%) ***Percent of production used for distillation***: 50 % ***Soil***: *Sables fauves* (Iron-rich sand) ***Production of armagnac per year***: 24 hl a.p. (12 barrels) ***Distiller***: Dargelos ***Distillation***: Armagnacaise ***Alcohol degree when leaving the still***: 52° ***Barrels***: Always new oak ***Time in new oak***: 5-6 years ***Oldest spirit still in cask***: 1983 ***Chai:*** In a humid barn, organized, dirt floor ***Stock***: 180 hl a.p. (90 barrels) ***Blended armagnacs available***: No ***Vintages available***: 1985, 1983 ***Reduction***: No

The storage conditions at Cavaillon are ideal: organized, humid, and with circulating air that helps prevent damp, off-aromas from developing within their rich spirit.

Dr. André Pitous inherited this legendary 28 hectare property from his grandfather Jean Lassis. During the post World War II years, he raised its already exalted level to new heights. Located just outside the tiny town of Lagrange and planted on pure *sables fauves*, the Domaine de Cavaillon produces armagnacs that are tremendously rich while also containing a fine texture that is nothing short of elegant.

Pitous was a doctor who worked in the nearby spa-town Barbotan-les-Thermes. In the early 1980's he retired and sold his entire stock (some of the most revered spirit in Gascony) to *négociants*, namely Darroze, Laubade, Sempé and Trépout. Then he decided to retire to Perpignan with his wife. Meanwhile, his daughter Dominique began overseeing production, albeit from a distance. Most vintages between 1983 and 1996 have been distilled, and now age in the same *chai* as the legendary vintages from the past.

What is the secret at Cavaillon? Bacco, Folle Blanche, *sables fauves* and lots of new oak, to begin with. Every vintage rests in new oak for between four and six years. This ensures plenty of tannin extraction and, of course, lots of color. Despite this barrel influence, these armagnacs retain all their fruit; in fact, beneath the chocolate/vanilla oak notes, rich, sweet fruit nearly spills out of the glass. At 15 years of age, the wood begins to melt into the fruit, yielding wonderful spice notes that dance across waves of *pruneau* and dried apricot.

In the mid-Eighties, half of the Bacco vines were replanted with Folle Blanche. Today both grapes are distilled and aged separately. At the present moment, the Folle Blanche is extremely influenced by oak. Only time will tell if the typical light, jovial aromas of Folle Blanche will rise above the dominating notes of chocolate and vanilla.

Armagnac fans should rejoice that the Pitous family are in the process of rebuilding their stock and preparing several vintages for the market. It is also heartwarming to know that their current spirits live up to their past reputation.

1989 Folle Blanche: Deep amber. Fine texture with lots of chocolate and a hint of coconut on the finish. Still heavily influence by wood, although with lots of potential.

1986 Bacco: Deep amber. Lots of wood notes, yet lovely prune-scented fruit in the mouth. Fine texture. Very long.

1985 Bacco: Deep, fine, sweet, rich. Lots of wood and a hint of nut on the finish.

1983 Bacco: Lovely amber. Lighter, spicy aromas. Elegant, fine. Lovely spice and integration of wood. A thoroughbred even with its wood influence. Plenty of sweet fruit in the mouth and not short of length.

Proprietors: René and Christian Sourbès ***Name of Property***: Simsat ***Vineyard size***: 8 ha (20 acres) ***Other production***: corn, grains, wheat, cows, sunflowers, wine ***Grapes used for armagnac***: Bacco (50%), Ugni Blanc (50%) ***Percent of production used for distillation***: 20 % ***Soil***: *Sablo-Limoneux*, *Sables fauves* (Sand and iron-rich sand) ***Production of armagnac per year***: 6-10 hl a.p. (3-5 barrels) ***Distiller***: Originally Broustet. Now St. Martin ***Distillation***: *Armagnacaise* ***Alcohol degree when leaving the still***: 54-55° ***Barrels***: Gascon and Limousin ***Chai:*** In an old barn, dirt floor, rustic. ***Stock***: 180 hl a.p. (90 barrels) ***Oldest spirit still in cask***: 1967 ***Blended armagnacs available***: No ***Reduction***: Very slightly after a few years, then left to reduce to 44°-45°

In addition to harvesting corn, cows, sunflowers, wheat, and grain, René Sourbès has been making armagnac for more than 50 years. His *chai* is a huge, ramshackle barn next to his house. Through the dim light one can vaguely see the huge cobwebs that cover various corners. The uneven dirt floor provides the necessary humidity for the slow evaporation of the 90 barrels inside.

Sourbès feels that the *sables fauves* gives his armagnacs a suppleness in their youth that one doesn't find on clay soil. His armagnacs always show a rich color, while in the mouth they show both good attack and fat while retaining a certain youthfulness.

1994: Lots of cinnamon and vanilla on the nose. Substantial fruit helps mask the elevated alcohol. Lots of new wood notes on the finish. Excellent potential if handled correctly.

1989 (6 years in new wood): Deep amber. Plenty of fruit on the nose with some vanilla. Soft texture. Lots of tannin on the finish, however.

1976: Deep amber. Almond-scented *rancio* on the nose. Round and rich in the mouth with a slightly dry finish. Still young.

1973: Hints of almond on the nose. Lots of fruit in the mouth along with some young wood. Still in development.

1967 (100% Bacco): Deep amber. Almond and vanilla on nose. Good attack, yet with a soft texture and well-integrated wood. Good pure length. Lovely armagnac.

Lannemaignan (Gers), population 118
Small village located on the border of the Gers and the Landes. A lovely church on the French list of historic monuments is located along the main road.

Proprietor: Paul Claverie ***Name of Property***: Baraillon ***Vineyard size***: 16.80 ha (41.5 acres) ***Grapes used for armagnac***: Bacco (33%), Colombard (33%), Ugni Blanc (34%). Some vintages made solely with Folle Blanche. ***Other production***: corn, soy beans ***Percent of production used for distillation***: 20% ***Soil***: *Sables fauves* (Iron-rich sand) ***Production of armagnac per year***: 40 hl a.p. (20 barrels) ***Distillation***: *Armagnacais* ***Distiller***: Loubère of Labastide d'Armagnac ***Alcohol degree when leaving the still***: 52° ***Barrels***: Regional oak ***Oldest spirit still in cask***: 1962 ***Stock***: 400 hl a.p. (200 barrels) ***Chai:*** Two: one damp, humid and rustic, the other newer and dryer. Both with dirt floors ***Blended armagnacs available***: No ***Vintages available***: 1900, 1918, 1923, 1924, 1933, 1944, 1958, 1960, 1962, 1963, 1965, 1967, 1970, 1972, 1973, 1974, 1975, 1976, 1979, 1980, 1981, 1982, 1983, 1984, 1985, 1986, 1987 ***Reduction***: No

Paul Claverie next to demi-johns of armagnac from the turn of the century.

Paul Claverie's family has occupied their present house since 1749. It is a typical Gascon property with ducks, geese, farm equipment and several primitive buildings surrounding their humble dwelling. When we sit down to talk in the dining room, Paul's wife, mother and daughter surround the table and listen intently.

Claverie's armagnacs are a blend of two properties; 4 hectares belonging to his sister in Le Frêche and 12 hectares surrounding the house. The armagnacs are distilled in Labastide by Loubère. Afterwards they go into 5,000 liter vats. When he can afford it, he buys new barrels or vats but this doesn't happen every year.

When barrel space opens up—perhaps after ten years—he transfers the armagnac from the vats into *pièces*. Once a year or so, he aerates the armagnacs to further promote oxidation. Every so often, he will blend all the barrels from an individual vintage to ensure consistent color and taste.

Claverie has two *chai* where he stores his armagnac. The newest—an unfinished cinder block structure—contains thirty barrels, many of which are recent distillations of Folle Blanche. It is hot and humid inside, and one almost sweats as they taste the armagnac. This climate works well to naturally concentrate the volume. The main *chai* is more rustic—armagnacs dating back nearly 40 years rest on the uneven dirt floor. Also within this *chai* are a number of bon-bonnes containing armagnacs distilled by Paul's father. The oldest, from 1900, was removed from the cask in 1951 by which time it had dropped to 42°.

Mr. Claverie is a traditionalist and sells only vintages that are at their natural degree. His armagnacs normally show a fine texture with slightly drying oak on the finish.

1979 Folle Blanche: Light almond note on the nose. Fine texture. Hint of vanilla in the mouth with some heat on the finish. Medium-bodied and long.

1976: Hint of almond on the nose. Slightly herbal in the mouth and with good length.

1974: Fine texture, with lots of spicy oak and pepper in the mouth. Very good length.

1970: Nice prune notes on the nose are overwhelmed by dry wood in the mouth. Several other vintages showed a similar problem.

1900 (50 years in oak): Very deep aromas of walnut, prune, and almond with a slight hint of fresh black pepper. Dry, smoky finish.

Proprietor: Christiane and Michel Lamothe ***Name of Property***: Domaine Le Bâsque ***Vineyard size***: 7 ha (17 acres) ***Other production***: corn ***Grapes used for armagnac***: Ugni Blanc (80%), Folle Blanche (20%) ***Percent of production used for distillation***: 100% ***Soil***: *sables fauves, sablo-limoneux* (Iron-rich sand and sand) ***Production of armagnac per year***: 20-30 hl of a.p. (10-15 barrels) ***Distiller***: Michel Lamothe himself ***Distillation***: *Armagnacaise* ***Alcohol degree when leaving the still***: 54° ***Barrels***: Allier ***Time in new oak***: 1-2 years ***Chai:*** In a barn, organized, and with a cement floor ***Stock***: 215 hl a.p. (108 barrels) ***Oldest spirit still in cask***: 1955 ***Blended armagnacs available***: VS (2-3 years), VSOP (5-6 years), *Hors d'age* (youngest: 10 years, 43-46°) ***Vintages available***: 1955, 1962, 1966, 1968, 1974, 1978, 1984, 1985 ***Reduction***: Commercialized armagnacs with *petites eaux*, vintages non-reduced

Michel Lamothe, unlike many of his neighbors in the Bas-Armagnac, has been able to place many of his armagnacs within markets around the world. Sales did not come overnight, however. Over the years he sent out hundreds of publicity letters; little by little, he built up a following in France. Many buy privately, although his armagnacs also move on a larger scale—through distributors in Scandinavia, Germany and the United States. He manages to sell around 165 cases a year.

Several decades ago, Lamothe studied enology in Bordeaux, then did an apprenticeship in Cognac. He returned to Lannemaignan, however, and until the early 90's worked as a water inspector for the department of Les Landes. Now that he is retired, he has more time to spend with his wife Christiane and work his product.

Lamothe produces his *vintages* traditionally—without reduction or additives. He likes to aerate his barrels at least once a year, and regularly tastes to keep track of oak dosage. There is always some sort of cuvée in production that needs to be monitored. Lamothe also produces commercial armagnacs of which, even though they pay the bills, he is not a tremendous fan. Vintages get the free run juice for distillation, he says, while the blends get the *vin de presse*. He is extremely up-front about his use of boisé for his blended releases unlike many producers. Still, his VS and VSOP are at least as good as those of any large *négociant* and deserve the success they've achieved.

Lamothe must be one of the few within armagnac that has recently replanted Bacco. Even though its demise is projected for 2010, Lamothe feels he can still get a decades worth of good vintages from the new vines. Unfortunately, none of his products will be passed on to future generations, as his son has no interest in taking over the domaine.

Le Bâsque's armagnacs normally offer forceful attack and retain a youthfulness that helps defy their age. They are medium-bodied, dry, and show lots of spice on the finish.

Hors d'age (41°): Very round and with good weight in the mouth. Fairly supple, and with a slight herbal hint on the finish.

1968: Lovely deep amber. Nice balance of fat and power in the mouth. Spicy oak creeps in on the finish.

1962: Fat aromas on the nose include orange and vanilla. Soft texture with a hint of almond brittle in the mouth. Still powerful on the palate.

Michel Lamothe amidst his beloved Bacco.

Our Lady Of The Cornfield, Lannemaingan, Gers

Lannepax (Gers), population 610

Lannepax (Lanae Pax, Paix de la Lande, or Country of the Landes) rests in the easternmost corner of the Bas-Armagnac. Its 652 inhabitants live along what was once part of a famous route between Bordeaux and the Pyrénées. Touristic highlights include a bastide from the 13th century, and the mouth of a river which, after passing underground through the Ténarèze , resurfaces in Lannepax. Called the "eye of the devil", it can be seen best from Cesar's bridge.

Proprietor: Alain Dauriac ***Name of Property***: Domaine de Gaston ***Vineyard size***: 12 ha (30 acres) ***Other production***: Cows, grain, oak trees ***Grapes used for armagnac***: Ugni Blanc (100%) ***Percent of production used for distillation***: 20-25% ***Soil***: *Boulbènes* (Sand with clay pieces) ***Production of armagnac per year***: 22 hl a.p. (11 barrels) ***Distiller***: Mr. Dauriac himself ***Distillation***: *Armagnacaise* ***Alcohol degree when leaving the still***: 57-58° ***Barrels***: Normally not new; older barrels refurbished ***Time in new oak***: Variable ***Oldest spirit still in cask***: 1980 ***Chai:*** In a barn, cement floor, fairly organized ***Stock***: 120 hl a.p. (60 barrels) ***Blended armagnacs available***: 8-year-old ***Vintages available***: 1980 ***Reduction***: With demineralized water to 42°

Alain Dauriac has experienced some hard times recently. Like many other farmers, the stagnation of the armagnac market has left him depressed. Sales are way down, stock is accumulating, and there seems to be no outlet for his aged goods. Armagnac just doesn't seem to be his best investment.

Consequently Dauriac has reduced his vineyards from 17 to 12 hectares, keeping his land at a level that he can manage himself without the need for outside help. The majority of his wine nowadays is sold in bulk, destined for table wine assembled in the center of France. This, along with some cows and crops, at least allows him sure revenue.

Armagnac, on the other hand, doesn't even cover the costs of production anymore. In fact, Dauriac hasn't even distilled the last couple of vintages. Since the recession of 1991, he has not bought much new oak either; instead, he has refurbished some barrels by having the heads and tails replaced with new wood. This helps give his spirit some color and flavor.

Not as much as he feels it needs, however, and boisé is normally incorporated into his blends. His two available armagnacs are reduced to 42° with demineralized water.

One senses some real Gascon spirit when speaking with Dauriac; he is independent, confident and proud of his roots. Yet with no *négociants* looking to buy stock of any sort, he is yet another forgotten producer who, unfortunately, heads closer and closer to obscurity without the prospect of any sort of financial recompensation.

8 Year Old: Amber. Slightly rustic on the nose. Hint of sweetness in the mouth, yet the flavors seem somewhat dilute.

1980: Deeper amber. Hints of caramel and spice on the nose. Medium-bodied in the mouth and without tremendous presence. Lacks some concentration yet finishes with surprising length.

Proprietor: Josiane and Didier Loss ***Name of Property***: Ouardère ***Vineyard size***: 45 ha (111 acres) ***Other production***: Cows, floc, red and white VDP ***Grapes used for armagnac***: Ugni Blanc (100%) ***Percent of production used for distillation***: 5 % ***Soil***: *Boulbènes* (sand with clay pieces) ***Production of armagnac per year***: 20 hl a.p. (10 barrels) ***Distiller***: St. Martin of Réans ***Distillation***: *Armagnacaise* ***Alcohol degree when leaving the still***: 52°-55° ***Barrels***: Limousin, Tronçais ***Oldest spirit still in cask***: 1982 ***Chai:*** In a barn, clean, organized, cement floor ***Stock***: 120 hl a.p. (60 barrels) ***Blended armagnacs available***: 3 Étoiles, VSOP, XO Vieille Réserve, *Hors d'age* ***Vintages available***: 1986, 1984 ***Reduction***: With distilled water to 42°

Even though the Loss family has resided at the same domaine for five generations, Didier is the first to distill its wine. The picturesque property, named Ouardère, was originally named *Gouardère* or *Guardian* because of its commanding view of the surrounding land. Somewhere along the line, some negligent notary forgot to write the first G and thus affected the domaine's name forever.

Loss buys new wood every year, insuring that every spirit obtains both quality tannin and true color. Aeration takes place once a year, at which time the armagnac is also slightly reduced. All spirits are eventually brought down to 42° before reaching the market.

A sense of optimism is evident at the property, and Didier's wife, in charge of communications, is both energetic and hospitable. A new tasting room is under construction, and the family now exports their excellent dry wines to most countries in Northern Europe.

Their armagnacs are available in many different bottle shapes, ranging from the Basquaise to intricate decanters. They are correctly made, consistent, and easy to understand and enjoy. In addition, they offer nice sweetness on the palate, notes of interesting wood spice and appreciable length.

XO-Vieille Réserve: Light floral note on the nose and nice sweetness on the palate. Soft, pleasing finish.

Hors d'age: Fatter in the mouth with a bit more attack. Soft mouthfeel and with slightly more length than the XO.

1986: Reticent nose. Palate offers good attack and lots of spice. Moderately long, peppery finish.

1984: More feminine-style than the 1986. High orange notes on the nose with additional notes of clove on the palate. Lightly floral *fond de verre*.

Larée (Gers), population 230
Tiny community several miles outside of Cazaubon.

Proprietor: Daniel Dubos ***Name of Property***: Domaine de Pujo ***Vineyard size***: 18 ha (44.5 acres) ***Grapes used for armagnac***: Bacco (100%) ***Other production***: Floc, soy beans, sunflowers ***Percent of production used for distillation***: 15-20% ***Soil***: *Boulbènes, sablo-limoneux* (Sand with clay pieces, sand) ***Production of armagnac per year***: 50 hl a.p. (25 barrels) ***Distillation***: *Armagnacaise* ***Distiller***: St. Martin ***Alcohol degree when leaving the still***: 54°-55° ***Barrels***: Gascon ***Blended armagnacs available***: VSOP (6 years old), Napoléon (9 years old), *Hors d'age* (12 years old) ***Oldest spirit still in cask***: 1940 ***Stock***: 200 hl a.p. (100 barrels) ***Vintages available***: 1986, 1979, 1974, 1973, 1970 ***Reduction***: With demineralized water to 40°

The Domaine de Pujo lies in the virtually non-existent town of Larée, once known for the legendary property of Joseph and Gérard Laberdolive, the Domaine d'Escoubes.

Seventy-seven-year-old Irenée Dubos remembers the days when *négociants* like Gélas, Janneau and Sempé were eager to distill his wine. Not the case now, he says; instead, most of the money comes from visitors who pass a week at Barbotan and stop by the house for a souvenir bottle of Gascon spirit.

For the past decade, the domaine has been run by Irenée's son Daniel. His wine is distilled by one of St. Martin's roaming alambics, then aged in partially new barrels. A complete range of commercial armagnacs are available, all reduced to 40° with demineralized water. In addition, a number of vintages are also available.

The armagnacs at Pujo are correctly made, and offer a commercially popular, soft mouthfeel without tremendous depth or complexity.

Hors d'age: Somewhat muted aromatics. Soft, supple texture. Hint of chocolate and anis. Correct, pleasing, commercial armagnac.

1973 (40°): Soft, supple, yet with somewhat dilute fruit. Somewhat short on the finish.

1970 (46°): Light aromatics include a touch of almond. Lots of attack in the mouth with notes of almond brittle. Medium-bodied and with some alcohol showing on the fairly short finish.

Le Vignau (Landes), population 391
Picturesque village located along the main route running from Aire-sur-l'Adour and Villeneuve de Marsan.

Proprietor: The Jordana-Lague Family ***Name of Property***: L'Arepic ***Vineyard size***: 7 ha (17 acres) ***Other production***: Corn ***Grapes used for armagnac***: Ugni Blanc (60%), Bacco (35%), Folle Blanche (5%) ***Percent of production used for distillation***: 50 % ***Soil***: *Boulbènes* (Sand with clay pieces) ***Production of armagnac per year***: 10 hl a.p. (5 barrels) ***Distiller***: Roumat ***Distillation***: *Armagnacaise* ***Alcohol degree when leaving the still***: 52° ***Oldest spirit still in cask***: 1974 ***Chai***: In a barn, organized, cement floor ***Stock***: 200 hl a.p. (100 barrels) ***Blended armagnacs available***: VS, VSOP (from 1988), *Hors d'age* (from 1985) (Reduced to 42° with *petites eaux*) ***Vintages available***: 1979, 1974 ***Reduction***: No

The Domaine de L'Arepic is run by 71-year-old Maurice Jordana, former commissioner of police in a number of French cities including Marseilles, Bordeaux and Mont-de-Marsan. When he retired, he settled in Le Vignau at the home where his wife Colette had been raised. At the same time he took over his father-in-law's armagnac production which started in the 1950's.

Distillation is traditional and at a low degree which helps preserve lots of fruit within the spirit. Once in barrel, the spirit is not worked very much; The younger blends are reduced, however, before they reach the public.

Jordana admits that they have never attempted to crack the market because their other occupations took precedence. Even now, he feels, armagnac doesn't seem to be a venture worth pursuing. His son owns a nearby café/restaurant and readily admits that 80% of the alcohol sales within the bar are of whiskey. And this, in the *Grand Bas Armagnac*!

Jordana has even decided to reduce his vineyard in 1998 by 50%. It's a shame because the armagnacs of L'Arepic show an incredible suppleness from an extremely early age. Even the VSOP contains a soft mouthfeel with lots of budding fruit. The vintages are extremely flattering in mouth, with intensely honeyed fruit and a tremendously soft, even sexy, mouthfeel. All of L'Arepic's armagnacs offer excellent value.

1979 (44°): Notes of grilled almond on the nose. Intense aromatics include prune, dried apricot and a light floral note. Additional notes of vanilla and honey in the mouth. Nice balance of fruit and alcohol. Extremely supple finish.

1974 (41°): Lovely almond notes on nose. Lots of sweetness on palate. Fat texture includes notes of dried plum and walnut. Honeyed mouthfeel. Very supple without much alcoholic kick.

Lias d'Armagnac (Gers), population 204

Small village located about four miles from Estang on the main route to Eauze.

Proprietor: Roger Bourdens ***Name of Property***: Domaine de Caumont ***Vineyard size***: 25 ha (62 acres) ***Other production***: red and white floc, VDP, kiwis, nectarines, corn ***Grapes used for armagnac***: Ugni Blanc (100%) *Production of wine per year*: 2,200 hl ***Percent of production used for distillation***: 20% ***Soil***: *Boulbènes* (Sand with clay pieces) ***Production of armagnac per year***: 32 hl a.p. (16 barrels) ***Distillation***: *Armagnacaise* ***Distiller***: Samalens in Laujuzan and Auban of Estang ***Alcohol degree when leaving the still***: 56° ***Barrels***: Mixture of Gascon and Limousin ***Oldest spirit still in cask***: 20 years ***Chai:*** In a refurbished barn, well-organized, cement floor ***Stock***: 87 hl a.p. (44 barrels) ***Blended armagnacs available***: *Hors d'age* (12 years old) *Oldest armagnac still in barrel*: 1976 ***Vintages available***: 1976, 1980, 1983 ***Reduction***: Reduced to 44° with *petites eaux*

The Domaine de Caumont lies about two miles off the main road between Eauze and Estang, just outside the small village of Lias d'Armagnac. Mr. Bourdens is the fourth generation to live at the property which now sports an attractive tasting room where visitors can sample Caumont's white wine, floc and, of course, armagnac.

The wine is normally delivered to either the Samalens property in Laujuzan or to the Auban distillery in Estang for distillation. The spirit is then returned, placed in cask, and left to age in their small yet relatively spacious *chai*. The barrels are racked and blended with the same vintage once a year, then reduced with demineralized water by about one degree. Occasionally Mr. Bourdens seeks the advice of an enologist, especially before creating his *Hors d'age* blend.

Caumont's armagnacs, although not of grand interest to the connoisseur, are correctly made and commercial in nature. They reach the market in modern, elongated bottles that come in a wide variety of sizes.

Hors d'age: Medium-body, with good attack, lots of spice and well-integrated wood on finish.

1983: More flattering nose with lots of vanilla and melted toffee aromas. Rich in the mouth yet with good penetration. Slightly dry, tannic finish that is not as long as one might expect.

1980: Charming nose with some creamy notes. Rich mouthfeel. Good attack with lots of spice. Tannin creeps onto the palate so that the armagnac finishes slightly dry.

Loubedat (Gers), population 122

Tiny hamlet located a few kilomètres from Cravencères. Colorful fields planted along the rolling hills makes for some lovely countryside.

Proprietor: Louis Oreja ***Name of Property***: Mauhic ***Vineyard size***: 13.5 ha (33 acres) ***Other production***: Cows, Corn ***Grapes used for armagnac***: Folle Blanche (80%), Ugni Blanc (20%) ***Percent of production used for distillation***: 15-20 % ***Soil***: *Sablo-limoneux* (Sand with clay pieces) ***Production of armagnac per year***: 15-20 hl a.p. (7-10 barrels) ***Distiller***: Dargelos ***Distillation***: *Armagnacaise* ***Distillation degree upon exiting the still***: 54°-55° ***Barrels***: Gascon and Limousin ***Time in new oak***: 8 months-1 year ***Oldest spirit still in cask***: 1966 ***Chai:*** Two, one with a cement floor, the other, more rustic, with dirt floor. ***Stock***: 160 hl a.p. (80 barrels) ***Blended armagnacs available***: No ***Vintages available***: 1987, 1981, 1975, 1969 ***Reduction***: To 45° with *petites eaux*

Louis Oreja is of Spanish decent, although he has resided in the Gers all of his life. When he took over the farm in 1966, his father sold what stock remained. Like that, Louis began from scratch and began building his own stock. Today his son Stephan looks after the new production; another generation continuing the tradition at the small farm.

Oreja claims that everyone has their own methods of working armagnac; he feels that a spirit at 50° shows too much alcohol, yet at 40° the aromas are lost. Consequently, one year before a vintage is to be released, it is reduced to 45°—a point which he feels best expresses the nuances of his product.

The spirit is worked barrel by barrel and the *assemblage* is made by taking a small proportion from barrels of the same vintage and letting them marry gradually. Both Louis and Stephan admit, however, that they are not great consumers of armagnac; surprising, perhaps, but fairly common amongst producers. At times it leads one to question how a product of good quality manages to reach the bottle.

At Mauhic, it does. Their armagnacs are rarely over-oaked and normally display light, somewhat floral aromatics with good, medium-bodied fruit in the mouth. The vintages, sold in Normand bottles, have different colored capsules depending on the year. A good *vin de noix* (wine, armagnac and leaves from a walnut tree) is also produced on the property.

1987: Amber. Lightly floral aromas, still with a hint of vine flowers. Lightly spiced oak, and with pleasing depth. Still young.

1981: Amber. Less floral, yet with a hint of vegetation in the mouth. Soft texture but with a vinous quality. Some heat on the finish.

1975: Amber. Light, fine aromatics that hint at flowers and toffee. Nice balance, and with a soft texture and some dryness on the finish. Good length.

1969: Light aromatics include notes of flowers and walnut. Nice balance in the mouth, with notes of maple. Not showing tremendous depth for its age.

Manciet (Gers), population 784

Located midway between Eauze and Nogaro, Manciet contains several crooked streets from which one can see the Pyrénées on a clear day.

Proprietor: Jean Cenac ***Name of Property***: Domaine de Laubuchon ***Vineyard size***: 20 ha (49 acres) ***Grapes used for armagnac***: Folle Blanche (50%), Ugni Blanc (50%). Vintages pre 1973 included a third each of Bacco, Ugni Blanc and Colombard. ***Other production***: Cows ***Soil***: *Boulbènes* (Sand with clay pieces) ***Production of armagnac per year***: 30-40 hl a.p. (15-20 barrels) ***Distillation***: *Armagnacaise* ***Alcohol degree when leaving the still***: 55° ***Distiller***: St. Martin ***Barrels***: Limousin, Gascon ***Chai***: Rustic, dirt floor, organized. ***Oldest spirit still in cask***: 1965 ***Vintages available***: 1965, 1966, 1967, 1968, 1969, 1970, 1973, 1989, 1990, 1991, 1992, 1993, 1994, 1995 ***Stock***: 200 hl a.p. (100 barrels) ***Reduction***: No

Jean Cenac was born in Manciet but brought up in the Gironde. Although he now owns the domaine that once belonged to his grandparents, he spends most of his time in the Charentes where he is a dental surgeon. A fan of fine spirits and fine things in general, his Gascon house is one of the few where you can find both a bottle of cognac and armagnac.

In November, St. Martin arrives with his alambic and fills between 12 and 15 barrels, about half of which are new. After vinification, 50% of Cenac's wine is sold to the coopérative in Nogaro. 80% of Laubuchon's remaining spirit is eventually sold to *négociants*, the most notable being Auxil. Like this Cenac is one of the few that makes consistent money from his armagnac production.

The armagnacs that remain at the domaine are always very rich in aromas and texture, and normally display good length. New oak has to be considered a partial reason for this, and flattering aromas often seduce the consumer toward the amber liquid in the glass.

1973 (from cask): Amber. Almond notes on nose. Somewhat charged with alcohol and not completely together in the mouth. Slightly floral hint with some richness beginning to develop in mouth. Still young.

1970: Flattering nose included some nuttiness, a fine texture and a slightly elevated level of alcohol.

1966: Deep amber. Flattering nose includes notes of coconut and vanilla. Smells fat. Rich in the mouth and with a lush texture. Lots of sweetness and a pleasingly long finish. Tasty stuff!

1965 (46°): Deep amber. Rich nose includes vanilla, wood spice and refined alcohol aromas. Maple syrup and nutty flavors dance upon an elegant texture. Impressive armagnac.

Mauléon d'Armagnac (Gers), population 328
Wonderfully aromatic pine forests dissect the fields of sunflowers, corn and vines surrounding the small center of Mauléon.

Proprietor: Jean and Christian Buffaumène (SCEA Buffaumene) ***Name of Property***: Domaine de Maupas ***Vineyard size***: 40 ha (99 acres) ***Other production***: Corn, sunflowers, Côtes de Gascogne, Floc ***Grapes used for armagnac***: Ugni Blanc (67%), Folle Blanche (33%) ***Percent of production used for distillation***: 10 % ***Soil***: *Boulbènes* (Sand with clay pieces) ***Production of armagnac per year***: 30-40 hl a.p. (15-20 barrels) ***Distiller***: St. Martin ***Distillation***: *Armagnacaise* ***Alcohol degree when leaving the still***: 54° ***Barrels***: Gascon ***Chai***: In a barn, cement floor, organized ***Stock***: 250 hl a.p. (125 barrels) ***Oldest spirit still in cask***: 1932 ***Vintages available***: 1982, 1979, 1975, 1964, 1942, 1932 ***Reduction***: With demineralized water to 45°.

Domaine de Maupas is one of the more picturesque properties in the Bas-Armagnac. Over the past decade, former Mauléon mayor Jean and his son Christian Buffaumène have replanted their old Bacco with Folle Blanche, a popular trend with those who want to continue their armagnac production. With this they have given up some fat in exchange for lighter aromatics, their developing product, currently in cask, is extremely encouraging.

The Buffaumène's have not bought much new oak recently and use limited amounts of wood chips and wood planks to add some tannin to their spirits—another trend because of its cost-effectiveness. Their armagnacs are reduced little by little to 45° and released only as vintages.

Armagnacs from the Domaine de Maupas always display rich color, medium-body and deep aromatics from ten years onwards. Maupas also produces a good Côtes de Gascogne white.

1986 Folle Blanche: Deep amber. Fine aromatics hint at vine flowers. Notes of almond brittle in the mouth. Delicate and fine, and with good pure length.

1982: Rich nose hints at maple syrup and alcohol. Fairly deep flavor. Decent fat but not very fine. Some hints of dry oak on the finish.

1979: Amber. Lots of aroma (orange, toffee, vanilla). Attractive fat on the palate. Slight hint of almonds and additional orange nuance on the finish. Good pure length. Very nice armagnac.

1975: Plenty of *rancio* (walnut, oak) on the nose with additional hints of mushrooms. Lots of oak in the mouth that continues through a very dry finish.

1964: Rich walnut *rancio* on the nose. Prune in the mouth. Lots of antique oak flavor on the finish without being overly dry.

1942: Plenty of aroma on the nose; walnuts, vanilla, prune. Lots of oak in the mouth but some fruit prevents it from being too dry. Impressive for its age.

Proprietor: Daniel Cames ***Name of Property***: Domaine de Lusson ***Vineyard size***: 15 ha (37 acres) ***Other production***: Corn, trees ***Grapes used for armagnac***: Ugni Blanc (60%), Bacco (30%), Folle Blanche (10%) ***Percent of production used for distillation***: 7% ***Soil***: *Sables, argilo-calcaires* (Sand, clay and chalk) ***Production of armagnac per year***: 10 hl a.p. (5 barrels) ***Distiller***: Punsola of Cravencères ***Distillation***: *Armagnacaise* ***Alcohol degree when leaving the still***: 52° ***Barrels***: Gascon ***Oldest spirit still in cask***: 1962 ***Chai***: Cement floor, organized. ***Stock***: 120 hl a.p. (60 barrels) ***Blended armagnacs available***: No ***Vintages available***: Most vintages from the 70's, 80's, and 90's ***Reduction***: No

At times, Daniel Cames wishes that he had sold more of his stock when the *négociant* firms were willing to buy. After all, important *négociants* like Darroze and Laubade once *cherry-picked* his stock, buying his best casks. However, since what many refer to as the *Gulf war crisis* in 1991, the negociants have not arrived. Mr. Cames is certainly at the retirement age; unfortunately, with low social security payments and a bank account in armagnac that pays no interest, he can't *afford* to retire.

The grand majority of his wine production is sold in bulk and he distills less than 10% of his harvest. Not long ago, Cames planted one hectare of Folle Blanche which he now distills separately, perhaps hoping that this grape will bring back the *négociants*. The 1993 vintage was certainly encouraging; lots of aromatics, spice and finesse. Still, the phone in the kitchen does not ring.

The armagnacs at Lusson are traditional; low distillation degree, long-term aging, no reduction. In an effort to homogenize a particular vintage, the armagnacs are aerated once every two years and placed in different casks. Many of the barrels in the *chai*, although less than ten years old, have parted with much of their tannin. The combination of light color, low tannin and high alcohol helps give the impression that the armagnacs at Lusson, in their present condition, are capable of extensive aging. One must not forget that the limestone soil under which a portion of their vine rests is certainly a contributing factor to this longevity.

1993 Folle Blanche: Amber. Lovely aromatics include hints of vanilla and notes of vine flowers. Round, rich flavors with pleasing wood-integration. Along the right path.

1986: Light amber. Flattering nose includes a hint of coconut. Fruit still muted; soft mouthfeel with some alcohol showing. Still young.

1977: Nose not fully open. Well-integrated oak in the mouth. Lots of body and alcohol. Pepper note surfaces with the oak on the finish.

1978: Amber with gold highlights. Fat beginning to develop. Hint of almond in the mouth. Good attack and balance. Well-integrated, non-obtrusive oak notes. Excellent length. Licorice note at the bottom of the glass.

Proprietor: The Castarède Family ***Name of Property***: Château de Maniban ***Vineyard size***: 16 ha (39.5 acres) ***Other production***: None ***Grapes used for armagnac***: Ugni Blanc (60%), Folle Blanche (25%), Colombard (15%) ***Percent of production used for distillation***: 100 % ***Soil***: *Boulbènes* (Sand with clay pieces) ***Production of armagnac per year***: 110 hl a.p. (55 acres) ***Distiller***: Alambic of the property and of St. Martin ***Distillation***: *Armagnacaise* ***Alcohol degree when leaving the still***: 52°-55° ***Barrels***: Limousin ***Time in new oak***: 1 year ***Oldest spirit still in cask***: 1983 ***Chai***: Rustic, dirt floor, organized ***Stock***: 400 hl a.p. (200 barrels) ***Blended armagnacs available***: VS (Gers), VSOP, Napoléon, *Hors d'age* ***Vintages available***: No ***Reduction***: To 40° with *petites eaux*.

The Château de Maniban (left) is a lovely property located near the village of Mauléon. Although grand, one would never see the domaine from the road. In fact, only a small, hand-painted sign informs the passerby of its presence. The château was once the summer retreat of members of the Toulouse parliament, but now is the property of the *négociant* firm Castarede.

The 16 hectares of vines are comprised chiefly of Ugni Blanc. The releases thus far have been strictly commercial: Gers is the name of their youngest armagnac, which is around three-years-old. A VSOP, Napoléon, and *Hors d'age* are also on the market. They are all well-made and without faults.

Folle Blanche has been harvested since 1985, and will soon be available as a single-varietal. There is talk that it will be released in a purer form, around 45°, but this seems doubtful considering Castarède's adherence to reducing everything, including vintages, to 40°.

It is sad that such a well-situated property should specialize only in commercial products. The 1983 tasted at 47° was immensely superior to their commercialized *Hors d'age* at 40°. Its nose of almond and vanilla was lovely, there was depth of apricot-like fruit, and the finish was both supple and long. A pity that this, like many of the domaine's releases, will reach the market in a dilute version that bears little resemblance to its former self.

Proprietor: GAEC des Coutons ***Name of Property***: Domaine Durroux ***Vineyard size***: 25 ha (62 acres) ***Other production***: corn, free range chickens, floc, white wine ***Grapes used for armagnac***: Bacco (70%), Ugni Blanc (30%) ***Percent of production used for distillation***: 18 % ***Soil***: *Boulbènes* (Sand with clay pieces) ***Production of armagnac per year***: 20 hl a.p. (10 barrels) ***Distiller***: Mr. Durroux himself ***Distillation***: *Armagnacaise* ***Alcohol degree when leaving the still***: 55° ***Barrels***: Some second-hand barrels each year that give some tannin ***Oldest spirit still in cask***: 1980 ***Chai***: In a corner of the vinification *chai*. Organized, cement floor, dry ***Stock***: 175 hl a.p. (88 barrels) ***Blended armagnacs available***: VSOP (9 years old) ***Vintages available***: 1983, 1985 ***Reduction***: To 48° with demineralized water

This large property sits on the route between Labastide to Mauléon. In addition to raising 20,000 free range chickens a year, the Durroux family also has plenty of corn surrounding the house. With regards to grapes, they are lucky in that they can market their excellent white wine as Côtes de Gascogne, which fetches a couple of francs more a bottle than the domaine next door, which is obliged to market their comparable wine under the *VDP de Terroir Landais* banner.

Distilling armagnac doesn't make much sense, says forty-year-old Jean-Marc Durroux. In fact, a new barrel now costs more than what the *negociants* are willing to pay for the newly distilled product inside. Corn, on the other hand, ultimately brings in more money. Unfortunately it is extremely impersonal. Sold to the coop in bulk, it's faceless. At least you work armagnac and the finished product has your name on it.

The passionate Durroux has distilled the property's armagnacs since 1983, using the alambic of neighbor Charles Garreau. Gas rather than wood heat is essential, he says, because it provides much more regularity. Distillation takes place at 55°; then the armagnac goes into previously used barrels.

Their armagnac *chai* lies just next to the fairly modern vinification area. Its warm, dry conditions do not allow for much alcohol evaporation. Consequently, even after 10 years of aging, the alcohol level has not budged—it's still at 55°. Difficult conditions in which to raise armagnac, yet, for the moment, the only conditions available.

Durroux's armagnacs tend to be medium-bodied and with good attack.; they show some decent soft fruit and very little wood influence.

1985 (48°): Deep amber. Sweet nose with some vanilla. Rich mouth remains soft, although some heat picks up on the spicy finish.

1983 (48°): Reticent nose. Medium weight, some sweetness on palate, although the lack of wood ultimately leads to a lack of complexity. Hint of orange peel on the finish.

Proprietor: Peter Hawkins ***Name of Property***: Domaine de Papolle ***Vineyard size***: 50 ha (124 acres) ***Other production***: Corn, sunflowers ***Grapes used for armagnac***: Ugni Blanc (50%), Folle Blanche (50%) ***Percent of production used for distillation***: 15 % ***Soil***: *Argilo-Calcaires, Argilo-Sablonneux* (Clay and chalk, clay and sand) ***Production of armagnac per year***: 30 hl a.p. (15 barrels) ***Distiller***: Dargelos ***Distillation***: *Armagnacaise* ***Alcohol degree when leaving the still***: 53° ***Barrels***: Limousin ***Time in new oak***: 12-18 months ***Oldest spirit still in cask***: 1973 ***Stock***: 400 hl a.p. (200 barrels) ***Blended armagnacs available***: VSOP, *Hors d'age* ***Vintages available***: 1985 (Folle Blanche), 1977, 1973 ***Reduction***: To 44° or 45° with distilled water

The Domaine de Papolle was bought in 1981 by Englishman Peter Hawkins, a civil engineer based in Northern France. He bought Papolle not only as an investment, but also because he and his French wife liked the Gers countryside. Today, however, he wonders if it was a wise purchase. According to him, there is too much competition with inexpensive white wines and the armagnac market is "dead".

Fortunately Hawkins, unlike many producers, is able to move a good deal of his product before it is even bottled. Samalens buys all of his Bacco wine which they later distill for their armagnacs. Larresingle also buys large quantities of aged spirits for their blends.

Hawkins property is indeed beautiful and tranquil; rolling hills display the fifty hectares of vine. Corn and sunflowers color another 70 hectares. The soil is a mixture of sand and limestone. A *chai* with the older spirits is near the attractive house. About two kilometers away, there is another *chai* which houses most of the young spirits. Lots of new wood is evident, and the space is organized. In short, one senses that the barrels will contain spirits of tremendous quality.

Yet whereas the blended armagnacs from Papolle offer lots of body and flavor and far surpass the minimum age requirements for commercial releases, the vintages rarely light up the night as one might expect. This is no doubt due to the fact that, like most market-minded properties, reduction mutes some of the aromas and minimizes whatever finesse could have existed naturally.

All things told, Papolle produces rich, commercialized armagnacs that are easily as good as similar-aged releases from most large houses. A pleasingly crisp Côtes de Gascogne white is also available in several international markets.

VSOP: Amber. Lots of aroma for a VSOP, especially at 40°. Excellent depth with a slight nutty hint. Heavy mouthfeel. Very good for its age (not surprising since the majority is from 1981).

Hors d'age: Amber with gold highlights. Rich nose hints at melted caramel/toffee/nougat. Soft mouthfeel with well-integrated alcohol. Pleasing depth. Good length. Well-made *hors d'age.*

1985 (Folle Blanche): Lighter, feminine armagnac with floral aromatics. Good attack in the mouth, and with a sweet mouthfeel. Good length.

1973: Amber. Rich aromas include floral notes. Good depth but undoubtedly feminine. Notes of almond brittle in the mouth. Some alcohol shows on the finish. Nice sweetness on the palate. Well-integrated wood on the finish.

Mauvezin d'Armagnac (Landes), population 100
Picturesque village whose church has been destroyed and reconstructed in various battles since 1569.

Proprietor: Societé GFA de Pichon-Longueville ***Name of Property***: Château de Briat ***Vineyard size***: 9 ha (22.23 acres) ***Other production***: *Eau de Vie* from 100% Colombard ***Grapes used for armagnac***: Bacco (56%), Folle Blanche (30%), Colombard (14%) ***Percent of production used for distillation***: 70 % ***Soil***: *Sables fauves* (Iron-rich sand) ***Production of armagnac per year***: 24 hl a.p. (12 barrels) ***Distiller***: Roumat ***Distillation***: Armagnacaise ***Alcohol degree when leaving the still***: 52° ***Barrels***: Limousin and Gascon ***Time in new oak***: 3 Years ***Oldest spirit still in cask***: 1979 ***Stock***: 260 hl a.p. (130 barrels) ***Blended armagnacs available***: *Hors d'age* (14 years old) ***Vintages available***: 1979, 1981, 1982, 1985 ***Reduction***: No

The Château de Briat has a long and impressive history; built in 1540, it first served as the hunting manor for Queen Jeanne d'Albret and her husband Henri III. Their son Henri de Navarre, later Henri IV, King of France, gave the château to one of his officers in 1587 as a reward for saving his life in battle. After changing ownership several times, the domaine was taken over by Baron Raoul de Pichon-Longueville in 1864.

The Pichon-Longueville family, who already owned the famous vineyard of the same name in Pauillac, used the estate as a country retreat while continuing the property's tradition of distilling a percentage of the harvest every year and accumulating stocks of armagnac.

When the Pichon-Longueville property in Bordeaux was sold,

the Château de Briat was retained by Baron Raoul de Pichon-Longueville, the maternal ancestor of the current owner Gilles de Luze.

De Luze, a former literary editor in Paris, now spends sixty percent of his time at the château in Mauvezin, a tiny yet attractive town located between Lagrange and Labastide. Seven hectares of vines are divided between Bacco, Folle Blanche, and Colombard; De Luze, unlike many other armagnac producers, is a firm believer in keeping yields low, and he is not opposed to cutting fruit to give a final harvest of 60 hl/ha.

Varietals are distilled separately to a low 52°, and all 10 *pièces* made at the property during a good year see new wood. After 2 or 3 years, they are transferred to older casks and, apart from an airing once a year, left to rest in the spacious yet primitive *chai.*

Topping up is not practiced; de Luze prefers to let the level fall and promote air contact which ultimately creates a spirit that is less aggressive and more concentrated. Assemblage of various grapes takes place after a minimum of four years and, at times, not until their tenth birthday.

With the glass in hand, the armagnacs of Briat do not let the consumer down. In fact, they epitomize the magical wonders that one can find floating in a glass of Gascon spirit. There is no consistency in taste; after all, grape blends and vintage conditions vary. What is consistent is tremendous quality; always lots of nose, plenty of new oak, a fine palate feel and excellent length. Only the current lack of agedstock prevents Briat from being among Armagnac's premier echelon.

... it, shortly before being transferred to the main storage area at Briat (right).

...che, 10% Colombard, 44°): Amber with extremely attractive ...s of licorice, toffee and oak. Excellent value.

1982 (Folle Blanche): Bright fruit (orange), almond and vanilla on the nose. Lots of oak. Fine texture, with a additional notes of chocolate and peppermint on the palate. Very inviting, warm length.

1981 (Bacco): Rich nose with notes of mashed almonds and plums. Fat in mouth yet with soft attack. Buttery texture. Hints of melted toffee, vanilla and coconut. Pleasing fruit on the finish, which is softer yet less long than the Folle Blanche.

1979 (50% Folle Blanche, 45% Bacco, 5% Colombard): Lots of new oak and floral notes on the nose along with a hint of orange and dried apricot. Good attack; playful, well-rounded fruit. Lots of finesse. Very long, and with lots of spice on the finish.

Montguilhem (Gers), population 256

Small town best known for its forest that once supplied oak for many of Armagnac's aging vessels. The town's church was built in the 14th Century.

Proprietor: M. B. Farbos-Cames ***Name of Property***: Clos de Moutouguet ***Vineyard size***: 10 ha (24.7 acres) ***Other production***: none ***Grapes***: Ugni Blanc (50%), Bacco (30%), Folle Blanche (15 %), Colombard (5%) ***Percent of production used for distillation***: 30-50% ***Soil***: *Boulbènes* (Sand with clay pieces) ***Production of armagnac per year***: 30 hl a.p. (15 barrels) ***Distiller***: *Distillerie des Côteaux de Gascogne* (Cutxan) ***Distillation***: *Armagnacaise* ***Alcohol degree when leaving the still***: 52-56° ***Barrels***: Gascon and Limousin ***Oldest spirit still in cask***: 1968 ***Stock***: 350 hl a.p. (175 barrels) ***Blended armagnacs available***: VS (5 year old), Napoléon (8 year old), *Hors d'age* (12 to 15 years old) ***Vintages available***: 1980, 1974, 1970, 1968 ***Reduction***: With *petites eaux* to 42°

The Farbos-Cames family once owned the Domaine de Papolle in Mauléon in addition to the Clos de Montouguet in Montguilhem. While they commercialized the armagnacs from Papolle, they simply stocked those at their other property. At the beginning of the Eightees, they sold Papolle to Peter Hawkins; in 1983, they began marketing the armagnacs from Montguillem.

A number of blended armagnacs are available in the United States (VS, Napoléon, Hors d'Age) as well as several vintages that, although slightly reduced, show deep and intense fruit. The marketing is handled by the Cames'son Bruno, who lives in New York City.

1968 (42°): Very deep amber. Lots of smoky oak on the nose along with sweet notes of hard caramel and subtle rancio. Good intensity on the palate while retaining a sweet, supple texture. Plenty of recurring oak/smoke notes ride along a creamy/nutty /prune-scented fruit. Smoke, earth and pepper notes pick up on the long finish.

Panjas (Gers), population 451

Panjas is home to one of the more important coopératives in the Bas-Armagnac as well as the headquarters of the biggest selling armagnac in France, Clés des Ducs. Pierre Cornet, a well-known regional distiller,was based in Panjas. The town's church was constructed between the 11th and 12th Centuries during which period a château, still in existence, was also built.

Proprietor: The Gessler Family ***Name of Property***: Domaine de Joÿ ***Vineyard size***: 72 ha (178 acres) ***Other production***: corn, conserves, VDP de Côtes de Gascogne ***Grapes used for armagnac***: Ugni Blanc (40%), Bacco (30%), Folle Blanche (30%) ***Percent of production used for distillation***: 10 % ***Soil***: *Boulbènes* (Sand with clay pieces) ***Production of armagnac per year***: 60 hl a.p. (30 barrels) ***Distiller***: St. Martin ***Distillation***: *Armagnacaise* ***Alcohol degree when leaving the still***: 56° ***Time in new oak***: 2-4 years ***Oldest spirit still in cask***: 1962 ***Stock***: 500 hl a.p. (250 barrels) ***Blended armagnacs available***: VSOP, Napoléon, XO, *Hors d'age* ***Vintages available***: 1984, 1979, 1976, 1962, 1942 ***Reduction***: Recent vintages to 42°. Older vintages non-reduced.

The Domaine de Joÿ makes one of the most exported wines from the Côtes de Gascogne. In less than a decade, they have jumped from 40,000 bottles a year to nearly 400,000, a good chunk of which goes to the Oddbins chain in Britain. Artist Ralph Steadman has incorporated the Gessler family, owners of the domaine, in to many of the Oddbins catalogue drawings.

Production is highly automated and nearly every week a full truck leaves for some European country. Brothers Olivier and Roland Gessler have recently raised their quality to new levels by cutting grapes to reduce yields and elevate sugar levels. This has allowed them to produce wines with more natural alcohol instead of adding the customary must to the fermenting wine.

Their armagnacs also get lots of attention. After dripping out of St. Martin's wood-fueled alambic at 56°, they go into oak casks, at least 50% of which are new. Their progression is monitored closely and they are aired at least once a year. Some of the armagnacs are placed into sanitized 220 liter wine barrels that once housed some of the brother's Gros Manseng experiments.

Reduction normally takes place a year or so before bottling and all armagnacs, including the recent vintages, are brought down to 42°. A large range of blended armagnacs are available, all of which show pleasing aromatics, lots of body and sweet fruit in the mouth.

Napoléon (6 years old): Notes of chocolate and almond on the nose. Nice fat in the mouth and some sweetness. Some alcohol shows on the finish.

XO (8 years old): Lighter, more jovial aromatics include an orange note. Feminine in the mouth, with notes of spice on the finish.

Hors d'age (12 years old): Nutty nose with a fat, soft mouthfeel. Finishes fairly short.

1984: Amber. Good attack with notes of orange and nut in the mouth. Slightly dry finish with some alcohol showing.

1979: Grilled almond on the nose. Lots of attack with well-integrated notes of spicy oak. Very good length.

Country Road between Nogaro and Le Houga

1976: Mashed, raw almond on the nose along with a chocolate note. Macho armagnac, with lots of richness in the mouth and a hint of old wood on the slightly tannic finish.

1962 (45°): Lots of oak and *rancio* on the nose and additional notes of sweet orange in the mouth. Well-hidden alcohol. Lots of old oak on the finish. Good length.

1942 (47°): Lots of oak on the nose. Fairly aggressive palate, with old oak notes continuing along the very dry finish.

Parleboscq (Landes), population 550

This small village has no less than seven churches, as well as two château, that of Laballe and the majestic Lacaze. Parleboscq lies on the border of Les Landes and the Gers, and its sandy soil gives lots of suppleness to its resultant armagnacs.

Proprietor: Noel Laudet ***Name of Property***: Domaine de Laballe ***Vineyard size***: 16 ha (40 acres) ***Other production***: white wine, floc ***Grapes used for armagnac***: Ugni Blanc (100%) ***Percent of production used for distillation***: 7-8% ***Soil***: *Boulbènes*, *Sables fauves* (Sand with clay pieces, iron-rich sand) ***Production of armagnac per year***: 5-10 hl a.p. (2-5 barrels) ***Distillation***: *Armagnacaise* ***Distiller***: St. Martin ***Alcohol degree when leaving the still***: 53° ***Barrels***: Regional and Limousin ***Time in new oak***: As long as possible ***Oldest spirit still in cask***: 1964 ***Chai***: Part of the château, dirt floor, organized ***Stock***: 60 hl a.p. (30 barrels) ***Blended armagnacs available***: VSOP (9-years-old), *Hors d'age* (12-years-old) ***Vintages available***: 1983, 1982, 1979, 1975, 1974, 1973, 1967, 1966, 1964 ***Reduction***: Demineralized water and *petites eaux* to 42°-44°

At the beginning of the 19th century, Jean-Dominique Laudet sailed to the Caribbean where he built a successful export business. In 1820, he returned to his native Gascony and purchased the Château de Laballe in Parleboscq. Since that time, armagnac has been produced on the property.

The most recent generation to produce is Nöel Laudet, one-time director of production at Château Beycheville in St. Julian. After leaving that post and running one of the Lafite-Rothschild agricultural properties near Paris, he returned to Gascony in 1980 and concentrated on the property's white wines and armagnac.

The château, reminiscent of a Bordeaux property, includes a well-aired *chai*. A modest stock of thirty barrels is housed within. Laudet purchases the occasional new barrel, but also refurbishes old barrels. Reduction for his commercial armagnacs is done with *petites eaux*; vintages are reduced gradually with demineralized water. Most armagnacs reach the market at around 42°.

Laballe's armagnacs, because of their reduction, tend to be less aromatic than those a few degrees stronger. In the mouth, they remain fairly linear. However, they do show decent fruit and a smooth texture.

1982 (42.5°): Amber. Not incredibly intense aromatics but with a touch of toffee. Hint of pepper in the mouth. Medium-body, and with a very accessible mouthfeel.

1976: Lovely deep amber color. Whiff of almond on the nose. Very round and soft in the mouth; in short, very smooth yet without tremendous delineation of flavor. Moderately long, agreeable finish.

1974: Less forthcoming on the nose. Lots of vanilla in the mouth with just a hint of dry wood. Round, supple mouthfeel with a pleasingly long finish.

1973 (less reduced, at 45°): Hint of almond on the nose. Richer mouthfeel with more penetration on the palate. *Pruneau*, vanilla and classy oak notes in mouth. More attack, and with some noticeable alcohol. Long finish.

1964 (from bonbonne): Almond and prune on the nose, along with some hints of coconut and tobacco. Some smoky oak in mouth adds complexity. Somewhat dry finish.

Proprietor: Jean-Pierre Sarrot ***Name of Property***: Domaine de Castagnet ***Vineyard size***: 12 ha (30 acres) ***Other production***: Corn ***Grapes used for armagnac***: Bacco (100%). Distilled first Folle Blanche in 1996. ***Percent of production used for distillation***: 8 % ***Soil***: Boulbènes (Sand with clay pieces) ***Production of armagnac per year***: 10 hl a.p. (5 barrels) ***Distiller***: Michaelouski ***Distillation***: *Armagnacaise* ***Alcohol degree when leaving the still***: 55° ***Barrels***: Gascon and Limousin ***Oldest spirit still in cask***: 1968 ***Stock***: 100 hl a.p. (50 barrels) ***Blended armagnacs available***: No ***Vintages available***: 1989, 1985, 1981, 1977, 1972, 1970, 1969 ***Reduction***: With distilled water to 43°

The Sarrot family has resided on the same property for over 3 centuries, and Jean-Pierre is the fifth generation to distill armagnac. Jean-Pierre is a humble farmer who varies crops depending on which pays the most, sells the majority of his grape production to either the coopérative or to *négociants*, and distills anywhere between 3 and 5 barrels a year—depending on the weather and his need for ready cash. Unlike many producers in the Bas-Armagnac who suffered early spring frosts, his loss in 1996 came from early June hailstorms that ripped apart many of his budding grapes and blossoming leaves.

His armagnac production is traditional; low distillation degree, some new oak, minimal intervention. He departs from the old school, however, just before bottling when he reduces his armagnacs to 43°. He reduces to this level because he feels the lower degree scares fewer clients, yet the product is not so dilute as to eliminate any aroma at all.

Castagnet's younger vintages, when tasted from bottle, showed good attack, some spicy aromas and good length. The older vintages showed similar characteristics with some budding fat. In short, they had more in common with the well-made Ténarèze than with the Bas-Armagnac (understandable, as the property lies extremely close to the Ténarèze border).

There was not much comparison, however, between the reduced product in the bottles and the unrectified versions in the *chai*. Without the addition of water, the spirit was more concentrated, had more powerful aromas and lovely integration of oak. Alcohol and fruit were completely in balance. The wood was well-integrated and the finish was long.

Like this, these lovely spirits began to resemble their proper *terroir*, the Bas-Armagnac.

1979 (47°): Lots of sweet, preserved fruit on nose. Hints of prune and apricot on palate help hide the alcoholic kick.

1970 (45°): Prune, vanilla and orange peel on the nose. Fat in the mouth, with lovely, soft length.

Perquie (Landes), population 294
Small village just outside of Villeneuve-de-Marsan, most known for the illustrious Château de Ravignan.

Proprietor: Guy Farbos de Luzan ***Name of Property***: Nautina ***Vineyard size***: 5 ha (12.35 acres) ***Other production***: Cows, corn ***Grapes used for armagnac***: Bacco (70%), Folle Blanche (30%) ***Percent of production used for distillation***: 20 % ***Soil***: *Sablo-Limoneux* (Sand) ***Production of armagnac per year***: 10 hl a.p. (5 barrels) ***Distiller***: Dargelos of Eauze ***Distillation***: *Armagnacaise* ***Alcohol degree when leaving the still***: 52° ***Barrels***: Gascon ***Oldest spirit still in cask***: 1972 ***Stock***: 78 hl a.p. (39 barrels) ***Blended armagnacs available***: XO ***Vintages available***: Most between 1972 and 1987 ***Reduction***: No

The Domaine de Nautina lies in the small town of Perquie, near the western limit of the Bas-Armagnac and just a stone's throw from the Château de Ravignan. The property, planted with a high percentage of Bacco on sandy soil, has helped make Nautina a known name amongst the *négociant* houses. Sempé and Janneau once used Nautina's wines as a source for their armagnacs. More recently, Auxil has put several of their vintages on the market.

Their armagnacs are traditional; low-distillation degree, regional oak, no reduction. Farbos de Luzan however, in contrast with some others, does not frequently rotate or top-up barrels. Instead, he lets them mature at their own rate with as little intervention as possible.

Nowadays, distillation does not take place every year; 1997, in fact, will be a wash. Between the year's frost and hail, not many grapes remain. "When a hail storm arrives, all you can do is pray," says Guy solemnly. He raises his head slowly and finishes in true Gascon style: "Pray that it hits the neighbor's property and not yours!"

Nautina's armagnacs tend to display good color and exhibit good balance between fruit and alcohol. Intensity of aromatics varies from year to year, and much of this has to do with quality of wood used from the outset. When Nautina gets it right, however, a profound richness or flavor fills the glass, with hints of prune and almond that persists nicely on the palate.

1991 (from barrel): Deep amber. Lots of new oak along with tremendous aroma and fruit in the mouth. Impressive for its suppleness, even at this age.

XO (an even blend of 1966 that had fallen below 40° and 1977 which brought the degree to 42°. The property's only blend): Medium-body, and without tremendous aromatics. Slight hint of nougat in the mouth. Fairly dry finish.

1980: Flattering nose included a hint of coconut. Nice fat in the mouth with good weight and a final note of almond.

1976: Light nose with a floral hint. Good body in the mouth, yet remains somewhat one-dimensional.

1975: Less aromatic than the 1972 but with pleasing toasted almond notes in the mouth.

1972: Rich nose with a hint of vanilla, coconut and marzipan. Nicely balanced vanilla and creamy oak, along with a dollop of prune. Finishes slightly dry.

Proprietor: The de Ravignan Family ***Name of Property***: Château de Ravignan ***Vineyard size***: 20 ha (50 acres) ***Other production***: Floc de Gascogne, raspberries in armagnac ***Grapes used for armagnac***: Ugni Blanc (50%), Bacco (30%), Folle Blanche (20%) ***Percent of production used for distillation***: 50 % ***Soil***: *Sables fauves, boulbènes* (Iron-rich sand, sand with clay pieces) ***Production of armagnac per year***: 25-30 hl a.p. (12-15 barrels) ***Distiller***: Roumat ***Distillation***: *Armagnacaise* ***Alcohol degree when leaving the still***: 52° ***Barrels***: Gascon and Limousin ***Time in new oak***: 1-2 Years ***Oldest spirit still in cask***: 1971 ***Stock***: 580 hl a.p. (290 barrels) ***Blended armagnacs available***: Armafizz (VSOP) ***Vintages available***: All from 1971 onwards ***Reduction***: No

The Chateau de Ravignan: arguably Les Landes' most beautiful dwelling, certainly home to one of its finest armagnacs.

Castles have graced the property of what is now the Château de Ravignan since the 12th century. The name Ravignan itself comes from the deep ravines surrounding the property that once served as a natural defense. The château was later occupied by feudal barons and partially destroyed during the religious wars of the Sixteenth century. In the mid-17th century, a Louis XIII manor was built on the property. In 1732 vineyards were planted. Around the same time, the property was sold to Jean La Croix who later took the name Ravignan.

Today the estate is managed by Jean-Henry d'Orglandes and his wife Christine along with her brother Baron Louis de Ravignan. The *chai* stands between the impressive château and a 16th century church. It has recently been expanded to house nearly 300 barrels. The area is cool and well-ventilated which helps promote oxidation.

Wood comes from both trees grown on the property and the Limousin forest. Ten to fifteen new barrels are made by Bartholomo each year after being air-dried for seven full years. Such quantities of oak insure good color and tannin dosage. Barrels are racked once a year and monitored frequently.

Ravignan has tremendous respect within the armagnac region. The distillation at a low degree insures lots of fruit, new oak gives wonderful structure, and long aging insures a natural concentration of flavors. A large array of subtle flavors always weave their way in and out of the glass, and their armagnacs normally receive top marks in important French magazines like *Gault-Millau* and *Revue des Vins de France.*

Ravignan also has a commercial product on the market called Armafizz. It is a VSOP level armagnac with a good dose of sugar syrup that has been reduced to 40°. It is meant to be consumed with Schweppes tonic water as a cocktail or *apéritif.*

Grass grows through the sandy soil within the Ravignan chai.

1982 (48°): Still young with regards to aromas. Texture beginning to develop in the mouth with a tad of sweetness on the palate. Fruit evocative of aged rum and spice; vanilla-scented wood is well-integrated. Still with plenty of alcohol—the definition of armagnac as a digestif! Good pure length.

1981 (47°): Hint of smoke on the nose. Chocolate and vanilla notes glide across the creamy texture. Lots of glycerin and a burst of alcohol on the long finish.

1980 (47°): Inviting nose hints at chocolate, prune and apricot-scented fruit. Very fine note of almond. Plenty of wood spice (pepper, clove) weaves its way over the palate. Lovely balance between wood, alcohol and fruit.

1979 (47°): Sweet plum, apricot, vanilla and marzipan on the nose. Pure flavors continue in the mouth with nearly perfect balance. Tremendous length. Excellent armagnac!

1978 (47°): Deep amber. Hint of orange, toffee and licorice on the nose. Nice creamy texture, with some fine spice and lovely nutty notes on the palate. Delicious armagnac.

1976 (47°): Rich aromatics with lots of oak, vanilla, almond and apricot. Soft, fruity mouthfeel with nice balance of alcohol and oak on the finish.

1975 (46°): Amber. Nose shows notes of vanilla, prune and peach. Medium-bodied, with a creamy texture and a finishing note of clove.

1973 (46°): Nicely-balanced nose with creamy vanilla, apricot and a hint of almond. Pure brown sugar note in the mouth meshes beautifully with sweet plum, vanilla and nuts. Extraordinary armagnac.

1972 (46°): Deep amber. Lots of *rancio* on the nose along with hints of coffee, vanilla and apricot. Supple mouthfeel with lots of vanilla/spice/oak notes on the palate. Long finish with hints of spice that recur.

1971 (46°): Deep amber. Sweet prune paste, vanilla and oak on the nose along with a touch of almond. Medium-to full-bodied, with a burst of alcohol on the palate. Smoky oak notes and recurring hints of vanilla on the very long finish.

1969 (45°): Deep amber. Wonderful nose includes hints of coconut, prunes and grilled almond. Round, rich flavors in the mouth with lots of fat. Soft, with spicy oak notes on the dry finish. Wow!

Proprietor: The de Poyferré family ***Name of Property***: Domaine de Jean du Haut ***Vineyard size***: 30 ha (74 acres) ***Other production***: none ***Percent of production used for distillation***: 75% ***Grapes used for armagnac***: Ugni Blanc (100%) ***Soil***: *silico-argileux, sables fauves* (Sand, iron-rich sand) ***Production of armagnac per year***: 30 hl (15 barrels) ***Distillation***: *Armagnacaise* ***Distiller***: Dargelos ***Alcohol degree when leaving the still***: 52° ***Barrels***: Oak from the property ***Time in new oak***: 15 years ***Oldest spirit still in cask***: 1979 ***Stock***: 200 hl a.p. (100 barrels) ***Blended armagnacs available***: Réserve (6 years old, reduced to 40°) ***Vintages available***: 1984, 1983, 1982, 1979 ***Reduction***: No

In 1975, Baron Jacques de Poyferré, owner of Domaine de Jouanda, obtained the Domaine de Jean du Haut and decided to replant its vineyards. Like at Jouanda, Ugni Blanc was the chosen grape, planted on the same *sables fauves* that had produced stunning armagnacs at the property since the beginning of the century.

The first harvest was in 1979 and production has remained extremely traditional. Dargelos lets the spirit drip out of her still at a low 52°, then the spirit rests in oak from the property for as long as possible. Whereas Jouanda's armagnacs are normally released after passing 20 years in wood, Jean du Haut's armagnacs reach the market sooner, perhaps after 10 years of aging. Even at this youthful age, the spirit is not reduced. It relies on the sandy soil, located between Perquie and the tiny hamlet of Gaube, for its impressively supple texture and sublime length.

An excellent commercial blend called *Reserve* is also available at the property.

1984 (47°): Deep aromas include prune, chocolate and coconut milk. Nice balance between fruit and wood and lovely integration of alcohol. Full-body. Excellent value.

1983 (48°): Wonderful balance between alcohol, fruit and tannin. Aromatic nose with a tad mor depth than the 1984. Supple texture, and a relatively long, smooth finish.

1982 (48°): Lighter, floral aromatics with a hint of spice. Light to medium-bodied, and feminine in nature.

1979 (47°): Lots of attack and more noticeable alcohol. Masculine style. Beginning to gain fat in the mouth, and with lots of developing vanilla aromas. Hint of pepper on the long finish.

Ramouzens (Gers), population 193

Located between Eauze and Vic-Fezansac, the soil in Ramouzens contains a high percentage of sand. Its inhabitants are proud of its bell factory, in operation since the last century.

Proprietor: Alain Lalanne ***Name of Property***: Domaine San de Guilhem ***Vineyard size***: 53 ha (131 acres) ***Other production***: VDP Côtes de Gascogne, Floc, sunflowers ***Grapes used for armagnac***: Bacco (80%), Ugni Blanc (20%) ***Percent of production used for distillation***: 15-20 % ***Soil***: *sablo-limoneux* (sand) ***Production of armagnac per year***: 70 hl a.p. (35 barrels) ***Distiller***: Dargelos ***Distillation***: *Armagnacaise* ***Alcohol degree when leaving the still***: 55°-58° ***Barrels***: Gascon, Limousin ***Oldest spirit still in cask***: 1970 ***Chai***: Organized, clean, dirt floor ***Stock***: 200 hl a.p. (100 barrels) ***Blended armagnacs available***: 5 years, 10 years, 20 years ***Vintages available***: 1979 ***Reduction***: With *petites eaux* to 45°

Alain Lalanne first bottled his wine in 1976 and now sells 250,000 to 300,000 bottles a year, making him one of the top sellers in the Côtes de Gascogne. His excellent wines are aromatic and fresh, and often display notes of exotic fruit.

Most of his armagnac production goes toward the 25,000 bottles of floc he sells each year. Between four and seven barrels are always put away to age, however, and all see a bit of new wood. His armagnacs rarely become over-oaked.

Like many successful wine producers, he continues to age armagnac almost for nostalgic reasons. He keeps things simple by reducing his four releases to 45°. Stylistically, Lalanne's armagnacs are medium-bodied, well-balanced, pleasing to drink and certainly compete with the blended releases of most *négociants*. 90% of his production is sold in France.

Ten-Year-Old: Nice aromas of crème brulée and a hint of licorice. Nicely balanced, medium-bodied style.

20-Year-Old: Creamier nose with more lush vanilla. Ten years has given this much more weight in the mouth. Very good length.

1979: Lots of vanilla on the nose. Good penetration of flavor with alcohol slightly more evident. Finishes with a sense of purity.

Réans (Gers), population 267

Réans is a small town that lies on the route between Eauze and Estang. If doing the speed limit, one passes by its few buildings within several seconds. The town's inhabitants know how to have a good time however; their village party at the beginning of September lasts a week and features meals and dances every night.

Proprietor: Yvan and Marc Saint-Martin ***Name of Property***: Domaine de St. Martin ***Vineyard size***: 42 ha (104 acres) ***Other production***: VDP Côtes de Gascogne, white floc, corn ***Percent of production used for distillation***: 15-20% ***Grapes used for armagnac***: Folle Blanche (65%), Bacco (35%) ***Soil***: *boullbènes, sables fauves* (Sand with clay pieces, iron-rich sand) ***Production of armagnac per year***: 50 hl a.p. (25 barrels) ***Distillation***: *Armagnacaise* ***Alcohol degree when leaving the still***: 55° ***Distillers***: Themselves ***Barrels***: Gascon ***Chai:*** Garage next to the house, cement floor, dry ***Stock:*** 120 hl a.p. (60 barrels) ***Oldest spirit still in cask***: 1949 ***Blended armagnacs available***: *Hors d'age (17 years old)* ***Vintages available***: 1962, 1949 ***Reduction***: With *petites eaux* to 42°

The St. Martin family have been distillers in the region for four generations. Their two wood-fueled alambics roam the countryside during the winter months and distill the grape production for over 50 independent producers.

Father and son have two properties they look after; 4 hectares in Mauléon and 2 hectares near the house in Réans. Most of their older armagnacs were made solely with Bacco; in light of the impending legislation regarding that grape's elimination, Folle Blanche has been planted over the past ten years.

Marc is convinced that the armagnacs that come from Mauléon are better than those from Réans. This added quality is due to slightly more sand and slightly more rain, which leads to wine that is more acidic and less alcoholic. Consequently the armagnac is slightly more supple, a touch sweeter and a bit longer. These armagnacs also seem to gain a bit more tannin from the oak and therefore a bit more color. New barrels are not bought frequently at St. Martin, yet often new heads are added to help rejuvenate the barrel and give it newfound life.

The armagnacs of St. Martin offer pleasing aromas, decent depth and extremely good value.

The father and son distilling team of Réans: Marc and Yvan St. Martin

Hors d'age: Amber with gold highlights. Lively fruit aromas with a slight floral hint. Supple finish with a touch of spicy oak.

1962: Rich nose with hints of aged wood and smoke. Prune in the mouth with some smoke on the finish. Supple mouthfeel with a hint of walnut on the finish.

1949: Deep amber. Walnut-scented *rancio* on the nose. Fat texture. Notes of old polished wood and deep caramel in the mouth. Some alcoholic heat on the finish but with very good length.

1976 (49° from barrel): Rich toffee and a hint of almond on the nose. Quite a bit of alcoholic heat in the mouth, along with some spicy oak. Notes of pepper on the finish.

Salles d'Armagnac (Gers), population 111

Salles is home to a 12th Century church. Dartigalongue's distillery is located off the main road, amidst the corn fields and vineyards.

Proprietor: Therese Hébert and Son ***Name of Property***: Château de Salles ***Vineyard size***: 28 ha (69 acres) ***Other production***: Corn, sunflowers ***Grapes used for armagnac***: Bacco (50%), Ugni Blanc (50%) ***Percent of production used for distillation***: 12 % ***Soil***: *Boulbènes* (Sand with clay pieces) ***Production of armagnac per year***: 30 hl a.p. (15 barrels) ***Distiller***: Punsola ***Distillation***: *Armagnacaise* ***Alcohol degree when leaving the still***: 56° ***Barrels***: Gascon and Limousin ***Time in new oak***: 2-3 Years ***Oldest spirit still in cask***: 1959 ***Chai:*** Part of the château; impressive for its size, dirt floor, organized ***Stock***: 220 hl a.p. (110 barrels) ***Blended armagnacs available***: *Hors d'age* ***Vintages available***: 1978, 1985 ***Reduction***: To 43° with distilled water

1987 was the first time Benoit Hébert and his father Michel distilled side by side. After Michel's sudden death in 1992, Benoit continued to distill every year in addition to looking after his father's stock. Today, he continues to be a busy man; father of three, board member at the Cave Coopérative in Nogaro, and farmer of corn and grapes. Recently a new tasting room was built within the château's impressive *chai* and signs have finally been put up on the road marking the domaine's sale of armagnac and floc as well as the property's *gîte*.

Benoit sells most of his grapes to the cave in Nogaro but always sets just over 10% aside which he uses for his own distillation. Mr. Punsola brings his alambic from neighboring Cravencères and lets the *eau de vie* drip out at 56°. From there it goes into a vat to blend for several days before being pumped into barrels; not many are new, but many have been refurbished by local *tonnelier* Dupont.

After about four years, the armagnacs of the same vintage are blended together once again, then placed into older casks. Apart from an airing once every couple of years, they rest in the humid yet well-ventilated *chai* until bottling.

The armagnacs at Salles mature at a very slow rate, mainly due to the fact that aging takes place in barrels that do not offer tremendous amounts of tannic material. The 1979, while displaying lots of fruit, lacked some tannic backbone. Earlier vintages like the 1962, however, were oaked perfectly, somewhat rare with armagnacs of that age.

More recent vintages have seen added investment in new wood, and consequently show more color and chocolate/vanilla notes at an early age.

1985: Amber. Light, balanced nose. Soft in the mouth and very supple. Somewhat dilute, but likable.

1962: Deep amber. Round notes of prune, quince, walnuts and spice. Excellent balance. Very long with extremely well-integrated oak. Impressive armagnac.

St. Justin (Landes) Population 917
Partially-walled village with several good restaurants, a couple of churches, and plenty of surrounding corn fields and vineyards.

Proprietor: Louis Dupuy ***Name of Property***: Lamoulette ***Vineyard size***: 3 ha (7.4 acres) ***Other production***: Pine trees ***Grapes used for armagnac***: Bacco (90%), Ugni Blanc (10%) ***Percent of production used for distillation***: 30 % ***Soil***: *sables fauves* (iron-rich sand) ***Production of armagnac per year***: 14 hl a.p. (7 barrels) ***Distiller***: Was Broustet until 1991. Now Lafontan ***Distillation***: *Armagnacaise* ***Alcohol degree when leaving the still***: 52° ***Barrels***: Gascon ***Time in new oak***: 2 Years ***Oldest spirit still in cask***: 1965 ***Chai:*** Three; dirt floors, humid, organized ***Stock***: 130 hl a.p. (65 barrels) ***Blended armagnacs available***: *Hors d'age* (27-years-old, non-reduced) ***Vintages available***: Most between 1970 and the present ***Reduction***: No

The Dupuy family has distilled at the Lamoulette property since 1871. Its current proprietor, eighty-eight year old Louis Dupuy, has been a producer of armagnac for well over half a century. Unfortunately, for health reasons, Dupuy is now obliged to pass his days and nights in a nearby clinic. His daughter Agnes and son-in-law Roger Beris now look after his affairs and uphold the domaine's level of quality.

Each year they distill four *pièces*; two are sold to *négociants* Lafontan and two are placed in one of their three *chai*, all of which are relatively dry. Once every two years they are aired. Even so, they tend to lose very little alcohol and even after twenty years hover around the 50° mark.

Fortunately lots of rich Bacco fruit helps hide the spirit's heady notes. What one get instead is classic Bas-Armagnac; plenty of color, good attack, lots of prune scents, well-integrated spicy oak notes and excellent length.

Dupuy's two *Hors d'age* are truly *Hors d'age*; one is around 25-years-old, the other around 35-years-old.

1986: Deep amber. Lovely nutty notes with accumulating prune-scented fruit. Medium-body, spicy and long.

1983 (51°): Supple, soft Bacco flavors. Somewhat hot, but still shows lots of fruit in the mouth.

1981: Nice almond-scented *rancio* arriving on the nose. Palate also shows some wood spice. Heat on finish is encircled by fruit.

1978 (49°): Deep nose shows lots of fruit. Nutty nuances on palate with a touch of smoky complexity. Developing fat carries some sweetness. Long finish.

Vrai Hors d'age (various 60's vintages, 49°): Fat in the mouth, with lots of spice. Lots of attack, notes of prune and just a hint of green wood. Very long armagnac.

Vrai Hors d'age (1969-1970 vintages, 49°): Nice attack with slightly younger fruit, lots of pepper and well-integrated oak. Beautiful.

Proprietor: Claude and Philippe Escoubets ***Name of Property***: Soube ***Vineyard size***: 6 ha (15 acres) ***Other production***: corn, honey ***Grapes used for armagnac***: Bacco (50%), Ugni Blanc (50%) ***Percent of production used for distillation***: 15 % ***Soil***: *sables fauves* (iron-rich sand) ***Production of armagnac per year***: 6 hl a.p. (3 barrels) ***Distiller***: Was Broustet. Now Lafontan ***Distillation***: *Armagnacaise* ***Alcohol degree when leaving the still***: 52° ***Barrels***: Limousin, Gascon, Tronçais ***Time in new oak***: 5-6 Years ***Oldest spirit still in cask***: 1970 ***Chai***: dirt floor, well-aired, organized ***Stock***: 64 hl a.p. (32 barrels) ***Blended armagnacs available***: 15-Year-Old ***Vintages available***: 1986, 1983, 1973, 1970 ***Reduction***: No

Claude Escoubets (no relation to René Escoubets from neighboring Labastide) first distilled in 1971 but didn't begin bottling until 1992. He sells most of his armagnac from his attractive property that once belonged to neighbor Louis Dupuy. His *chai* rests in an old barn; inside he has also created a *musée du paysan* displaying farm equipment used over the past couple of centuries.

Like most producers in Les Landes, Escoubets feels the impending disappearance of Bacco is nothing short of sad. "Bacco made the reputation of Armagnac," he claims. "What's more, it only needs to be treated five times a year. Ugni Blanc and Folle Blanche need to be treated 12 times a year. In short, further cost with less result."

Escoubets makes sure that all his armagnacs see some new wood; he also airs his armagnacs once or twice a year, during which time he changes barrels while keeping the same vintage intact. His armagnacs always show good color from an early age, yet at times accumulate too much tannin. When they are not too influenced by oak, his spirits show bright fruit notes with wonderfully-integrated notes of *rancio*.

1985: Deep amber. Lots of fruit and oak on the nose. Flattering vanilla aromas in the mouth, along with a moderately tannic finish.

1980: Lighter citrus and vanilla aromas. Hints of almond and orange in the mouth, with some accumulating fat on the palate. Less influenced by wood yet with a well-integrated vanilla note. Long finish. Excellent armagnac.

1970 (100% Bacco): Notes of prune, licorice and walnut on the nose. Round, supple mouthfeel. Notes of prune and spiced orange in the mouth. Smoky complexity rides along the surface. Very long and very good.

Sarragachies (Gers), population 271

Small village between Riscle and Nogaro that was the home of many Seigneurs during the Middle-Ages. Remnants of wine storage vessels have been found in the local Gallo-Roman villa and the town's 11th Century church has recently been restored.

Proprietor: The Perissé Family ***Name of Property***: Malartic ***Vineyard size***: 25 ha (62 acres) ***Other production***: corn, ducks, wheat, red and white Floc ***Grapes used for armagnac***: Bacco (100%) ***Percent of production used for distillation***: 10% ***Soil***: *boulbènes* (sand with clay pieces) ***Production of armagnac per year***: 10-12 hl a.p. (5-6 barrels) ***Distiller***: St. Martin ***Distillation***: *Armagnacaise* ***Alcohol degree when leaving the still***: 60°-63° ***Barrels***: Regional. Very little new oak ***Oldest spirit still in cask***: 1977 ***Stock***: 120 hl a.p. (60 barrels) ***Chai***: cement floor, dry, organized ***Blended armagnacs available***: No ***Vintages available***: 1982, 1981, 1980, 1979, 1977 ***Reduction***: With *petites eaux* to 40°

Roger Perissé is now in his 70's and shares the property with his son Bernard and grandson Sebastien, a trained enologist. Their 25 hectare property was once planted with nothing but Bacco, but each year a percentage of these old vines is ripped up and replanted with Ugni Blanc. Recent distillations now include 70% Ugni Blanc.

The Perissés sell nearly 70% of their grape production to the Cave Coopérative in Nogaro, another 20% to the Cave de St. Mont, and have St. Martin distill what remains—normally around 5 or 6 barrels a year. New wood is rarely employed nowadays. In fact, no one at the property can remember the last time a new barrel was purchased!

When informed that the armagnacs are reduced from their high distillation temperature to 40° as well, one doesn't expect much from the property's armagnacs.

Yet surprises do indeed happen; all of Malartic's armagnacs displayed good fat, sweet notes of orange and spice and a soft texture. In short, rich, well-crafted, commercial armagnacs.

1981: Amber. Hint of orange and spice. Relatively sweet with vanilla notes. Lacks some attack and finishes sweet. Pleasant.

1979: Amber. Deeper, more flattering aromas of vanilla and a hint of coconut. Sweet in the mouth, with medium to full-body. Extremely soft. Pleasing vanilla notes on the finish.

1977: Hint of orange and vanilla on the nose. Very soft, smooth mouthfeel. Creamy texture, with lots of sweet fat. Some dry tannin creeps in on the finish.

Sorbets (Gers), population 203

This small village, like many surrounding it, was destroyed and rebuilt several times during the vicious battles of the Middle-Ages.

Proprietor: Jean-Jacques Lesgourgues ***Name of Property***: Château de Laubade ***Vineyard size***: 105 ha (260 acres) ***Other production***: oak forest, sunflowers ***Grapes used for armagnac***: Ugni Blanc (50%), Bacco (25%), Colombard (17%), Folle Blanche (13%) ***Percent of production used for distillation***: 100% ***Soil***: *boulbènes, sables fauves* (sand with clay pieces, iron-rich sand) ***Production of armagnac per year***: 900 hl a.p. (450 barrels) ***Distiller***: Château de Laubade themselves ***Distillation***: *Armagnacaise* ***Alcohol degree when leaving the still***: 60° ***Barrels***: Gascon and Limousin ***Oldest spirit still in cask***: 1974 ***Chai***: 9 warehouse-sized structures, organized, cement floors ***Stock***: 5,600 hl a.p. (2,800 barrels) ***Blended armagnacs available***: VSOP, *Hors d'age* ***Vintages available***: All since 1974 ***Reduction***: With *petites eaux* to 40°

Jean-Jacques Lesgourgues is the director of a seed company in Les Landes which has experienced tremendous commercial success. In 1974, he bought the Victorian-influenced Château de Laubade, formerly owned by the French ambassador Noulens. Lesgourgues kept Noulens' mixture of styles (Toulouse brick, Bâsque porches, Normandy wood) and began rebuilding the property which had been somewhat neglected since Noulens death in 1940.

Today the 170 hectare property is covered with 105 hectares of vines along with a large collection of eclectic art pieces which Lesgourgues commissions each year. Mr. Lesgourgues also owns several wineries in Bordeaux which helps fund such expenditures.

All 105 hectares of the property's grapes are distilled, making Laubade the largest armagnac producing property...by far. Their large alambic distills the alcohol to 60°; after six months in wooden vats, it is transferred to oak casks. They are carefully monitored by *Maitre de Chai* Eric

Artigalongue, who trained with Loubère is Labastide before arriving at Laubade in 1984. Barrels are aired and changed as he sees fit.

Laubade is a giant in comparison with other producers in the area and is easily the largest independent seller. Several warehouses hold their impressive stock. They invest tremendous sums each year in new oak, thus reducing their need for additives. Laubade does, however, reduce most of their armagnacs to 40°; for the purists, minimally reduced releases made of purely Bacco, Ugni Blanc and Folle Blanche are available in small quantities.

Armagnacs from before 1974 are also released by Laubade through their *négociant* label. These were bought from small produces within the communes of Cravencères, Mauléon, Panjas, and Bourrouillan. With these, however, the name Laubade always appears on the small label under a large label that simply states "Bas-Armagnac".

Laubade's vintages tend to be rich in aromas and full-bodied on the palate. Also available abroad are two other brands, *Labiette-Castille* (the same as Laubade's VSOP) and *Duc de Loussac* (a younger, more commercial armagnac).

VSOP: Nicely balanced nose with well-integrated alcohol. Notes of vanilla in the mouth with a lightly-spiced finish. Well-made.

Hors d'age: Slightly heavier mouthfeel with some notes of brown sugar. Elegant.

1984 Bacco (45°): Round, rich nose with notes of prune, apricot, vanilla and a hint of almond. Nice fat in the mouth, and with a moderately long finish.

1984 Ugni Blanc (45°): Less aromatic than Bacco, yet finer in the mouth. Not as supple as Bacco and certainly not as fat. Decent length.

1976: Rich vanilla notes on the nose. Spicy, round palate. A hint of green wood. Good length.

1967: Rich nose with lovely almond and walnut-scented *rancio*. Hints of dried apricot in the mouth along with some spice. Round mouthfeel and well-integrated wood on the finish.

1943: Lots of walnut-scented *rancio* and an orange note on the nose. Well-integrated scents of antique wood. Slightly dry finish.

Toujouse (Gers), population 177
Tiny community without a café, but home to an interesting museum dedicated to the history of the Gascon paysan.

Proprietor: Madeleine Capin ***Name of Property***: Tarride ***Vineyard size***: 1.14 ha (2.82 acres) ***Grapes used for armagnac***: Bacco (40%), Ugni Blanc (40%), Colombard (20%) ***Percent of production used for distillation***: 80% ***Soil***: *sables fauves* (iron-rich sand) ***Production of armagnac per year***: 8-10 hl a.p. (4-5 barrels) ***Distillation***: *Armagnacaise* ***Alcohol degree when leaving the still***: 53° ***Distiller***: Jean Capin ***Barrels***: Gascon ***Time in new oak***: 2 years ***Oldest spirit still in cask***: 1965 ***Chai:*** Rustic, dirt floor, organized ***Stock***: 60 hl a.p. (30 barrels) ***Blended armagnacs available***: No ***Vintages available***: 1985, 1982, 1976 ***Reduction***: No

Jean Capin is a retired carpenter whose specialty was doors, windows, furniture and kitchens. Every winter, he helped his father-in-law distill the year's modest harvest. When he took over the property, he also took control of the property's own alambic—a lovely artifact that takes nearly twenty-four hours to produce one barrel of spirit.

Mr. Capin is one of members of the old school of armagnac production. He distills his own spirit at a low temperature, doesn't buy much new wood, and basically lets the spirit rest in barrel until bottling time. His *chai* is humid; therefore he loses alcohol at a more rapid rate than volume. A sign announces the sale of armagnac near his road but he hasn't gotten around to putting up a sign marking his property. Consequently, many of his sales come from people who have already visited the domaine.

The armagnacs of Tarride tend to be light in color and remain fairly young considering their age. They are in no way aggressive and a licorice component is often noticeable on the finish.

Definition of an artisan: Jean Capin distills his tiny production every year in this small capacity armagnac alambic.

1976: Amber with gold highlights. Hint of almond on the nose. Medium-body and soft on the palate. Hint of buttery *rancio*, yet not tremendously concentrated. Good length.

Villeneuve-de-Marsan (Landes), population 2,107

Old bastide town which is capital to the Armagnac Landais. The church dates to the 13th Century, and a number of restaurants, including that of Hélène Darroze, are located in the centre-ville.

Villeneuve-de-Marsan marks the end of the grape growing region and the full-blown beginning of the famous Landes pine forests.

Proprietor: Yves Laburthe ***Name of Property***: Menjot ***Vineyard size***: 2 ha (5 acres) ***Other production***: cows, corn ***Grapes used for armagnac***: Bacco (50%), Ugni Blanc (50%) ***Percent of production used for distillation***: 20% ***Soil***: *sables-fauves* (iron-rich sand) ***Production of armagnac per year***: 8 hl a.p. (4 barrels) ***Distiller***: Roumat ***Distillation***: *Armagnacaise* ***Alcohol degree when leaving the still***: 52° ***Barrels***: Regional ***Time in new oak***: 2-4 years ***Oldest spirit still in cask***: 1969 ***Chai:*** Dirt floor, organized ***Stock***: 18 hl a.p. (9 barrels) ***Blended armagnacs available***: No ***Vintages available***: 1976, 1974, 1969 ***Reduction***: No

Yves Laburthe is nearing the end of his armagnac road. In 1981 he retired; the farm was taken over by his son who in 1991 decided to discontinue production of armagnac altogether. The old Bacco vines were ripped up several years ago and the field is currently vacant; at some point it will probably be planted with corn or something that brings in sure money each year.

The domaine is located along the route between Bordeaux and Lourdes, and a billboard announcing the sale of armagnac tends to bring in lots of tourists en route to the religious Mecca. Even so, Yves claims, sales are sporadic; 15 bottles one day, 5 the next, then three weeks without a sale. Fortunately he has a faithful clientele that return each year to deplete a bit more of his traditional, non-reduced stock. Nowadays he has less than ten barrels left.

Three vintages are for sale at the domaine; a 1976, 1974 and 1969, all which fall between 44° and 47°. They are all medium-bodied, have pleasing nuances of prune and chocolate, and offer attractive, warm length.

1976: Deep amber. Medium-bodied with lots of attack. Without the depth of flavor expected from an armagnac of this age, yet pleasingly spicy. Nice warm length.

1974: Walnut notes on nose. Nice spice on the palate with a hint of chocolate. Lacks some concentration. Finishes with moderate length.

1969: Notes of walnut *rancio* on nose. Lots of prune in the mouth. Medium-bodied on the palate. Slightly dry yet long finish that includes spice and walnuts.

The Ténarèze

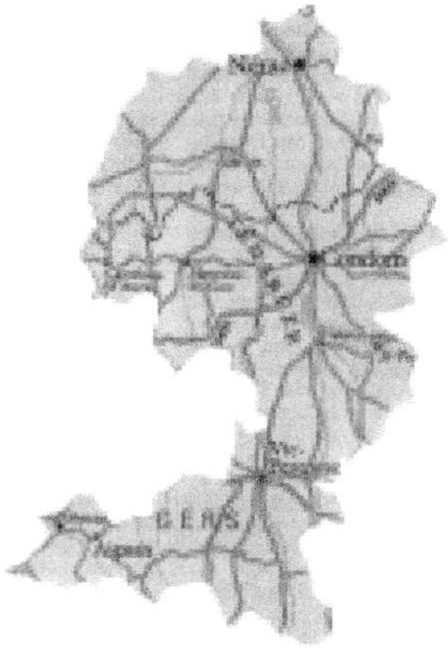

For many years armagnac consumers have held a misconception that the Ténarèze is inferior to the Bas-Armagnac. This has led to a further generalization that anything from the Bas-Armagnac is good and anything from the Ténarèze is mediocre. While it is true that certain zones of the Bas-Armagnac do produce extremely fine *eau de vie*, others produce fairly course spirit. In reality, many armagnacs from the Ténarèze far surpass the quality of many Bas-Armagnacs.

What is the difference, exactly, between the Ténarèze and the Bas-Armagnac? To begin, the soil; in contrast to the top areas of the Bas-Armagnac whose base is sand, the base soil in the Ténarèze tends to be *argilo-calcaire*, or a blend of clay and limestone. This hard soil-base is less acidic than sand and retains water better. Its composite particles are extremely fine and compact—in short, fairly firm and ungiving. In some ways, the resultant spirit tends to reflect these traits in its youth. For this reason, many people describe young Ténarèze as being firm and flat.

In addition, the slightly higher temperatures and less frequent rain in the Ténarèze helps make the region more conducive to *vin de qualité* or quality wine—to be drunk rather than distilled. In contrast to most producers in the *Grand Bas-Armagnac*, many producers in the Ténarèze make highly aromatic and pleasing table wines as well as extremely fruity floc.

Many producers in the Ténarèze have no problem in selling out their production of *Vin de Pays de Côtes de Gascogne*. In fact, so good is that market that many domaines prefer to save their best grapes, once reserved for armagnac, for this table wine. Unfortunately this new priority has ultimately led to a slight decline in quality at a few domaines throughout the Ténerèze.

The grapes used for armagnac is another major difference between the Ténerèze and the Bas-Armagnac. Bacco does not seem to perform as well on hard soils as it does on sandy soil. Consequently the majority of the vineyards in the Ténerèze are planted with Ugni Blanc or Colombard instead of Bacco, as in the Bas-Armagnac.

The evolution curve between the two sub-regions is quite different as well. Whereas a Bas-Armagnac tends to develop fairly rapidly, a Ténarèze normally remains firm until its 10th birthday. At this point it begins to show a bit more fat and depth of flavor. Many Bas-Armagnacs, around their 20th birthday, begin to consume too much wood and become slightly over-oaked. The majority of Ténarèze armagnacs, on the other hand, carry their age a bit better, gaining in complexity with each passing year and continuing to soften perhaps until their 30th or 40th birthdays.

There are a number of domaines in the Ténarèze that produce first-rate armagnac. Understandably, if one is to truly be a *connoisseur* of armagnac, one needs to experience the spirits from both regions.

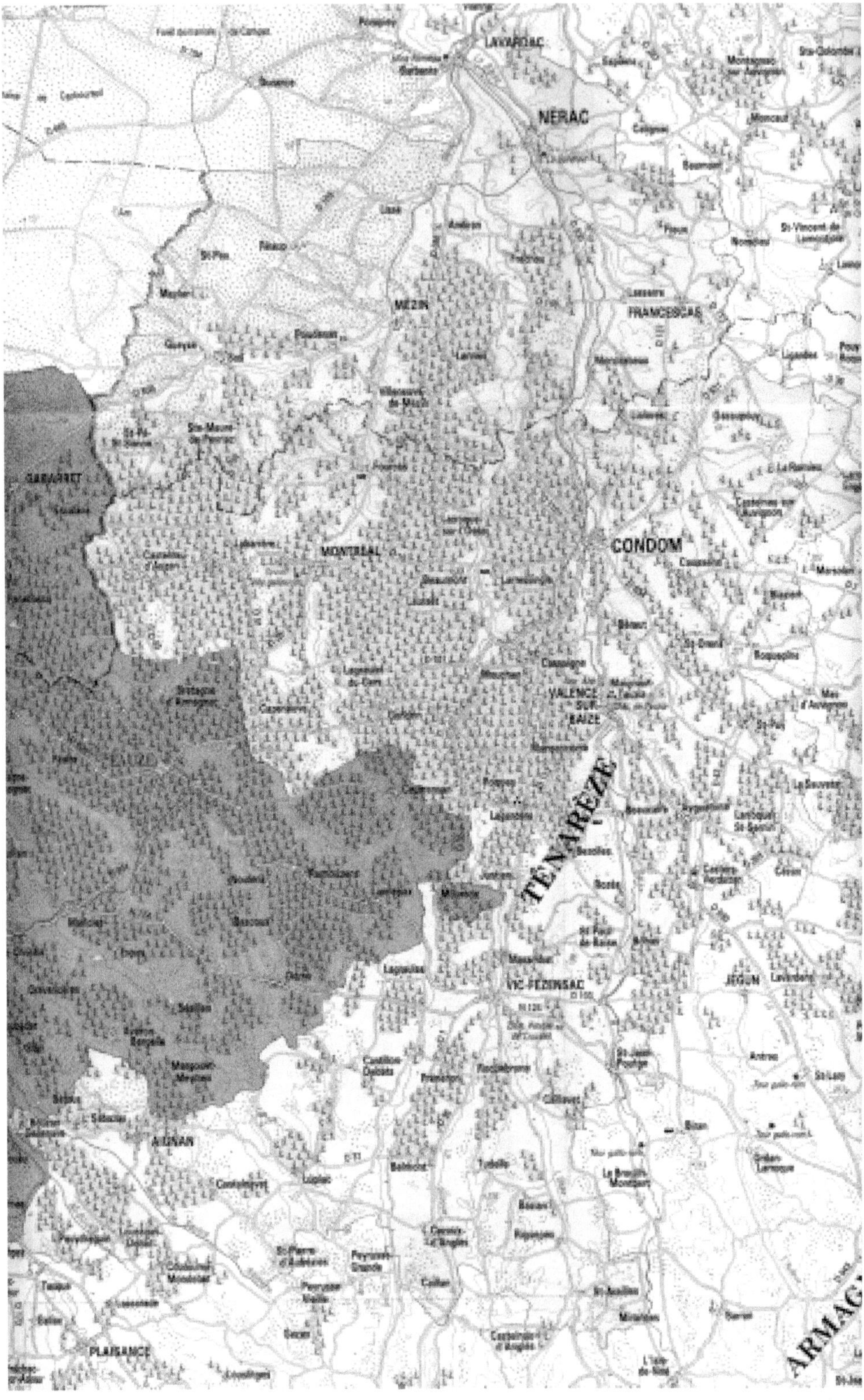

The Ténarèze

Aignan (Gers), population 921

Aignan was the first capital of Armagnac. Nowadays its 940 inhabitants are proud of its eleventh and twelfth century church and its Roman portal. Nearby one can visit the tenth century church at Croute, the gothic church at Sabazan and the chapel in Fromentas.

One of the three coopératives that comprise the Producteurs of Plaimont is in Aignan. Their wines of Cotes de St. Mont, Madiran and the Côtes de Gascogne offer excellent price/quality rapore, and the modern facility is open to the public every day.

Proprietor: Ernest Larrieu ***Name of Property***: Les Escasses ***Vineyard size***: 12 ha (29.65 acres) ***Other production***: wheat, sunflowers ***Grapes used for armagnac***: Bacco (40%), Colombard (40%), Ugni Blanc (20%) ***Soil***: *argilo-calcaire* (clay with a high proportion of limestone) ***Distillation***: *Armagnacaise* ***Alcohol degree when leaving the still***: 52° ***Distiller***: With their personal alambic ***Barrels***: Gascon ***Chai:*** Organized, cement floor, dry ***Oldest spirit still in cask***: 1976 ***Stock***: 50 hl a.p. (25 barrels) ***Vintages available***: 1976 ***Reduction***: No

Ernest and Ema Larrieu at their home near Aignan.

Ernest Larrieu has not distilled armagnac for over 20 years. Understandable, considering that Larrieu was born in 1903, making him the oldest producer that still sells armagnac in bottle. His wife Ema, a spry 89, continues to take care of the business side of things. At their house, located just outside Aignan near the Fromentas chapel, one finds their alambic tucked away in a corner of the garage and, in a small *chai* next door, the 20 barrels of stock that remain.

The 1976 vintage was placed into 25-year-old barrels after it was distilled, which accounts for its light hue and absence of domineering oak notes. The dry conditions within his *chai* have kept the alcohol level at 48°. Larrieu's armagnacs are traditional in style and display a sense of naturalness.

The Aignan coopérative also markets a white Côtes de Gascogne under the *Domaine des Escasses* label. It is made from mostly Colombard and displays lots of forward fruit.

1976 (48°): Light amber. Hints of mushroom-scented oak on nose. Lots of attack, medium-bodied, and with hints of wood spice. Fairly hot finish.

Ayguetinte (Gers), population 162

The name of this small town arose after a particularly bloody battle during the Barbarian invasions when the river running through the town was literally tainted with blood or, in patois, "aigo tinto".

Proprietor: The Maestrojuan family ***Name of Property***: Domaine Bordeneuve-Entras ***Vineyard size***: 32 ha (79 acres) ***Other production***: Wheat, Sunflowers, VDP Côtes de Gascogne, Floc ***Grapes used for armagnac***: Ugni Blanc (50%), Colombard (50%) ***Percent of production used for distillation***: 20 % ***Soil***: *argilo-calcaires* (clay with a high proportion of limestone) ***Production of armagnac per year***: 70-80 hl a.p. (35-40 barrels) ***Distiller***: Gimet ***Distillation***: *Armagnacaise* ***Alcohol degree when leaving the still***: 60°-61° ***Barrels***: Center of France ***Chai***: Organized, cement floor, dry ***Oldest spirit still in cask***: 1987 ***Stock***: 140 hl a.p (70 barrels) ***Blended armagnacs available***: 10-Year-Old ***Vintages available***: No ***Reduction***: Demineralized water to 50°

In the late-sixties, Michel Maestrojuan, the son of a Spanish Basque refugee and French mother, abandoned his medical studies and returned to his hometown of Beaucaire to work on the family farm *Bordeneuve*. In 1981, he bought a property a couple of miles away in Ayguetinte called Entras. A mixture of white and red vines were planted on the property and when they bore useable fruit several years later, Bordeneuve-Entras was created.

In addition to bottling wine, floc and armagnac, the Maestrojuan's also produce a vatted table wine which they sell to locals. During my visit, a half dozen people came to the spacious, clean, and renovated property with four gallon jugs to search for their weekly *pinard* or everyday wine. It was encouraging to see such activity, as most Gascon farms seem commercially dormant nowadays. Lying on the route between the Auch Cathedral and The Abbaye de Flaran—the two biggest tourist attractions in the Gers—also helps sales. In fact, several thousand people stop every year at the picturesque property overlooking the rolling countryside of the Gers.

Profits from the domaine's critically acclaimed wines and floc have enabled the Maestrojuan's to invest in new wood every year for their armagnacs. This enables them to get plenty of natural color and tannin. Distillation is by Gimet to a relatively high 60°, and the armagnacs are reduced gradually to 50°. Maestrojuan claims that this strong proof helps guard the typicity of a *vrai* armagnac.

The Maestrojuan's market their oldest armagnac, currently the 1987, as a ten-year-old called *Vieille Réserve*. Unfortunately, they haven't set barrels of older vintages aside, making it impossible to monitor the domaine's aging potential.

Vieille Réserve: Amber with gold highlights. Nice aromatics include a hint of nougat. Medium bodied in the mouth, with a sense of force. Even at 50°, the alcohol is neither overwhelming nor dry. Finishes with moderate length.

Calignac (Lot et Garonne), population 481

Blink and you'll miss it: Calignac lies about five miles outside Nérac along the route to Agen.

Proprietor: The Lascombes Family ***Name of Property***: Domaine de la Lapeyrade ***Vineyard size***: 5 ha (12.35 acres) ***Other production***: sunflowers, wheat, corn, grapes for Buzet wine ***Grapes used for armagnac***: Ugni Blanc (100%) ***Soil***: *boulbènes, argilo-calcaires* (sand with clay pieces, clay with a high proportion of limestone) ***Production of armagnac per year***: 15 hl a.p. (7-8 barrels) ***Distiller***: Michalouski ***Distillation***: *Armagnacaise* ***Alcohol degree when leaving the still***: 53° ***Barrels***: Variable, although each vintage sees some new oak ***Chai:*** Organized, cement floor, humid ***Oldest spirit still in cask***: 1968 ***Stock***: 200 hl a.p. (100 barrels) ***Blended armagnacs available***: 10-year-old (1986, 15-year-old, 1981) ***Vintages available***: From 1968, on demand ***Reduction***: With demineralized water to 45°

We talk about drawing a fine line when we talk about the property of the Lascombes family. Grapes are planted on both sides of the road running between Nérac and Agen; one side has Merlot and Cabernet Franc—destined for the coopérative in Buzet. If they were planted on the other side, they would be considered simply *vin de pays*. The East side is planted in Ugni Blanc—for Ténarèze. Distilled grapes from the west side of the road would be Haut-Armagnac. The Lascombes' know which side of the street to plant their grapes on...

Mr. Lascombes has a relatively small production yet, over the past 25 years, he has been putting away three or four casks per year. Being so close to the Haut-Armagnac, I didn't expect much with regards to quality. But when I tasted his 10 and 15-year-olds, I was pleasantly surprised. With both, there was lots of fruit, acceptable complexity and some length. When I viewed Mr. Lascombe's *chai*, I was immensely impressed. Modern, double rows of new barrels on cement tiers with each year clearly marked—order normally seen only in *négociant* houses!

Mr. Lascombes, a farmer in his fifties, has barrels of various sizes; some are 400 liters, others 300 and others 220. A good deal of his stock used to be sold to Janneau; since the mid-eighties, however, his only relationship with the *négociant* is to buy used barrels. This, in addition to the 1 or 2 new *pièce* he buys each year, insures that his product gets a good dose of tannin and color.

Lascombes' armagnacs tend to reflect their Ténarèze origins; they are firm, yet tend to gain fat after the twelve-year mark. They are not incredibly profound, yet they do contain a wonderful balance between alcohol, fruit and tannin coupled with a lovely sense of power and grace.

1986: Light color. Rich nose hints at soft fruit. Soft fruit confirmed in the mouth. Good length with a hint of licorice.

1981: Amber. Fairly fat, soft mouthfeel with hints of spice. Decent depth and length for its age. Nice round mouthfeel with a hint of spice on the finish. Pleasing, natural feel with the impression that fat waits around the corner. Hint of orange marmalade on the finish.

1978 (43.8°): Best of the lot. Excellent balance of wood, fruit and alcohol. Nice power, with a hint of complexity (almond). Muscular, but with some flesh. Nice Ténarèze.

1976: Hint of almond on the nose. Good pure flavor with a somewhat spicy finish. Still young.

1973: Deep color. Nice deep vanilla notes on the nose. Lots of vanilla in the mouth with some fat. Slightly overoaked; fortunately the oak is of quality.

1970: Deep amber. Oak on nose with a hint of walnut. Slightly too much oak. Some nice fruit notes manage to peak through, however.

Castelnau d'Auzan (Gers), population 1,062

Situated at the intersection of three départements (Gers, Landes and Lot et Garonne), Castelnau, meaning new castle in the land of Eauze, was rebuilt during the middle ages. Remains of an ancient Roman community are preserved in nearby Pouchégu. The town center possesses a number of interesting churches, including St. Jean Baptiste de Beziey, built at the end of the Middle Ages, Rioupeyroux, Notre Dame de Pibèque, and the neo-gothic Saint-Martin. The vineyards surrounding the town have always been important as a source of fruit to many négociants. The largest foie gras factory in the northern Gers lies on the outskirts of town.

Proprietor: Pierre Laporte ***Name of Property***: Domaine de Pouchegu ***Vineyard size***: 14 ha (34.5 acres) ***Other production***: corn, sunflowers, floc ***Grapes used for armagnac***: Bacco (100%) ***Percent of production used for distillation***: 15% ***Soil***: *sables fauves, boulbènes (iron-rich sand, sand with clay pieces)* ***Production of armagnac per year***: 12-15 hl a.p. (6-8 barrels) ***Distillation***: *Armagnacaise* ***Alcohol degree when leaving the still***: 54° ***Distiller***: Michalouski ***Barrels***: Limousin ***Chai***: Organized, cement floor, dry ***Oldest spirit still in cask***: 1973 ***Blended armagnacs available***: No ***Vintages available***: 1972, 1974, 1979 ***Reduction***: No ***Stock***: 190 hl a.p. (95 barrels)

The Domaine de Pouchegu has produced armagnac for over 100 years. The small, attractive, family-run property lies along the route between Castelnau and Eauze. It is a pleasing place to visit, with a nice view of the countryside along with a relatively modern *chai* and tasting room.

Pierre Laporte (left) states that an armagnac shouldn't be released before its tenth birthday. Younger than that and it is really just a brandy. New oak is essential for ultimate quality, he reckons, and he makes sure all his armagnacs are in some way influenced by freshly-constructed barrels. No reduction takes place, and the armagnacs are marketed at a relatively high 48°. One doesn't sense this alcohol, however, as it is normally submerged beneath plenty of fruit.

Laporte frequently wins competitions and his armagnacs are among the best in the Ténarèze. They always show rich fruit and subtle spice, and nicely blend material with finesse. As the property lies just on the border of the Ténarèze and the Bas-Armagnac, it is as natural a blend of both regions as one can get.

1979 (48°): Flattering nose with lots of rich vanilla cream and toasted coconut on nose. Good fruit in the mouth with a soft, lush texture. Hint of cocoa in the mouth. Smooth finish hides the alcohol.

1974 (48°): Amber. Muted floral notes on nose. Less fat on palate than some vintages. Notes of chocolate and orange. Lots of attack without much fat. Less impressive than other vintages.

1972 (48°): Amber. Hints of butterscotch and flowers on the nose. Medium-bodied, with some fat and natural sweetness. Very well-integrated oak. Lots of firm, alcoholic attack. Good length. Undoubtedly rests a Ténarèze.

1962 (46°): Sweet nose includes hints of quince, butter, aged vanilla, and a floral note. Pleasant *rancio*. Some antique oak notes continue on the long finish.

Caussens (Gers), population 557

Caussens is a mid-sized village located along the rolling roads between Condom and Lectoure.

Proprietor: Chambre d'Agriculture du Gers ***Name of Property***: Château de Mons ***Vineyard size***: 30 ha (74 acres) ***Other production***: Sunflowers, Wheat, VDP, Floc ***Grapes used for armagnac***: Ugni Blanc (95%), Folle Blance (5%) ***Percent of production used for distillation***: 17% ***Soil***: *boulbènes, argilo-calcaire* (sand with clay pieces, clay with limestone pieces) ***Production of armagnac per year***: 30 hl a.p. (15 barrels) ***Distiller***: Gironi ***Distillation***: *Armagnacaise* ***Alcohol degree when leaving the still***: 60° ***Barrels***: Allier and Limousin ***Chai***: Organized, cement floor, dry ***Oldest spirit still in cask***: 1978 ***Stock***: 200 hl a.p. (100 barrels) ***Blended armagnacs available***: 8, 12, and 20-year-old ***Vintages available***: 1965, 1969, 1973, 1979 ***Reduction***: With *petites eaux* to 40°

The Château de Mons is an experimental domaine owned by the Agricultural Department of the Gers. Recent experimentation includes the distilling of the region's lost grapes; Jurançon Blanc, Clairette, Plainte de Grèce, and Meslier as well as armagnacs aged in 200 liter barrels made of American oak.

The château's armagnacs are distilled at Gironi's distillery in Mouchan to a relatively high 60°. Director Michel Pourquet then reduces immediately to 52° with *petites eaux*, claiming that this helps eliminate some of the unpleasant aromas caused by low-degree distillation. The *3 Etoiles* and the 8-year-old are aged in Allier oak with a heavy toast—which helps give them lots of color and vanilla. The armagnacs meant for the long term are aged in Limousin with a lighter toast. The barrels are aired once a year and gradually brought down to 40°.

Over the past fifteen years, Pourquet has seen the château's production fluctuates greatly, basically due to market demand. "It's a shame we practice polyculture here," he states, "because if something isn't selling, we can always concentrate on another crop. We've let the armagnac market fall because other markets around it have grown. Whatever doesn't sell for the moment is simply put on the back-burner."

The Château de Mons' armagnacs tend to be full-bodied, with lots of flavor, a heavy mouthfeel, and well-integrated wood. They deliver lots of bang for the buck, but remain somewhat monolithic and lacks some finesse. In short, they are good value, commercial armagnacs.

8-year-old: Fairly rich nose hints at toffee and nougat. Not deep, but fairly rich VSOP- level armagnac. Decent sweetness on the palate with a moderately-long finish.

12-year-old: Hint of brown sugar on the nose. Medium to full-bodied and weighty on the palate. Correct.

20-year-old: Not intensely aromatic but with a smooth texture. No evidence of *rancio* for such age. Nice sweetness on the palate along with a hint of orange on the finish.

1979: Amber. Light, floral aromatics. More attack and more penetrating on the palate than the blends. Lacks some depth, however, and shows some heat on the finish.

Cazeneuve (Gers), population 139

Tiny village located on the border of the Ténarèze and the Bas-Armagnac. Cazeneuve is most famous for the Tour de la Mothe, which once divided two other regions, that of the Agenais and the English. The tower originally belonged to the Pardaillan family, one of whom was later a companion of Jeanne de Arc.

Proprietor: Veuve Hector Théaux and R. Filartigue ***Name of Property***: Domaine de Sans ***Vineyard size***: 25 ha (61.75 acres) ***Other production***: sunflowers, wheat, corn, cows, wine ***Grapes used for armagnac***: Colombard 40%, Ugni Blanc 40%, Bacco 20% ***Percent of production used for distillation***: 5% ***Soil***: *argilo-calcaires, sables* (clay with limestone pieces and sand) ***Production of armagnac per year***: 5-10 hl (2-5 barrels) ***Distillation***: *Armagnacaise* **Alcohol degree when *leaving the still***: 54°. Earlier vintages at 52° ***Distiller***: Gimet ***Barrels***: Early vintages from the property. Most recent from Allier. ***Chai:*** Rustic, dirt floor, humid ***Oldest spirit still in cask***: 1932 ***Blended armagnacs available***: No ***Stock***: 80 hl a.p. (40 barrels) ***Vintages available***:1935, 1941, 1943, 1945, 1946, 1962, 1968, 1969, 1974, 1975 ***Reduction***: No

The chai is the office: Jacques Théaux amidst bills, correspondence and barrels of 50- year-old armagnacs.

Visiting the Théaux property is like taking a step back in time. Located off a small backroad in the nearly non-existent village of Cazeneuve, the family house sits below grapevines and is constructed with exposed beams of wood. The *chai* is located within a larger barn, which one enters after climbing a few steep steps.

The Théaux family has lived here for nearly 150 years. Hector, well-known and liked farmer and the first to sell the domaine's armagnac, died in 1995. One of his best customers was André Daguin, who used many older Théaux vintages for his *négociant* label.

Today Hector's son Jacques runs the business. One gets the impression when entering the *chai* that very little has changed since the domaine's inception. Jacques' desk sits amidst mushroom-covered barrels, full of handwritten notes and tattered pieces of paper. The area is dimly lit with several weak lightbulbs hanging overhead. A hand pump, used for the occasional racking of barrels, lies atop some rusted metal shelves. The floor is uneven; hardened dirt, packed down by generations of footsteps. Even display bottles have cobwebs running between them. The area rarely sees natural light. This is a *chai* in its most rustic form.

Théaux's armagnacs are basically left on their own to age. "A great Ténarèze needs between twenty and forty years," states Théaux. "One just has to have the patience."

New wood is very rarely employed; consequently the armagnacs gain color , vanilla and spice at an incredibly slow rate. A 1988, after nine years in barrel, still had a color and floral youthfulness that most armagnacs possess after one year in new oak.

For this reason, the older vintages are not dominated by secondary aromas; there is always lots of fruit below the almond-scented *rancio*. The wood is commonly well-integrated and the color normally a pure deep amber. Forty-year-old armagnacs could pass for half that. Fifty-year-old armagnacs still show some signs of youthfulness. These are armagnacs that defy their age!

Outside the *chai*, the Gers was experiencing one of the its common Spring thunderstorms. Inside, however, as Jacques siphoned numerous samples from his great stock of Ténarèze, the rain seemed very far away.

1969: Amber with gold highlights. Lots of vanilla and almond on the nose. A little more alcohol showing makes it slightly dry, but the fruit ultimately wins out. Lightly-spiced finish and excellent length. Enjoyable armagnac.

1962: Lovely amber color. Almond *rancio* on nose. Vanilla and coconut in the mouth with just a hint of wood dryness. Very supple finish.

1946: Vanilla cream and a hint of coconut on the nose. Gentle spice, creamy and exotic in the mouth with a lush, fat texture. Just a touch of woodsmoke on the finish. Excellent balance. Defies its age!

1946 (from a different barrel made of wood from the property): Amber with red highlights. Slightly more attack, noticeable alcohol and tannin. In short, a tighter structure than the other barrel.

1943: Deep amber with red highlights. Almond on the nose. Jammy orange and dried plum in the mouth. Almond paste on the finish.

1941: Deep amber with red highlights. Lovely walnut *rancio* with a deep nose that hints at prune. Very round in the mouth with just a hint of smoke and pepper. Good length.

1935: Deep amber with red highlights. Almond-scented *rancio* and pepper on the nose. Apricot, peach pit and prune in the mouth. Touch of wood smoke on the finish.

1932: Vanilla and apricot on the nose. Wood and alcohol are well-integrated. Lively in the mouth. Hint of smoke and herbs on the finish add complexity.

Condom (Gers), population 7,717

Condom is the second largest community in the Armagnac region behind Auch. It is built around the Baise River which, when navigable, was an important thoroughfare for armagnacs making their way toward Bordeaux. The main touristic sight of the village is the immense St. Pierre Cathedral which dates to the fifteenth century. Most impressive are its gothic cloister and pipe organ. The scenic 15th century walled village of Larressingle lies a few miles outside of town.

Today a number of armagnac négociant houses are located in Condom (Larressingle, Ryst-Dupeyron, Janneau) and readily accept visitors. The town's humorous name in English means nothing to the French: rather than condom, capote is their name for prophylactic.

Proprietor: François Faget ***Name of Property***: Château de Pomès-Péberère ***Vineyard size***: 40 ha (99 acres) ***Other production***: VDP Côtes de Gascogne, floc ***Grapes used for armagnac***: Ugni Blanc (90%), Bacco (10%) ***Percent of production used for distillation***: 25% ***Soil***: *argilo-calcaires* (clay with a high proportion of limestone) ***Production of armagnac per year***: 100 hl a.p. (50 barrels) ***Distillation***: *Armagnacaise* ***Distiller***: Mr. Faget himself ***Alcohol degree when leaving the still***: 60° ***Barrels***: Gascon ***Chai:*** Organized, cement floor, dry ***Oldest spirit still in cask***: 1964 ***Stock***: 900 hl a.p. (450 barrels) ***Blended armagnacs available***: *VSOP* (7 years), *Napoléon* (10 years), *Hors d'age* (20 years old) ***Reduction***: With *petites eaux* to 42° ***Vintages available***: 1941, 1950, 1964, 1965, 1966. Released at 42°

François is the fourth generation Faget to produce wine at the Château de Pomès-Péberère, located on the route between Fourcès and Condom. His father Louis invented a pruning system known as the Faget system, which helps allow for a vine's optimum exposure to the sun. François, in addition to making excellent dry white wine, floc, and armagnac, has also served as president of the BNIA in Eauze.

Faget's stock, housed in an organized, well-aired *chai,* is considerable. Four lines of barrels are each stacked four high. Faget distills at a relatively high 60° with an alambic he owns. The spirit begins its life in a large *tonneau*, where it is immediately reduced by about five degrees. It then goes into relatively new barrels where it ages naturally. Every few years the armagnacs are reduced by a couple more degrees, and they all reach the market at 42°.

Faget is one of the few producers in the Condom canton with a wide array of vintages available. All are medium to full-bodied and with lots of oak. His *Napoléon* and *Hors d'age* are excellent, partially because their ages far surpass the minimum requirements. These are always made with a blend of four or five vintages and account for about 70% of his armagnac sales.

As a side note, his white Côtes de Gascogne is also extremely pleasing; bursting with fruit reminiscent of white peach, melon and orange, and without the aggressive herbaceousness often found in other white wines from the region.

10 Year Old: Amber. Hints of well-integrated oak in the mouth. Relatively sweet, with a hint of almond. Supple, commercial, and well-crafted Ténarèze.

20 Year Old: Walnut and licorice on the nose. Nice sweetness on the palate with some accumulating fat. Moderate length.

1966: Nice aromatics hint at walnut and orange. Lots of fat in the mouth, yet manages to retain some elegance. Feminine style Ténarèze.

1965: Walnut and maple on the nose. Lots of oak on palate which ultimately overwhelms fruit.

1964: Rich, creamy nose includes walnut and prune. Nice balance on palate, with excellent attack, rich mouthfeel, and admirable length. Hint of smoke creeps in on the finish.

1961: Elevated level of oak on the nose along with noticeable levels of alcohol. Dry, oaky finish.

1950: Lots of oak and smoke in the mouth. Some fat on the palate, but ultimately suffocated by dry oak.

1941: Admirable amounts of fruit remain in this full-bodied, vanilla and oak-scented, pre-war armagnac. Although it finishes slightly dry, it is impressive for its age.

Proprietor: Société Magnol ***Name of Property***: Domaine de la Brette ***Vineyard size***: 9 ha (22 acres) ***Other production***: sunflowers, wheat, soy beans, tourism ***Grapes used for armagnac***: Ugni Blanc (100%) ***Percent of production used for distillation***: 20 % ***Soil***: *argilo-calcaire* (clay with a high proportion of limestone) ***Production of armagnac per year***: 20 hl a.p. (10 barrels) ***Distiller***: Michalouski ***Distillation***: *Armagnacaise* ***Alcohol degree when leaving the still***: 55° ***Barrels***: 30-40% new/year, some from the property ***Chai:*** Organized, cement floors, humid ***Oldest spirit still in cask***: 1963 ***Stock***: 900 hl a.p. (450 barrels) ***Blended armagnacs available***: *Hors d'age* (15-17 years old) ***Vintages available***: 1970, 1969, 1966, 1964 ***Reduction***: With *petites eaux* to 42°

The Magnol family, inventors of electrical meters used throughout Europe, bought this picturesque property in 1961 and began producing armagnac in 1963. Armagnac was distilled every year and "put away for a rainy day". In 1993, Mr. Magnol's daughter, Monique, and her husband, Johannes Gerzabek, were given the opportunity to take over the property. Monique, a former French professor, and Johannes, a former flight coordinator, had lived in Vienna with their three children. Given the possibility of full-time country life, the family decided to relocate to Condom and run the domaine. In addition, they constructed a gîte that now includes several cabins and rooms spaced along the scenic property.

The Austrian Gerzabek has learned his trade quickly. He buys new wood every year, airs his younger barrels every twelve months, and regularly monitors their progress. Several *chai* house his considerable stock. He leaves the barrels at their natural degree until about a year before they are to be bottled. Then he gradually reduces their degree with *petites eaux*, giving the blend adequate time to become a whole.

The armagnacs of Magnol always show good attack and good depth. Some armagnacs, nearly a quarter century old, still need time, an occurance typical with producers in the Ténarèze. "I think the spirits from the Bas-Armagnac develop quickly, yet also disintegrate quickly," states Gerzabek. "In contrast, those from here develop slowly yet also fall apart at a slower rate."

One often hears that an armagnac evokes the aroma of violets. Although many producers might claim that their armagnacs contain this nuance, the fact is that this ethereal scent is extremely rare. Alas, with both the 1964 and the extremely limited 1963, the odor of wild violets did indeed arise, dance around in the glass, and finally leave, quickly replaced by rich odors of vanilla and nuts. Bravo!

Hors d'age: Light nose with a floral hint. Lots of oak in the mouth. Hint of sweetness on the finish.

1971: Lots of wood notes on nose. Good attack, along with some developing fat in the mouth.

1964: Light floral note on the nose (violet). Not quite as rich in the mouth as expected, yet with an intriguing creamy note. Hints of oak on the finish.

1963: Deep amber with red highlights. Deep aromas with a highlight of violet. Additional aroma of almond and vanilla. Nice fat in the mouth with a creamy coconut nuance. Hint of smoke on the finish. Flattering yet complex; extremely interesting Ténarèze.

Fourcès (Gers), population 324

This often photographed village possesses a rare circular bastide that dates back to the 13th century. In 1388, Charles VII destroyed the original castle. It was replaced in the 15th century by a castle that now houses a hotel and restaurant. During the last weekend of April, Fourcès is host to a flower festival that is well-known throughout the region.

Proprietor: Yves Duflo ***Name of Property***: Domaine du Carpoulet ***Vineyard size***: 42 ha (104 acres) ***Other production***: None ***Grapes***: Ugni Blanc (80 %), Colombard (20%) ***Percent of production used for distillation***: 20% ***Soil***: boulbènes (sand with clay pieces) ***Production of armagnac per year***: 60 hl a.p. (30 barrels) ***Distiller***: Mme. Dargelos ***Distillation***: *Armagnacaise* ***Alcohol degree when leaving the still***: 53° ***Chai***: Modern, cement floor, dry ***Barrels***: Limousin, Gascon ***Oldest spirit still in cask***: 1974 ***Stock***: 2,000 hl a.p. (1,000 barrels) ***Blended armagnacs available***: VO, VSOP, Napoléon, Vieille Réserve, *Hors d'age* ***Vintages available***: ***Reduction***: With *petites eaux* to 40°

The Domaine du Carpoulet is an attractive property located just outside the charming town of Fourcès. Its proprietor, Yves Duflo, divides his time between the Gers and Guadeloupe, where he has several other business interests. Since 1974, he has distilled a good portion of his harvest and his stock now consists of nearly 1,000 barrels. In fact, his *chai* can no longer contain his holdings and consequently he has not recently distilled.

The quality of armagnacs at Carpoulet is excellent. The boulbènes soil yields a softer spirit than many in the area, and every spirit sees new wood. Some of the unreduced vintages, while still containing powerful alcohol levels, show good depth of flavor and excellent length.

A full line of blended armagnacs are available which rival those of many *négociant* houses.

Gondrin (Gers), population 1,042

This mid-size town, located between Condom and Eauze, lies on the route of Saint Jean de Compostelle. Most locals visit Gondrin during the summer because of its large municipal swimming pool and lake.

Proprietor: Janine and Gilles Baumann ***Name of Property***: Domaine des Cassagnoles ***Vineyard size***: 65 ha (161 acres) ***Other production***: None ***Grapes used for armagnac***: Ugni Blanc (100%) ***Percent of production used for distillation***: 10-15% ***Soil***: *argilo-calcaires* (clay with a high proportion of limestone) ***Production of armagnac per year***: 50-80 hl a.p. (25-40 barrels) ***Distiller***: Gironi ***Distillation***: *Armagnacaise* ***Alcohol degree when leaving the still***: 58-62° ***Barrels***: Gascon, Vosges, Limousin ***Chai:*** Organized, cement and dirt floor, humid ***Oldest spirit still in cask***: 1980 ***Stock***: 250 hl a.p. (125 barrels) ***Blended armagnacs available***: 3 Year Old, 10 Year Old, 15 Year Old ***Vintages available***: No ***Reduction***: To 42° with *petites eaux*

The Domaine de Cassagnoles is one of the leading producers of white Côtes de Gascogne wines. They sell well over half-a-million bottles per year, and about 25,000 go to the United States. The white wine, always based around Colombard but with an increasing percentage of Gros Manseng, is exuberantly fruity and clean. While Tariquet is still the reference within the Côtes de Gascogne, Cassagnoles is vying for the crown.

Gilles Baumann is originally from Alsace and his wife Janine is from nearby Montréal-du-Gers. They first distilled armagnac in 1974 and have since built up stock to about 125 barrels. Ugni Blanc is the only grape employed, and distillation (at a relatively high degree) takes place at Gironi's distillery in nearby Mouchan. A number of different woods are employed for the aging; at times regional, at times Limousin, and at times in used wine barrels from Vosges. The armagnac vintages remain separate until a year or so before the bottling, at which time they are assembled. Reduction with *petites eaux* takes place during various stages along the way. Their three releases normally reach the market between 43° and 40°.

The armagnacs from Cassagnoles are not as exciting as their wine, yet they are commercially correct and sell fairly well (5000-6000 bottles per year). In fact, they have recently had to discontinue their *5 Year Old* because not enough stock existed to cover its demand. A younger *3 Etoiles* has since taken its place.

Their market is undoubtedly aided by their wine success, as often armagnac cases are tacked on to an existing wine order. Their attractive bottles also attract the consumer who is looking for a special gift.

5 Year Old: Not tremendously aromatic. Hint of toffee in the mouth, without tremendous depth. Commercially correct.

10 Year Old: A bit more depth, although still fairly ungiving. Slight note of almond on the finish.

15 Year Old: Somewhat muted aromas. Touch of almond brittle in the mouth along with a hint of fat. Just now beginning to soften.

Proprietor: Corentin Mao ***Name of Property***: Marquisat ***Vineyard size***: 50 ha (124 acres) ***Other production***: white wine, white floc ***Percent of production used for distillation***: 30% ***Grapes used for armagnac***: 60% Ugni Blanc (30-40 years old), 40% Colombard (15-20 years old) ***Soil***: sables, boulbènes (sand, sand with clay pieces) ***Production of armagnac per year***: 50 hl a.p. (25 barrels) ***Distillation***: *Armagnacaise* ***Distiller***: Lassalle of Gondrin (owned by Mr. Mao's son, Jean-Bernard) ***Alcohol degree when leaving the still***: 58-62° ***Barrels***: Gascon ***Chai***: Organized, cement floor, dry ***Oldest spirit still in cask***: 1968 ***Stock***: 200 hl a.p. (100 barrels) ***Reduction***: Less than one degree, and only to simplify labeling ***Blended armagnacs available***: *Hors d'age* (14 years old) ***Vintages available***: 1972, 1977, 1979

When one thinks of Gascon names, one doesn't think of Mao. Indeed, the name Mao is of *Breton* orgin, but the family has resided just outside of Gondrin for four generations. In 1953, Corentin Mao (left) sold his last cow and decided to concentrate solely on vines. He sold his wine *en vrac* until 1969 when he decided to bottle himself. Today his son Jean-Bernard runs the Lassalle distillery nearby.

According to Corentin, the Ténarèze produces the best armagnac. "Bas-Armagnac is fruity the first five years, but after that it's a bit flat. Here we start hard, but get rounder with age. It's a question of *terroir*."

Corentin (at left) is a traditionalist who firmly believes that an armagnac must age itself. Sure, one airs it once in a while, but to achieve a pure product, "one has to have patience. Caramel and water are shortcuts which are practiced widely," he states, "but in my opinion, are in no way acceptable. A pure product is never reduced and should fall naturally to between 45-50°. With reduced spirits you don't get the *fond de verre*. There's just too much water inside."

Corentin briefly shakes a bottle and watches the bubbles along the armagnac's surface. "Look how the bubbles remain for nearly ten seconds," he states. "With reduced armagnacs, the bubbles disappear within seconds."

Mao also believes that a barrel is made to age its own armagnac. At times he airs his armagnacs and rotates barrels, but several years before bottling, he likes to replace the spirit into the barrel where it began its life. Like that the spirit comes full circle.

"Even though most of our money comes from the sale of wine, armagnac is my true passion," says Corentin. "And each time I fill a bottle, I have a little sip from the barrel. Like that I can constantly revive my memories."

Hors d'age (48°): Amber with gold highlights. Slightly hot on nose. Hints of caramel and fruit. Slightly spicy and green on the finish.

1979 (48°): Hint of almond, coconut, buttery vanilla on nose. Prune and apricot-scented fruit with good depth and lightly-spiced oak. Good finesse.

1977 (48°): Slightly less developed on the nose than 1979. Slight hint of almond with more fruit in the mouth than on the nose.

1976 (50°): Fat nose hides alcohol. Slightly smoky, with a touch of almond on nose. Creamy, vanilla-scented texture. Hint of pepper on the finish. Pure *fond du verre*.

1972 (48°): Almond-scented *rancio* on the nose with a hint of marzipan paste. Rich nose defies alcohol level. Good fat in the mouth, with hints of butterscotch, herbs and walnut.

Lagraulet (Gers), population 395

Located on the route between Montréal and Gondrin, this picturesque village offers panoramic views of the surrounding countryside.

Proprietor: Michel Duffour ***Name of Property***: Domaine de St. Lannes ***Vineyard size***: 32 ha (79 acres) ***Other production***: red and white Côtes de Gascogne, red and white Floc ***Grapes used for armagnac***: Ugni Blanc (100%) ***Percent of production used for distillation***: 15% ***Soil***: *argilo-calcaires* (clay with a high proportion of limestone) ***Production of armagnac per year***: 25 hl (12 barrels) ***Distillation***: *Armagnacaise* ***Alcohol degree when leaving the still***: 57° ***Distiller***: Michalouski ***Barrels***: Allier ***Chai:*** Dirt floor, organized, humid ***Oldest spirit still in cask***: 1977 ***Stock***: 50 hl a.p. (25 barrels) ***Blended armagnacs available***: No ***Vintages available***: 1977, 1979, 1981, 1983, 1983, 1985, 1986 ***Reduction***: *petites eaux* to 42°

One of the biggest success stories over the past ten years has been the ascension of Michel Duffour as Gascon *vigneron*. His powerfully aromatic white Côtes de Gascogne has won numerous medals in competitions all over France and now sells upwards of 200,000 bottles a year. Made from 80% Colombard, the nose displays a pungent herbaceousness reminiscent of Sauvignon Blanc with additional hints of melon and lime. There is decent flesh in the mouth and the finish, unlike some wines of the region, is dry. It is an ideal *apéritif* wine, yet also a super accompaniment to shellfish.

Duffour's parents bought the property in 1953. His father practiced polyculture; corn, sunflowers, and cows provided their income. In 1971, Michel began planting grapes. The majority is Colombard, but there are also parcels of Ugni Blanc, Gros Manseng, Tannat, Cabernet Sauvignon, Cabernet Franc, Merlot and, most recently, Chardonnay.

Duffour is much more comfortable talking about his wines than his armagnac; likewise, as is the case with many successful wine producers, his qualitative and financial success with table wine has diminished his enthusiasm for armagnac. Consequently he does not distill every year; when he does, it is normally used in his floc. In fact, over the past decade, only one of his harvests has been destined for vintage armagnac.

Even so, the quality of his armagnac in barrel is excellent. The time it spends in new oak is relatively long yet, perhaps because it is aged in the softer Allier, the spirit is not overoaked. His armagnacs are medium-bodied, with lots of fruit on the nose and palate. The finish is lightly spicy without being overbearing.

1981 (44°): Deep amber. Slight hint of almond which begins to hint at *rancio*. Notes of vanilla, caramel and dried apple in the mouth. Moderate depth. Good length with pepper on the finish.

1986 (48°): Amber with red highlights. Rich nose shows lots of prune and creamy vanilla. Hints of spicy oak and licorice in the mouth, along with a good deal of alcohol. Shows lots of potential.

Proprietor: Jean-Marie Lapisse ***Name of Property***: Houres ***Vineyard size***: 14 ha (35 acres) ***Other production***: wine, grains, cows ***Percent of production used for distillation***: 20% ***Grapes used for armagnac***: 20% Bacco, 15% Colombard, 15% Folle Blanche, 50% Seyve-Villard ***Soil:*** *boulbènes* (sand with clay pieces) ***Production of armagnac per year***: 40 hl a.p. (20 barrels) ***Distiller***: Mur of Labarrère ***Distillation***: *Armagnacaise* ***Alcohol degree when leaving the still***: 52°-55° ***Barrels***: Gascon ***Chai:*** Rustic, dirt floor, humid ***Oldest spirit still in cask***: 1975 ***Stock***: 70 hl a.p. (35 barrels) ***Blended armagnacs available***: *Vieille Réserve* (20 years old) ***Vintages available***: No ***Reduction***: to 42° with *petites eaux*

The owner of this property, Gabriel Lapisse, passed away in 1992. He was the fourth generation to produce armagnac on the property, which is reached by a small country road running between Cazaneuve and Lannepax.

Today his widow, Jeanne-Marie, sells what remains of the stock. The last distillation took place in 1983, and less than thirty barrels remain. To facilitate matters with the tax board, only one armagnac is currently on the market, a 20-year-old *Vieille Réserve* which is actually from the 1977 vintage.

Vines still exist around the property, but the Lapisse's daughter prefers to sell them to a *négociant* in Bordeaux. Madame Lapisse speaks fondly of old times when they sold to *négociants* such as Janneau, Larressingle, and Gelas. Nowadays, as is the case with many independent producers, no one is interested in aged stock. She reckons that now, less than half a barrel is sold per year.

"When we had to buy a tractor or when we got central heating," Madame Lapisse remembered, "we sold a barrel to a *négociant* to pay the bill."

"That's all finished now," she continued, disillusioned. "I get $400 a month from social security. How can I live on that? Sure I have a house, but you have to keep it up. We once stocked armagnac because we thought it would pay for our retirement. Not true. Now I have to can preserves to help make ends meet."

Still, life goes on for Madame Lapisse and her fond memories make the journey a little bit easier. "I remember a tree fell down on the property and my husband called me over. 'Smell this,' he said, holding a chunk of moist oak to my nose. And I'll be damned if it didn't smell of *pruneau*—just like our armagnac."

It is interesting to note that nearly 50% of Houres' older armagnacs were made with the grape *Seyve-Villard*, a rarely-found hybrid developed after the phylloxera which in turn was replaced with Bacco by most properties.

Madame Lapisse also offered me a rare treat—a pre-phylloxera armagnac distilled in 1850. For as long as her memory serves her, the armagnac was in a glass bonbonne at 37°. In 1992, she decided to bottle what remained.

This ageworthy armagnac was chestnut with red highlights and showed very deep walnut-scented *rancio* on the nose. Notes on the palate were reminiscent of polished sandalwood and prune, the texture was soft, and the finish pleasantly long.

Vieille Réserve (from the 1977 vintage, 42°): Slightly floral nose with a hint of spice. Medium-body, with hints of prune and pepper. Well-integrated wood. Moderately long finish.

Proprietor: Jean Réon ***Name of Property***: Domaine de Moura ***Vineyard size***: 25 ha (62 acres) ***Other production***: corn, sunflowers, wheat, cows ***Grapes used for armagnac***: Bacco (70%), Colombard (30%) ***Percent of production used for distillation***: 5% ***Soil***: *boulbènes* (sand with clay pieces) ***Production of armagnac per year***: 12 hl a.p. (6 barrels) ***Distiller***: Michalouski ***Distillation***: *Armagnacaise* ***Alcohol degree when leaving the still***: 56° ***Barrels***: Allier and some oak from the property ***Chai:*** Organized, dirt floor, humid ***Oldest spirit still in cask***: 1970 ***Stock***: 92 hl a.p. (46 barrels) ***Blended armagnacs available***: No ***Vintages available***: 1968, 1970, 1974, 1977, 1986 ***Reduction***: With demineralized water to 42°

Jean Réon is the third generation to produce armagnac at this small property located a few miles outside of Gondrin. Unlike many other producers in the Ténarèze, Réon favors a high percentage of Bacco in his armagnacs, which he feels his *boulbènes*-based soil favors.

Polyculture is practiced at the domaine, and only a small percentage of the grape harvest is distilled every year. The rest of his wine is sold *en vrac*. He is making a concerted effort to sell his armagnacs, and often sells them at evening fairs and markets. The 31-year-old Réon has won several medals in armagnac competitions in Eauze, and *négociant* Jean-Pierre Gimet has bought several vintages for his neighboring firm.

Certain casks of Réon's armagnacs are unreduced while others have been brought down to 42° with demineralized water. In 1996 all of his spirit saw the effects of new oak, and remain extremely promising in cask.

1995: Good fat in the mouth with a viscous, oily texture. Wood beginning to dissolve nicely into the spirit. Excellent potential.

1989: Nice sweetness on palate, wood beginning to integrate itself. Good length.

1974: Some almond-scented *rancio* on the nose. Medium-body and not yet layered with flavor. Decent length.

1970: Interesting nose with more complexity than the 1974. Oak, vanilla, *rancio*. Prune-scented fruit along with some dry oak in the mouth. Moderately tannic finish.

Lannes (Lot et Garonne), population 364

Lannes is located just outside Mézin along the route to Condom. Its church dates to the 13th Century. It was annexed in 1972 with Villeneuve-de-Mezin, where today one can visit its 12th Century church.

Proprietor: The Langalerie Family ***Name of Property***: Château de la Grangerie ***Vineyard size***: 15 ha (37 acres) ***Other production***: *pruneau*, wheat, corn, floc ***Grapes used for armagnac***: Ugni Blanc (100%) ***Percent of production used for distillation***: 30 % ***Soil***: *argilo-calcaire* (clay with a high proportion of limestone) ***Production of armagnac per year***: 30-40 hl a.p. (15-20 barrels) ***Distiller***: Michalouski ***Distillation***: *Armagnacaise* ***Alcohol degree when leaving the still***: 55° ***Barrels***: Gascon ***Chai:*** Organized, dirt floor, humid ***Oldest spirit still in cask***: 1978 ***Stock***: 130 hl a.p. (65 barrels) ***Blended armagnacs available***: 3 Étoiles (48°) ***Vintages available***: 1989, 1986, 1982, 1978 ***Reduction***: Minimally with demineralized water

The people of Lannes certainly have some of the most interesting storage conditions in Armagnac. The Langalerie family lodge their barrels in this picturesque monastery on their property.

The Château de la Grangerie has belonged to the de Langalerie family for over 250 years. Once a monastery, its attractive chapel now houses the 50 or so barrels that have been distilled since 1974. The dirt floor and humid conditions within the ancient chapel permits a fairly rapid evaporation of alcohol. The domaine's policy to purchase a good percentage of new oak allows for the essential, natural added flavorants.

Much of the grape production is sold to the cooperative in Poudenas, where Robert de Langalerie works as an enologist. 50% of the domaine's distilled product, passed through the alambic by the local Michalouski, goes toward the domaine's floc and excellent *pruneau a l'armagnac*. The other part rests in the *chai*, aired occasionally and reduced by approximately half-a-degree a year.

The armagnacs of La Grangerie are very typical of the Ténarèze; their usage of new oak, however, helps add some depth of flavor to their spirits. They have several ruptures in stock, which perhaps forces premature vintages toward the public. Auxil, a *négociant* with admirable instincts, currently markets a couple of their vintages.

1989 (46°): Light amber. Fairly hard, typical of the Ténarèze at this age. Still lacks depth, although with some notes of nutty oak in the mouth. Lots of attack. Hot finish.

1986 (45°): Amber. Shy nose shows some alcohol. Rests fairly-one dimensional in the mouth, although with some accumulating fat. Still hot.

1982: Deep amber (noticeably darker): Lots of wood in the mouth (chocolate, cinnamon) and with gaining depth. Still showing alcohol and lots of new wood, and consequently fairly disjointed. Sweet fruit beginning to surface. To follow with interest.

1978 (42°): Amber. Hint of orange marmalade on the nose. Some flattering notes of vanilla and orange in the mouth. Slightly softer than the other releases, but still fairly ungiving. Nicely-integrated wood and alcohol, however. Decent length.

Proprietor: The Maurer Family ***Name of Property***: Domaine de Brichot ***Hectares of vines in production***: 38 ha (94 acres) ***Other production***: sunflowers, soy beans, wheat ***Grapes***: Ugni Blanc (100%) ***Percent of production used for distillation***: 5 % ***Soil***: *argilo-calcaires* (clay with a high proportion of limestone) ***Production of armagnac per year***: 20 hl a.p. (10 barrels) ***Distiller***: Michalouski ***Distillation***: *Armagnacaise* ***Distillation degree upon exiting the still***: 56° ***Barrels***: Gascon and Limousin ***Oldest spirit still in cask***: 1962 ***Stock***: 600 hl a.p. (300 barrels) ***Blended armagnacs available***: 3 Étoiles (4 years old), VSOP (5 years old), *Hors d'age (12 years old)* ***Vintages available***: 1962-1992 ***Reduction***: With distilled water to 40°

Good-sized armagnac property located not far from the center of Lannes. Armagnac makes up a small percentage of the domaine's production, and their releases are of sound, commercial quality. A large range of vintages is available, most of which are released at 40°.

Hors d'Age: Creamy coconut notes in the mouth. Full-bodied, with a slightly sweet finish.

1975: Amber. Good attack with a pleasing sweetness that remains on the palate. Without tremendous depth but with some pleasing peppery notes on the finish.

Proprietor: Michel Kauffer ***Name of Property***: Domaine de Cazeaux ***Vineyard size***: 20 ha (50 acres) ***Other production***: wheat, corn, sunflowers, floc ***Grapes used for armagnac***: Ugni Blanc (100%) ***Percent of production used for distillation***: 15% ***Soil***: *argilo-calcaires* (clay with a high proportion of limestone) ***Production of armagnac per year***: 20-25 hl a.p. (10-12 barrels) ***Distillation***: *Armagnacaise* ***Distiller***: Michel Kauffer himself ***Alcohol degree when leaving the still***: 55° ***Barrels***: Tronçais, Gaillac ***Chai:*** Organized, cement floor, dry ***Oldest spirit still in cask***: 1972 (25 years) ***Stock:*** 260 hl a.p. (130 barrels) ***Blended armagnacs available***: VS (6 years old), VSOP (9 years old), *Hors d'age* (14 years old). All reduced to 40° with *petites eaux* ***Vintages available***: 1972 (44°) ***Reduction***: No

The Domaine de Cazeaux, located on the crest of a hill overlooking colorful sunflower, wheat, and vine fields, has been run by the Kauffer family for four generations. Like many other properties in the Mézin canton, they are not frequently damaged by frost. In contrast, they are more susceptible to hailstorms, the force of which frequently rips both grapes and leaves apart.

Michel Kauffer has his own alambic with which he distills. Over the years, he has built up a considerable stock that now numbers around 130 *pièces*. They are housed in long columns of barrels stacked four high in an attractive *chai* next to the house. Its appearance is a blend of the artisan and the industrial.

Kauffer lets his spirit drip out of the alambic at 55°. It sees some form of oak for about six years (occasionally planks), then is placed in older barrels where a reduction with *petites eaux* begins. The final reduction takes place about a year before bottling.

Kauffer also makes excellent wines that are released as *Vin de Pays de l'Agenais*. In addition, his floc often receives medals during competitions. His armagnacs, while certainly older than the minimum requirements, remain firm most of their life. Whether this is due to the hard soil or the lack of new wood is debatable. They are, without doubt, Ténarèze from the old school.

Hors d'age (12-15 years old): Aromatics fairly closed. Trace of sweetness on the palate along with a slight floral note. Firm finish with a slight astringency.

1972: Hint of almond an slight creamy note displays evidence that the spirit is finally beginning to soften. Palate remains fairly firm with just a touch of sweetness showing. Still has lots of attack and seems younger than its age because of its lack of oak.

Proprietor: Paul Dubourdieu ***Name of Property***: Broustet ***Vineyard size***: 7 ha (17.5 acres) ***Other production***: wheat, cows, prunes, sunflowers, corn, floc ***Grapes used for armagnac***: Ugni Blanc (60%), Folle Blanche (15%), Colombard (15%), Jurançon (15%) ***Percent of production used for distillation***: 100 % ***Soil***: *argilo-calcaires*, boulbènes (clay with a high proportion of limestone, sand with pieces of clay) ***Production of armagnac per year***: 40-50 hl a.p. (20-25 barrels) ***Distiller***: Michalouski ***Distillation***: *Armagnacaise* ***Distillation degree upon exiting the still***: 52 ° ***Barrels***: Gascon ***Chai:*** The great outdoors! ***Oldest spirit still in cask***: 1981 ***Stock***: 300 hl a.p. (150 barrels) ***Blended armagnacs available***: 3 Etoiles (3 years old), VSOP (5 years old), *Hors d'age* (10 years old), 15 year old ***Vintages available***: No ***Reduction***: No

In comparison with other armagnac producers, Paul Dubourdieu is what one might call... *eccentric*. One doesn't say this because his cows roam in the driveway. Or because his chickens and geese nest their young next to the front door. Or that half his house seems to have collapsed.

No, one really says this because, in comparison with every other armagnac producer who has a proper *chai* which protects his barrels, Dubourdieu ages his armagnacs outside. That's right,

A true original, Paul Dubourdieu (above) exposes his barrels to the elements outside his decaying barn.

outside, in the sun of Summer, the snow of Winter, and the rains of Spring and Fall.

The seventy-nine-year-old Dubourdieu says that his idea to age barrels outside came to him one winter when he lacked space inside his normal *chai* for the last barrel. He placed it outside and checked its progress a year later. He was completely convinced that the barrel outside was better than the rest. He then moved other barrels outside, and noticed a continuity within their superior quality. Soon his *chai* became the great outdoors.

Dubourdieu, who has distilled nearly every year since 1940, loses about 40% of his volume over the course of ten years, mostly during the summer. During the cold winter months, the alcohol level diminishes gradually. Apart from topping up with the same vintage, Paul lets nature take its course once the armagnacs are in barrel. No reduction, no additives. Pure, unadulterated Ténarèze.

Exposure to the elements takes its toll on the barrels, most of which are deeply colored with painful looking splinters of wood adorning their rough surface. He normally keeps them covered with corrugated sheet metal, but when I arrived, most casks were in direct sunlight and one was even missing its bung-hole cork!

Dubourdieu's unorthodox form of aging helps concentrate his armagnacs and basically accelerates their aging. Unlike many spirits from the Mézin canton, Paul's were supple after only ten years. They showed concentration and lots of forward fruit. The wood was present, but in no way dominant.

Legend has it that one fall day after the family had killed several pigs and was in the process of preparing their meat, Paul's mother died. Paul, as butcher, could not leave the meat unattended as it would certainly spoil. Instead, he placed his mother on an adjoining table where she stayed until the primary job was finished. Yes, Armagnac has characters that can be taken straight out of Faulkner.

One will not see advertising for the domaine. In fact, there are no signs indicating its sale of alcohol. Just outside of the tiny village of Lannes along a small country lane, if one looks hard enough, they will simply find a small sign marking the property name, Broustet.

10 Year Old (48°): Pleasing, spicy aromatics. Good attack, with admirable concentration for its age. Soft texture, and without much tannin or wood influence.

15 Year Old (46°): Rich amber. Nice palate feel with lots of fat. Good balance between alcohol and fruit. Slightly green woodspice on the finish. Excellent concentration of flavor without aggressive tannin. Admirable length.

An *eau de vie de prune* is also available at the property, as well as a similar version aged in oak for eight years. Another delicious regional specialty, *pruneau a l'armagnac*, is also available.

Larroque-Sur-Osse (Gers), population 254

Charming feudal village whose hilltop setting was once the home of nobles. The 13th century Tour de Luzan and the 15th century church are of interest to the passerby. The fields are manicured like a garden, and views from small hills nearby are both picturesque and memorable.

Laroque-sur-l'Osse

Proprietor: Michel Depis and Jocelyne Sampietro ***Name of Property***: Le Péto ***Vineyard size***: 4 ha (10 acres) ***Other production***: white wine ***Grapes used for armagnac***: Ugni Blanc (70%), Colombard (30%) ***Percent of production used for distillation***: 25% ***Soil***: *argilo-calcaires* (clay with a high proportion of limestone) ***Production of armagnac per year***: 10 hl a.p. (5 barrels) ***Distillation***: *Armagnacaise* ***Distiller***: Gironi of Mouchan ***Alcohol degree when leaving the still***: 55° ***Barrels***: A mixture; some from the region, some from the center of France ***Chai:*** Organized, cement floor, humid ***Stock:*** 120 hl a.p. (60 barrels) ***Oldest spirit still in cask***: 1979 ***Blended armagnacs available***: VSOP (8 years), *Hors d'age* (16 years), both reduced to 42° with *petites eaux* ***Vintages available***: 1979, 1981, 1982, 1988 ***Reduction***: distilled water to 42°

The Domaine de Péto has been part of the Depis family since the first World War. The family has produced armagnac for three generations, yet bottling did not begin until 1974. Located on the crest of a hill, the property commands an attractive view of surrounding multi-colored crops, while the vineyards lie on each side of the entrance drive.

Today, Jocelyne Sanpietro and her brother Michel Depis look after the property and stock. Mr. Depis is employed during the week by an electronics firm in Bordeaux, but his true love is armagnac. Consequently, he returns each weekend to Péto to look after the stock. His sister lives next to the domaine and runs everyday affairs.

Distillation does not occur every year; with sales of alcoholic beverages down, less and less has been distilled recently. The oldest barrel is from the 1979 vintage; Mr. Depis feels that armagnacs reach their peak between 15 and 20 years and that keeping a tremendous stock of older vintages does not warrant the qualitative payoff.

The wine is fermented at the property, then distilled by Philippe Gironi at his distillery in Mouchan. The spirit is housed in a converted horse stable that holds about seventy barrels. An *eau de vie* is also available, in addition to a VSOP, *Hors d'age*, and several vintages. The *Hors d'age* accounts for about 70% of their sales.

No caramel is used to enhance the color of the firm's armagnacs; consequently they display fairly light hues. All are reduced to 42° with *petites eaux*.

The armagnacs of Peto are not heavy, but very complete and with good depth of character. The VSOP, at 8 years of age, has a bit more development than other VSOP's on the market.

Eau de Vie (only about 50 bottles made a year from Ugni Blanc): Floral notes on the nose with a hint of white pepper. Alcohol creeps in on the finish.

VSOP: Amber with gold highlights. Lightly floral nose along with deep notes of caramel. Smooth palate with a hint of white pepper. Spice picks up on finish. Good pure length.

Hors d'age (1982): Amber with orange highlights. Lightly smoky nose. Richer mouthfeel than VSOP and with some additional floral hints. Good balance. Hint of spice on the finish.

1981 (from barrel, 45°): Hints of almond on the nose. Some prune, black pepper and herbal notes in the mouth. Lots of spice on the finish.

1979 (from barrel, 42°): Amber with gold highlights. Almond and marzipan on the nose. Rich texture with faint hints of butter and vanilla. Very pleasing *rancio*. Excellent integration of oak. Nice length. Very good armagnac.

Proprietor: Michel Fezas ***Name of Property***: Domaine de Chiroulet ***Vineyard size***: 28 ha (69 acres) ***Other production***: floc, red wine, white wine, gîte ***Grapes used for armagnac***: Ugni Blanc (100%) ***Percent of production used for distillation***: 15% ***Soil***: *argilo-calcaires* (clay with a high proportion of limestone) ***Production of armagnac per year***: 34 hl a.p. (17 barrels) ***Distillation***: *Armagnacaise* ***Alcohol degree when leaving the still:*** 60° ***Distiller***: Michalouski ***Barrels***: *Tonneau* made with oak from the property ***Chai:*** Organized, cement floor, dry ***Oldest spirit still in cask***: 1973 ***Stock***: 280 hl a.p. (140 barrels) ***Blended armagnacs available***: Reserve (8-10 years old) ***Vintages available***: 1979 ***Reduction***: with *petites eaux* to 42°

Michel Fezas is yet another armagnac producer pissed off with the market. He deplores the fact that the consumption of whiskey heavily outweighs the consumption of armagnac within the region. A certain *snob appeal* is part of the reason, he feels. The same snobbism that makes a person order a port instead of a floc, or a minor Bordeaux instead of a top Côtes de Gascogne. So many people would rather consume something that has a known name even if the product, in short, lacks character or personality.

Consequently the amount of armagnac he reserves for aging has plummeted. Instead, he uses most of his distillation for his superb floc, recently given the gold medal at the Eauze competition and the *Coup de Coeur* by *Guide Hachette*. His son Philippe, a Toulouse-trained enologist now working at Seguin-Moreau cooperage in Cognac, has certainly influenced the quality of the domaine's wine production. He now makes one of the best red Côtes de Gascogne available, comprised of a high percentage of Merlot and aged in new oak barrels. Concentrated with cherry, currant, vanilla and coffee nuance, and with a lush texture that glides across the palate, it is nothing short of wonderful and a benchmark for quality wines from the region.

In comparison with their soave wines and floc produced at the lovely, picturesque property, Chiroulet's armagnacs remain slightly hard and, although showing some adequate sweetness, do not demonstrate tremendous dimension; in short, a *typical* Ténarèze.

Master of floc and wine, respectively: Michel and Philippe Fezas at Chiroulet

Réserve: Aromatic and fairly supple for its age. Nice natural sweetness and correctly made, yet lacking real depth and finesse.

1979: More attack and force on nose with notes of caramel and vanilla. Some fat beginning to develop on the palate but without tremendous depth. Still seems young for its age.

Proprietor: Olivier Fourtet ***Name of Property***: Ferragus ***Vineyard size***: 14 ha (35 acres) ***Other production***: red and white floc, wine sold *en vrac* ***Grapes used for armagnac***: Ugni Blanc (100%) ***Percent of production used for distillation***: 15% ***Soil***: *argilo-calcaires* (clay with a high proportion of limestone) ***Production of armagnac per year***: 50-60 hl a.p. (25-30 barrels) ***Distillation***: *Armagnacaise* ***Alcohol degree when leaving the still:*** 58° ***Distiller***: The Fourtet family ***Barrels***: Tronçais and Allier ***Chai:*** Organized, cement floor, dry ***Oldest spirit still in cask***: 1972 ***Stock:*** 240 hl a.p. (120 barrels) ***Blended armagnacs available***: 3 Star, VSOP, *Hors d'age* ***Vintages available***: 1977 ***Reduction***: With *petites eaux* to 42°

Ferragus is a pretty property located along the route between Condom and Fourcès, next to the Osse River. Within the domaine's *chai* lies a wood-fueled alambic built in 1901. In comparison with other rustic alambics in the region, the Fourtet's is polished, clean and beautiful.

Their armagnacs are of a commercial nature, sold young, reduced to 42° and treated with aged boisé. Their three releases show good color, a smooth mouthfeel and moderate length.

The domaine's flocs are excellent. The white, perhaps because of its Semillon content, shows lots of fruit both on the nose and in the mouth. The red is replete with ripe cherry and herbs. Very well made and a lovely *aperitif.*

Lauraët (Gers), population 215

Tiny village located on the route between Montréal and Mouchan.

Proprietor: Joël Fourteau ***Name of Property***: Domaine du Bourdieu ***Vineyard size***: 21 ha (52 acres) ***Other production***: Red and White floc ***Grapes***: Ugni Blanc (90%), Bacco (10%) ***Percent of production used for distillation***: 10% ***Soil***: *argilo-calcaires* (clay with a high proportion of limestone) ***Production of armagnac per year***: 19 hl a.p. (8 barrels) ***Distillation***: *Armagnacaise* ***Distiller***: With the alambic of the property ***Alcohol degree when leaving the still***: 55° ***Chai:*** Organized, cement floor, dry ***Oldest spirit still in cask***: 1974 ***Stock:*** 60 hl a.p. (30 barrels) ***Blended armagnacs available***: *Hors d'age* (11 years old, 50°) ***Reduction***: No

The Domaine de Bourdieu was purchased by the Fourteau family in 1878. Owner Joël Fourteau now lives in Lille, and his son Jean-Luc runs the 21 hectare property, located about 4 miles south of Montréal-du-Gers. Much of the property's sales comes from visitors passing through the region, who have the chance to see the property's alambic and sample both their floc and armagnac.

Only one armagnac is available for purchase; an 11 year old *Hors d'age*, released at its natural degree. Very little new wood is used at Bourdieu. In fact, no barrels were in sight. Instead, the armagnacs all go into grand *tonneaux* where they stay for their entire lives.

One must respect Bourdieu's adherence to tradition by distilling their own product and not cutting their armagnac's purity with water. However, until they invest in new barrels to naturally give them color and flavor, their armagnacs will never turn the head of the true connoisseur.

Hors d'age (50°): Amber. Not intensely aromatic. Decent depth of flavor in the mouth with some sweetness. Fairly soft despite its elevated alcohol level. Fleeting hint of nuttiness, and a note of heat on the finish.

Mézin (Lot et Garonne), population 1,455

Hillside village located just over the Lot-et-Garonne border on the route from Montréal to Nérac. An interesting cork museum can be visited and the Garcia family runs La Belle Gasconne, an excellent restaurant in nearby Poudenas.

Proprietor: Maurice Tadieu ***Name of Property***: La Ferme de Gagnet ***Vineyard size***: 6 ha (15 acres) ***Other production***: ducks, conserve, prunes, cows, corn ***Grapes***: Ugni Blanc (80%), Colombard (20%) ***Percent of production used for distillation***: 30 % ***Soil***: *argilo-calcaires* (clay with a high proportion of limestone) ***Production of armagnac per year***: 7 hl a.p. (3-4 barrels) ***Distiller***: Michalouski ***Distillation***: *Armagnacaise* ***Alcohol degree when leaving the still***: 56° ***Barrels***: Gascon and the center of France ***Oldest spirit still in cask***: 1981 ***Chai:*** Organized, cement floor, dry ***Stock***: 70 hl a.p. (35 barrels) ***Blended armagnacs available***: No ***Vintages available***: 1981, 1982, 1983 ***Reduction***: No

The Tadieu family run an attractive *gîte* just outside the town of Mézin. There are plenty of ducks on the property, and each year 1000 are fattened up, then used for the region's culinary specialties. Three armagnacs are also available from the property, all naturally made and sold with vintage dates.

No new oak is used at Gagnet and the spirit is aged in used barrels. Even so, they do not use woodchips or boisé; consequently the armagnacs are fairly light in color. At 52°, they are also some of the stronger armagnacs on the market.

Maurice Tadieu's son-in-law David Lorenzon will soon be responsible for the property's armagnac production. Having served an apprenticeship with Gilles Baumann at Domaine des Cassagnoles, David has been toying with the idea of becoming more interventional; reducing his armagnacs and using boisé to give some additional tannin and create a more accessible product.

Gagnet's armagnacs, without the color, tannin, or flavor derived from oak, tend to be somewhat immature even after 15 years. It would be extremely interesting to taste these same armagnacs at twice their age, once some concentration has developed and the aromas begin to surface over the alcohol.

1983 (52°): Light amber with gold highlights. Slightly austere nose offers some scents of caramel. Medium-bodied, with some strong alcohol surfacing on the finish.

1982 (52°): Light amber. Trace of richness on the palate with just a hint of chocolate. Very little oak influence. Still young, but shows good potential.

1981 (52°): Light amber. Some floral notes on the nose. Medium-body, with a trace of spicy oak. Still not real concentrated.

Montréal-du-Gers (Gers), population 1,235

This charming town is thought to be the first bastide in Gascony, dating back to 1289. The XIIIth century Gothic church lies just to the side of the town square, where the market takes place on Fridays. A museum on the town's square houses many finds from Seviac, the gallo-roman villa nearby.

Discovered by a farmer plowing his field in the mid-1800's, Seviac has proven to be one of the largest archeological finds in the Southwest with scores of impressive mosaics dating back to the second century. The village party takes place at the beginning of August, although 1997's festivities began in June when the town's rugby team won the fourth division championship of France for the third time in 20 years.

Proprietor: Veuve Ladavèze and Sons ***Name of Property***: Domaine de la Boubée ***Vineyard size***: 28 ha (69 acres) ***Other production***: sunflowers ***Grapes***: Ugni Blanc (60%), Plainte de Grèce (15%), Colombard (15%), Folle Blanche (10%). Varietals are distilled and aged separately ***Percent of production used for distillation***: 50 % ***Soil***: *boulbènes* (sand with clay pieces) ***Production of armagnac per year***: 100 hl a.p. (50 barrels) ***Distiller***: Earlier vintages Gimet. More recently, Michalouski ***Distillation***: *Armagnacaise* ***Alcohol degree when leaving the still***: 54-56° ***Barrels***: One-third new per year. Regional and Limousin ***Chai:*** Several. All organized, cement and dirt floor, humid and dry ***Oldest spirit still in cask***: 1942 ***Stock***: 200 hl a.p. (100 barrels) ***Blended armagnacs available***: VSOP, *Hors d'age* ***Vintages available***: 1984, 1982, 1980, 1978, 1942 ***Reduction***: To 42° with distilled water

Domaine de la Boubée takes its name from the soil surrounding it—sand with a large percentage of *boulbènes* (clay pieces) or *boubée* for short. Jean Ladevèze farms the 28 hectares passed on to him by his mother, the Veuve Ladevèze. Ugni Blanc comprises 70% of the plantings, and the remainder is split evenly between Folle Blanche, the rare Plainte de Grèce (which he claims resembles Folle Blanche in weight and suppleness), Colombard (used for table wine) and Gros Manseng (used for floc). The wines, once distilled by Gimet, are now distilled by Patrick Michalouski's traveling alambic. A good chunk of his production is bought by Larresingle in nearby Condom.

Much of the Ladevèze business comes from commercialized armagnacs, which are carefully reduced to 40° with *petites eaux*. These are aged for between 9 months and a year-and-a-half in new 400 liter barrels made with Tronçais oak, then transferred to older barrels.

Ladaveze has two *chai*. The first, with two levels, is where the armagnacs begin their life. The dry upper level insures that the spirits lose some volume and begin to concentrate. Later, they are changed to the lower level which is slightly more humid. Finally, they are transferred to a *chai* next door which is extremely humid, ensuring that the optimum amount of alcohol is lost in as natural a manner as possible.

These commercialized armagnacs, above all the *Hors d'age*, are typically well-balanced and with admirable natural sweetness on the palate. Unfortunately, there are large ruptures in stock during the years when Boubée should really be showing its best (the Fifties through the Seventies).

Hors d'age (A blend of 10 to 20 year old armagnacs, with an average of 15 years, 42°): Amber. Lots of spice on nose, along with hints of caramel and some floral notes. Good balance of wood and alcohol in the mouth. Licorice picks up on the finish, along with a trace of white pepper.

1983 (50°): Light amber. Rich chocolate notes in the mouth along with vanilla. Gaining fat yet still shows lots of alcohol. Typical, young Ténarèze at the adolescent stage.

1978 (42°): Nose hints at prune paste and caramel. Light quince notes. Accumulating fat in mouth, although displays lots of attack. Long finish.

1976 (42°): Hazelnut, almond paste, and vanilla on the nose. Rich mouth includes prune, licorice and a floral note on the finish. Very long and very good.

1942 (43°): Amber. Extremely rich nose with overtones of quince enveloped within layers of prune and vanilla. Medium-bodied, with hints of polished, antique wood. Still shows good attack. Note of creamy vanilla show through the slightly dry finish. Long.

Proprietor: Gaston Béraut ***Name of Property***: Château de Pellehaut ***Vineyard size***: 140 ha (346 acres) ***Other production***: corn, wheat, animals, cows, red wine, white floc ***Grapes***: Folle Blanche (5 years old), Ugni Blanc (25 years old) ***Percent of production used for distillation***: 5-10% ***Soil***: *argilo-calcaires, boulbènes* (clay with a high proportion of limestone, some sand parcels with pieces of clay) ***Production of armagnac per year***: 9-10 hl a.p. (5 Barrels) ***Distillation***: *Armagnacaise* ***Distiller***: Michalouski ***Alcohol degree when leaving the still***: 52°-55° ***Stock***: 1,000 hl a.p. (500 barrels) ***Barrels***: Allier, Limousin, Bourgogne, Gascon ***Chai:*** Several. Organized, cement floors, dry and humid ***Oldest spirit still in cask***: 1974 ***Blended armagnacs available***: 3 Etoiles (3 year old Folle Blanche, reduced with *petites eaux* from 1978 to 1982, 46°) Five Year Old, 10 Year Old, 20 Year Old (From 1973 and 1974 vintages) ***Vintages available***: 1974 to the current date ***Reduction***: Certain casks unreduced, others reduced to 43°-45° with *petites eaux*.

On a beautifully situated property overlooking the town of Montréal-du-Gers lies the Château de Pellehaut. Purchased by Gaston Béraut shortly after the Second World War, he has slowly developed one of the largest single properties in the region.

Béraut's sons Mathieu (at right) and Martin now take care of winemaking and the *élevage* of armagnac. Both are intelligent and enthusiastic about their product, and between them have studied enology at Toulouse and apprenticed at Tariquet in Eauze, Beycheville in Bordeaux and Au Bon Climat in California.

Both are fond of experimentation and are barrel fermenting-Chardonnay as well as making some reds in quality oak. Likewise, they are experimenting with different types of wood for the armagnacs (Gascon, Allier, Limousin, Bourgogne) as well as with different distillation degrees (52° and 55°) and different amounts of reduction. In contrast to many rustic aging areas to be found in armagnac, their two organized *chai* are also their laboratories.

Folle Blanche is of extreme interest to the brothers Béraut, mostly because of the its floral, peppermint-scented bouquet, but also because it shows well in its youth. As their younger armagnacs outsell their older products by a considerable amount, only Folle Blanche has been distilled since 1992. All armagnacs at Pellehaut before this date were made solely with Ugni Blanc.

Their armagnacs made with Ugni Blanc, like many others in the Ténarèze, take longer to develop and begin to bloom around their 15th birthday. Their commercialized armagnacs include an *Hors d'age* distilled in 1983 and a 20 year old, which is a blend of the 1973 and 1974 vintages.

The armagnacs are aged on two properties, about four miles apart. The youngest spend their first five years on the upper level of one *chai* next to the house, then are transferred to the other *chai* during their intermediate years. The older vintages finally make their way back to the lower level of the initial *chai*. Their stock is impressive; nearly 1,000 hl a.p. They have reduced distillation drastically and now produce between six and 10 *pièces* a year, basically the amount that covers their sales and evaporation.

The armagnacs of Pellehaut show tremendous quality and are frequent prize winners in various competitions. They are certainly a property to watch.

Folle Blanche 1995 (Bourgogne oak): High floral nose, hint of quince.

Folle Blanche 1995 (Allier oak): Lots of wood-vanilla, clove, smoked meats. Fruit masked by wood for the moment.

Folle Blanche 1994 (distilled at 52°): Lots of chocolate-scented oak provides a foundation for fine, orange-scented fruit. Pleasing white pepper notes on the finish.

VSOP (assemblage of 78, 82, 83, 88, 89 vintages): Pleasing amber. Vanilla notes in the mouth, along with a high orange note. Balanced, supple and with nice sweetness. Correct.

1988: Deep amber. Fat fruit in the mouth with well-integrated alcohol.

1986: Budding fat, hint of almond, very good length. Excellent potential.

10 Year old (1983): Hint of orange, nice sweetness in the mouth, yet without tremendous depth. Correct and pleasing *Hors d'age*.

1979 Ugni Blanc (50% Single, 50% Double-distillation, 45°): Rich nose with good fat. Lots of aromatics include prune paste, almond brittle and butterscotch. Hints of cocoa surface above very appealing and lovely-integrated wood notes. Lively, and with good depth. Slight hint of coconut on the finish. Good length.

1979 Ugni Blanc (unreduced, 48°): Plum, creamy vanilla, hard caramel on the nose. Excellent balance in the mouth, with a sweet core of inner fruit. Hints of pepper on the long finish.

1978 (45°): Almond and marzipan on the nose. Fat in the mouth with a hint of prune. Excellent length.

1977 (47°): Lovely balance between wood, alcohol and fruit. Toffee notes, along with a lovely hint of clove-scented oak in the mouth. Lots of finesse on the palate. Excellent length.

1974 (48°, Limousin and Gascon oak): Rich fruit, with hints of dried apricot, orange and licorice. Fat texture. Excellent armagnac.

1974 (reduced to 45°): Pleasing aromatics yet slightly dilute and with less length than the former.

Proprietor: Jean-Pierre and Claudine Labenne ***Name of Property***: Jean de Montréjo ***Vineyard size***: 30 ha (74 acres) ***Other production***: wheat, sunflowers, floc, white, red, and sparkling wine ***Grapes***: Ugni Blanc (60-70%), Colombard (30-40%) ***Percent of production used for distillation***: 15 % ***Soil***: *argilo-calcaires* (clay with a high proportion of limestone) ***Production of armagnac per year***: 6-10 hl a.p. (3-5 barrels) ***Distiller***: Michalouski ***Distillation***: *Armagnacaise* ***Alcohol degree when leaving the still***: 63° ***Barrels***: Not many new; barrels occasionally refurbished ***Chai:*** Organized, cement floor, humid ***Oldest spirit still in cask***: 1945 ***Stock***: 150 hl a.p. (75 barrels) ***Blended armagnacs available***: 3 Etoiles (1992), VSOP (1990) ***Vintages available***: 1986, 1985, 1981, 1979, 1977, 1969, 1962, 1959, 1958, 1952, 1945, 1932 ***Reduction***: To 42° with *petites eaux* or distilled water

Jean de Montréjo is located about five miles from Montréal-du-Gers in the small hamlet of Balarin. Winemaking is now attended to by son Nicolas Labenne (left), supervisor of production at Château Calon-Ségur in St. Estèphe as well as first-line starter for the 1997 champion rugby team from Montréal.

Each year between 3 and 5 barrels of armagnac are distilled by one of Michalouski's alambics to a relatively high 63°. The spirit drips into used *pièces*, a few of which have been refurbished with new tops and bottoms. They then rest in the *chai* at their natural strength. Once every two years, the same vintage is aired, blended together and rediffused into different barrels. Because of the small amount of new wood employed,

Jean de Montréjo's armagnacs tend to show light amber tones even after 12 years in barrel.

The property's armagnacs, like those of Théaux in Cazeneuve, are not sprinters but long-distance runners. They begin to show some signs of class around their 20th birthday and come into their own around age 35. Wonderful examples of Ténarèze built to endure the long haul, accumulating oak over the course of several decades and gaining complexity ever so slowly.

Barrels in the *chai* are not reduced, and several vintages from each decade going back to the forties are available. Their younger vintages are reduced with rainwater to 42°. They tend to display nice fat and sweetness, and admirable length. They also display very good value.

Excellent rosé and red Côtes de Gascogne as well as a floc bursting with red fruit are available at the property.

1979 (54°): Very pretty nose includes flattering notes of coconut and chocolate. Building fat, with less alcohol showing. Good length with orange and pepper notes that rest on the palate.

1962: Amber. Prune and vanilla notes on the nose. Fat, supple texture. Hints of spice and vanilla on the finish with well-integrated oak. Pretty armagnac.

1958: Prune and spice on the nose. Hints of mushroom-covered oak in the mouth, along with a note of orange. Still fairly young, and with lots of life ahead.

1945 (49°): Orange and melted toffee on the nose. Hint of polished antique oak in the mouth, along with some oak tannin. Very long and elegant for its age.

1932: Lots of oaky complexity on nose. Some old oak notes in the mouth still ride upon some attractive fat. Fairly low alcohol level. Impressive for its age.

Proprietor: The Gabriel Family ***Name of Property:*** La Caillavère ***Vineyard size***: 40 ha (99 acres) ***Other production***: sunflowers, wheat ***Grapes used for armagnac***: Ugni Blanc (80%), Colombard (20%) ***Percent of production used for distillation***: 25-30% ***Soil***: *argilo-calcaires* (clay with a high proportion of limestone) ***Production of armagnac per year***: 70-80 hl a.p. (35-40 barrels) ***Distiller***: Themselves ***Distillation***: *Armagnacaise* ***Alcohol degree when leaving the still***: 52°-53° ***Barrels***: Limousin ***Oldest spirit still in cask***: 1978 ***Stock***: 1,200 hl a.p. (600 barrels) ***Chai:*** Organized, cement floor, humid ***Blended armagnacs available:*** A full range is imminent ***Vintages available***: 1978, 1979 ***Vintage Reduction***: No

Raymond Gabriel was a medical doctor in Guadeloupe, but he so loved the Gascon countryside that, in 1976, he decided to buy an attractive property located on a hillside between the village of Montréal and the Château de Pellehaut. He would spend four months a year at the property, and always oversee the distillation. Over the course of twenty years, he managed to accumulate 600 barrels, occasionally selling some of his wine to a *négociant* but never selling a bottle.

In 1996, Doctor Gabriel unexpectedly died and passed on his stock to his children. Today, daughter Solanges Gabriel, a doctor herself, occasionally travels from Guadeloupe to the Gers while attempting to give the domaine some commercial direction. Her raw ingredients are ideal because her father held back no expense: He bought an alambic for the property, distilled his armagnacs at a low degree, and invested tremendous amounts in new oak (20-30 new barrels per year). Apart from being rotated to more neutral barrels after several years, the armagnacs were basically left to mature at their natural degree.

The 1979 vintage was one of the most forward Ténarèze I came across. It was full of rich fruit and spicy oak nuance. The 1978 showed similar qualities. In short, they are flattering spirits—something rare with Ténarèze. Consumers will be spoiled when Cavaillon's vintages finally reach the market.

1979: Amber. Melted toffee and almond on the nose. Fat in the mouth, with notes of quince and spicy oak. Lovely viscosity. Excellent length.

1978: Amber. Notes of chocolate and almond on the nose. Full-body. Melted toffee and a hint of prune. Chocolatey wood on the finish, along with a touch of heat. Excellent length.

Nérac (Lot et Garonne), population 7,015

This large town located between Mézin and Agen has a rich historical heritage: it was the site of one of Jeanne d'Albret's château and one of the childhood homes of her son, Henri IV, King of France.

Proprietor: Jean-Pierre Herrail ***Name of Property***: Château Pierron ***Vineyard size***: 28 ha (69 acres) ***Other production***: corn, sunflowers, wheat, Buzet wine, floc ***Grapes used for armagnac***: Ugni Blanc (90%), Colombard (10%) ***Percent of production used for distillation***: 0-50% ***Soil***: *boulbènes* (sand with clay pieces) ***Production of armagnac per year***: 0-30 hl a.p. (0-15 barrels) ***Distiller***: Michalouski ***Distillation***: *Armagnacaise* ***Alcohol degree when leaving the still***: 52° ***Barrels***: Allier, Gascon ***Oldest spirit still in cask***: 1968 ***Chai:*** Organized, cement floor, dry ***Stock***: 60 hl a.p. (30 barrels) ***Blended armagnacs available***: 10, 20, and 25 Year Old ***Vintages available***: 1968, 1973, 1974, 1977, 1978, 1979, 1980, 1982, 1983, 1984, 1985, 1986, 1987, 1988, 1989, 1990 ***Reduction***: With *petites eaux* to 40°

Château Pierron lies just outside Nérac, at the northern limit of the Ténarèze. Once a fairly large producer of armagnac, the attention of the domaine now lies mostly with their production of excellent Buzet wine. Their stock has diminished to a mere 30 barrels and no distillation took place in 1996. Recently the majority of the 8 hectares (20 acres) devoted to armagnac vines was ripped up, and now a mere 2.5 hectares (6 acres) remains, much of whose eventual spirit will be used for floc.

It's a shame because the armagnacs that remain from their heyday during the 60's and 70's show very good depth of flavor and sweetness. This is perhaps due to its low distillation degree and the domaine's policy of using new oak.

Nowadays much of their stock has been diverted to blends of 10, 20 and 25 years, much of which is sold in the proprietor's native Belgium. The armagnacs are reduced gradually to a commercial 40°. Even so, Pierron's armagnacs with at least 10 years still display lots of nose and texture, something fairly uncommon with the majority of blended armagnacs.

Their older vintages and blends display lots of body, well-integrated wood and spicy length.

20 Year Old: Lots of wood spice on the nose with a moderately fat texture. Supple fruit reminiscent of prune and quince on the palate, with a touch of dry oak on the finish.

1970: Spicy oak on the nose with a touch of almond. Fat in the mouth, with lots of length. Pretty vintage.

25 Year Old: Note of walnut on the nose, with some antique wood buried under a wave of sweet fruit. Hint of antique, dry wood creeps in on the finish.

1968: Interesting nose hints at *rancio* and vanilla. Lots of old oak in the mouth surfaces above the fruit. Dry, oaky finish.

Saint-Puy (Gers), population 595
The Château de Monluc, located in the center of town, can be visited. A small museum also details the history of wine in the region.

Proprietor: The Lassus Family ***Name of Property***: Château de Monluc ***Vineyard size***: 115 ha (284 acres) ***Other production***: sparkling wine, Pousse Rapière, wine, floc ***Grapes used for armagnac***: Ugni Blanc (90%), Colombard (10%) ***Percent of production used for distillation***: 20 % ***Soil***: *argilo-calcaires* (clay with a high proportion of limestone) ***Production of armagnac per year***: 200 hl a.p. (100 barrels) ***Distiller***: Gimet ***Distillation***: *Armagnacaise* ***Alcohol degree when leaving the still***: 62° for aged armagnacs, 64-65° for the VSOP, 68° for the Pousse Rapière. ***Chai***: Organized, cement floor, dry ***Barrels***: 80% Allier, 20% Regional ***Oldest spirit still in cask***: 1958 ***Stock***: 300 hl a.p. (150 barrels) ***Blended armagnacs available***: VSOP, *Hors d'age* ***Reduction***: With *petites eaux* to 40°

Saint Puy is home to the 16th-century Château de Monluc, a lovely castle that sits atop the crest of a hill with a commanding view that spreads over a patchwork of multi-colored fields. Today the château is owned by the Lassus family, inventors of the regional specialty *Pousse-Rapière*.

Pousse-Rapière or *sword thrust* is a liquor made with orange, sugar, armagnac and a "secret" blend of spices. For the Gascon version of a *Kir Royal*, it is mixed with sparkling wine and a slice of orange.

Château de Monluc also produces white, red, and rosé Côtes de Gascogne. Their biggest seller, however, is there sparkling wine; in fact, more than half a million bottles leave the property each year. The majority of their young armagnac goes into the *Pousse- Rapière* liquor. Some is aged in a *chai*, however, and commercialized at 40°.

VSOP: Hints of vanilla, tobacco and licorice on the nose. Good balance in the mouth and not at all heavy.

Hors d'age: Deeper nose hints at orange jam, plum and herbs. Hints of older wood in the mouth carries through a slightly dry finish.

1979: Jammy nose with a hint of almond and smoke. Slightly harder in the mouth with some licorice and well-integrated wood. Firm finish indicative of the Ténarèze.

1973: Amber with gold highlights. Nice attack, but fairly short. Slightly dry wood carries through the finish.

Sainte Maure de Peyriac (Lot et Garonne), population 327

Small community located in the northern part of the Ténarèze. Its church dates to 1852.

Proprietor: SCEA Darréon et Fils ***Name of Property***: Au Bourg ***Vineyard size***: 10 ha (24.7 acres) ***Other production***: wheat, corn, beans, floc ***Grapes used for armagnac***: Ugni Blanc (60%), Colombard (40%) ***Percent of production used for distillation***: 30 % ***Soil***: *boulbènes* (sand with clay pieces) ***Production of armagnac per year***: 30 hl a.p. (15 barrels) ***Distiller***: Michalouski ***Distillation***: *Armagnacaise* ***Alcohol degree when leaving the still***: 54°-55° ***Chai:*** Organized, cement floor, dry ***Barrels***: From the region ***Oldest spirit still in cask***: 1961 ***Stock***: 230 hl a.p.(115 barrels) ***Blended armagnacs available***: VSOP, *Hors d'age* ***Vintages available***: No ***Reduction***: To 44° with *petites eaux*

The Darréon family make traditional armagnacs in the small town of Ste.Maure de Peyriac, located in the Lot et Garonne *département*. They are traditionally distilled by the region's most popular distiller, Patrick Michalouski, then aged in spacious, cement-paved *chai*.

They use both 400 liter *pièces* as well as 600 liter barrels more commonly found in the Gaillac region to age their spirits. They market only two armagnacs; a *VSOP* that averages 7 years, and an *Hors d'age* that is 20 years old. Both are reduced to 44° for two reasons. States Madame Darréon: "An armagnac at 44° offers more aroma without scaring a consumer with too much alcohol. And, perhaps more importantly, we also pay slightly less tax with less alcohol."

Darréon's armagnacs are well made, yet display much of the toughness inherent to the Ténarèze. Their *Hors d'age*, only slightly more expensive than their VSOP, offers very good value.

VSOP: Amber. Not intensely aromatic. Medium body with a hint of licorice on the finish.

Hors d'age: Amber. Pronounced difference in aroma. Deeper fruit, with just a hint of almond. Nice weight, and with good attack. Good integration of oak. Dry, alcohol-charged finish.

Proprietor: Labeyrie et Fils ***Name of Property***: GAEC de Janin ***Vineyard size***: 50 ha (124 acres) ***Other production***: corn, wheat, floc, wine ***Grapes used for armagnac***: Ugni Blanc (100%) ***Percent of production used for distillation***: 16% ***Soil***: *argilo-sablonneux* (clay and sand) ***Production of armagnac per year***: 30 hl a.p. (15 barrels) ***Distillation***: *Armagnacaise* ***Distiller***: Michalouski ***Alcohol degree when leaving the still***: 55° ***Chai:*** Organized, dirt floors, humid ***Barrels***: From the center of France ***Oldest spirit still in cask***: 1946 ***Stock***: 320 hl a.p. (160 barrels) ***Blended armagnacs available***: 3 Etoiles (3 years old), VSOP (7 years old), *Hors d'age* (13 years old). Reduced to 45° with demineralized water ***Vintages available***: 1946, 1947, 1970, 1971, 1973, 1974, 1976, 1978, 1979, 1980 ***Reduction***: No

Jean-Paul and Eric Labeyrie are the third generation of armagnac producers on the Janin property. The family started bottling their armagnacs in 1964 and saw a tremendous surge in the market between 1975 and 1991. During this golden age, they sold the equivalent of six barrels per year. Nowadays, that figure has dropped to between one and two. In fact, with regards to income, armagnac now accounts for a mere 5% of family's annual earnings. Fortunately they sell over 90% of their wine *en vrac*, which enables cashflow.

Ugni Blanc is the only grape distilled, and the spirit exits Michalouski's alambic at 55°. Not a tremendous amount of new oak is used; boisé is occasionally employed to give some color and tannin. The armagnacs are aired once a year, blended amongst the same vintage, then returned to different barrels. This helps provide some necessary homogeneity.

The vintages at Janin tend to be medium-bodied, fairly high in alcohol and irregularly oaked. In short, fairly tough Ténarèze that need lots of time to develop. The 1978 vintage seems to be on the right path.

A couple of vintages from the 1940's are also available.

1978 (50°): Deep amber. Beginning to develop some fat, and with a hint of almond brittle in the mouth. Fruit still wades beneath a tide of alcohol. Very good potential.

1970: Deep amber. Nose has some depth; prune, vanilla. Lots of oak in the mouth, which the remaining fruit barley manages to escape.

1946: Rich nose hints at prune, vanilla, walnut. Notes of smoke in the mouth along with dry oak. Slightly astringent finish. An armagnac to smell rather than drink.

St. Pé St. Simon (Lot et Garonne), population 199

Pine trees, vineyards, soy beans and sunflowers...not much else in this small town between Mézin and Gabarret.

Proprietor: Léon Beyries ***Name of Property***: La Hauresse ***Vineyard size***: 9 ha (22 acres) ***Other production***: corn, sunflowers, white wine ***Grapes used for armagnac***: Ugni Blanc (50%), Bacco (25%), Colombard (25%) ***Percent of production used for distillation***: 10-15 % ***Soil***: *sables* (sand) ***Production of armagnac per year***: 7-8 hl a.p. (3-4 barrels) ***Distiller***: Michalouski ***Distillation***: *Armagnacaise* ***Alcohol degree when leaving the still***: 53°-55° ***Chai:*** Organized, dirt floor, humid ***Barrels***: Gascon, Limousin ***Oldest spirit still in cask***: 1964 ***Stock***: 90 hl a.p. (45 barrels) ***Blended armagnacs available***: VSOP, *Hors d'age* ***Vintages available***: 1970, 1964 ***Reduction***: Distilled water to 43°

La Hauresse is a small property that lies 8 kilometers east of Gabarret and 20 kilometres west of Mézin. Unfortunately for 65-year-old Léon Beyries, his property lies within the latter canton. When tasting his armagnacs, however, it is clear that they have much more in common with those of the neighboring Bas-Armagnac than with those of the Ténarèze. In addition, Beyries armagnacs have more in common with the *Bas* than just about any armagnac tasted from the Gers.

Beyries sandy soil is most probably the reason for this, although a healthy Bacco content, especially with the older vintages, also plays a role. The grapes are vinified together, distilled by one of Michalouski's *ambulant* alambics, then placed in barrels in a barn next to his house. They sit untouched until it is time to assemble a blend.

The commercial releases of Beyries (pictured above with his wife) always contain armagnacs nearly double the minimum requirements and offer excellent value. His vintages are naturally made and not normally reduced.

VSOP: Light amber. Rich nose that hints at nut, nougat, vanilla. Fairly rich mouthfeel with a layered texture, well-integrated wood and a moderately long finish.

Hors d'age (70% Bacco, a blend of 1974-1975 vintages): Hint of almond-scented *rancio* on the nose. Rich vanilla, deep caramel and prune in the mouth, with just a touch of dry wood on the finish. Moderately fat, supple texture. Excellent value.

1970: Amber with gold highlights. Hint of orange on the nose. Good attack, with plenty of alcoholic structure. Fruit remains somewhat feminine and light. Finishes with a kick of more masculine alcohol.

1964: Walnut on the nose. Fat fruit in the mouth with a trace of dry wood. Slightly dry finish is salvaged by a dollop of prune-scented fruit.

Valence-Sur-Baïse (Gers), population 1,157
Hillside bastide constructed in 1274 that passed between the English and the French over the course of several centuries. Nearby is the historic Abbaye de Flaran, one of the best preserved monasteries in France.

Proprietor: Mme. Jacqueline Palthey ***Name of Property***: Château du Busca-Maniban ***Vineyard size***: 12 ha (30 acres) ***Other production***: wheat, sunflowers, corn ***Grapes used for armagnac***: Ugni Blanc 90%, Colombard 10% ***Percent of production used for distillation***: 15% ***Soil***: *argilo-calcaires* (clay with a high proportion of limestone) ***Production of armagnac per year***: 60 hl a.p. (30 barrels) ***Distillation***: *Armagnacaise* ***Alcohol degree when leaving the still***: 60° ***Distiller***: Gironi ***Chai:*** Organized, cement and dirt floors, dry ***Barrels***: Regional ***Time in new oak***: 3 years ***Oldest spirit still in cask***: 1946 ***Stock***: 450 hl a.p. (225 barrels) ***Blended armagnacs available***: VS, VSOP, Napoléon, *Hors d'age* ***Vintages available***: 1975, 1973, 1968 ***Reduction***: With *petites eaux* to 43°

The Château du Busca-Maniban is one of the most beautiful remaining examples of Gascon architecture. The castle was commissioned in 1649 and was once the residence of the Marquis de Maniban. It also served as the home of magistrates of the Languedoc parliament during the 17th and 18th centuries.

Since 1802, the château has been owned by the family of Madame Palthey, who now divides her time between the Gers and Switzerland. The château is as impressive on the inside as it is from the outside. Tapestries hang upon the huge stone walls and a maze of hallways connect the various rooms.

Busca-Maniban has produced armagnacs since the Seventeenth century. What is thought to be the oldest distillery house in the region lies on the property; however, all the domaine's armagnacs are now distilled by Philippe Gironi at his nearby facility to a relatively high 60°. Busca-Maniban's biggest seller is their *Napoléon*, which averages seven years of age. It is reduced to 40°.

The best armagnacs tasted were the vintages from cask that had not been reduced. With these, the alcohol levels were between 43° and 46°, but there was enough depth of fruit to compensate for the higher levels of alcohol.

Napoléon: Hints of licorice, cocoa, light alcohol aromas. Pleasing, balanced armagnac of moderate depth.

1975 (46.3°): More concentrated aromas of almond, hint of dried apricot, peach and prune. Slightly dry finish. Decent length.

1968 (44°): Nice amber color with gold highlights. Fat, rich nose with hints of brown sugar. Finish is slightly herbal.

HAUT ARMAGNAC PRODUCERS

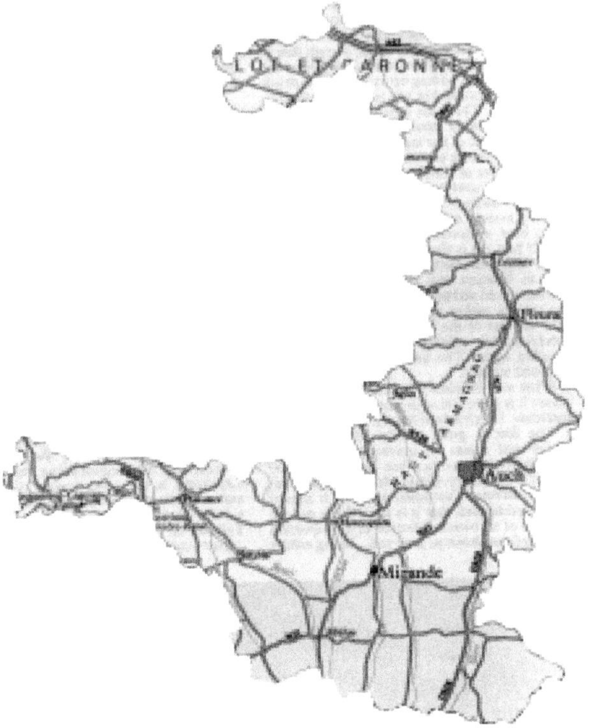

Even though the Haut-Armagnac encompasses nearly 50% of the Armagnac region, it is responsible for less than one percent of its production. In fact, one is hard-pressed to find more than scattered patches of vines in the Haut-Armagnac except for those near Plaisance—which are mostly used for the coopérative wines in Plaisance, and in Maumusson—the heart of Madiran.

Nowadays, only three producers remain in the Haut-Armagnac that sell more than half-a-barrel of armagnac a year. No *négociant* I spoke with claimed to use any Haut-armagnacs in their blends. The soil is the main reason for most people's disinterest: hard because of its elevated limestone content, its resultant spirit tends to be flat and lack depth. Instead of grapes, most farmers plant their fields with sunflowers, wheat, soy beans and corn.

While the quality of their spirit certainly falls behind that of the Western part of the region, their landscape is miles ahead; beautiful rolling hills are ablaze with color, while each curve in the road leads to a view more beautiful than the last.

Bassoues d'Armagnac, population 454

Picturesque village near which St. Fris was mortally wounded during an encounter between two tribes in 732. In the 10th Century, his sarcophagus was found by local shepherds who transferred it to the town's chapel where it can still be seen today. The town's bastide dates to the 13th Century, the church to the 15th Century.

Proprietor: Mr. Della Vedove ***Name of Property***: Domaine de Bilé ***Vineyard size***: 6 ha (15 acres) ***Other production***: wheat, corn, soy, sunflowers, peas, beans, white floc ***Grapes used for armagnac***: Ugni Blanc (100%) ***Percent of production used for distillation***: 40% ***Soil***: *argilo-calcaire* (clay with a high proportion of limestone) ***Production of armagnac per year***: 15 hl a.p. (7-8 barrels) ***Distillation***: *Armagnacaise* ***Distiller***: Coopérative de Vic-Fezensac ***Alcohol degree when leaving the still***: 60° ***Chai***: Organized, cement floor, dry ***Barrels***: None of the armagnacs see new oak ***Oldest spirit still in cask***: 1975 ***Stock***: 100 hl a.p. (50 barrels) ***Blended armagnacs available***: No ***Vintages available***: 1979, 1983, 1989 ***Reduction***: Distilled water and *petites eaux*

In 1962, Mr. Della Vedove moved from Lannepax in the Bas-Armagnac to his current farm between Marciac and Montesquiou in the Haut-Armagnac. Perhaps it was Della Vedove's Italian roots or his childhood memories of grape vines, but in 1968 he decided to plant vines. He set aside some money from his other crops each year and in 1973 had his wine distilled for the first time.

Today he continues to harvest grapes. They are brought to the *coopérative* in Vic, changed into wine, and later distilled with one of the coop's three alambics. Spirit is delivered to the farm several months later (although not necessarily the distillation from the wine he delivered, but perhaps from both the Bas-Armagnac and Ténarèze) and lodged in used barrels that lay in his small yet attractive *chai*.

Some of the barrels are in the traditional form, yet others contain 250 liters, the size Della Vedove claims was common during the latter part of the 18th century. Once every couple of years, he airs the spirit and allows it to breath. All of the property's armagnacs are slowly diluted with *petites eaux* and reach the market at 40°

Della Vedove likes the fruit that surfaces with armagnacs that are between 15 and 20 years old. Armagnacs with lots of age are not necessarily better, he states, just different. The domaine's armagnacs are never overwhelmed with too much oak or alcohol. They are correctly made, commercial armagnacs. Not surprisingly, most of the property's sales come from tourists who pass the farm en-route to view the 13th century bastide in nearby Bassoues.

1983: Surprisingly rich nose. Some sweetness in the mouth. Little wood influence. Lots of sweetness in the mouth. Moderate length.

1979: Pleasing sweetness of fruit on the nose. Smooth and sweet in the mouth with no rough edges. Very pleasing armagnac.

Préchac (Gers), population 133

Once the home of Antoine de Monlezun, governor of Armagnac during the 15th Century. The town's Fountain of Saint-Pé was famous as its water was thought to be beneficial for those with urinary diseases. Today one can visit a recently restored 19th Century church.

Proprietor: Claude Posternak ***Name of Property***: Château de Néguebouc ***Vineyard size***: 8 ha (20 acres) ***Other production***: None ***Grapes used for armagnac***: Ugni Blanc (50%), Folle Blanche (25%), Colombard (20%), Plainte de Grèce (5%) ***Percent of production used for distillation***: 100% ***Soil***: *boulbènes* (sand with clay pieces) ***Production of armagnac per year***: 40 hl a.p. (20 barrels) ***Distillation***: *Armagnacaise* ***Distiller***: ***Alcohol degree when leaving the still***: 53°-57° ***Barrels***: Limousin and Alsacian ***Oldest spirit still in cask***: ***Stock***: 120 hl a.p. (60 barrels) ***Blended armagnacs available***: Simple Distillation, Cuvée du Château ***Vintages available***: None ***Reduction***: Eau de Vie to 46°, armagnacs to between 43° and 45°.

Claude Posternak was an advertising executive in Paris before moving with his wife and three daughters to the Château de Néguebouc in Préchac. Posternak, a descendent of the Russian writer, has since become the leading spokesperson for the beleaguered Haut-Armagnac.

Posternak specializes in a series of *eau de vie* that are made with different varietals. Unlike many producers, Posternak harvests his grapes a week before maturity to help guard their acidity level. He only uses the first press juice and distills extremely early, normally during the third week of October. The wine enters the still as cold as possible, which further concentrates its aromas.

Posternak distills each varietal separately to different strengths, depending on the wine's initial alcohol level. Finally, each varietal is aired in stainless steel tanks in an effort to lessen some heavy esters.

The result? Highly aromatic *eau-de-vie* that truly show the varietal differences of the armagnac grapes before they enter the cask and are influenced by other factors: The Colombard shows good body and a fragrant herbal note. The Folle Blanche is delicate with a light floral note and hint of white pepper. The Ugni Blanc shows lots of body but has the least aromatic character. This trio is released in a 3 pack sampler and consumers are encouraged to drink them in different ways: as an *apéritif*, with various plates (like foie gras) or in between courses as the *trou gascon.*

Two blends are also released by the domaine, both of which put to rest the myth that no good armagnac is to be had east of the Ténarèze.

Cuvée de Château (70% Ugni Blanc, 20% Colombard, 10% Folle Blanche, 44.5°): Fruity nose hints at vanilla and melted toffee. Full-body, but lacking a little finesse.

Terraube (Gers), population 435

Terraube is the home of the beautiful 10th Century Château de Terraube, later enlarged during the 13th, 14th, and 15th Centuries. The château has been in the hands of the de Galard family since the beginning.

Proprietor: Victor de Galard ***Name of Property***: Château de Terraube ***Vineyard size***: 3 ha (7.4 acres) ***Other production***: None ***Grapes used for armagnac***: Ugni Blanc (100%) ***Percent of production used for distillation***: 100% ***Soil***: *argilo-calcaires* (clay with a high proportion of limestone) ***Production of armagnac per year***: 20 hl a.p. (10 barrels) ***Distillation***: Double-distillation ***Distiller***: Gimet of Cazeneuve ***Alcohol degree when leaving the still***: 72° ***Barrels***: Gascon and Limousin ***Stock***: 170 hl a.p. (85 barrels) ***Blended armagnacs available***: Réserve (10 years old) ***Reduction***: With distilled water to 42° ***Vintages available***: No

The small vineyards surrounding Terraube have been used to produce armagnac for several centuries. All of the chateau's Ugni Blanc production is taken to Gimet's distillery in Cazeneuve, passed twice through a *Charentaise* still, then returned to Terraube where it ages in small casks. Only one release is available, a 6 to 10-year-old blend called *Réserve*.

Réserve: Light amber color. Notes of pear, apple and caramel on the nose. Medium-body and without tremendous intensity. Pleasing commercial armagnac.

Le Tour de Lamothe, Cazeneuve

SELECTED ARMAGNAC NEGOCIANTS

The Négociant System

Traditional Armagnacs from a single vintage often provide unique and, indeed, mind-boggling complexity. Blends of various years can also provide wonderful drinking that is not only devoid of rough edges, but also consistent. Blends are most commonly released by *négociant* houses and, like in Cognac, comprise about 85% of Armagnac sales. *Négociants* do not normally have vines of their own; instead they buy partially or fully-made products, then commercialize them under a single brand name. Martell and Remy Martin are examples in Cognac. Johnnie Walker is an example in Scotland. Janneau is an example in Armagnac.

These houses normally have the experience and ability to seek out, blend, and commercialize a product whose parts, otherwise, would have difficulty reaching the market on their own. While an independent producer hopes to bottle and sell perhaps half a cask over the course of a year, he hopes to sell a cask or two in one fell swoop to a *négociant*. Of course he will receive less money for selling in bulk, but he also receives an immediate payoff and has a hell of a lot less paperwork. These *négociant* are important because they provide the money which allows the small producer to pay his bills and produce again the next year.

Most *négociant* houses are located in the center of the Armagnac region, not far from Condom or Eauze. Others are distillers by trade yet age and release some aged armagnacs on the side (Auban in Estang and Loubère in Labastide). Some *négociants*, however, are not even located in the Armagnac region. Interestingly, many are located in Cognac, including Cerbois (run by cognac *négociants*), and the less frequently seen A de Fussigny and Prunier.. Others are owned by cognac giants, including Gerland (owned by Camus). Still others are owned by drinks conglomerates, like Marquis de Caussade, Marquis de Montesquieu, Lapostolle, St. Vivant and Cles des Ducs.

Négociants operate in a number of ways:

a) They buy wine from growers, distill it with their own alambics, then age, blend and bottle it in their cellars (the case with Delord, Samalens, Dartigalongue, and Janneau). It is rare that a *négociant* house will buy only grapes from a grower; few have vinification equipment.

b) They can buy young armagnacs in a large quantities or in vats, normally from independent producers or coopératives. Then they age, blend, and bottle them in their cellars (the case with Larresingle, Cles des Ducs, Sempé, Trepout, Veuve Goudoulin).

c) They can purchase entire barrels of armagnac, transfer them to their own *chai*, and raise it until they feel it worthy of release (like Darroze, Gelas and Auxil).

d) They can buy certain aged vintages from independent producers or *negociants* and market them under their brand name (just about all *négociants*). Today it is common for *négociants* to buy between each other. Like that it is entirely possible for a vintage to be distilled in Bourrouillan by the Dufrechou family in 1968, purchased by Papalourey in 1991, and later sold to Trepout in 1997. This vintage is then bottled with the Trepout label and distributed around the world.

Many of these armagnacs are introduced to the *négociants* by agents known as *courtiers* who operate in much the same way as a literary or talent agent. They are sent samples which they screen; through experience, they know which types of armagnac interests each house. They negotiate a price with the producer, then the house. If the armagnac is useful to them, it is purchased.

Once the *négociant* has received the spirit, they blend, reduce, and market the product as their own. Many *négociants* have a number of brand names or *marques*. This enables them to release the same product in various countries under different names (so as not to piss off an importer), or create releases that have differing amounts of sugar, caramel, or alcohol without jeopardizing the established image of the house. At last count, there were over 350 *marques* available worldwide.

Styles between houses are less different than one might expect, however. Their major differences are with regard to body; Caussade, Cles des Ducs, and Trepout tend to favor heavier armagnacs, while Janneau, Sempé, and Larresingle strive for lighter armagnacs that are *easy* to consume.

Unfortunately, most *négociant* play to the mainstream's taste, rather than concentrating on products that display character or a unique sense of *terroir*. They strive for consistency; as one *maitre de chai* at a major *négociant* house stated, "We attempt to make our product on an excellent rather than outstanding level, because some years we might not have the goods to recreate an outstanding product and people will view this inconsistency as a flaw."

Another criticism with *négociants* is their general policy of reducing their spirits to 40° or 42°. While perhaps acceptable with young, commercially-oriented blends (which are not very serious anyway), the reduction of a vintage is reprehensible. Imagine a barrel that has remained untouched in the cellar of a producer for a few decades and that has relied on nature to bring it down to 45°. Suddenly it is reduced to 40° with the addition of 30 liters of water in one fell swoop. Why?

The answers are simple. Less tax to pay and additional volume to sell. If one adds 30 liters of water to something to bring it down to a *tame* degree, they immediately have thirty more liters to sell. For old vintages, this means a lot of extra money. Couple that with the amount of tax paid (tax on French spirits is calculated by its alcoholic degree, higher alcohol equals higher tax and vice-versa) and the profit margin becomes even wider.

In short, reduction comes down to nothing but greed on the *négociant's* part. No bottle that carries a vintage date should have an alcohol content of 40° or 42°. Even though its taste might be acceptable, a vintage at this degree should always be viewed with cynicism. It almost always means that reduction of some sort has taken place. And when reduction has taken place disrupting a spirit's natural harmony, chances are other *corrections* have also been made—those being boisé, sugar and caramel, the amounts of which ultimately dictate the style of a *négociant*.

In general, however, *négociants* release armagnacs that are, at worst, acceptable brandies and, at best, great—especially when they come from prime land, are well-aged *and* tactfully blended.

Because of this, one should not avoid the output of a big house just because they are *a big house*. Indeed, the work of a master blender operating with quality goods can produce a memorable, if not unforgettable, *digestif*.

The following negociants are located within the Armagnac region. Darroze and Auxil, both based in Les Landes, have been included, however, because of their vast selection of traditional releases from independent domaines located in some of Armagnac's most highly regarded areas.

ADEX (LA MAISON DE L'ARMAGNAC)

Village: Castelnau d'Auzan ***House founded***: 1996 ***Proprietor***: Chateau de Bordeneuve ***Brand Names***: Baron de Sigognac, Vaghi ***Percentage of armagnacs distilled on the property***: 80% ***Percentage bought***: 20% ***Sales per year (bottles)***: 30,000 ***Stock***: 300 hl a.p. (150 barrels) ***Region where base material originates***: 70% Bas-Armagnac, 30% Ténarèze ***Distillation type***: *Armagnacaise* ***Barrels***: Limousin ***Blended armagnacs reduced to***: 40° ***Vintage armagnacs reduced to***: 40° ***Production sold in France***: 15% ***Production exported***: 85%

This firm rose from the ashes of the Vaghi firm *La Maison de l'Armagnac* which experienced severe financial problems in the mid-1990's. ADEX (Armagnacaise de Distribution et d'Exportation) is now owned by the Guasch family of Eauze and run by Thomas Guasch. Fabrice Vaghi is currently the *maitre de chai.*

ADEX distributes a wide variety of commercial blends and vintages, some under the Vaghi name and others under the Baron de Sigognac and Baron de Pibrac labels. All are reduced to 40° and have relatively wide distribution throughout the world.

1985 (40°): Barrel mushrooms on the nose. Soft and sweet in the mouth, with recurring barrel notes. Short.

1978 (40°): Pleasing vanilla-scented oak, toffee, a hint of barrel mushrooms. Adequate length.

1973 (40°): Soft toffee, along with a hint of nuts and mushrooms. Very soft mouth, lacks some penetration. Decent length.

AUXIL

Village: Saint-Geours-de-Marenne ***House founded***: 1978 ***Proprietor***: Societé Auxil Fatima ***Percentage of armagnacs distilled on the property***: 0% ***Percentage bought***: 100% ***Brand name***: Castelsegur ***Sales per year (bottles)***: 15,000 ***Stock***: 190 hl a.p. (95 barrels) ***Region where base material originates***: Bas-Armagnac (Hontanx, Manciet, Le Frêche, Lannemaignan) ***Distillation type***: *Armagnacaise* ***Blended armagnacs reduced to***: 40° or 45° ***Vintage armagnacs***: Non-reduced ***Production sold in France***: 90% ***Production exported***: 10%

Large *négociant* firm founded by a Christian brotherhood known as *Les Freres de Fatima.* Located near the Basque coast, their headquarters lie a good hour outside the armagnac region in the town of Saint-Geours-de-Marenne. The firm specializes in the production of pastis, as well as the distribution of single malt scotches and armagnacs.

Their brand name, Castelsegur, comprises 50% of their armagnac sales. Three releases are available for the mass market, all from grapes grown and distilled in the Bas- Armagnac and reduced to 40°. *L'Hermitage*, a 5-year-old, *Reserve des Moins*, ranges from 8 to 15 years-of-age, while the *XO* is a blend of armagnacs between 12 and 20-years- old, minimally reduced to 45°. 50% of their sales are from single vintages.

They are to be applauded for these vintages, which normally come from individual properties in the *Grand Bas-Armagnac.* Like Darroze, the property name and bottling date is listed prominently on the label, something which helps document the authenticity of the spirit inside. They are released at cask strength and are excellent examples of traditional armagnac.

Reserve des Moins: Light, pleasing floral notes on the nose. Medium-body. Caramel notes on the palate, with a smooth, pleasing finish.

XO: Rich nose hints at dried brown fruits and spice. Full-bodied palate, with light hints of *rancio.* Nice length. Excellent commercial armagnac.

The following armagnacs are bottled in their orginal state and marketed by Auxil:
Domaine de Lagoue (Hontanx) 1984
Domaine de Cazenave (Le Frêche) 1982

Domaine de Jean du Haut (Perquie) 1983, 1979
Domaine de Beroy (Castandet) 1976, 1973
Domaine de Laubuchon (Manciet) 1975, 1970
Domaine de Beauregard (Le Bourdalat) 1974
Domaine de Luzan (Perquie) 1966
Domaine Le Durre (St. Gein) 1965
Domaine de Bordenave (Hontanx) 1962
Domaine de Nöel (St. Justin) 1946, 1949
Chateau de Gaube (Gaube) 1964, 1959, 1956
Domaine de Rincaulet (Maulèon) 1929

In addition, Auxil also releases vintages from two properties in the Ténarèze:
Domaine de la Grangerie (Lannes) 1980
Domaine de Tambouriat (Cassaigne) 1963, 1962

CASTARÈDE

Village: Lavardac ***House founded***: 1832 ***Proprietor***: The Castarède Family ***Percentage of armagnacs distilled on the property***: All since 1984 ***Percentage bought***: All current vintages ***Sales per year (bottles)***: 45,000 ***Stock***: 400 hl a.p. (200 barrels) ***Region where base material originates***: Nogaro, Manciet, Bourrouillan, Castex d'Armagnac, Mauléon ***Distillation type***: *Armagnacaise* ***Distiller***: *Themselves and St. Martin of Réans* ***Type of Oak***: Gascon, Limousin ***Blended armagnacs reduced to***: 40° ***Vintage armagnacs reduced to***: 40° ***Production sold in France***: 50% ***Production exported***: 50%

Castarède is the oldest *négociant* firm in the Armagnac region, founded in 1832 by Jules Nismes. Strategically located near Baïse River (which empties into the Garonne), they were also the first domaine to ship their armagnacs to Bordeaux and beyond. This warehouse is still owned by Castarède, but in a more symbolic than practical fashion.

Nowadays Castarède distills all of its younger product at their property in Maulèon, the Château de Maniban. (See also Château de Maniban). These are comprised of Ugni Blanc and Colombard, distilled once to 55°. The spirit starts its life in large wooden vats, is reduced, then placed in barrels where it ages. Every few years it is further reduced, blended and prepared for the market.

Castarède's commercial armagnacs are round and tend to emphasize their fruit. The majority of their vintages are Bacco-based and bought from reliable producers in the central and eastern parts of the Bas-Armagnac. They always reach the market at 40°.

CHÂTEAU DE MAILLIAC

This *négociant* firm has been closed since the mid-Nineties, yet was once widely available abroad. Its remaining stock was sold to the cognac firm Coirvoisier, who is now in the process of selling to other *negociants*. Parts of this château, located in Montréal-du-Gers, have been in existence since the middle ages. It was most recently run by the Bertholon family, who bought the majority of grapes from local growers.

While Château de Maillac was in full-swing, its wines were double-distilled, then the spirit was housed in new oak for 6 to 12 months. After reduction to 50°-55°, the armagnac was transferred to older oak and gradually reduced 3% at a time with distilled water. The result was a fiery, yet aromatic, armagnac. The firm's pride and joy was an armagnac distilled exclusively from Folle Blanche, grown on the sandy soil at the far western corner of the Bas-Armagnac.

The Chateau de Maillac still exists, yet its armagnacs have made their way to the Charente.

CLES DE DUCS

Village: Panjas ***House founded***: 1900 ***Proprietor***: Remy-Cointreau ***Percentage of armagnacs distilled on the property***: 0% ***Percentage bought***: 100% ***Sales per year (bottles)***: 571,000 ***Stock***: 9,000 hl a.p. (4,500 barrels) ***Region where base material originates***: 50% Ténarèze, 50% Bas-Armagnac from the communes of Gondrin, Panjas, St. Mont, Aignan, Labastide ***Distillation type***: *Armagnacaise* ***Barrels***: Limousin and Tronçais ***Size of aging vessels***: 80% 400 liter barrels, 20 % Vats ***Oldest armagnac still in pièce***: 1942 ***Blended armagnacs reduced to***: 40° ***Production sold in France***: 70% ***Production exported***: 30%

Cles de Ducs was started near the turn of the century and has since changed owners several times. Its most influential owner has been Izarra, the liqueur producer from the Basque country who for years fortified their liqueur with armagnacs from Cles des Ducs. Over fifty years ago, they finally decided to buy the company and distribute their product from their home base in Bayonne.

In 1980, Cles des Ducs was sold to Cointreau, and ownership was passed to Remy-Cointreau at the beginning of the 1990's.

Cles des Ducs is easily the largest selling armagnac in France and very close to the top with regards to the international market. 95% of their armagnacs are on the VS and VSOP levels; consequently one would be hard pressed not to find a bottle of Cles des Ducs in a French supermarket.

At the two large *chai* in Panjas, they have three storage areas that hold a total of nearly 3,000 barrels. Cles des Ducs prefers to keep their warehouses relatively warm which promotes the respiration of the spirit through the wood.

Cles des Ducs owns no stills of their own. Much of their *eau de vie* comes from cooperatives in Panjas and Aignan. Gimet is another large source, and his contributions come from Labastide d'Armagnac and Gondrin. All are distilled one time only.

The grape blend is the same for each level of armagnac; 40% Ugni Blanc, 40% Colombard, 15% Bacco, and 5% Folle Blanche. Half comes from the Bas-Armagnac and half from the

Ténarèze.

Most of the wood barrels are made near Condom from wood grown in Tronçais or Limousin. *Maitre de Chai* Philippe Lezama insists that at least 50% of the recently distilled spirit sees at least 6 months of new oak.

Apart from the rare vintages, all armagnacs are gradually reduced to 80 proof. All are assembled from numerous barrels. "There are not many single armagnacs," states Lezama. "Like people, most armagnacs want to get married, to share their life with others."

The older armagnacs of Cles des Ducs tend to have a viscous mouthfeel along with rich, mature fruit and elements of *rancio* (partially from age, partially from permitted additives). This round, fat character is sure to please fans of full-bodied spirits.

VSOP: Amber with gold highlights. Light fruit on the nose, with hints of vanilla. Fairly smooth mouthfeel, yet slightly hot on the finish..

Napoléon: Hints of almond on the nose. Notes of plum jam and apricot in the mouth, with a very viscous texture. A huge step up from the VSOP.

XO: Highly aromatic nose hints at almond and walnut, along with pepper, clove, and tobacco. Good richness in the mouth, with good integration of fruit and wood. Good length. Well-made commercial armagnac.

21 Year Old (tasted 1995): Very thick texture, with hints of orange and spice. The wood is well-integrated, and the finish is smooth and long. Seductive armagnac.

25 Year Old (the production of the 21 year old was discontinued in 1997, replaced instead with a 25 year old, also known as their Hors d'Age): Extremely advanced *rancio* on the nose; walnuts, mature port, aged vanilla. Very rich texture, yet too much oak gives a dry palate with loads of tannin. Decent length, but with simply too much oak in the mouth.

1973 (46°): Amber with gold highlights. Lighter color than blends. Some prune and pepper and with a hint of apricot. Good integration of alcohol and good length.

DARROZE

The affinity between the Darroze name and quality cuisine dates back several generations. During the 1920's, Jean Darroze became the first trained chef of the family after apprenticing at some of the top restaurants in France. His exposure to cuisine came from his mother, a cook, and his father, a baker, both of whom ran the inn of Villeneuve-de-Marsan. When Jean returned to Villeneuve in 1928, he achieved success fairly quickly, soon becoming one of the top chefs in the Southwest. His upgraded restaurant featured traditional Gascon cuisine and specialized in game birds like becasse and ortolan. With the help of Raymond Baudouin, founder of the Revue de Vins de France, Jean Darroze began building a wine list that soon rivaled the top restaurants of France. In exchange for Baudoin's wine advice, Jean Darroze taught him about armagnac and sampled him on the restaurant's enormous collection, all bottled by neighboring producers.

His son Francis started working at the restaurant when he was 18; he participated in the tasting conversations between his father and Baudoin, but his principle interest at the time was rugby. When Jean retired, Francis took over as maitre d'hotel and became more involved with the restaurant. Of course he continued his father's tradition of searching for armagnacs from small, regional producers to serve to customers after the meal (see menu on the following page).

In 1973, Francis came across a small armagnac-producing property and decided to buy an entire barrel rather than the customary pot gascon. He bottled the armagnac himself and gave several bottles to various restaurateur friends around France. Before long, those friends began asking for more.

Word began to spread. Clients at France's top restaurants were soon enamored by the traditional armagnac packaged with the simple brown label. The restaurants began buying bottles to serve to their discriminating guests. Darroze's side-business began to gain popularity. Soon bottles were being shipped to the top restaurants of Europe.

Francis soon began researching another property. This time he was caught between two. He decided to buy them both and age them at his mother-in-law's property several kilometres outside of the Armagnac region in Roquefort. Before long, thirty barrels filled the chai.

1976: Anatole Saint-Jean, owner of racehorses and eleveur of armagnac, decides to sell some 300 barrels—his entire stock—at the Domaine de St. Aubin. Made with pure Bacco and raised just outside the Bas-Armagnac town Le Houga, it is a négociant's fantasy! Saint-Jean, aware of Darroze's integrity, decides to sell it all to the restaurateur. It is one of the most important purchases in armagnac history, and certainly lays the foundation for the Darroze firm.

Today the name Darroze is known and respected around the world. Seeing that they distill no product of their own, they are considered négociants, certainly a pejorative tag when put in the same boat with some others who dilute and traffic their spirits. The truth is, under the roof of their modern chai, constructed in 1982, lies one of the most superb collections of armagnac ever assembled. Specializing in vintages from the hotbeds of the top regions in the Bas-Armagnac, walking through the Darroze chai can be likened to walking through an Armagnac hall of fame!

Every barrel has the property name chalked into its side like the engravings on championship trophies; Jouanchicot, Guillemouta, Coquillon, Juliac, aux Ducs; attached tags clearly mark the minute lessening of degree over the years. The casks are all worked separately; if the alcohol is slightly out of balance, it is racked and exposed to some additional air. If it lacks tannin, it is temporarily exposed to new wood. If it has consumed its optimum tannin, it is transferred to a barrel that no longer gives flavoring components. In general, however, most of the armagnacs rely on slow oxidation to concentrate and ultimate release the spirit's wonderful aromas.

vous présente sa sélection
de véritables Eaux-de-vie Régionales du Bas-Armagnac

(Certaines bouteilles sont en cave depuis plus de quarante ans)

Propriétaires	Année	Degré	Origines	Prix le verre 2 cl. environ
Sélection Jean Darroze (10 ans de fût)		50°5		7,50
*Domaine Roumégoux	1961	51°	Hontanx (en fût d'origine de 400 litres)	8,50
*Domaine d'Ognoas Départemental	1962	47°	Arthez-d'Armagnac	8,50
*Domaine Roumégoux	1942	49°5	Hontanx (en fût d'origine de 400 litres)	10
*Domaine J.-B. Boingnères-Lafitte	1928	48°	St-Vidou	20
*Domaine Jean Dibos	1942	47°8	Le Frêche	20
*Domaine de Capdepont	1942	48°5	Bourdalat (en fût d'origine de 400 litres)	20
*Domaine de Pariot	1934	47°8	Gaube	25
*Domaine de Roumégoux	1938	49°5	Hontanx (en fût d'origine de 400 litres)	20
*Domaine Marcel Bonneau	1939	46°	Montégut	20
*Domaine Labarthe	1937	48°2	Arthez-d'Armagnac	30
*Domaine Victor Lugardon	1924	48°5	Mauléon-d'Armagnac	30
*Domaine J.-B. Boingnères-Lafitte	1920	48°5	St-Vidou	30
*Domaine Lugardon	1918	40°	Mauléon-d'Armagnac	30
*Château de Muret	1941	48°	Gaube	30
*Domaine Dufour	1924	48°8	Arthez-d'Armagnac	30
*Domaine d'Ognoas Départemental	1942	48°	Arthez-d'Armagnac	30
*Domaine Rincaulet Beyrie	1933	47°5	Mauléon-d'Armagnac	40
*Domaine Rincaulet Beyrie	1923	47°	Mauléon-d'Armagnac	40
Château de Poyferré	1913	40°	Arthez-d'Armagnac	40
*Domaine Rincaulet Beyrie	1918	47°	Mauléon-d'Armagnac	40
Domaine Laberdolive	1904	40°	Labastide-d'Armagnac	40
Domaine Laberdolive	1919	40°	Labastide-d'Armagnac	40
*Domaine Claverie	1900	48°	Lannemaignan	40
*Domaine du Miquer	1900	47°	Hontanx	40
*Domaine Rincaulet	1918	46°5	Mauléon-d'Armagnac	40
*Domaine Rémazeilles	1900	47°	Arthez-d'Armagnac	40
*Docteur Pitous (Barbotan)	1904	46°5	Lagrange	40
Domaine Laberdolive	1878	40°	Labastide-d'Armagnac	40
*Château de Muret	1906	47°5	Gaube	50
*Domaine Rémazeilles	1904	47°5	Arthez-d'Armagnac	50
*Domaine A. Claverie	1900	47°8	Hontanx	50
*Domaine Galabert	1893	48°	Bourdalat	50
*Domaine Queyroux	1900	47°5	Arthez-d'Armagnac	50
*Domaine Capin	1890	46°8	Gaube	50
*Domaine Dufour	1893	47°5	Arthez-d'Armagnac	50
*Domaine Rincaulet Beyrie	1893	47°	Mauléon-d'Armagnac	50
*Domaine Dupeyron	1900	47°	Le Frêche	50
*Docteur Pitous	1898	46°5	Lagrange	50
*Château de Muret	1873	46°8	Gaube	50

En dehors des Heures de Service, notre clientèle peut demander à voir vieillissement naturel des Armagnacs. Le nombre des visiteurs en cave est limité à quatre.

Reduction is the enemy of an armagnac purist, and therefore a dirty word at Darroze headquarters. Likewise, sugar syrup, boisé, and caramel are regarded as being sleazy ways of making a quick buck. One thing is certain at Darroze; an armagnac takes time and patience, yet also careful attention. Contrary to what some people might think, an armagnac does not make itself. It must be guided along the way, led by the hand with not only love but understanding.

Several producers (Deyres, Cazenave) sell the majority of their production to Darroze every year. About 60% of Darroze armagnacs, however, come from estates that no longer produce. Their land, in most cases, no longer contains vines. Although the exact percentages are unclear, it is certain that Bacco was their dominant grape and that they were distilled at a low degree. The remaining 10% of the firm's stock is bought through agents who happen to stumble upon a superb find first.

Francis Darroze recently retired, and his spirited son Marc now runs the firm with expertise. He has expanded distribution to North and South America, Asia, and increased their presence on Europe's top tables.

Today, the Darroze name is much better known for armagnac than it is for food: their stock totals some 380 barrels, aged on two different floors. The top is somewhat dry, accelerating the loss of volume. The bottom level is more humid, which helps diminish the level of alcohol. Another chai, located next door, is extremely humid and houses several dozen barrels.

Darroze releases still sport the classic brown label and red wax seal. The label always bears the name of the original domaine, giving full respect to the property from which the armagnac came. Even before it became law, the back label always documented bottling date.

The firm currently markets armagnacs from nearly 45 properties. Their quantities do not, however, last forever. If two barrels are bought from a particular year, after evaporation one might expect for 900 bottles to reach the market. Understandably, when they're gone, they're gone.

Of course, there is always another unique release that is true to its terroir which will replace it on the market. And one can always feel confident that the amber liquid within the next bottle will, like its predecessor, also be completely authentic, as well as rare and collectible.

Réserve Spéciale (Darroze's only commercial release, a blend of three properties between 10 and 14 years of age, and reduced to 43°): Fairly unevolved, one dimensional nose that remains flat. Caramel notes in the mouth along with a damp note and some finishing heat.

Serie Rare (a blend of two properties, both distilled in 1965): Deep nose hinting at plums, apricot, vanilla. Extremely well-integrated oak in the mouth with lots of pepper. Excellent balance between alcohol, wood and tannin. Long and very good.

Various Properties Marketed By Darroze

The majority of the Darroze stock is comprised of several vintages from several dozen domaines scattered across the Bas-Armagnac region. A purchase price is normally negotiated between Darroze and the producer; afterwards, the barrels are purchased, transferred to the *chai* in Roquefort and observed.

The firm has a special agreement with other producers; a large percentage of each year's distillation is purchased in return for guaranteed cash. Darroze, like other *négociants*, also buys small quantities of older vintages which are stored in bon-bonnes.

Many of these domaines no longer exist; perhaps the owner died and the family decided to sell the property or replant with corn or another crop. In most cases, the recent vintages come from domaines that still exist. Many of these producers also market some vintages from their own property. However as the wood, aging techniques and storage conditions differ, so does the final result.

Further information can be found on the producers marked with an asterisk in the Bas-Armagnac directory.

Domaine de La Bataille (La Frêche, Landes)

Seven hectare estate planted on sables fauves in the heart of the Grand Bas-Armagnac. Old vine Bacco and Ugni Blanc are divided evenly and distilled at 52°, then aged in regional oak.

Armagnacs from La Bataille are always overflowing with fruit; the prune, banana, and apricot flavors have lovely-integrated spice notes.

1966 (44°): Lots of fruit on the nose, along with noticeable alcohol. Peach, apricot, prune, cinnamon, hints of licorice. Lively in the mouth, with lots of spice. Additional notes of licorice. Smooth tannins of good quality, and very good length.

1950 (41.5°): Complex nose, mixing lots of fruit (orange, prune, quince) with cinnamon, licorice and acacia. Deep fruit in the mouth, without any aggressiveness. Mellow and long.

1949 (45°): Slightly different style for the domaine, with an elevated wood-level on the nose along with licorice, damp earth and prune notes. Lots of finesse in the mouth, with hints of smoke, *rancio* and damp earth. Very earthy, complex and good armagnac.

Marc Darroze...continuing his father's unending quest for quality.

1945 (42°): Dried prune and apricot on the nose, along with cinnamon and licorice. Very explosive and lively in the mouth, with similar notes as those found on the nose.

1943 (41°): Exceptional balance between the aromas of wood, alcohol and fruit. Lots of prune in the mouth, with hints of white and dark chocolate. Extremely well-balanced.

Domaine de Bel Air (Lacquy, Landes)

1966: Evolved nose shows floral notes (acacia) as well as licorice and almond. Alcohol and tannin still fairly strong on palate. Plenty of licorice and pepper on the finish.

Domaine de Bidaous (Hontanx, Landes)

1973: Very expressive nose shows apricot, prune and vanilla notes. Similar flavors in mouth, along with a touch of earthiness. Alcohol and wood in excellent balance. Good pure length.

Domaine de Capdepont (Le Bourdalat, Landes)

1.6 hectare property that was planted with old vine Bacco on sables fauves, distilled at 53° and aged in regional oak. The Domaine de Capdepont no longer exists.

Because of a very humid chai, the armagnacs of Capdepont matured quickly and showed hints of rancio at a young age. Because of low alcohol levels, these armagnacs are extremely flattering and normally display a sexy mouthfeel.

1966 (40°): Fine nose with hints of *rancio* (walnuts, almonds,) prune, tobacco and licorice. Excellent balance in the mouth, with delicate tannin and well-integrated alcohol. Lots of fruit, including quince, honey, figs, coffee, mocha and an earthy note. Good length.

1964 (40°): Fine nose with lots of fruit, including quince, prune, orange jam and spicy oak. Almost syrupy in the mouth, with notes of honey and orange. Fine tannin and alcohol in balance, giving the spirit's tremendous fruit some structure. Excellent.

1954 (41°): Plenty of licorice and vanilla on the nose, along with leather and coffee. Wonderful concentration of fig and prune, and with an extremely long finish.

Domaine de Coquillon (Le Frêche, Landes)

Located in a town known for producing fine armagnacs, this extremely small property had just over 3 hectares of vines planted in 1950. Bacco comprised 60% of the plantings, while Ugni Blanc comprised 40%. The property was owned by the recently departed Albert Faget, whose grandson, Gilles Bartholomo, is the area's favored cooper.

The varietals were distilled separately by Roumat, and the eaux-de-vie dripped from the alambic at 53°. The assemblage took place after distillation, and the spirit remained in new wood for at least four years.

The property is known for nurturing fat and round armagnacs, with lots of prune, coffee and spice notes, in addition to the early development of rancio. A wonderful place to begin one's exploration of traditional armagnac.

1986 (51.5°): Somewhat aggressive nose that combines notes of apricot, vanilla, caramel and orange peel. Palate beginning to gain fat.

1985 (51.5°): Hints of peach and bitter orange; in short, lots of fruit. Plenty of spice in the mouth, along with some new wood aromas still not completely integrated. Excellent potential.

1983 (50°): Nose still marked by new wood aromas (chocolate, cocoa, vanilla). Lots of spice on the palate, including prune, licorice, clove and pepper. Good length.

1980 (49°): Nose: Fig, quince, prune, walnut, vanilla. Good attack with additional hints of cinnamon and licorice. Very good balance between tannin, alcohol and aromas.

1979 (49°): Aromas of fruit preserved in syrup (prune and raspberry) as well as vanilla. Lots of flavor and fat for its age. Prune, licorice and chocolate on the palate. Very flavorful and long.

1977 (49°): Very expressive nose, with notes of prune, roasted coffee, toast, gunflint, licorice, vanilla and chocolate. Complex in the mouth, with slightly dry tannin. Dry finish.

1976 (43.5°): Nose: Prune, quince, toast, leather and almond. Lots of finesse on the palate.

1975 (46°): Exotic nose hints at banana and almond paste. Full-bodied and feminine, with plenty of fat and supple tannin. Hint of licorice on the finish. Very long.

1974 (47°): Brilliant chestnut color. Spicy oak on nose, as well as mocha, chocolate, cocoa and coffee. Prune, fig, and quince in mouth, with additional hints of licorice, coffee, coconut and walnut. Wonderful balance between rich aromas, round tannins and integrated alcohol. Wood present, but not dry. Very good length. Super armagnac!

1973 (48°): Deep, open aromas include prune, quince, toast and leather, along with hints of *rancio*. Very good structure in mouth, with rich fruit, smooth tannin, and well-integrated antique oak notes.

1972 (48°): Honey, white peach, fig—lots of sweet fruit. Plenty of wood spice in mouth (pepper, clove) which is intricately balanced by vanilla, cinnamon and a hint of almond. Very long.

Domaine aux Ducs (Le Bourdalat, Landes)

Six hectare domaine owned by the Deloi family for generations. Located in the center of the Grand Bas-Armagnac, the sables fauves-based soil was planted with 100% Bacco whose vines averaged 40 years of age.

Distillation was by Mr. Lasserre of Hontanx. The spirit was aged in new oak from the region for its first five years, then transferred to older casks until bottling time.

Earthy armagnacs, often evoking scents of gun flint and acacia. Layers of preserved fruit rise above this complex length, balanced with the spirit's well-integrated tannin.

1978 (48.5°): Mahogany with golden highlights. Forthcoming aromatics that bring pepper, chocolate, coffee, licorice and toast to mind. Additional hints of gun flint. Full-bodied mouth is well-structured; additional notes of cinnamon and pepper continue on the long finish.

1961 (44): Mahogany with golden highlights. High-pitched fruit includes preserved orange and apricot. Supple mouthfeel with additional notes of cinnamon, cocoa and baking chocolate. Nice length.

1960 (43°): Mahogany, with chestnut highlights. Lots of wood on the nose, along with roasted coffee, chocolate, licorice, prune, quince and caramel. Silky tannins support this armagnac's considerable weight. Fine texture and excellent length.

1958 (41°): Mahogany, with golden highlights. Earthy, rich aromas of fig, licorice and damp soil are balanced by sweeter aromas of cocoa, quince and caramel. Lots of wood in the mouth, behind which remains a spirit with silky, round tannins and excellent richness.

1955 (42°): Golden color with brown highlights. Classy nose once again balances earthiness with lighter aromas of acacia, orange peel, cinnamon and vanilla. In the mouth, everything is in harmony; the fruit (prune, apricot, fig, quince), the alcohol and the silky tannins. Wonderful armagnac!

1942 (41.5°): Mahogany, with chestnut highlights. Viscous texture masks any sign of alcohol but yields lots of jammy fruit (apricot and quince) along with considerable *rancio*. Silky tannins struggle beneath the fruit creating a somewhat flabby finish.

1941 (40.5°): Mahogany with brown reflections. After aeration, a superb nose is released that includes notes of vanilla, quince, cinnamon and coffee. The alcohol gives this spirit continued life—even at over fifty years of age! Prune, cinnamon, clove and menthol aromas persist on the long finish.

Domaine d'Eauze (Eauze, Gers)

1965 (46.5°): Deep amber with red highlights. Some heat on the nose. Penetrating aromas of prune and vanilla. Similar flavors persist in the mouth.

Domaine d'Eyres (Arthez, Landes)

1973: Deep amber with gold highlights. Rich nose includes prune, licorice, vanilla and cinnamon. Flavors continue on the rich palate, along with a lovely hint of orange peel.

Domaine de Gaube (Gaube, Landes)

1967 (44°): Chestnut with gold highlights. Dried apricot and figs on the nose, along with licorice, vanilla and walnut. Silky, fine tannin on the palate. Excellent length.

1966 (46°): Deep amber with chestnut highlights. Nose includes aromas of vanilla, antique wood and dried fruits. Medium-bodied, with additional notes of pepper, cinnamon and clove. Polished antique-oak notes finish slightly dry. Traditional, rustic armagnac.

Domaine de Guillemouta (Le Frêche, Landes) *
Often understated and extremely complex armagnacs that always contain lots of finesse. High levels of alcohol are normally submerged beneath a wave of fruit. An herbaceous complexity is normally present, along with hints of dried fruits and spice.

1982 (48°): Amber with dep amber highlights. Nose soars from the glass atop a wave of alcohol: prune, vanilla, licorice. A fig note sneaks in on the finish. Still young, but with excellent potential. Long finish.

1981 (47°): Complex nose that includes good quality oak, mint, white pepper, licorice, leather and prune. Plenty of flavor in the mouth; licorice, mint, white pepper, pine, almond, walnut. Excellent length.

1980 (48°): Extremely fine, herbal aromas on nose (fern, linden tea) along with coffee and chocolate notes. Supple mouth, with flavors that include dried fig, walnut, almond and licorice. Well-integrated tannin.

1979 (47°): Lovely amber color. Well-balanced nose includes hints of *rancio*, hay, apricot, quince and dried fig. Good depth of flavor in mouth, with additional spicy oak, pepper and licorice. Very penetrating spirit, and with good length.

1978 (50°): Lots of alcohol on the nose, along with fern, mint, dried flowers, licorice and pepper. Very supple tannin in the mouth that allows lots of flavor; prune, quince, dried fig, mint and white pepper. Very long.

1977 (50°): Good balance between alcohol and aromas. Floral hints on nose, along with prune, licorice, coffee, chocolate. Vanilla, cinnamon and licorice in mouth, with smooth, well-integrated tannin.

1976 (47°): Lots of fine aromas on the nose; licorice, white pepper, mint, dried flowers, mint, prune, quince. Good structure in the mouth, and with well-developed tannins. Deep flavors of vanilla, caramel, dark chocolate. Good length.

1975 (47.5°): Deep, rich aromas that include prune, quince, vanilla, orange and honey. Similar flavors in the mouth, followed by hints of clove, cinnamon and mint. Tannins are well-structured. Good length.

1974 (47.5°): Aromas of quince, prune, dried fig, mint and white pepper. In the mouth, licorice, vanilla, white pepper and fig flavors. Slightly drying tannin on the finish.

Domaine de Jeanblanc (Hontanx, Landes)
20 hectare domaine with soil comprised of sand and clay. Jeanblanc used only Bacco for their armagnacs and distilled at 56° .

1962 (44°): Mahogany color with chestnut highlights. Some heat on the nose. With aeration, interesting aromas surface: dried apricot, fig, cinnamon, licorice. Supple in the mouth, with delicate tannin. Additional notes of quince and pepper become evident on the moderately long finish.

Domaine de Jouanchicot (Domaine de Dupont): (Mauleon d'Armagnac, Gers)
Six hectare property owned by Dr. Jacques. Dupont—under whose name the domaine is referred

to in America—and whose distribution is handled entirely by the Darroze firm. The property was planted exclusively with old-vine Ugni Blanc—an anomaly for Darroze as the majority of their armagnacs are made with Bacco.

Ugni Blanc grown on the tawny-colored sand yields an elegant and interesting armagnac that always contains class: White peach and flowers normally surface within the first few years, while years later exotic nuances of banana and mango occasionally arise. The armagnacs of Jouanchicot are always interesting to compare with Bacco-based armagnacs, if only to see what pure Ugni Blanc does when grown on sand and when distilled by the armagnac method.

1977 (48°): Prune and a hint of *rancio* on nose. Additional notes of orange peel and pepper. Very smooth, and with good length.

1976 (47°): Prune and flowers along with spicy oak. Additional notes of vanilla, caramel and white peach in the mouth. Very fine and long.

1975 (45°): Delicate aromas (dried fig, licorice, cinnamon and a floral note) in complete balance with wood that never becomes aggressive. Hint of pear and tobacco in the mouth, and alcohol that is in no way obtrusive. This armagnac is all about balance.

Barrels containing infant armagnacs and demi-johns containing pre-World War II vintages rest together on the upper level of Chez Darroze.

1974 (45°): Prune, dried fig, orange peel, and vanilla on the nose. Fat and smooth in the mouth, without excessive wood tannin. Hints of spice on the long finish.

1972 (44.5°): Amber with chestnut highlights. Profound nose that includes vanilla, caramel, cinnamon and chocolate. Round and balanced mouth, with smooth tannin. More vanilla and caramel on the finish, along with clove and cinnamon notes.

1970 (42°): Dried figs, mint and licorice on the nose. Lots of finesse. Notes of white and dark chocolate in the mouth, along with some vanilla. Well-sculpted tannins.

1969 (41.5°): Notes of quince, vanilla and wood spice on the nose. Extremely supple mouthfeel with an additional hint of apricot. Finishes with very soft tannin.

1968 (41°): Nose: Prune, fig, quince, along with spice (clove and white pepper). Similar notes in mouth, along with vanilla and acacia. Good balance between alcohol, tannins and aromas.

1967 (44°): Beautiful amber with red tints. Peach and apricot on the nose, along with some white pepper and cinnamon. Very delicate and not quite as giving as other armagnacs from the property. Some vanilla and acacia in mouth. Very silky tannins. Long finish.

1964 (43°): Wonderful nose shows complex aromas of prune, cinnamon and licorice. Similar flavors continue in the mouth atop very well-integrated tannin. Good stuff!

1963 (42°): Deep amber with red highlights. Very nice balance on the nose with plenty of dried fruit (apricot, quince), tobacco, hazelnut and oak. Very soft tannins allow the fruit to glide across the palate. Finishing notes include licorice and cinnamon. Nice length.

1957 (40.5°): Dried fruit notes on nose include apricot, white chocolate and vanilla. Plenty of prune in the mouth along with cinnamon and cocoa. Some drying tannin on the finish.

Domaine de Jouatmaou (Le Frêche, Landes) *

The armagnacs of Jouatmaou offer a grab-bag of aromas that normally begin to mesh at about 15 years of age when the tannin has integrated with its considerable fruit.

1985 (51°): Notes of peach, caramel and licorice on the nose. Rich mouthfeel, with plenty of prune, licorice, mint, pepper and spice. Long finish.

1984 (52°): Complex nose hints at almonds, walnuts, vanilla, acacia, licorice and pepper. Good balance between fine tannins and flavors in the mouth; vanilla, prune, quince and walnut. Good length.

1983 (47°): Lots of wood on the nose, as well as licorice, nuts, prune and toast. Very complex—rare for such a young armagnac. Plenty of fat in the mouth along with flavors of quince, prune and vanilla. Finishes with silky tannins.

1982 (51°): Lots of spice on the nose (white pepper, clove). Fine aromas of prune, quince, fig, tobacco and leather. Similar flavors in the mouth, with an additional hint of toast. An armagnac with lots of personality, although the tannin is still not fully-integrated.

1981 (48.5°): Complex aromatics include dried fig, almonds, tobacco, leather and toast. Smooth tannin in the mouth, and good balance with fruit flavors. Good length.

1980 (48.5°): Real fine nose, with lots of aromatics (toast, leather, prune, quince, cinnamon). Apricot and quince notes ride along a velvety texture. Very good length.

1979 (47.5°): Slightly muted nose that offers aromas of coffee, bitter chocolate, leather, prune, walnut and licorice. Good balance between smooth tannins, fruit aromas (prune, coffee, walnut, licorice) and alcohol. Very long and very good.

1978 (46°): Nose is dominated by nutty aromas and spice including pepper and cinnamon. Well-balanced mouth, with dried fruits and smooth tannins. Still not at its peak.

1977 (48°): Aromas of toast, dried fig and nutty notes that hint at *rancio*. In the mouth, licorice, vanilla and toast. Extremely long finish.

1976 (46.5°): Nice aromatic complexity with aromas that include quince, white chocolate and vanilla. Plenty of fat in the mouth—vanilla, caramel and prune flavors dominate. Lots of pepper and licorice on the finish. Very good armagnac.

Chateau de Juliac (Betbezer, Landes) *

Rich, fat armagnacs made for long-term aging. Sexy and seductive yet rarely hot, the passing years simply concentrated the spirit, adding complexity without infringing its vivaciousness.

1954 (45.5°): Chestnut color. Spicy nose, with lots of alcohol, although not in any way aggressive. An abundance of licorice, cinnamon and vanilla-scented wood in the mouth.

1951 (46.5°): Chestnut color with gold and red tints. Evolved nose that hints at caramel, spice and a note of *rancio*. Good structure and balance in mouth between alcohol and tannin, fruit and *rancio*. Opens up wonderfully with aeration.

Domaine de Laburthe (Lacquy, Landes)

1981: Rich aromatics hint at baked apple, acacia, fern, pear and quality toffee. Apricot, an herbal note, licorice and spice notes surface on the palate. Well-integrated wood. Very good length.

1980 (49°): An herbal note on the nose is reminiscent of acacia. Apricot and pear on the palate with a nice tannin/alcohol balance. Long finish.

1979 (45°): Amber with gold highlights. Nose: Dried fruit (apricot, prune) along with nuts (almond) and lots of spice (cinnamon, white pepper). Palate: Similar flavors with an additional note of leather. Very long.

1978 (40.5°): Nice combination of quince and prune, vanilla and almond. Very soft on the palate due to low alcohol level. Moderate length.

1977 (47°): Lots of nose (acacia, pear, hint of prune). Additional herbal note in the mouth as well as a touch of dried apricot. Long finish.

1976: Deep amber. Lots of vanilla and caramel aromas. Plenty of fat in the mouth, with hints of prune and licorice, as well as a spicy note on the long finish.

Domaine de Lagoué (Hontanx, Landes)

1981: Amber. Interesting nose evokes high-pitched citrus notes and flowers. Mouth shows good richness while managing to maintain finesse. Good length.

1980: Nose shows hints of mint and licorice. Once again combines a rich mouthfeel while managing to maintain finesse. Vanilla and spice on the long finish.

Domaine de Lusson (Mauléon d'Armagnac, Gers) *

The best word to describe Lusson is elegance: lots of finesse, complex aromas like dried flowers and bitter orange, and a wonderful balance between alcohol, spicy wood notes and fine tannins.

1970 (48°): Golden color with amber hints. Fig and prune dominate the nose, with some secondary notes of licorice. The mouth is very different from the nose; almonds and walnut, then licorice and spice. Silky finishing tannin.

1967 (45°): Elegant aromas include dried flowers and licorice. Elegance continues in the mouth, with a surprisingly rich texture. Classy armagnac.

Domaine de Mahu (Labastide d'Armagnac, Landes) *

As can be expected with most well-stored armagnacs of this age, a walnut character often surfaces with the Mahu bottlings. This and other rancio notes are wonderfully balanced by rich, viscous fruit that nearly conceals what tannin remains.

1949 (41.5°): Deep, very pleasant nose. Very complex aromas that include honey, vanilla, prune and citrus fruits. An abundance of prune, white chocolate and licorice notes in the mouth, with well-integrated tannin and excellent balance.

1948 (42°): Fairly closed on nose; with aeration, prune, chocolate and spice aromas surface. Complex mouth includes notes of chocolate, licorice and smoky oak. Very long finish.

1947 (42°): With aeration, plenty of aromas surface in the glass: fig, prune, coffee, chocolate. Fat mouthfeel, and with well-integrated tannin. Some vanilla and spice surfaces on the long finish.

1946 (43°): Light chestnut color with orange tints. Notes of mocha, coffee and grilled almonds on the nose, along with some earthy notes. Good fat in the mouth, with a supple texture which carries additional flavors of licorice, vanilla and walnuts. Excellent length.

1945 (42.5°): Aromatic nose includes dried figs, walnuts, almonds, vanilla and spice. Very round in the mouth, with nearly perfect balance between alcohol-aromas-tannin. Very long.

1941 (40°): Chestnut color with red tints. Fruity nose, with hints of orange, prune and banana, along with notes of wood spice. Apricot, prune and quince jam surface in the mouth. Good balance and very round.

1939 (44°): Deep chestnut color. Rich nose suggests chocolate, vanilla, licorice, white pepper and walnuts. Very fat and round in the mouth, with a velvety texture and high quality tannins. Shows additional flavors of quince jam, licorice, dried figs and prunes. Excellent length.

Domaine de Martin (Hontanx, Landes) *

Armagnacs from the Domaine de Martin always contain a very expressive nose, often hinting at prune, quince, vanilla and honey. Forward fruit helps make these armagnacs enjoyable in their youth.

1986 (51.5°): Amber with darker highlights. Lots of alcohol on the nose, With aeration, notes of dried apricot and orange peel. Still needs some time.

1985 (51.5°): Interesting, rich aromas include chocolate, coffee, fig and quince. Lots of alcohol on the palate which is, surprisingly, in balance with the fruit and tannin at this stage.

1984 (50.5°): Light amber color. Aromas of vanilla, prune, and a bourbon/nutty note. Flavors accentuated in the mouth by the alcohol. Very forceful, feisty even. Good pure length, relying on material rather than wood notes.

1983 (51.5°): Pale amber color. Expressive nose hints at spice; pepper, cinnamon and vanilla. Vanilla continues in mouth, merging into licorice. Very long.

1982 (51.5°): Pale amber with gold highlights. Hints of honey, peach, pear and pepper on the nose. Rich flavors of prune, honey and vanilla in the mouth. Well-integrated spicy oak on the finish.

1981 (50°): Prune, fig, vanilla, spice...Chocolate, clove, coffee and spice on the long finish.

1980 (46.5°): Golden amber with dark highlights. Aromas of prune, honey, quince, vanilla, licorice, pepper. Well-integrated wood and tannin. Fat notes of quince, prune and dried apricot in mouth. Extremely supple finish.

1979 (45°): Bright amber. Vanilla, caramel, cinnamon, quince, prune and dried fig on the nose. Fat in mouth, with well-integrated tannin. Spicy finish.

1976 (47.5°): Deep chestnut. Pruneau, coffee, cocoa on the nose. Lots of fat on the palate with a slightly dry, oak-driven finish.

1974 (46°): Amber with brown highlights. Deep and exciting aromas of banana, quince, prune, vanilla and cinnamon. Prune, quince and vanilla in the mouth. Well-integrated tannin. Good length.

Domaine de Monturon (Le Bourdalat, Landes)

1976: Intense fruit on the nose shows myriad flavors: preserved orange, mango, banana, *pruneau*. Similar fruit surfaces on the palate, along with wood notes that include licorice and cinnamon. Alcohol and wood in good harmony, yet outweighed by the fruit. Wonderfully exotic armagnac!

Domaine de Mouliot (St. Justin, Landes)

1959: Deep amber with chestnut shades. Pungent nose includes aromas of prune, oak, cinnamon and clove. Full-bodied, viscous texture with extremely supple tannins. Additional notes of white chocolate, licorice and prune in the mouth. Good length.

1924 (45°): Dark chestnut color. Rich aromas hint at dried fruit (fig, prune) and damp earth. Lots of wood on the palate does not overwhelm the sweet, viscous fruit. Good length.

Domaine de Peyron (Labastide d'Armagnac, Landes)

Domaine de Peyron covered 3 hectares and was planted with a large percentage of Bacco on sables fauves, but also contained parcels of Ugni Blanc and Colombard resting on chalk and limestone-based soil. The vines averaged 40 years of age, the wine was distilled at 52°, and the spirit was aged in a mixture of oak from the region and that of Limousin.

Peyron's armagnacs often contain lots of wood spice and finesse, adjectives often used to describe cognac. Because of this, Domaine de Peyron becomes a good place for the cognac aficionado to start his exploration into armagnac.

1974 (45.5°): Somewhat muted aromas of dried fruit (apricot, almond) and gunflint. Supple texture, with hints of quince, pine, white pepper and spice. Additional notes of vanilla, licorice and cinnamon. Excellent length.

1973 (47.5°): Nose is aromatic without being forceful. Spice, dried fruit and gunflint— very typical of the property. Sweet notes of prune and licorice in the mouth. Good length.

1970 (47°): Attractive amber color. Extreme aromatics that include preserved plums and a hint of *rancio*. Good balance in the mouth, with similar flavors as those found on the nose. Very long.

1968 (42.5°): Lots of wood on the nose, along with hints of coffee, chocolate, truffle and licorice. Additional notes of walnuts and almonds surface. In the mouth, excellent balance between the alcohol, flavors (mocha, prune) and tannins, which are smooth and delicate. One of the best armagnacs from the property.

1967 (44.5°): Dried fig, walnut, gunflint, and *rancio* on the nose. Lots of Bacco-influenced character in the mouth; prune, apricot, spice. Extremely well-integrated tannin, and with exceptional length.

Domaine de Peyrot (Ste. Christie d'Armagnac, Gers)

1932 (47°): Mahogany with red highlights. Tremendous aromatics include prune, licorice, vanilla and cinnamon. Soft, almost syrupy in the mouth where more exotic flavors emerge: mango, pepper, cinnamon and licorice. Good length.

1930 (46.5°): Prune, vanilla, cinnamon and notes of *rancio* on the nose. Good liveliness on the palate despite the spirit's age. Spicy notes of pepper and licorice continue on the finish.

1904 (42°): Mahogany color with chestnut highlights. Prune and cinnamon on the nose, along with notes of *rancio* and a hint of acacia. Extremely soft tannin and viscous mouthfeel with good length.

Domaine de Picpout (Panjas, Gers)

Three pre-World War II vintages from the Domaine de Picpout are marketed by Darroze. Made from Ugni Blanc and Folle Blanche from 30 year old vines, the spirits dripped from the alambic at 57° and were aged in regional oak.

Picpout's armagnacs combine viscous suppleness with an undercurrent of youthful liveliness.

1918 (44°): Fairly discreet nose that offers subtle aromas of prune and damp earth. Fairly youthful in the mouth, with supple tannins.

1915 (43°): Exotic, spicy notes on nose, along with earthy hints of mushrooms. Slightly more restrained in the mouth, with some earthiness and spice.

1914 (43°): Very expressive nose that shows prune and a hint of quince. Wonderful marriage between wood and fruit in the mouth.

Domaine de Pinas (Le Frêche, Landes)

Three-and-a-half hectare estate planted solely with old-vine Bacco on sables fauves. Distilled by Roumat at 53° and aged in regional oak.

Plenty of floral aromatics show in Pinas' fine armagnacs, which also contain delicate tannin and surprising length.

1972 (48°): Lots of floral and nut aromas on the nose, as well as a note of alcohol. Very supple, with nutty flavors and a hint of flowers on the finish.

1971 (46°): Pear, white flowers, acacia and gunflint on the nose. Lots of fat in the mouth, with round, good-quality tannin. Apricot, quince, vanilla and cinnamon notes persist on the long finish.

Domaine de Rieston (Perquie, Landes) *

Small property owned by Jean-Luc Deyres, whose father Guy owns the Domaine de Martin next door. Rieston's one-and-a-half hectares are planted exclusively with 50 to 60-year-old Bacco. Deyres distills the spirit, then transfers it to the Darroze chai to be aged. The armagnac spends a relatively long time in new oak (8 years) which allows it maximum tannin accumulation. The second part of its life is spent in old barrels. It is here that the tannins become refined and the spirit comes into its own.

Rieston's armagnacs are expressive and always show spicy oak flavors that are regularly supported by substantial material. These armagnacs are fat and complex, yet also retain a certain finesse.

1985 (52°): Intricate notes of prune, licorice and vanilla on the nose. Similar flavors in the mouth with a firm hit of alcohol on the finish.

1979 (46°): Deep nose, with lots of complexity. Hints of mocha, fig, earth and oak. In the mouth, additional notes of licorice, coffee and chocolate. Good balance and good length.

1976 (45.5°): Lots of wood on the nose. Underneath, hints of prune, fig and walnut. Full-body in mouth, with more prune, licorice, fig. Excellent length.

1975 (46°): Good complexity on nose; walnut, vanilla, cinnamon, fig, prune, pepper. Flavors continue in the mouth. Lots of fat balanced by quality tannins. Exceptional length. Super armagnac!

1974 (45°): Lots of aromatics; licorice, mint, peach, banana, apricot, vanilla, cinnamon. Very good balance in the mouth, with round and fine tannin buttressing flavors that include quince, ripe peach and vanilla. Hint of heat on the finish, although overwhelmed by rich, soft fruit.

1973 (46°): Complex nose, with hints of walnuts, almonds and mocha. Less expressive than some later vintages. In contrast, lots of flavor in the mouth (mango, prune, walnut, vanilla), smooth tannin and extraordinary length.

1971 (43°): Lots of wood on nose. With aeration, aromas of nuts, chocolate and coffee surface. Fairly fat in the mouth, with more chocolate and coffee and lots of wood tannin. Good length.

1970 (45°): Dried apricot and prune on the nose, along with vanilla and cinnamon. Less wood than some armagnacs from this property. Lots of alcohol and character, and with good length.

1968 (44°): Lots of finesse on nose; fig, licorice, walnut—no single aroma dominates. Plenty of richness in the mouth, with hints of pepper and clove. Tannins provide a nice balance to the fruit. Very long.

Domaine de Saint Aubin (Le Houga, Landes)

Large property formerly owned by Anatole Saint-Jean, who raised race horses in addition to growing grapes. Each year, all of these grapes would be distilled into armagnac. Before he died, he decided to sell his entire stock—some 300 barrels—from the years 1958 to 1982. Darroze bought the entirety of this stock in what was to become their flagship armagnac.

The armagnac is made from 100% Bacco from vines averaging 18 years. It was distilled at 53° and aged in regional oak.

When one drinks St. Aubin, one drinks one more glass of what remains; unfortunately, after the death of Saint-Jean, the vines were ripped up and replaced with additional pasture for grazing horses.

St. Aubin's full-bodied, masculine armagnacs are sometimes exotic, often spicy and, at their best, complex.

1982 (49.5°): Complex nose without being hot. Prune and licorice on the nose. Hint of quince. Very fine tannin and with a touch of *rancio*.

1981(51.5°): Very aromatic, with hints of vanilla, fig and prune. Spicy notes in mouth (clove, pepper, vanilla) along with hints of coffee. Very long.

1980 (48.5°): Lots of alcohol on nose. With aeration, hints of orange, pineapple and apricot surface. Plenty of flavor in the mouth, along with an abundance of spice. Lots of personality.

1978 (49.5°): Prune, apricot and almond paste on the nose. Flavors continue in the mouth, with additional hints of honey and a noticeable alcohol level. Medium-body. Spice builds on the finish.

1975 (43.5°): Wood on nose, along with honey, acacia and prune. Not necessarily complex, but fat and full-bodied. Hints of spice and earth on the finish. A very rustic armagnac.

Although the vineyards have been replaced by additional horse pasture, the chai at St. Aubin still stands. The armagnacs once housed within now rest at Chez Darroze, Roquefort.

1973 (50°): Fruit on the nose nearly soars from the glass; honey, coffee, white chocolate, apricot, ginger. Vanilla, coffee, prune, cinnamon, and a hint of smoke in the mouth. A seamless texture and also very long. Nearly perfect armagnac.

1971 (44.5°): Deep nose, with hints of wood, walnuts, cinnamon, almonds, prunes. Fig and prune in the mouth along with honey and ginger. Elegant, but marked by forceful tannins.

1968 (48.5°): Excellent balance between fruit and alcohol on nose. Exotic aromas of banana and mango. Very fat in mouth, and exceptionally smooth. Extremely long and extremely good.

1967 (48°): Lots of wood aromas on the nose (walnuts, almonds, vanilla, licorice, cinnamon). Wood notes continue in the mouth, yet the palate does not become dry. Prune, fig, licorice. Good length.

1966 (46.5°): Complex nose hints at coffee, cocoa, quince and oak. Very fat, with prune and a hint of *rancio* in mouth. Fine, palate-coating tannin. No aggressiveness. Very long. Splendid.

DARTIGALONGUE

Village: Nogaro ***House founded***: 1838 ***Proprietor***: Jean-Pierre Dartigalongue ***Percentage of armagnacs distilled on the property***: 100% ***Percentage bought***: 10% (mostly older vintages) ***Sales per year (bottles)***: 90,000 ***Stock***: 1,250 hl a.p. (625 barrels) ***Region where base material originates***: 50% from property in Salles. The rest from the surrounding villages, most notably Nogaro, Panjas, Le Houga ***Distillation type***: 75-80% *Armagnacaise*, 20-25% double-distillation ***Barrels***: Limousin 60%, Gascon 40% ***Oldest armagnac still in piece***: 1912 ***Blended armagnacs reduced to***: 40° ***Vintage armagnacs reduced to***: 40° ***Production sold in France***: 34% ***Production exported***: 66%

The ultra-modern Dartigalongue distillery amidst the vineyards of Salles.

The Dartigalongue firm was started in 1838 and initially achieved financial success by shipping drums of armagnac to the Netherlands, Britain and the United States. In 1870, a 30 hectare property was purchased in nearby Salles d'Armagnac. Named Lacroutz (cross in *patois*), this was soon transformed into a brand name for Dartigalongue: *La Croix de Salles*.

There is no actual difference between the armagnacs marketed with the Dartigalongue label and those with the Croix de Salles label. The wine is all distilled on the property in neighboring Salles in a new, state of the art alambic that works through a computer system. 10-12 barrels can be filled each day, which nearly quadruples the rate of traditional alambics. Next to this 20 foot column are a couple of *Charentaise* stills which churn out the alcohol at a higher degree.

With this new still, Dartigalongue has been able to expand his market tremendously. In fact, armagnac now accounts for only 20% of his revenue. 80% comes from huge quantities of wine that he distills and later sends *en vrac* to other European countries. For the German market, for instance, 30 hectoliters are produced each day during the distilling season. These later make their way into German brandies or liquors. Tremendous quantities are also sent to Sweden and Norway.

After distillation, Dartigalongue's armagnacs are aged in the *chai* in Nogaro. Very few new barrels are bought each year, although each barrel gets five kilos of wood chips which help add tannin and color to some of the younger spirits.

All armagnacs are eventually reduced to 40°. Vintages account for very little of the output. In fact, many of these are bought in small quantities from *courtiers*, then placed in bon-bonnes in the warehouse.

Dartigalongue occasionally associates with the famous; François Mitterand used to visit the domaine when visiting his son in Sion, and the Queen of Norway recently bought a large quantity of 1937 for her 60th birthday.

80% of Dartigalongue's sales are armagnacs less than six-years-old. His commercial armagnac with the most character, however, is undoubtedly the *Hors d'age*.

Hors d'age: Deep amber color. Notes of preserved apple, toffee, vanilla, and pepper on nose. Medium-fat texture with lots of wood notes. Additional hints of tobacco and herbs on finish. Good length. A good example of its type.

15 Year Old: Light amber. Hints of apricot and caramel. Generous mouthfeel but with moderate depth of flavor.

1962: Hint of almond on the nose along with a light varnish note. Pepper note on the finish.

1959: Richer nose emphasizes more fruit (apricot and prune). Lots of drying oak in the mouth which leaves the palate very dry. Somewhat difficult to drink.

DELORD

Village: Lannepax ***House founded***: 1925 ***Proprietor***: The Delord Brothers ***Percentage of armagnacs distilled on the property***: 100% ***Percentage bought***: 0% ***Sales per year (bottles)***: 200,000-250,000 ***Stock***: 1,500 hl a.p. (750 bottles) ***Region where base material originates***: 50% Lannepax, 25% from Betbezer and Labastide, 25% from Parleboscq, Maulèon, St. Julien, Lagrange and Eauze ***Distillation type***: *Armagancaise* and *Double-Chauffe* ***Barrels***: 80-90% Limousin, 10% Gascon ***Oldest armagnac still in piece***: 1958 ***Blended armagnacs reduced to*** : 40° ***Vintage armagnacs reduced to***: 40° ***Production sold in France***: 50% ***Production exported***: 50%

Jacques and Pierre Delord are the third generation to be involved in this family *négociant* firm located in Lannepax. The family owns 20 hectares of vines in Lannepax which accounts for about 50% of their source material. The rest of the bought wines come from excellent growing areas in the Bas-Armagnac. In fact, along with Samalens and Darroze, Delord is the only *négociant* firm to use only Bas-Armagnac fruit.

Ugni Blanc is the main component of the firm's armagnacs, comprising 70% of the blend. Bacco comprises a further 20% while Colombard fills out the remaining 10%.All distillation takes place on their property. Two traditional alambics are used which produce an alcohol of 52°-58°. The VS and VSOP, which together account for 65% of their sales, also see a third of double-distilled armagnac converted with their two *Charentais* stills.

Japan, Malaysia, and Australia remain important export countries for Delord. They also bottle an armagnac for a well-known boutique in Paris.

Aging takes place in a warehouse behind the offices. We tried a glass of the 1996 vintage from two vats, one which was double-distilled and one which was continuously distilled. The differences were outstanding. The single distillation showed lots of fruit in the mouth, with good fat and a hint of herbs. It tasted slightly sweet. In contrast, the double-distilled product was fairly neutral on the nose and extremely alcoholic in mouth. Delord stated that the continuous product does not accept reduction very well. Time is its best friend. In contrast, the spirit that was double-distilled can be cut drastically without too much effect, making it much easier to mold into any form you liked.

All of the firm's armagnacs are reduced to 40°. This makes it much easier for tax reasons, claims Jacques, but also more appealing to a widespread public. "We don't strive for complexity or tremendous character with our armagnacs," he adds. "We like them round in the mouth, and without astringency or aggressiveness. Without doubt, this is much easier to achieve with a blend than with a single vintage."

Hors d'Age: Light alcohol and wood notes on the nose. Fat in the mouth, with an extremely supple texture. Moderately long finish.

GELAS

Village: Vic- Fezansac ***House founded***: 1865 ***Proprietor***: Pierre Gelas ***Percentage of armagnacs distilled on the property***: 25% ***Percentage bought***: 75% ***Sales per year (bottles)***: 300,000 ***Stock***: 4,000 hl a.p. (2,000 barrels) ***Region where base material originates***: Delord, Cave de Panjas ***Distillation type***: *Armagnacaise* ***Barrels***: Limousin (90%), Gascon (10%) ***Oldest armagnac still in piece***: 1937 ***Blended armagnacs reduced to***: 40° ***Vintage armagnacs***: Non-reduced ***Production sold in France***: 80% ***Production exported***: 20%

Philippe Gelas now runs this family business founded by his grandfather in 1865. Most of the spirit to be used in their commercial blends comes from the Bas-Armagnac and is bought either from the *négociants* Delord in Lannepax or the well-run *coopérative* in Panjas.

When I visited the *négociant's* modern headquarters in Vic-Fezansac, I politely suggested that I start with the *VSOP* and *Hors d'Age*, knowing that the firm had commercial products.

"Don't worry about *that* stuff," said the energetic Philippe while bringing in half-a-dozen bottles of single-property armagnacs, dating between 1950 and 1979. "If you want to talk about quality, traditional armagnac, we have to talk about these".

Like Darroze and Auxil, Gelas also commercializes vintages from various properties. Unlike the others, however, Gelas uses different labels for each domaine, therefore accentuating their rarity. Of course, these armagnacs are bottled at their natural strength.

One is the Chateau de Martet, located in Sauboires, just outside Manciet. Owned by the Gelas family, the 15 hectare property is planted with 60% Bacco and 40% Ugni Blanc. The yields at the domaine are purposely kept low and the grapes are distilled and raised separately. It is normally bottled at about 20 years of age and is a frequent prize winner.

Each of the releases were impressive; they were all flattering, showing lots of fat in the mouth, emphasizing fruit and displaying some *rancio*. They are not, however, dominated by secondary aromas and excessive oak, qualities that often make a twenty-year-old armagnac excessively dry and difficult to drink.

Chateau de Martet 1977 (46°): Hints of almonds and citrus fruit on nose, with a slight touch of mocha. Prunes and orange in the mouth.

Chateau de Martet 1976 (46°): Lots of creamy vanilla and almond on the nose. Lovely new oak spice along with a hint of toasted coconut in the mouth. Fat texture. Notes of dry oak on the finish. Pleasing *fond-du-verre*.

Domaine de Miquer (Hontanx) 1979 (46°): Cinnamon and almond notes on the nose. Some fat in the mouth, yet with a fine texture. Good sweetness in mouth and with nice length.

Chateau La Beroje (Hontanx) 1975 Bacco (46°): Hint of almond *rancio* on the nose. Lots of fat in the mouth, along with vanilla. Somewhat rustic style—typical of Bacco—yet with good length.

Chateau Massot (Castex) 1969—bottled 1982 (45°): Fruitier nose, with hints of prune, apricot and quince. Hints of white chocolate and vanilla in the mouth.

Domaine de Pantagnan (Subehargues) 1965 Folle Blanche: Lighter, more elegant in the mouth. Hints of orange and sandalwood, a very refined, subtly-spiced oak. Light whiff of smoke on the finish. Feminine in style.

Domaine de Seviac (Montréal) 1964 Folle Blanche: Walnut and spiced-sandalwood on the nose. Good attack, but with lots of elegance on the palate. Nice length.

Domaine de Pantagnan (Subehargues) 1950 (43°): Rich nose includes prune, butterscotch and walnuts. Wonderful balance of fruit and tannin. Excellent armagnac.

GIMET

Village: Cazeneuve ***House founded***: 1920 ***Proprietors***: The Gimet Family ***Percentage of armagnacs distilled on the property***: 100% ***Sales per year (bottles)***: 20,000 ***Stock***: 500 hl a.p. (250 barrels) ***Distillation type***: *Armagnacaise* and Double-Distillation ***Barrels***: Various types ***Oldest armagnac still in barrel***: 1944 ***Blended armagnacs reduced to***: 40° ***Vintage armagnacs reduced to***: 44° or 45° ***Production sold in France***: 100%

This family firm was founded in 1920, but it wasn't until the fifties that it gained real prominence. It was at that time that the recently deceased Roger Gimet referred to himself first as *Gimet le Paysan (the Country Boy)*, then *Gimet, Le Roy des Armagnacs! (The King of Armagnac)*! Little by little, on the border of the Ténarèze and the Bas-Armagnac in the virtually non-existent town of Cazeneuve, he built a *négociant* business which, among locals, became one of the area's most loved.

Today Roger's son Jean-Pierre is most known as a distiller, and his distillery houses two continuous stills and two Charentaise-type stills. During the last two months of the year, he distills wine for about thirty producers and several large *négociant* houses including Janneau and Larresingle. All of the wine is brought to the distillery with the firm's truck; it is distilled then returned in the same truck to the property. If the customer wants something to be released within two to five years, they normally request the *double-chauf*. For longer-term aging, one of the alambic *armagnacaise* is used. Gimet is content to do what the customer requests.

The well-liked and regarded Gimet also releases his own armagnac produced from grapes grown on the property surrounding the distillery. The vineyard, called *Balentin*, is planted with 70% Ugni Blanc and 30% Colombard on *boulbènes* soil. Two blends are available: the *Hors d'age* is 10-years-old while the *Vieille Reserve* contains armagnacs that are 20 years old. Several vintages are also available, the oldest being from 1944.

Hors d'Age: (40°): Light amber. Moderately sweet palate with a soft texture.

Vieille Reserve (40°): Amber. Nose hints at almond paste and prune. Pleasingly sweet on the palate with a nice integration of wood. The finish is moderately long. A reduced blend that has managed to keep its flavor.

1960 (46°): Amber. Spicy aromatics with a hint of orange. Medium-bodied and with good attack. Lots of spice on the finish.

JANNEAU

Village: Condom ***House founded***: 1851 ***Proprietor***: Fabio Massimo Giovinetti ***Percentage of armagnacs distilled on the property***: 70% ***Percentage bought***: 30% ***Sales per year (bottles)***: 360,000 ***Stock***: 16,000 hl a.p. (8,000 barrels) ***Region where base material originates***: 55% Bas-Armagnac (Manciet, Mauléon, Hontanx), 45% Ténarèze (Montréal, Larroque-sur-l'Osse, Lannes) ***Distillation type***: 70% double-distillation, 30% *Armagnacaise* ***Barrels***: Limousin and Tronçais ***Size of aging vessels***: 450 liter barrels and vats ***Oldest armagnac still in piece***: 1962 ***Blended armagnacs reduced to***: 40° ***Vintage armagnacs reduced to***: 43° ***Production sold in France***: 17% ***Production exported***: 83%

The Janneau firm was founded in 1851, making it one of the oldest firms in the region. Located in Condom (capital of the Ténerèze), it is also one of the biggest *négociant* firms (controlling about one-eighth of the market.) Etienne Janneau, the founder's grandson, died in 1946 after running the company for four decades. Power was passed on to his son Pierre. In the 1960's, Pierre, in need of financial support, sold one-third of the firm to the cognac firm Martell. More shares were later sold, although the family held on to the majority of stock.

When Martell was taken over by Seagrams, Janneau fell very low on the multi-national's marketing agenda. Family disputes between Janneau *pere et fils* did not help matters. In 1997, the company left the Janneau family's possession when it was sold to the Italian importer Fabio Massimo Giovinetti.

While operating in his native Italy, Giovinetti raised sales of Glen Grant whisky from 50 cases to 450,000 cases over the course of several decades. He was also the first in Italy to import Macallan, which is how he came into contact with their marketing director, Willy Phillips. Phillips, a reserved yet acute Scot, raised Macallan's sales from 6,000 to 180,000 cases over the course of 20 years, the slow, hard and honorable way. When Macallan switched hands, he, along with the other Macallan noses, lost their jobs. In a way, Giovinetti lucked out. Phillips accepted his pitch to be the managing director for Janneau.

Janneau controls more than one-third of the Armagnac market in Britain and, overall, ranks second in export sales. When double-distillation was reinstituted within the region in 1972, Janneau was one of the first to resume the practice and it still accounts for more than two-thirds of their production.

They generally buy wine from local growers (75% Ugni Blanc and 25% Bacco) and distill it in their own cognac-type stills purchased in 1973. Some additional double-distillation is provided by their neighbor Chiaradia in the industrial section of Condom. In addition, Gimet provides them with *eau-de-vie* that has been continuously-distilled, a quantity that accounts for only 25% of their volume.

Their stills and main warehouses are located about three miles from central Condom. The barrels are piled five high and six deep and arranged on metal tiers. It is modern and industrial and somewhat reminiscent of the powerhouses in the Charente.

All of the firm's spirit begins its life in barrels that still give flavorant material; after a year, these are assembled in a vat, reduced by 6-7 degrees, and rediffused into older wood. This practice continues each year until the armagnacs have reached 40° and are ready for bottling.

The older vintages that will ultimately be blended are reduced at a slower rate and normally contain a higher percentage of Bacco that has been continuously distilled. In addition, Janneau also buys limited quantities of old armagnacs that are housed in their double-tiered 19th century cellar.

François Heron has been Janneau's *maitre de chai* for over two decades. In no uncertain terms, he is convinced that double-distillation is the way to go for commercial armagnacs. Single-distilled armagnacs take too long to develop, he feels, while with the *double-chauf*, the resultant spirit is lighter and displays more class—attributes he feels the consumer prefers.

Janneau's armagnacs are both light and elegant, especially up to their 15-Year-Old blend. From the *Reserve de la Maison* on, however, they exhibit more fat and traditional armagnac *muscle*.

With the recent changes in ownership, the future direction of Janneau is still uncertain. Will Phillips introduce sherry barrels to the Armagnac region? Only time will tell...What is certain is that with stock ten times that of their sales per year, Janneau certainly have the base materials to create wonderful blends.

Sélection (100% Double distillation): Lacks some nose. Light and round on the palate, with a hint of sweetness on the finish. Correct.

Réserve de la Maison (70% Continuous Distillation, 50% Bacco, 15 to 25-years-old): Some walnut notes on the nose along with hints of prune. Just a touch of antique wood in the mouth, intricately covered with lush fruit. Fat texture. Rich finish. Very well-made blend.

1976: Fat texture with hints of prune and well-integrated oak notes. Hint of sweetness. Pleasing.

1962 (purchased from courtier): Deep amber. Walnut paste on the nose. In the mouth, lots of old oak is intricately woven with notes of rich prune.

Domaine de Tucom 1970 (a domaine once marketed by the firm): Light, sweet floral nose leading to rich smooth caramel on the palate. Additional notes of violets and wood give this good depth and weight.

Domaine de Mouchac (a firm still owned by the Janneau family) 1979 La Frêche (45°): Wonderfully layered nose includes vanilla, prune, and a floral note. Remarkably pure *pruneau* in the mouth. Lovely armagnac.

LARRESINGLE

Village: Condom ***House founded***: 1837 ***Proprietor***: The Papalourey family ***Percentage of armagnacs distilled on the property***: 0% ***Percentage bought***: 100% ***Sales per year (bottles)***: 350,000 ***Stock***: 2,800 hl a.p. (1,400 barrels) ***Region where base material originates***: 65% Ténarèze, 35% Bas-Armagnac ***Distillation type***: *Armagnacaise* ***Blended armagnacs reduced to***: 40° ***Vintage armagnacs reduced to***: 40° ***Production sold in France***: 30% ***Production exported***: 70%

In the early 1800's, the Papalourey family operated a shipping business based in Normandy. Items in demand included fortified wines and brandies; occasionally the youngest Papalourey son descended to Gascony to purchase some of the local *eau de vie*. Once while in the Gers, he met a girl from Lectoure, fell in love and married. He decided to stay in the region while continuing to ship armagnac north to Normandy. He finally created his own *négociant* business in 1837.

In 1897, this couple's son, Gabriel Papalourey, bought the walled village of Larresingle near Condom, which dates to 1250. The name of this village was then established as the *négociant* name. Although the village was sold several years later, the brand name stuck. In the early 1900's, Larresingle became the first Armagnac firm to sell its product in bottles rather than in cask.

The firm is now run by Gabriel's grandson Maurice and his son Arnaud (pictured at left), the fourth and fifth-generation Papalourey. Its offices and stock are housed in central Condom in a former Carmelite convent. Larresingle has no stills of its own, and either contracts wine for distillation, buys young armagnacs from the local coopératives in Nogaro or Panjas, or buys older vintages from individual producers. They have recently departed from their use of double-distilled products and now use only armagnacs which have been distilled once. Softness in their younger blends comes from Bacco, while the major component of their Ténarèze purchases is Ugni Blanc. Gimet is their preferred distiller, and they buy much of their wine from the towns of Castelnau d'Auzan, Larroque-sur-L'Osse, Montréal-du-Gers, Cassaigne, Parleboscq and Mauléon.

"Our strength is our ability to blend," says Arnaud Papelourey. In fact, eight to twelve different armagnacs normally comprise the Larresingle blends. Reduction is performed with demineralized *petites eaux*, aged six months and carrying a 25° strength.

Aged armagnacs bought from selected growers are reduced slightly, then marketed with the Larresingle name or one of their brand names. These include: Chapoulie, Comte de Laffite, Comte de Lanauze, Comte Royer de Bravard, De Salem, De Verly, Duc de Birac, Duc de Seviac, Lacasagne, Marquis de Lacassagne and Sainsbury among others.

VSOP (7-8 year old armagnacs, 40°): Amber. Restrained aromatics, yet a nice, soft mouthfeel includes a light hint of nut. Smooth finish. Good, commercial VSOP.

XO (European market, 40°): Not tremendously aromatic, but with lots of fat and richness in the mouth, surely due to elevated percentage of Bacco. Hints of melted caramel and quality toffee in the mouth. Nice, rich finish.

Ténarèze Tres Vieille Armagnac (XO in the USA, 20 years old, 43°): Deep amber. Reticent nose offers light aromas of chocolate and spice. Well-integrated wood, with notes of oak and pepper. Silky smooth in the mouth, with a hint of accumulating fat. Good balance, admirable length.

Bas-Armagnac (20 years old, 43°): Fatter and smoother in the mouth, although not heavy. Less oak than Ténarèze. Easy to drink. Moderately long.

MARQUIS DE CAUSSADE

Village: Eauze ***House founded***: 1980 ***Proprietor***: Groupe CCG (Companie Commercial de Guillet) ***Percentage of armagnacs distilled on the property***: 90% ***Percentage bought***: 10% ***Sales per year (bottles)***: 450,000 ***Stock***: 6,500 hl a.p. (3,250 barrels) ***Region where base material originates***: Eauze, Cazaubon, Montréal, Parleboscq ***Distillation type***: *Armagnacaise* ***Barrels***: Limousin ***Blended armagnacs reduced to***: 40° ***Production sold in France***: 33% ***Production exported***: 67%

An aerial view of the Marquis de Caussade facility: this is about as close as Armagnac gets to a Charente-type operation.

In the 1930's, Elliott de Caussade created a *négociant* firm and began selling armagnacs under his family's name. Success was fairly rapid and, in 1936, the first *bottle* of armagnac was taken to the United States on the maiden voyage of the Normandie.

In 1944, Elliott was killed and the firm was taken over by a friend. Shortly thereafter, the name was sold to the Bartissol group who, in turn, bought up the area's most ambitious *coopérative*, the *Union de Cooperatives Viticoles de l'Armagnac*. With one signature, over 6000 growers who accounted for 35% of the region's total production of white wines were united under one banner.

Financial mismanagement proved disastrous to the *coopérative* in the 1970's. In 1980, the *Credit Agricole* bank took possession of the coop. Five million francs later, Michel Coste, a former managing director of the cognac firm Otard, acquired 65% of the company including its modern premises and control of the largest stock of aged armagnacs in the region.

Today, the majority of wines are bought within the Eauze canton and transformed into *eau de vie* at the firm's distillery in Cutxan. Two of their three stills pump out about twenty-five barrels a day at a relatively high 60°. Ugni Blanc is the favored grape and comprises nearly 80% of their blends.

Managing director Michel Verron states that Caussade has nearly eliminated releasing vintages because there is too much variance between them. Caussade no longer releases armagnacs with the denominations XO or Reserve either. Instead the firm has opted for a policy that releases armagnacs with specific age minimums, allowing them to give the customer a firm idea of what they are receiving. Currently available are a 7-year- old, 10-year-old, 17-year-old, 21-year-old, 30-year-old and 50-year-old. The ages are, of course, minimums.

The firm worked hard to establish a logo. In the end, they opted for a blue butterfly, not only because this variety flies the highest but also because the butterfly is analogous with armagnac; it starts as something crude (moth or rough spirit), is lodged in a vessel (cocoon or barrel) and finally transformed into something beautiful (butterfly or armagnac).

Stylistically the house releases armagnacs that offer fairly light aromas, lots of body and sweetness in the mouth, well-covered alcohol, and a relatively short finish. For total sales, they are in the top five for total armagnac sales.

The *VSOP* is somewhat sweet in the mouth, but offers full body. The *10 Year Old* possesses lots of fruit, a rich mouthfeel, and enjoyable persistence. The *17 Year Old* is very smooth in the mouth, with slightly more alcohol showing and slightly more length. The *21 Year Old* has some notes of nutty *rancio* on its fat nose, very subdued alcohol, and a rich, soft texture. And the *30 Year Old* shows notes of mashed almond, hints of orange, and fairly low alcohol, yet finishes shorter than one might expect.

MARQUIS DE MONTESQUIEU

Village: Eauze ***House founded***: 1936 ***Proprietor***: The Pernod-Ricard Group ***Percentage of armagnacs distilled on the property***: 100% ***Percentage bought***: None ***Sales per year (bottles)***: 200,000 ***Stock***: 7,500 hl a.p. (3,725 barrels) ***Region where base material originates***: Properties of the domaine near Campagne d'Armagnac. ***Distillation type***: Apart from Extra, 100% *Armagnacaise* ***Barrels***: Limousin ***Size of aging vessels***: Vats and 400 liter *pièces* ***Blended armagnacs reduced to***: 40° ***Vintage armagnacs***: Non-reduced ***Production sold in France***: 50% ***Production exported***: 50%

Marquis de Montesquieu was founded in 1936 by Pierre Montesquieu, the *Comte of Fezansac*. Since the 1960's, the firm has been sold twice, first to the *aperitif* firm *Suze*, and in 1965 to *Pernod.*

In 1966, the Pernod drinks conglomerate bought the Chateau de Campagne d'Armagnac, located about 7 miles from the firm's base in Eauze. Vines were planted and wine was distilled for the first time in 1970.

During the mid-80's, when sales hovered around the half-million bottle mark, half of the wine that Montesquieu distilled was bought from towns surrounding Eauze, both in the Ténarèze and Bas-Armagnac. Today, with annual armagnac sales slumping (200,000 bottles) and stock mounting, all of their distilled product comes from the properties surrounding Campagne. 90% of the grapes are Ugni Blanc. The remaining 10%, Folle Blanche. Madame Dargelos uses all three of her alambics to distill the firm's wine to a relatively high 60°.

Montesquieu has a tremendous amount of armagnacs on the market. All see some new oak. Reduction to 40° is gradual. Their *chai*, called the *Cathedral*, now houses over 3,500 barrels.

The armagnacs of Montesquieu are certainly directed at a commercial market; their master blend, the *Reserve Cathedrale* (30 years old and not for sale) represents the basic taste of the domaine. All other armagnacs are constructed to follow this taste, yet at younger stages of development. They always offer a pleasing mouthful of flavor, with a layered texture and a submerged level of alcohol. In short, easy to enjoy, commercial armagnacs. They are often seen in duty-free shops.

Four vintages are also available on the market; those from the 60's were bought from the Nogaro or Panjas sectors of the Bas-Armagnac, whereas those since 1970 have come from the property in Campagne. These are bottled at a higher degree and are of more interest to the connoisseur.

Napoléon (5 years old): Nice sweetness in mouth with some developing fat. Pleasing, commercial armagnac.

XO (9 years old): Hint of commencing *rancio* on nose. Lots of fat fruit in the mouth (prune, melted toffee) along with some enticing almond notes.

Extra (9 years old with 25% double distillation): Lacks the nose of the other armagnacs and shows more attack. Ultimately less fat and less sweet; lighter, highly commercial style.

Hors d'Age (15 years old): More natural mouthfeel, and without a heavy texture. Some evidence of old oak in the mouth, although well-covered by fruit. Lacks some attack, but nonetheless has very appealing length.

1972 (43°): Lots of lovely *rancio* notes on the nose. Medium to full-bodied, with nice integration of alcohol. Soft texture. Hints of almond and cinnamon on the finish. Nicely made vintage.

1965 (46°): Natural flavors include antique wood generously covered by prune-scented fruit. Very traditional style. Lots of purity as well as length. Finishes dry with recurring notes of oak.

RYST-DUPEYRON

Village: Condom ***House founded***: 1905 ***Proprietor***: Jacques and François Ryst ***Percentage of armagnacs distilled on the property***: 0% ***Percentage bought***: 100% ***Sales per year (bottles)***: 160,000 ***Stock***: 1,800 hl a.p. ***Region where base material originates***: Eauze, Nogaro, Cazaubon ***Distillation type***: *Armagnacaise* ***Barrels***: Gascon and Limousin ***Oldest armagnac still in piece***: 1946 ***Blended armagnacs reduced to***: 40° ***Vintage armagnacs reduced to***: 40° ***Production sold in France***: 30% ***Production exported***: 70%

Ryst-Dupeyron was founded around the turn of the century by Joseph Dupeyron. The offices, bottling area and one *chai* are housed in Château Cugnac, located in central Condom. The house is now run by Dupeyron's grandson, Jacques Ryst.

The firm owns no alambics and buys most of their newly distilled product from the coopératives in Eauze, Nogaro, and Cazaubon. 70% of their product comes for the Bas-Armagnac while the remainder comes from the Ténarèze. No Bacco is employed; instead the grapes are divided evenly between Colombard, Ugni Blanc and Folle Blanche. Between 200 and 300 barrels of spirit are purchased each year.

Another *chai* is located across the river on the other side of Condom. Here lies most of the company's stock, judiciously looked after by *maitre de chai* Bernard Domecq. All armagnacs see some new oak, although not normally for more than 18 months. Each barrel is racked at least once a year, and the *chai* is well-ventilated.

Armagnacs are kept at their natural alcoholic degree until a year or so before they are to be bottled; those tasted were pure and of extremely high quality. Afterwards, the barrels are emptied into larger wooded vats and carefully reduced in stages with *petites eaux*. Here they obviously lose some concentration and ultimate length.

Still, on the *négociant* level, Dupeyron's armagnacs are of very good quality. They always show lots of aroma with deep vanilla notes, have a nice round mouthfeel and good sweetness.

1981 (56°): Amber with gold highlights. Some fat in the mouth, with lots of promise for future development. Lightly-spiced finish.

1974 (45°): Amber. Creamy, deep vanilla notes on nose. Nice fat, with hints of prune and high-quality wood. Well-integrated alcohol. Good weight on the palate, with a rich, round mouthfeel. Well-made vintage.

1958: Deep amber. Roasted almond, nougat on nose, along with some maple syrup and orange peel. Plenty of rich fruit on the palate.

1946: Lots of walnut *rancio* on nose. Some smoke in the mouth, along with the taste of old wood. Preserved fruit notes prevent this from being over-the-hill.

SAMALENS

Village: Laujauzan ***House founded***: 1882 ***Proprietors***: The Samalens family ***Percentage of armagnacs distilled on the property***: 99% ***Percentage Bought***: 1% ***Sales per year (bottles)***: 250,000 ***Stock***: 8,000 hl a.p. (4,000 barrels) ***Region where base material originates***: Bas-Armagnac, especially Mauléon, Laujuzan, Larée, Lias, Perquie and Le Frêche. ***Distillation type***: 60% *Armagnacaise*, 40% *double-distillation* ***Barrels***: Gascon and Limousin ***Size of aging vessels***: Vats and 400 liter *pièces* ***Oldest armagnac available***: 1888 ***Commercial armagnacs reduced to***: 40°-45° ***Vintage armagnacs reduced to***: 45° ***Production sold in France***: 25% ***Production exported***: 75%

Samalens was founded by former wood merchant Jean Samalens in 1882 in his hometown of Laujuzan, near Panjas in the Gers. Nowadays it is his great-grandsons, cousins Philippe and Pierre Samalens, that run the business. The Samalens own no vines of their own, but buy wine from 15 farmers in the Bas-Armagnac region. They are, in fact, one of the two major *négociant* houses that uses only fruit grown in the Bas-Armagnac for all of their releases (the other being Delord).

The relationship with their growers is both close and long. The majority of their wine comes from Mauléon, Laujuzan, Lias, Le Frêche and Larée. The wines are not distilled by single varietal but together. Ugni Blanc normally accounts for 70% of the blend. The remaining thirty percent is divided equally between Folle Blanche, Bacco and Colombard. Less than half-a-percent of their stock has not been distilled on the property; the occasional barrel is bought from time to time from one of their faithful suppliers.

The old distillery was built before the turn of the century during which time it housed four continuous alambics. Always innovators, Samalens was the first house to fuel their alambics with gas and, in 1973, became the first to install four *Charente*-style stills whose double-distillation helps the younger armagnacs show better in their youth. To accomodate them, they also built a new *chai* that currently holds all eight stills.

Single-distillation still accounts for 60% of their output. Whereas barrels once came from oak grown on the property, resources now prohibit this; now Gascon and Limousin oak is employed, air dried for 5-6 years and made by *tonnelier* Bartholomo in Le Frêche.

Several aging *chai* lie on the Samalens property, some of which are relatively warm and allow for rapid volume evaporation but slow alcohol evaporation. Others are very cool, which allows for a higher rate of alcohol reduction.

The grand majority of their armagnacs are reduced with *petites eaux* aged in traditional oak casks. Most are reduced gradually to 80°; the older blends normally reach the market at 42°. Some of the vintages are not reduced and are released at 45°.

Maitre de chai Philippe Samalens worked as an intern for many cognac firms including Remy Martin and Delamain. Now in his mid-thirties, he has been the blender at his family's firm for nearly ten years. He reckons that the production of a good armagnac is 25% earth, 25% grapes, 25% quality of oak, and 25% *savoir faire*. He is much more interested in blends than straight vintages. And although he knows that some purists will condemn him for these thoughts, he has often proved them wrong in a simple manner: he hands them a glass of one of his blends that averages twenty years and a vintage of another that is exactly twenty-years-old. He claims his critics normally concede quickly.

Samalens, like the other armagnac houses, are certainly commercially minded: the 3 Étoiles and VSOP account for nearly 90% of the firms's production. With the VSOP and XO, the firm strives for a light, feminine style that is very supple in its youth. The older blends are certainly the firm's most impressive yet they sell the least. These armagnacs are always rich in fruit and display a pronounced level of almond-scented *rancio*. A few vintages are also on the market, most of which have been reduced by less than one degree.

25% of their Samalens armagnac is consumed in France while 75% is exported. Japan is by far their largest buyer (which might account for their elaborate bottle design), followed by the European countries and then the States.

VSOP (6-8 years old, 67% single, 33% double distillation): Bright amber color. Hints of toffee, orange and white pepper. Possesses good initial sweetness and becomes very round in the mouth. Impressive persistence for its age. One of the better VSOP armagnacs on the market.

Napoléon (10-12 years old, 67% Armagnacaise, 33% double-distillation): Bright amber color. Lots of fruit on nose; prune, apricot, vanilla and spice. Good balance of fruit, wood and tannin.

Rare (more carefully selected Bas-Armagnac with a 10 year minimum. 100% Armagnacaise): Amber color. Prune and vanilla on the nose. Additional notes of pepper and licorice, along with a pine note.

Reserve Imperiale XO (Average age 15 years, 100% Armagnacaise): Deep amber with orange highlights. Rich, deep nose with aromas of plum, vanilla, honey, and almonds. Hints of licorice ride along the thick palate. Good length.

Vieille Relique (Average age 18 years, youngest brandy 15 years, 100% Armagnacaise): Amber with gold reflections. Complex nose combines clove, licorice, tobacco, smoke and lots of nut. Good weight in the mouth, with rich prune, oak and smoke notes on the finish.

Relique d'Age Inconnu (a type of solera-system armagnac, built up from years and years of Vieille Relique lot ends. Average age undetermined, minimum age 20 years. 100% Armagnacaise): Chestnut color. Plum and vanilla on the nose, along with orange and peach notes. Lots of oak on the palate, along with tobacco, licorice and hints of almond. Very round and long.

Relique Ancestrale (a blend of vintage armagnacs with 25% of the blend coming from 1891. Youngest: 15 years. 100% Armagnacaise, 44°): Mahogany color with chestnut reflections. Lots of plum and vanilla on the refined nose, along with plenty of *rancio*. Rich, thick texture, with additional flavors of fruitcake, licorice and pepper. Very round in the mouth, with well-masked alcohol. Well put together.

1952 (38 years in wood, 45°): Deep amber. Alcohol masked by aromas of prune, vanilla and quince. Lots of licorice and vanilla on the palate. Very long.

1930 (42.5°): Chestnut color. Huge legs, tremendous viscosity. Just a hint of heat. Prune, apricot, vanilla and oak in the mouth.

1888 (transferred to vat in 1957, then to glass containers in 1982, 40°): Mahogany with red highlights. Rich, full-bodied nose replete with *rancio*. In the mouth, viscous texture carries intense notes of smoke, pepper and spice which ride atop a solid foundation of preserved prune.

SEMPÉ

Village: Aignan ***House founded***: 1934 ***Proprietor***: Jean-Pierre Thenon ***Percentage of armagnacs distilled on the property***: 0% ***Percentage bought***: 100% ***Sales per year (bottles)***: 200,000 ***Stock***: 3000 hl a.p. (1,500 Barrels) ***Region where base material originates***: 80% Bas-Armagnac, 20% Ténarèze ***Distillation type***: *Armagnacaise* ***Barrels***: Gascon, Limousin ***Maitre d'chai***: Gerard Pujau ***Blended armagnacs reduced to***: 40° ***Vintage armagnacs reduced to***: 40°-42° ***Production sold in France***: 50% ***Production exported***: 50%

The Sempé firm was founded in 1934 by 20-year-old Henri-Abel Sempé who went on to become a long-serving senator in the Gers. In 1994, the company went into liquidation and its doors were temporarily closed. In early 1997, the firm was bought by Jean-Pierre Thenon, a businessman from Toulouse who, thus far, has not changed the firm's commercial direction.

The firm owns 12 hectares near its headquarters in the Ténerèze region—6 hectares in Sabazan and 6 hectares in Aignan. In the past they distilled some of their own spirit; since 1991, however, they have bought all their young spirits from the coopératives, especially those in Eauze, Panjas, Aignan and Vic-Fezansac, or from Gimet in Cazeneuve. The grape blend with their young releases is normally 70% Ugni Blanc, 15% Bacco, 5% Folle Blanche and 10% Colombard. They once incorporated some double-distillation into their blends; distillation now, however, is 100% *Armagnacaise*.

The new armagnacs normally start their life in a large *tonneaux* where they are blended. After several days, they go directly into 400 liter casks where they rest for up to two years. Once again they are transferred to the *tonneaux* and reduced, then placed back in older barrels. After several more years, they are placed back in the *tonneaux* and reduced again.

70% of Sempe's sales are of armagnacs less than seven-years-old. Like at most *négociant* houses, reduction is employed for all of their releases.

A tremendous array of vintages are available, many of which are bought in small quantities and placed in glass demi-johns. These normally come from various properties in the Bas-Armagnac and consequently display different styles; they are normally reduced to between 40° and 42°.

VSOP (5-6 years old): Light, slightly floral aromatics. Decent weight in the mouth with nice fruit on the palate.

Hors d'age (14 years old): Hints of caramel, nougat and orange on the nose. Medium-bodied and with an agreeable finish.

1973: Lovely almond notes on the nose mesh seamlessly with vanilla-scented oak and rich toffee. Lush, smooth mouthfeel reminiscent of fine nougat. Finely crafted and a pleasure to drink.

1968 (42°): Lightly floral aromatics with a hint of orange; not tremendously expressive. Medium-bodied and without strong, penetrating fruit. Moderately long finish.

1965: Amber, lots of *rancio* on the nose with hints of prune. Full-bodied, rich mouth with layers of flavor filled with character.

1960: Walnut on the nose, with additional notes of prune and vanilla. Extremely pleasing. Fat, lush texture with lots of flavor. Well-integrated wood. Good length.

TREPOUT

Village: Vic- Fezansac ***House founded***: 1941 ***Proprietor***: Societé Marcel Trepout and sons ***Percentage of armagnacs distilled on the property***: 0% ***Percentage bought***: 100% ***Sales per year (bottles)***: 20,000 ***Stock***: 250 hl a.p. (125 barrels) ***Region where base material originates***: 70% Bas-Armagnac, 30% Ténarèze ***Distillation type***: *Armagnacaise* ***Barrels***: Gascon and Limousin ***Oldest armagnac still in piece***: Most old spirits in demi-johns ***Blended armagnacs reduced to***: 40°-42° ***Vintage armagnacs reduced to***: 40°-43° ***Production sold in France***: 70% ***Production exported***: 30% (60-80 cases a year go to USA)

Small yet excellent *négociant* firm located in an old chapel once used by monks from the neighboring Chateau de Notre Dame in Vic-Fezansac. In 1941, Marcel Trepout took over for his father and extended sales north to Paris. One of his first sales was to the owner of the restaurant at the Eiffel tower who bought three bottles, then six, and finally a case. Gradually, word of Trepout's armagnac began to spread through the better restaurants in Paris.

One day Trepout's accounted asked him why he had not been paid for sales to the Eiffel tower for over six months. Trepout responded that the publicity had been so good that he didn't want to ask for the money!

Trepout retired in 1969 and his son Jean-Pierre took over the business. After various domestic squabbles, he left to form his own *négociant* firm, also located in Vic-Fezansac. Since 1984, the firm has been run by Marcel Trepout's son-in-law, Georges Dareux. Sadly, Marcel Trepout passed away in early 1997.

Dareux buys from three or four brokers who offer him samples from properties on a periodic basis. When a vintage from one source has finished, they seek a different source that is representative of an armagnac of that age. Because of this, the same vintage bought several years apart might not taste exactly the same. Dareux states, "If one trusts the Trepout label, they will be rewarded with an excellent product. Whether it comes from the Bas-Armagnac or the Ténarèze, or if it is made from Bacco or Ugni Blanc is *not* the most important thing with us. We only offer the consumer things that are naturally made, with good attack and some fat. One just has to have confidence in our products".

Trepout offers a full range of products, from 3 Étoilles to vintages from 1830. Unlike many *négociant* firms, their older blends and vintages account for nearly 80% of their sales, and just about every vintage from 1900 to 1986 is available.

Hors d'Age (20 years old, 42°): Amber. Hints of almond on the nose. Nicely balanced fruit (prune, apricot). Elegant. Hints of well-integrated wood. Pleasingly dry, and with good balance. One of the best *hors d'age* on the market.

Apotheose (30 years old, 40°): Amber with gold highlights. Prune, almond, vanilla and a hint of walnut on the nose. Rich, smooth mouthfeel with excellent balance; well-integrated oak on the long finish. Overall, an excellent blend that has lots to offer.

1955 Vintage (42°): Amber with gold highlights. Hints of toffee, licorice, almond and spice. Mouth shows licorice, vanilla, chocolate, white pepper and touches of orange. Lots of pepper on the finish, with a fleeting glimpse of *rancio*. Overall, nice balance between fruit, tannin, and alcohol, and soft on the palate. Most impressive, however, is the spirit's length. This armagnac is very long.

VEUVE GOUDOULIN

Village: Courrensan ***House founded***: 1935 ***Proprietor***: Madame Goudoulin ***Percentage of armagnacs distilled on the property***: 0% ***Percentage bought***: 100% ***Sales per year (bottles)***: 30,000-40,000 ***Stock***: 500 hl a.p. (250 barrels) ***Region where base material originates***: Eauze, Panjas, Estang, Montguillem, Perquie, Cazaubon, Nogaro, Mauléon, Hontanx ***Distillation type***: *Armagnacaise* at 55°-56° ***Barrels***: Mostly Limousin, some regional ***Oldest armagnac still in piece***: 1953 ***Blended armagnacs reduced to***: 40° ***Vintage armagnacs reduced***: 1or 2 degrees ***Production sold in France***: 50% ***Production exported***: 50%

This relatively small *négociant* firm is found just outside the small town of Courrensan, located between Gondrin and Lannepax. Following the death of her husband, Madame Goudoulin started the company in 1935, mainly to commercialize her late husband's stock.

A warehouse was built in 1983 to house the increasing number of barrels, which are normally bought from either coopératives or small producers in select areas of the Bas- Armagnac. In fact, over 90% of the firm's product comes from the Bas-Armagnac.

The director of the firm, Christian Faure, feels that the high proportion of fruity spirit from the Bas-Armagnac minimizes the need for boisé or sugar syrup, which might be necessary if more Ténarèze was employed.

Even though the firm has been in existence for sixty years, their spacious warehouse gives the visitor the impression that the company is very new, unlike many *négociants* whose quarters are cramped and dark.

Their commercialized armagnacs, reduced to 40°, have slightly more age than others on the market with the same denominations. They tend to be very soft and round, with very pleasing and inviting aromas. The vintages are minimally reduced; one, a wonderful Folle Blanche from a single property in Hontanx, is bottled at its natural degree.

VSOP (8 years old): Fairly light in color. Pleasant milk chocolate notes surface on the palate.

Hors d'Age (15 years old): From the 1979 vintage, this displays a very open nose with a slightly deeper and creamier chocolate note.

1981 Folle Blanche (from Hontanx, 46°, bottled 1994): Very lovely amber with gold highlights. Almond notes on the nose. Peach, orange peel and some creamy vanilla in the mouth. Refined mouthfeel. Elevated alcohol meshes well with a fat, creamy finish. Excellent armagnac.

1934: Deep amber. Lots of rich *rancio* on the nose, with the taste of antique wood in the mouth. Slightly over-oaked.

1914 (Distilled by Mr. Goudoulin and bottled in 1987): Maple syrup on the nose with hints of walnut and smoky oak. Slightly dry but with good length.

Christian Faure of Veuve Goudoulin displays the firm's demi-john collection. Many armagnac producers and négociants keep small quantities of older vintages in these wicker-covered bottles which not only protect the spirit from taking on too much wood but also from dropping below the 40 degree alcohol minimum. It is common practice for négociants to buy between each other nowadays; what is in this cellar may eventually end up on the market under someone else's name.

Les Caves Coopératives

A coopérative is a collective of growers who share a production facility run by qualified professionals. Since the end of the 1940's, coopératives have played an important role within the Armagnac region. Many farmers without enough grapes, finances or desire to bottle their product often sell their harvest to the local coopérative.

How do coopératives operate? After the harvest, these group-owned enterprises collect the harvested grapes from a farmer's property. These grapes are weighed and an average sugar content is established. Based upon a set price that year, the farmer's cut is placed into an account at the coopérative. Like this, the coopérative is like a bank to many farmers. At any time in the future, the farmer may withdraw all or part of his money as he wants. In addition, he may also buy wine or armagnac from the coopérative and use the money from his account as payment. For its work, the coopérative takes a percentage of the initial payment..

After buying the grapes, the coopérative uses its modern equipment to vinify the wine. The majority of this wine is sold to *négociants* around France and Europe and normally reaches its final destination in a large tanker truck. Part of the wine is distilled and then placed in casks where it ages peacefully. Coopératives normally have an impressive stock of armagnac and are *ideal* sources for *négociants* to find large quantities of ten-year-old armagnac or small quantities of forty-year-old armagnac.

In addition, the coopératives normally market their products with a specific brand name, under which it also sells other wine-based products like wine, floc and armagnac-based cocktails.

There is much to be said, both good and bad, regarding coopératives. On the positive side, they provide the majority of grape growers with funds to continue growing grapes. In contrast to much equipment found on a farm, coopératives often have sophisticated vinification and distillation equipment, which make for healthy, vibrant wines and spirits without defects. Storage conditions are typically ideal and the quality of the oak used is excellent.

On the down side, every farmer's product is treated similarly, something that often makes the final release lack a distinct personality that can come from a certain parcel of land. In addition, the grapes used are not always of the best quality. What's more, many of the commercialized products have been tailored to meet market demand: reduced to 40° and adjusted with the enologists tools.

For the connoisseur, the barrels of unreduced stock within the warehouse often provide interest while the releases on sale in the attached *salle de vente* usually do not.

The coopératives have had problems in the past. In the late 1960's the coopérative in Panjas burned to the ground, and all its stock went up in flames. In the late 1970's, all the coopératives grouped together to form the *Union des Coopératives Viticoles de l'Armagnac (UCVA).* With aspirations to conquer the international market, the UCVA suddenly found themselves in control of nearly one-third of the region's production. However, mismanagement led to fiscal problems that soon proved so great that the UCVA filed for bankruptcy in 1980.

Little by little, the individual coopératives have restructured themselves and again are well-run. The coopératives account for about a 40% of the Armagnac production and half of the stock in the region, while their bottle sales account for about 6% of the overall market.

Coopératives are divided into several regions and the members, although it is not obliged, generally live not far from the coop. The technical statistics of the Eauze *cave* is indicative of many coopératives:

Coopérative Armagnacaise Viticole d'Eauze (C.A.V.E.)

Founded: 1957 ***Current Members***: 280 ***President***: Michel Désangles ***Hectares Harvested***: 1,100 ha ***Grapes***: Bacco (50%), Ugni Blanc (50%) ***Armagnac production per year***: 500 hl a.p. ***Armagnac sales per year:*** 300 hl a.p. ***Distillation***: *Armagnacaise* with 5 alambics fueled by natural gas ***Barrels***: Limousin and Gascon (1,800 barrels plus 50-60 vats) ***Stock***: 4,600 hl a.p. ***Oldest barrel***: 1924 ***Brand Name***: *Le Chevalier Gascon* ***Available Product***: 3 Etoiles, VSOP, *Hors d'Age* ***Vintages available***: 1970, 1965, 1962, 1960, 1958, 1955, 1949, 1944 ***Other products available***: Red and White Floc de Gascogne, sparkling wine, and products with an armagnac base: Ambrée (a liqueur made with armagnac and mandarin orange juice), Lou Traouc (a cocktail made with fruit juice and armagnac)

The Cave Coopérative at Panjas, long known for its armagnacs of excellent quality.

These coopératives also exist in the region:

Cave Coopérative de Cazaubon (Bas-Armagnac)
Cave Coopérative de Panjas (Bas-Armagnac)
Cave Coopérative de Nogaro (Bas-Armagnac)
Cave Coopérative de Villeneuve de Marsan (Gerland) (Bas-Armagnac)
Cave Coopérative de Castelnau d'Auzan (Ténarèze)
Cave Coopérative de Condom (Ténarèze)
Cave Coopérative des Coteaux du Mézinais S.C.A. (Ténarèze)
Cave Coopérative d'Aignan (Ténarèze)
Cave Coopérative de Vic-Fezansac (Ténarèze)
Cave Coopérative de Riscle (Haut-Armagnac)

Several releases from coopératives are available in the United States, including those from the Gerland coop (most recently owned the Cognac firm Camus) which go under the banner of *Marquis de Puységur. Armagnac de Montal*, once a *négociant* firm in its own right, is now marketed by the coopérative in Nogaro.

Rating The Producers

Outstanding Producers
Château du Lacquy (de Boisseson)
Château de Ravignan (de Ravignan)
Domaine Boingnères (Lafitte)
Domaines de Jaurrey and Pillon (Laberdolive)

Excellent Producers
Chai de Muret (Corderoy/Debains)
Château de Briat (de Luze)
Domaine de Cavaillon (Pitous)
Domaine de la Coste (Lacourtoisie)
Domaine de Guillemouta (Cazenave)
Domaine de Jean du Haut (de Poyferré)
Domaine de Jouanda (de Poyferré)
Domaine de Lamoulette (Dupuy)
Domaine de Larriou (Dando)
Domaine de Lassabatju (Blondeau)
Château de Martet (Gelas)
Château de Miquer (Lasserre)
Domaine d'Ognoas (*Département* des Landes)
Domaine de Sans (Théaux)

Very Good Producers
Château La Béroje (L'Huillier)
Château de Castex (St. Pastou)
Château de Laubade (Lesgorgues)
Château de Pellehaut (Béraut)
Château Pierron (Herrail)
Château de Pomes-Péberère (Faget)
Château de Tariquet (Grassa)
Château du Prada (de Bouglon)
Domaine de L'Arepic (Jordana)
Domaine de Baraillon (Claverie)
Domaine de Le Basque (Lamothe)
Domaine de la Boubée (Ladevèze)
Domaine de la Brette (Magnol)
Domaine de Caillavère (Gabriel)
Domaine de Gaube (Serres)

Domaine de Guéchet (Chevalley)
Domaine de Jouatmaou (Lacave)
Domaine de l'Hérité (Sempé)
Domaine de Hourtica (Tarbes)
Domaine de Lapeyrade (Lascombes)
Domaine de Larroudé (Tastet)
Domaine de Laubesse (Lacoste)
Domaine de Laubuchon (Cénac)
Domaine de Lusson (Cames)
Domaine de Maouhum (Lasseignou)
Domaine de Martin (Deyres)
Domaine de Nautina (Farbos de Luzan)
Domaine de Paguy (Darzacq)
Domaine de Pouchegu (Laporte)
Domaine de Saoubis (de Mandalaere)
Domaine de Soube (Escoubets)

Good Producers
Château de Castandet (de Coutard)
Château Garreau (Garreau)
Château de Juliac (Cassagne)
Château de Laballe (Laudet)
Château de Maniban (Castarède)
Château de Millet (Dèche)
Château de Mons (Département du Gers)
Château de Neguebouc (Posternak)
Clos de Moutouguet (Cames)
Domaine de Bacoge (Labarbe)
Domaine le Béroy (Duhurc)
Domaine de Bordeneuve (Guasch)
Domaine la Bouc (Clavé)
Domaine Broustet (Dubourdieu)
Domaine le Cantaloup (Donnefoi)
Domaine du Carpoulet (Duflo)
Domaine de Castagnet (Sarrot)
Domaine de Coutchot (Ponge)
Domaine de la Grangerie (Langalerie)
Domaine de la Hauresse (Beyries)
Domaine de Jean de Montréjo (Labenne)
Domaine de Joÿ (Gessler)

Domaine de Lagajan (Geogeacaracos)
Domaine de la Lartigue (Lacave)
Domaine de Mahu (Couerbe)
Domaine de Malartic (Périssé)
Domaine de Marquisat (Mao)
Domaine de Mauhic (Oreja)
Domaine de Maupas (Buffaumène)
Domaine de Menjot (Laburthe)
Domaine de Papolle (Hawkins)
Domaine de Pariot (Lafargue)
Domaine a Parot (Lartigolle)
Domaine de Péré (Dufréchou)
Domaine de San de Guilhem (Lalanne)
Domaine de Sandemaignan (Guérard)
Domaine de Simsat (Sourbès)

Average Producers
Château de Busca-Maniban (Palthey)
Château de Joutan (Plouvier)
Château de Monbel (d'Agrain)
Château de Monluc (Lassus)
Château de Salles (Hébert)
Château de Terraube (de Galard)
Domaine de Bilé (Della Vedove)
Domaine de Bordeneuve-Entras (Maestrojuan)
Domaine du Bourdieu (Fourteau)
Domaine au Bourg (Darréon)
Domaine de Boutille (Dubuc)
Domaine de Brichot (Maurer)
Domaine de Cassagnoles (Baumann)
Domaine de Caumont (Bourdens)
Domaine de Cazaux (Kauffer)
Domaine de Chiroulet (Fezas)
Domaine Durroux (Durroux)
Domaine des Ecasses (Larrieu)
Domaine de Ferragus (Fourtet)
Domaine de Gagnet (Tadieu)
Domaine de Gaston (Dauriac)
Domaine de Houres (Lapisse)
Domaine de Janin (Labeyrie)

Domaine de Moura (Réon)
Domaine de Ouardère (Loss)
Domaine de Péto (Depis)
Domaine de Pujo (Dubos)
Domaine de St. Lannes (Duffour)
Domaine de St. Martin (St. Martin)
Domaine de Tarride (Capin)

Rating The *Négociants*

Outstanding Négociants
Francis Darroze

Excellent Négociants
Auxil
Gelas
Samalens
Trepout

Very Good Négociants
Castarède
Dartigalongue
Delord
Janneau
Larresingle
Marquis de Montesquieu
Ryst-Dupeyron
Sempé
Veuve Goudoulin

Good Négociants
ADEX
Clés des Ducs
Les Roy des Armagnacs
Marquis de Caussade

Glossary

Alambic Charentaise: A pot still, most commonly found in the Charente, used for the double-distillation of wine.

Alambic Armagnacaise: A continuous still, most commonly found in the Armagnac region, used for the single-distillation of armagnac.

Alcool pur: Literally, pure alcohol. Pure alcohol is 100% or 100° alcohol, or alcohol of 200 proof. Traditional armagnac comes out of the still at 52°-55° or 104-110 proof, and within five years will have naturally reduced to around 50° or 100 proof. Therefore, 2 liters of 50° alcohol actually contains 1 liter of *pure* alcohol. Likewise, 400 liters of 50° alcohol is the equivalent of 200 liters of pure alcohol. Armagnac barrels are generally around 400 liters in size. Henceforth, if full with 50° spirit, we can say that they contain 200 liters of pure alcohol, or *2 hectolitres d'alcool pur.*

Aperitif: A beverage typically consumed before one eats. It is meant to stimulate the palate and prepare it for the food that is to follow. The most popular aperitifs include: Floc, Ricard, Pernod, Kir, Champagne, Beer, Martini, Campari, Souze, and various dry cocktails.

Appellation d'Origine Controlée (A.O.C.): The highest of the government-enforced classifications concerning wines and spirits. Appellation laws insist that the products from a certain area conform with certain regulations, including the grapes from which it was made, yields of the vine, treatment of the wine, etc. Although not guaranteeing exceptional quality, these releases should be above-average and retain an established level of quality.

Barrique de Cognac: A 350 liter barrel, most commonly made with Limousin or Tronçais oak.

Bonbonne: A glass jar covered in wicker or straw that normally holds between 25 and 30 liters. Older armagnacs are normally stored in these *bonbonnes*, also known as demi-johns, so as to prevent them from obtaining further oak influence.

Bonne-Chauffe: Second and final distillation when a pot still is used to make brandy. The spirit normally exits the still at 72° or 144 proof.

Brouillis: The first distillation when two are to be used, normally exiting the still at a strength of 36° or 72 proof.

Bureau National Interprofessional d'Armagnac (BNIA): The governing body of armagnac, which supervises the production and sale of armagnac as well as advertising the spirit in both French and foreign markets.

Chai: The area of the domaine where the grapes are pressed, fermented and turned into wine. An above ground storage space for either wine barrels or barrels containing spirit.

Congeners: Flavoring elements once present in wine that have been carried into the spirit. With time, congeners normally lend tremendous complexity to the spirit. Additional distillation tends to limit the amount of congeners present in a spirit.

Courtier: Agent or broker of armagnacs, normally operating between the producer and the *negociant*.

Digestive: A beverage meant to be consumed after the meal, whose alcoholic strength helps aid digestion. The best example is, of course, armagnac.

Eau de Vie: Any spirit distilled from fruit, ie. grapes, cherry, pear, apple, kirsch, plum, apricot, raspberry, etc.

En Vrac: Translated from French, *vrac* means bulk. Wines or spirits sold *en vrac* means that they are sold in large quantities that will later be blended or resold under a different name. The majority of wine that a negociant will blend or distill is normally bought *en vrac* because its price is always less expensive than something bought in bottle. Most armagnac producers will sell part of their production *en vrac* and keep the rest for themselves. Their *en vrac* sale at least gives them an immediate cashflow.

Finesse: Literally "fineness," normally with regards to a spirit's texture. Spirits that exhibit finesse seem to dance across the palate while delivering all the flavorants that something with more body would possess.

Floc de Gascogne: Regional *aperitif* made with 2/3 unfermented grape juice and 1/3 armagnac that has been aged for one year. Floc comes in both white and red versions (called rosé), and is best served chilled. The equivalent in the Cognac region is called *Pineau des Charentes*.

Gîte: French equivalent of a bed and breakfast, normally located on a farm in the countryside. Regional food is frequently available for midday and evening meals.

Grand Bas-Armagnac: An *un-official* sub-region of the Bas-Armagnac that encompasses most of the Landais towns *and* thought to produce the finest *eau-de-vie*. This expression *may not* be used on labels because it is not an actual appellation.

Heads: The first part of the spirit that exits the still. These are normally discarded, although they may be kept and re-distilled.

Hectoliter: 100 liters or approximately 26½ gallons.

Lees: The solid debris left in vat after fermentation has taken place. This includes skins, grape pits, stems and yeast cells.

Maitre de Chai: Normally the one who oversees all facets of aging, including racking, reduction and blending. Most commonly referred to in English as the cellar master.

Malolactic Fermentation: A secondary fermentation, during which time the wine's malic acid is transferred into lactic acid. Most wines that are distilled do not pass through *malo*, as wines with a high level of malic acid tend to produce better *eau de vie*.

Négociant: Dealer of armagnacs, normally purchasing existing armagnacs and then marketing them under their own name. Larresingle, Sempé, and Janneau are all *négociants*.

Part des Anges: A somewhat humorous term given to the amount of spirit which evaporates within the *chai*. Literally, *The Angel's Share*, because the evaporating spirit heads upward, as if to heaven.

Patois: Dialect of the natives. Every region of France, Italy and Spain have local dialects that can change within thirty or forty miles. Most older armagnac producers will remember having spoken nothing but *patois* when they were kids. Nowadays, however, not many kids are able to speak their local *patois*. It is but another part of a vanishing heritage.

Petites Eaux: A mixture of brandy and water which is normally around 20° or 40 proof. When a producer reduces the alcoholic strength of his spirit, *petites eaux*, also called *vieux faibles*, are less shocking to the new balance of the spirit than if water alone is used.

Pièces: Barrels used to store armagnac, normally between 400 and 420 liters in size.

Primary Aromas: Aromas that exist during a spirit's infancy and youth: the fruit is often bright, floral overtones are often present and the vanilla notes are young, .

Rancio (rahn-si-oh): Technically, oxidation of acids within the spirit which is caused by years of breathing through the barrel. To the spirit's fan, *rancio* displays itself with a slight oxidized or maderized note—somewhat like aged port. It often carries with it the aromas of grilled nuts (almond, walnut, hazelnut) and should lend a note of complexity to the spirit. Another expression of rancio is the oxidation of vanilla that has come from the oak and infused itself within the spirit. The aromas most commonly related with this form of rancio are those of coconut milk or butter.

Rancio can be recognized as early as ten years of age, but most normally surfaces between the spirit's 15th and 20th birthday. While *rancio* certainly adds another dimension to spirits, it should never outweigh the remaining fruit.

Secondary Aromas: Aromas that arrive as a spirit matures: primary fruit begins to condense and become preserved or *confit*: vanilla notes evolve into those of nuts and rancio.

Stock: The amount of spirit owned by a producer or negociant. This figure is normally referred to in *hectolitres of alcohol pur*.

Tails: The final part of the distillation batch, mostly comprised of water and not normally kept.

Terroir: A vineyard area with particular physical characteristics (soil, sub-soil, climate, micro-climate) that play an important role in determining the nature and taste of the wine or spirit produced there.

Tonnelier: Cooper or barrel-maker. His workshop is a *tonnellerie*, cooperage or wood shop.

Tonneau: Large, closed container used for aging, blending and storing armagnac, also referred to as *cuve*. Normally made of wood that gives little, if any, flavoring material.

Trou Gascon: *Eau de vie* of armagnac, normally served between courses of a meal. The burst of alcohol acts to create room (the Gascon hole) for the next course.

Index

A Parot 123
Abbaye de Flaran 214, 244
Abd-el-Rhaman 42
accent of the Gascon people 21
acidity 27, 28, 34, 111
acids 47, 88-9, 94, 110
Acquitanian 23
Adam, Edouard 42
ADEX (La Maison de l'Armagnac) 252
aeration 60, 94
alambic 10, 34, 37, 41, 61
alambic *armagnacais* 41, 45, 297
alambic *charentaise* 44
alambic plates 46
alcohol 89
alcohol reduction 59
alcool pur 297
alcoolmètre 47
alembic 10
Algeria 116, 125, 143
Alizé 106
alkalinity 27
Allier 53, 131, 141, 237
Alsace 223
American oak 217
American rootstock 37
amontillado sherries 94
Ampelographie 75
angel's share 59, 299
Antoine de Bourbon 19
Antoine de Mellet 42
AOC (Appellation d'Origine Controlée) 37
apéritif 41, 81, 107, 297
Appellation d'Origine Controlée (A.O.C.)
41, 297
Aquitaine 23
Arab 20
Arles 14
Armafizz 198
Armagnac Blanc 81
Armagnac de Montal 292
Armagnac *Gersois* 115
Armagnac *Landais* 115
Armagnac/Cigar matching 108-9
Armagnacais 20
Arminiac 9
Arminius 9
Arnaud, Patrick 118, 151
Arnaud-de-Villeneuve 41
aromas 93-94
asparagus 12
assemblage 65
Atlantic Ocean 31
Au Bon Climat 237
Au Bourg 242
Auban, Yvan 122, 166, 251
Auch 11, 23, 220
Auch Cathedral 214
Aurian, Philippe 106
Auxil 157, 186, 196, 228, 251, 253, 276

Bacco (22-A) 33, 35, 37-39, 75, 78, 80,
85-86, 110, 116, 142, 212, 226
Bacco, François 37, 75
Bacoge 162
Baïse River 73, 74, 220, 254
balance 94
Balarin 238
Balentin 277
Baraillon 177
barbarians 23
Barbotan 137
Barcelonne 24
barley 86
Barolo 9
Baron de Pibrac 253
Baron de Sigognac 144, 252, 253
barrel rotation 65
barrels 51
barrique de Cognac 297
Bartholomo, Gilles 55, 197, 261, 285
Bas-Armagnac 20, 26, 27, 28, 31, 75,
85, 111, 115, 117, 195, 211-2, 218,
247, 275, 282-4, 288
Basque 12, 14, 214, 253, 255
bastides 23
Batz, Charles de 20

Baudoin, Raymond 148, 257
Baumann, Gilles 222, 223, 235
Bayonne 14, 74, 122, 255
Béarn 14
bécasse 13, 257
Belgium 127, 240
Béraut, Gaston 236, 237
Béraut, Martin and Mathieu 237
Beris, Roger 204
Berthelot 42
Bertholon 254
Beyries, Leon 243
black oak 52
black rot 40
black truffles 12
Blondeau, Francis 156, 162
boisé 57, 67, 68, 69, 110, 179
Boisseson, de 171
bonbonnes 89, 275, 297
bonne-chauffe 297
Bordeaux 9, 47, 73-4, 117, 179, 190, 194, 206, 209, 220, 225, 232, 237, 254
Bordeneuve 143
botrytis 14
Bouglon, Philippe de 165
boulbènes 28
Bourbon, Antoine de 19
Bourdens, Roger 184
Bourgogne 53, 237
Boutille 137
brandewijn 73
brebis 105
Bretagne 24
Bretagne d'Armagnac 130
Brin d'Amour 156
brouillis 44, 297
Broustet 229
Brown-Foreman 82
Brumont, Alain 14, 141
Brunello 9
Brunswick 42
Buffaumène, Jean and Christian 186
bullfight 14, 15
Bureau National Interprofessional d'Armagnac (BNIA) 76, 77, 81-85, 87, 92, 139, 153, 220 297
Burgundy 9
Buzet 14, 215, 240
Cabernet Franc 14, 105, 215, 225
Cabernet Sauvignon 14, 105, 225
Cahors 14
calcium 27
California 79, 237
Calignac 215
Calvados 10, 41
Cames, Daniel 187
Camus 251, 292
Canada 37
Capin, Jean 208
Capin, Madeleine 208
caramel 67, 224
Carbon-14 87
Carré des Feuillants 11
Cassagne, Pierre 125
cassoulet 12
Castarède 74, 188, 254
Castelsegur 253
Catholicism 19, 20, 24
Caussade, Elliott de 281
Caussade, Marquis de 252
Cave Coopérative de Aignan 292
Cave Coopérative de Castelnau d'Auzan 292
Cave Coopérative de Cazaubon 292
Cave Coopérative de Condom 292
Cave Coopérative de Nogaro 292
Cave Coopérative de Panjas 292
Cave Coopérative de Riscle 292
Cave Coopérative de Vic-Fezansac 292
Cave Coopérative de Villeneuve de Marsan 292
Cave Coopérative des Coteaux du Mézinais S.C.A. 292
Cave Coopérative de Nogaro 206
Cave Coopérative de St. Mont 206
Caves Coopératives 290
caviar 104
Cazenave, Jean-Jacques 145, 259
Cenac, Jean 185
central forests 52
cépages nobles 148
cèpes 12, 13
Cerbois 251
Chablis 108

chabrot 13
chai 47, 49, 54, 56, 59, 60, 86, 87, 88, 113-4, 297
Chai de Muret 154, 293
Chambre d'Agriculture du Gers 217
Champagne 79, 157
Chaptal 42
chaptilization 34
charcuterie 12, 18
Chardonnay 141, 225
Charentaise still 42
Charente 38-9, 59, 68, 73-4, 77, 87, 185, 255, 279, 284
Charles the Bad 42
Charles VII 222
Château Beycheville 194, 237
Château Calon-Ségur 238
Chateau de Bonas 42
Château de Bordeneuve 143, 252
Château de Briat 104, 108, 190, 293
Château de Busca-Maniban 295
Chateau de Campagne d'Armagnac 282
Château de Castandet 62, 133, 295
Chateau de Castelmore 20
Château de Castex d'Armagnac 134, 294
Château de Gaube 152, 154, 254
Château de Joutan 295
Château de Juliac 125, 127, 146, 267, 294
Château de la Grangerie 227
Château de Laballe 295
Chateau de Lacaze 84
Château de Lacquy 113, 171
Château de Laubade 39, 108, 206, 293
Château Leoville-Poyferré 119
Château de Malliac 144, 157, 254
Château de Maniban 188, 254, 295
Château de Martet 108, 276, 293
Château de Millet 294
Château de Miquer 293
Château de Monbel 135, 295
Château de Monluc 241, 295
Château de Mons 39, 217, 295
Château de Neguebouc 248, 294
Chateau de Notre Dame 287
Château de Pellehaut 59, 104, **236-7**, 239, 293
Château de Pichon-Longueville 190
Château de Pomès-Péberère 220, 294
Château de Ravignan 49, 108, 113, 195, **197-199**, 293
Château de Salles 203, 295
Château de Sandemaignan 136
Château de Tariquet 104, 105, 108, 141, 223, 237, 293
Château de Terraube 295
Château du Busca-Maniban 244
Château du Lacquy **171-174**, 293
Château du Prada 165, 293
Château Garreau 166, 295
Château Joutan 127
Château La Béroje 60, 157, 277, 294
Château Margaux 94
Chateau Massot 277
Château Millet 105, 139
Château Monluc 105
Chateau Montus 14
Château Petrus 87
Château Pierron 240, 294
Chateau Yquem 87
Chevalley, Robert 138
Chez Simone 13
Chiaradia 278
chocolate 108, 113
Cigar Aficionado 82, 108
cigars 108-109
Clairette 39, 217
Clavé, Michel 163
Claverie, Paul 177
clay 26, 27, 28
Clés des Ducs 67, 192, 251, 252, 255
Clos de Moutouguet 108, 192, 295
Cognac 9, 10, 33, 38, 41, 44-45, 53, 68, 73-74, 76, 78-80, 82, 87, 89, 101, 104, 179, 233, 251
Cohiba 108
Cointreau 101, 106
Coirvoisier 144, 254
Coke 82
Cologne 24
Colombard 33, 35, 37, 47, 78, 104, 110, 141, 212, 214, 223, 225, 236, 248
color 91, 92
Comte of Fezansac 282
coñac 82
confit de canard 12, 14, 104
congeners 77, 297

Consumption, general changes in 81
continuous still 41, 45
Cooking of Southwest France, The 12
Coopérative Armagnacaise Viticole d'Eauze (C.A.V.E.) 291
corn 85-86, 116
Cornet, Pierre 192
corrida 15
Coste, Michel 281
Côtes de Gascogne 14, 82, 130, 139, 141, 186, 190, 201, 212, 213, 214, 220, 223, 225, 232, 233, 239, 241
Cotes de St. Mont 213
coup 65
Courbu 14
course Landaise 14-16, 47
courtier 113, 144, 275, 298
Courvoisier 74
Coutard, Francis de 133
Coutchot 152
Credit Agricole 281
crème de cassis 106
crème de mûres 106
Crèmes a l'Armagnac 106
croustade (apple tart) 12, 13
Cutxan 281
Cuvée Bois 141

Daguin, André 11, 219
Daguin, Ariane 12
d'Agrain, Madame Jeanne 135
d'Albret, Jeanne 19, 139, 190
Dame Blanc 39
Dando, André 127, 128
Dareux, Georges 287
Dargelos, Madame 46, 47, 140, 144, 282
Darreon 242
Darroze 60, 111, 144, 158, 175, 187, 251, 253, **257-273**, 275, 276
Darroze, Francis 125, 145, 146, 170, 259
Darroze, Helene 209
Darroze, Jean 257
Darroze, Marc 260
D'Artagnan 12, 19, 20
Dartigalongue 41, 108, 157, 203, 251, 274
Dartigalongue, Jean-Pierre 274
Darzacq, Albert 126
Dauriac, Alain 181
Davidoff 108
Dax 14, 16
Déche, Francis 139
degree 10
Delamain 78
Della Vedove 247
Deloi 262
Delord 157, 251, 275, 276
demi-john 70
demineralized water 65
Departement des Landes 117
Depis, Michel 231
Desangles, Michel 291
Dewars 81
Deyres, Guy 158, 259
digestive 81, 298
distillation 41, 65, 113, 116
distilled water 65, 69
Dom Perignon 87, 157
Domaine a Parot 294
Domaine au Bourg 295
Domaine aux Ducs 262
Domaine Boingnères 38, 41, 59, 104, 108, 115, **147-150**, 293
Domaine Bouscassé 14
Domaine Broustet 295
Domaine de Bacoge 295
Domaine de Baraillon 108, 293
Domaine de Beauregard 254
Domaine de Bel Air 261
Domaine de Beroy 254
Domaine de Bidaous 261
Domaine de Bilé 247
Domaine de Bordenave 254
Domaine de Bordeneuve 104, 294
Domaine de Bordeneuve-Entras 105, 214, 295
Domaine de Boutille 295
Domaine de Brichot 228, 295
Domaine de Caillavère 294
Domaine de Capdepont 261
Domaine de Cassagnoles 105, 295
Domaine de Castagnet 195, 294

Domaine de Caumont 184, 295
Domaine de Cavaillon 175, 293
Domaine de Cazeaux 105, 229
Domaine de Cazenave 253
Domaine de Chiroulet 105, 232
Domaine de Coquillon 257, 261
Domaine de Coutchot 295
Domaine de Dupont 264
Domaine de Ferragus 295
Domaine de Gagnet 105
Domaine de Gaston 181, 295
Domaine de Gaube 154, 155, 263, 293
Domaine de Guechet 138, 294
Domaine de Guillemouta 145, 257, 263, 293
Domaine de Houres 295
Domaine de Hourtica 294
Domaine de Jalousie 141
Domaine de Janin 295
Domaine de Jaurrey 166, 293
Domaine de Jean du Haut 108, 119, 200, 254, 293
Domaine de Jeanblanc 264
Domaine de Jouanchicot 247, 264
Domaine de Jouanda 108, 119, 200, 293
Domaine de Jouatmaou 266, 293
Domaine de Joÿ 192, 294
Domaine de La Bataille 260
Domaine de la Boubée 39, 59, 235-6, 294
Domaine de la Brette 221, 294
Domaine de la Coste 169, 293
Domaine de la Grangerie 254, 295
Domaine de la Hauresse 294
Domaine de la Lapeyrade 215
Domaine de la Lartigue 105, 130, 294
Domaine de Laballe 194
Domaine de Labrune 166
Domaine de Laburthe 267
Domaine de Lagajan 294
Domaine de Lagoué 253, 268
Domaine de Lamoulette 293
Domaine de Lapeyrade 294
Domaine de L'Arepic 183, 294
Domaine de Lassabatju 156, 293
Domaine de Laubesse 294
Domaine de Laubuchon 185, 254, 293
Domaine de Le Basque 293
Domaine de le Greau 129
Domaine de l'Herité 129, 294
Domaine de Lusson 187, 268, 294
Domaine de Luzan 254
Domaine de Mahu 268, 294
Domaine de Malartic 294
Domaine de Maouhum 151, 293
Domaine de Marquisat 294
Domaine de Martin 59, 269, 293
Domaine de Mauhic 294
Domaine de Maupas 186, 294
Domaine de Menjot 295
Domaine de Miquer 277
Domaine de Monturon 269
Domaine de Mouchac 279
Domaine de Mouliot 270
Domaine de Moura 226, 295
Domaine de Nautina 59, 293
Domaine de Nöel 254
Domaine de Paguy 39, 126, 293
Domaine de Pantagnan 277
Domaine de Papolle 190, 192, 294
Domaine de Pariot 152, 294
Domaine de Péré 128, 129, 295
Domaine de Peto 295
Domaine de Peyron 270
Domaine de Peyrot 270
Domaine de Picpout 271
Domaine de Pillon 166, 293
Domaine de Pinas 271
Domaine de Pouchegu 216, 293
Domaine de Pouy 141
Domaine de Pujo 182
Domaine de Ravignan 197
Domaine de Rieston 110, 158, 271
Domaine de Rieux 141
Domaine de Rincaulet 254
Domaine de Saint Aubin 272
Domaine de San de Guilhem 294
Domaine de Sandemaignan 294
Domaine de Sans 218, 293
Domaine de Saoubis 123, 293
Domaine de Seviac 277
Domaine de Simsat 295
Domaine de Soube 294
Domaine de St. Aubin 108, 272-3
Domaine de St. Lannes 224, 295
Domaine de St. Martin 201, 295
Domaine de Tambouriat 254

Domaine de Tucom 279
Domaine d'Eauze 263
Domaine des Cassagnoles 222, 235
Domaine des Ecasses 295
Domaine des Escasses 214
Domaine des Roches Freres 105
Domaine d'Escoubes 166, 182
Domaine d'Eyres 263
Domaine d'Ognoas 108, 115, 151, 293
Domaine du Bordieu 234
Domaine du Carpoulet 222, 294
Domaine du Martin 158
Domaine Durroux 189
Domaine la Bouc 295
Domaine Laffitte 56
Domaine Le Bâsque 178
Domaine le Beroy 294
Domaine le Cantaloup 294
Domaine le Durre 254
Domaine San de Guilhem 201
Domecq, Bernard 283
Don Tomas 109
Donnefoi, Pierre 137
Dordogne 12, 52
d'Orglandes, Jean-Henry 197
double-distillation 41, 43-45, 47, 68, 77-79, 110, 169
Dubos, Daniel 182
Dubourdieu, Paul 229
Dubuc, Jean-Louis 137
Duc de Loussac 207
ducks 12, 85
Duffour, Michel 224
Duflo, Yves 222
Dufrechou 128, 251
Dufrechou, Henri 129
Dufrechou, Pierre 128, 129
Duhurc, Guy 122
Dumas, Alexander 19
Dunkerque 20
Dupeyron, Joseph 283
Dupont, Jacques. 264
Dupont, Michel 123, 203
Dupuy, Alain 113
Dupuy, Louis 204, 205
Dutournier, Alain 11
early landed cognacs 87
eau de toilette 65
eau de vie 40-42, 47, 67, 104, 106, 142, 144, 191, 211, 232, 248, 255, 298
écarteur 15
Egypt 41
élevage 65
en vrac 298
England 73, 87, 102, 124
enologist **65-69**, 88
escargots 14
Escoubets, Claude and Philippe 205
Escoubets, René 205
estate-bottled armagnacs 110
esters 47, 77, 110

Faget, Albert 261
Faget, François 220
Fahrenheit 42
Farbos-Cames, B. M. 192
Faure, Christian 288, 289
Fer Servadou 14
fermentation 34, 65
Ferragus 233
fête 14
Fezas, Michel 232
Fezas, Philippe 233
Filartigue, R. 218
finesse 94, 298
finish 96
flambé 12
Floc de Gascogne 14, 47, 81, 101, 104, 116-117, 201, 214, 228, 233-4, 239, 240, 298
Floc de l'été 105
foie gras 12, 13, 82, 105, 108, 127, 216, 248
Folle Blanche 33, 35-6, 38-40, 75, 78, 80, 104, 110, 125, 141, 142, 236, 237, 248, 255
fond de verre 96, 224
Fonseca 87
Fountain of Saint-Pe 248
Fourteau, Joël 234
Fourtet, Olivier 233

Francis I 145
Franks 23
Fronde War 20
Fronton 14
frosts 27, 31
fruit 89, 111
Fruit d'Amour 156
Fruits Macerated In Armagnac 105

Gabriel, Raymond 113, 239
Gabriel, Solanges 240
GAEC des Coutons 189
Gaillac 39
Gamay 105
ganadero 15, 47
garbure 13
Garcia 234
garlic 12
Garreau, Charles 166, 189
Gascon oak 78
Gascony 9, 11, 15, 19, 20, 23-4, 31, 36, 38, 42, 52-53, 111, 237
Gault-Millau 14, 198
geese 12, 85
Gelas 74, 157, 159, 182, 225, 251, 276
Gentilhomme de Gascogne 140
Georgacaracos, Constantin 140
Gerland 106, 162, 251, 292
Germany 20, 76, 124
Gers 12, 20, 31, 40, 52, 74, 84, 105, 115-6, 118, 216, 219
Gerzabek, Johannes 221
Gessler, Olivier and Roland 193
Gier 42
Gimet 214, 236, 277, 278, 286
Gimet, Jean-Pierre 226
Gimet, Roger 277
gin 45, 101
Giovinetti, Massimo Fabio 278
Gironi, Philippe 217, 223, 232, 244
gîte 298
glassware 111
Glen Grant 278
Goudoulin, Madame 288
grain 51
Grand Bas-Armagnac 211, 253, 298
Grand Marnier 101, 106, 251
grapes 86, 116
Grassa, Pierre 141
Grassa, Yves 143
gravel 28
gray rot 33
Great Britain 20
Greek dynasty 41
Gros Manseng 14, 39, 104, 141, 172, 193, 223, 225, 236
Gros Plant 36
Groupe CCG 281
Guadeloupe 143, 222, 239, 240
Guasch, Jean-Claude 143
Guasch, Thomas 253
Guérard, Michel 11, 136
Guide Hachette 233

hail storm 31
Hamilton 108
Haut-Armagnac 26, 75, 117, 215, 246, 248
Hawkins, Peter 189
heads 44, 45, 298
Hébert, Benoit 203
Hébert, Therese 203
hectoliter 298
hectolitre d'alcool pur 117
Hennessey 74, 78
Henri III 19, 190
Henri IV 19, 24, 190, 240
Hermann 9
Heron, François 279
Herrail, Jean-Pierre 240
highlights 92
Holland 20, 73
Hors d'age 68-9, 110, 220
Hotel de France 11
Houres 225
Hourtica 170
Hugenots 19
humidity 59
humidity of the *chai* 94
Hundred-Year War 24

Indivision Corderoy/Debains 154
Italy 20
Izarra 255

jambon de Bayonne 12
Janin 242
Janneau 74, 81-2, 108, 123, 157, 182, 196, 220, 225, 251, 252, 277-8
Janneau, Etienne 278
Japan 68
Jean de Montrejo 238, 295
Jeanne de Arc 218
Johnnie Walker 81, 251
Jordana, Maurice 183
Jurançon 14, 39, 42, 108
Jurançon Blanc 39, 217

Kauffer, Michel 229
kiwi plants 144

La Belle Gasconne 234
La Bouc 163
La Caillavère 239
La Croix de Salles 274
La Ferme de Gagnet 234
La Flor Domenicana 108
La Gloria Cubana 108-9
La Grande Passion 106
La Hauresse 243
La Croix, Jean 197
La Maison de l'Armagnac 253
La Rochelle 73
La Table des Cordeliers 12
Labarbe, André 162
Labenne, Nicholas and Jean-Pierre 238
Laberdolive 108, 113, **166-168**
Laberdolive, Gerard 166, 182
Labeyrie, Jean-Paul and Eric 242
Labiette-Castille 207
Laburthe, Yves 209
Lacave, Francis 130
Lacave, Roger and Bernard 146
Lacoste, Claude and Josette 159
Lacourtoisie, Claude 54, 169
Ladevèze, Veuve 235
Ladevèze, Jean 60, 236
Lafargue, Claudine 152
Lafargue, Jacqueline 152
Lafite-Rothschild 87, 144, 194
Lafitte, Léon 41, 147
Lafitte, Marguerite 148
Lafitte, Martine 148
Lagajan 140
Lalanne, Alain 201
Lamothe, Michel 178
Lamoulette 204
Langalerie 227
Languedoc 36, 38
Lannes, Jean 20
Lapisse, Jean-Marie 225
Laporte, Pierre 216
Lapostolle 251
Larresingle 74, 78, 108, 190, 220, 225, 236, 251, 252, 277, 279
Larrieu, Ema and Ernest 213
Larriou 127
Lartigolle, Pierre 123
Lascombes 215
Lassalle distillery 223
Lasseignou, Jean-Claude 151
Lasserre, Jacques 161
Lasserre, Paul 158, 160, 262
Lassis, Jean 175
Lassus family 105
Laubade 175, 187
Laudet, Jean-Dominique 194
Laudet, Nöel 194
Le Béroy 122
Le Canteloup 137
Le Gascon 107
Le Maison des Paysans 151
Le Miquer 160
Le Péto 231
Le Roy des Armagnacs 277
Le trou Gascon 104
lees 298
length 95, 96
Les Escasses 213
Les Freres de Fatima 253
Les Landes 11, 15, 16, 20, 55, 74, 84, 11

Les Prés d'Eugenie 11
Lesgourgues, Jean-Jacques 206
Lezama, Philippe 256
L'Hermitage 253
L'Huillier, Bernard 60, 157
Lille 234
limestone 20, 26, 27, 28, 31, 88, 115
Limousin oak 52-53, 78, 111, 141, 223, 237
Limoux 39
liqueurs 41
Liria, Pepin 15
Loire 23, 36
Lomagne 20
Lorenzon, David 235
Loss, Josiane and Didier 181
Lot et Garonne 12, 39, 216, 234, 242
Lou Traouc 291
Loubedat 184
Loubère 207, 251
Louis XIII 197
Louis XIV 20
Lourdes 209
Lupiac 20
Luzan, Guy Farbos de 196
Luze, Gilles de 191
Macallan 89, 278
Macanudo 108-9
Madeira 94
Madiran 14, 141, 213, 246
Maestrojuan, Michel 214
magret 11-12, 104
maitre de chai 298
Majestic 108
maladie du bois 61
Malartic 205
Malbec 14, 37, 82
malolactic fermentation 298
Mandelaëre, Maurice de 124
Manrique, Laurent 12
Mao, Corentin 223
marine sediment 26
Marquis de Caussade 67, 251, 281
Marquis de Montesquieu 84, 251, 282
Marquis de Puysegur 292
Martell 74, 251, 278
Massif Central 26
Mauhic 184
Maumusson 246
Maurer 228
Maury 108
Mauzac 39
Mediterranean Sea 31
Mellet, Antoine de 42
melons 14
Mendic 36
Menjot 209
Merlot 105, 215, 225, 233
Meslier 217
Meslier St. Francis 40
Michalouski, Patrick 46, 47, 228, 236, 238, 242
Midouze River 74
Mielan 24
Mitterand, François 275
Mixed Drinks made with armagnac 107
Möet 157
Monbel, Raymond de 135
Monguilhem (forest) 52
Monlezun (forest) 52, 56
Monlezun, Antoine de 248
Mont-de-Marsan 14, 15, 16, 74
Montbazillac 124
Montecristo 108-9
Montesquieu, Pierre 282
Montesquiou 247
Montpellier 41
Moore, Benjamin 67
Moors 23
Mosaics 41
Muret, Mademoiselle de 154
mushrooms 88
Musketeers 19, 20
Muslim religion 41

Nantes 73
Napoléon 99
Napoléon Bonaparte 20
Nautina 196
Navarre 19
négociant 33, 41, 52, 59-60, 67-70, 74, 76-7, 79, 81-5, 86-7, 110, 113, 116, 251, 298
Négrette 14
Nismes, Jules 254

Nismes-Delclou 74
Noah 75
non-alcohols 46
Normandy 280
Northern Africa 23, 41
nosing 93
Notre Dame de Pibeque 216
Novempopulanie 23

oak 25, 88, 92
oak chips 71
Oreja, Louis 184
ortolan 257
Otard 281
Ouardère 181
oxidation 34, 51, 61, 94
oysters 108

paella 14
Palladin, Jean-Louis 12
palombes 18
Palthey, Jacqueline 244
Papalourey, Gabriel 280
Papalourey, Maurice 280
Papelourey 251
Paradis 70
Pardaillan 218
Paris 11, 20, 248
Parker, Robert 39, 82
Parleboscq 75, 194
part des anges 299
Partagas 108-9
pasodobles 16
pastis 253
patois 21, 104, 299
Pau 19
Pauillac 190
perfume 65
Perigord 12
Perissé, Roger 206
permitted additives 47, 57, 65, 69
Pernod 101, 282
Pernod-Ricard 282
Perrier 105
petanque 127
petites eaux 65, 78, 126, 139, 141, 194, 217, 223, 283, 299
pH level 27
Philip, King II 19
Phillips, Willy 278
phylloxera 33, 37, 39, 40, 75, 76, 141
Pichon-Longueville, Baron Raoul de 190
Picpoul 36
pièce 119, 129, 131, 299
pieds noirs 20, 116, 125, 143
Pilgrims 42
pine forests 26
pine trees 116
Pineau des Charentes 81, 101, 104
Piquepoult 33, 36
Pitous, Dr. André, 175
Plainte de Grèce 33, 39, 217, 236
Plantignac 107, 153
Plouvier, Michel 127
Point-de-Bordes 74
polombière 18
polyculture 217
Ponge, Michel 152
Pope Clement V 41
pork roast 92
Port 41, 83
Posternak, Claude 248
pot still 34, 41, 45, 77
Pouchégu 216
Poudenas 228, 234
Pourquet, Michel 217
Pousse-Rapière 105, 138, 241
Poyferré, Jacques de 119, 200
primary aromas 94
Prince de Gascogne 105
producers of armagnac 113
prohibition 75
proof 10
Protestant 19, 24
Provence, 38
pruneau 37, 92
pruneau a l'armagnac 228, 231
pruneau d'Agen 105
prunes 12
Pujau, Gerard 286
Punch 108
Pyrénées 12, 14, 18-20, 23, 26, 42, 52, 105

quercus silicus 52, 54
Quillard 39
racking 25, 60
rancio 47, 62, 80, 85, 94, 128, 130, 138, 139, 142, 145, 173, 205, 210, 219, 256, 282, 284, 285, 286, 288, 299
Rancio® 68, 69
Ravignan, Baron Louis de 197
reduction 25, 60, 65, 77, 94, 110
Remy Martin 111, 251
Remy-Cointreau 255
Rendu 75
Réon, Jean 226
Réserve 99, 110
Reserve Cathedrale 282
Reserve des Moins 253
Réserve Spéciale 99, 148, 259
Restaurant Jean-Louis 12
Revue des Vins de France 148, 198, 257
Rhone 14, 79
Ribeira del Duero 79
Ricard 101
Riedel 91, 111
Rioja 79
Rioupeyroux 216
Roman empire 23
Romanée-Conti, Domaine de la 97
Romeo y Julieta 108
Roquefort 60, 105, 259, 273
Roumat 49, 261
Roux, Michel 106
Royal Jamaican 108
rugby 17, 113
rum 82
Ryst, Jacques and François 283
Ryst-Dupeyron 220, 283

SA C.T.S. Thermes de Barbotan 136
Sabazan 213, 286
sables fauves 28, 52
Saint Jean de Compostelle 222
Saint-Geours-de-Marenne 253
Saint-Jean, Anatole 257, 272
Saint-Martin 216
Saint-Martin, Yvan and Marc 47, 130, 139, 182, 186, 193, 201-202, 206
Salerne 41
sales, of armagnac in France 103
sales, of armagnac abroad 103
sales, cognac abroad 103
sales, cognac France 103
sales, cognac leaders 102
salmis de palombes 13
Samalens 108, 144, 157, 184, 190, 251, 275, 284
Samalens, Jean 284
Samalens, Philippe 285
Samalens, Pierre 284
Sampietro, Jocelyne 231
sand 27, 28, 31, 115
Sarrot, Jean-Pierre 195
Sauvignon Blanc 141, 225
Scandinavia 20, 101
Schweppes 105
Scotch 89, 107
Scotland 251
Seagrams 82, 278
secondary aromas 63, 94, 111
Seguin-Moreau 233
Segur, Marie-Claude 92
Seillan, Jules 75
Semillon 234
Sempé 81, 82, 106, 163, 175, 182, 196, 251, 252, 286
Sempé, Henri-Abel 286
Sempé, Jean-Paul 129
Serie Rare 259
Serres, Jean-Pierre 154
Seviac 235
Seyve-Villard 226
simple-chauffe 41
Simsat 176
single malt scotch 253
single-distillation 68, 78-9, 110
smoked salmon 104
snifter 91
Societé Auxil Fatima 253
Societé Magnol 221
soil 26, 113
solera system 83
Soube 205
Sourbès, René and Christian 176
Southdown Wines and Spirits 67
soy beans 86

Spain 19, 20, 23, 42, 68
spider's legs 46
Springbank 87
St. Estéphe 238
St. Fris 247
St. Jean Baptiste de Beziey 216
St. Jean-de-Luz 20
St. Julien 119
St. Pastou 134
St. Pierre Cathedral 220
Steadman, Ralph 192
stock 83, 102, 117, 299
stylistic consistency 83
subsoil 28
sugar 68, 77, 85, 94, 110
sugar syrup 68, 69, 71
sulfur 34
sunflowers 86, 116
Super Tuscan 47
Suze 282
Switzerland 138

3 Etoiles 99
Tadieu, Maurice 234
tails 44, 45, 299
Tannat 14, 105, 225
tannin 51, 52, 53, 55, 61, 68, 87, 89, 91, 95, 111
Tarbe, Hubert and Marthe 170
Tarride 208
Tastet, Alain 144
Tasting Armagnac 91
Tawny Port 94
taxes 60, 65, 81
Ténarèze 20, 26, 28, 34, 38, 47, 75, 92, 111, 115, 117, 195, 212, 215, 218-9, 228, 233, 241, 247, 254, 278, 282-3, 288
terrebouc 28
terrines 92
terroir 25, 88, 299
tertiary aromas 94
texture 61, 93
Theaux, Jacques 218, 239
Theaux, Veuve Hector 218
Thenon, Jean-Pierre 286
Tignac 107, 153
toasting barrels 54
toffee 111
tonneaux 64, 152, 299
tonnelier 51, 53, 56, 299
Topographie des Vignobles du Gers et de l'Armagnac 75
topping up 59
torula compniacensus 59
Toulouse 12, 14, 23, 31, 237
Tour de la Mothe 218
Tour de Luzan 231
Trebbiano 38
Trepout 124, 144, 175, 251, 252, 287
Trepout, Marcel 287
troisième mi-temps 17
Trończais 52, 53, 78, 236
trou gascon 248, 299
Tuscany 38

Ugni Blanc 33, 35, 37, 68, 78, 80, 104, 110, 116, 119, 141-2, 212, 215, 223, 225, 236-7, 242, 248

Union de Coopératives Viticoles de l'Armagnac 281, 290
United States 21, 102-3

V.D.L.Q. P. R. D 104
V.S.O.P. 99
Vaghi 144, 252, 253
Vaghi, Fabrice 253
Valois, Marguerite de 19
vats 64
VDP de Terroir Landais 189
Vega Sicilia 87
Verdier 42
Verron, Michel 281
Veuve Goudolin 159, 251, 288
Vielle-Saint-Girons 151
vieux faibles 299
Vin de Noix 106, 185
Vin de Pays 211, 215
Vin de Pays de Côtes de Gascogne 38
Vin de Pays de l'Agenais 229
Vin de Pêche 106

vin de presse 179
Vin Jaune 94
vintage 78
Vintage armagnac 83
vintage years 87
violet 92
Visigoth 23
vitus labrusca 37
vitus vinifera 37
vodka 45, 82, 101
volatile acids 60
Vosges 223

walnuts 109
Washington DC 12
water 224
wheat 86, 116
whiskey 41, 45, 81, 101
wild boar 12
wild pigeons 12
Wine Enthusiast 82
Wine Spectator 82
Wines and Spirits 82
Wolfert, Paula 12
wood chips 56, 67
wood planks 57
worldwide Total Sales 101

yeast 34

XO 99

PHOTOGRAPHIC ACKNOWLEDGEMENTS

Most of the photographs taken in this book were by Charles Neal. A handful of photographs were reproduced from armagnac promotional material within which they were not credited. Those concerned can contact the publisher and a credit will be included in any further editions.

With kind thanks to the BNIA for use of the maps on pages 120-121 and 212.

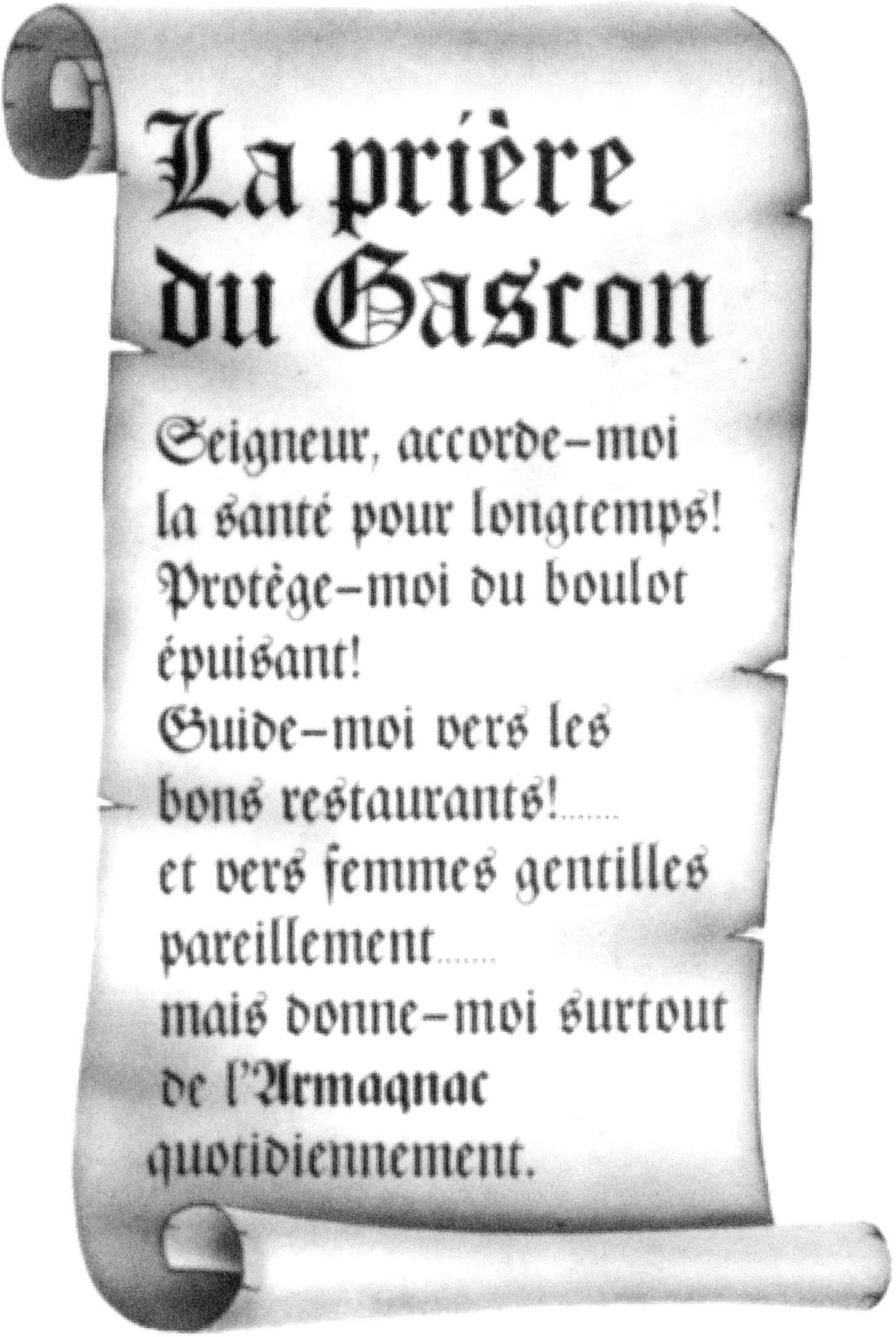

"Give me a long, healthy life, dear Lord, and keep me away from tiring employment
Yet guide me to great restaurants, nice women and things of enjoyment.
But more than anything, O Lord I pray, give me armagnac everyday!"—The Gascon Prayer

Printed in Great Britain
by Amazon

41187439R00183